TRADING BEAUTY

TRADING BEAUTY
Art Market Histories from the Altar to the Gallery

Valentina Castellani

Gagosian

To Gianluca

CONTENTS

Foreword by Massimiliano Gioni 9

1. Church, Royalty, Bankers: The Patronage Model from the Middle Ages through the Early Baroque Period 12

2. The Dutch Golden Age and the First Free Market 36

3. At His Majesty's Service: The Monopsony Model under Louis XIV of France 52

4. Leonardo's *Salvator Mundi* and Aspects of the Old Masters Market 62

5. Paul Durand-Ruel and the Birth of the Impressionist Market 94

6. From Cézanne to Picasso: The Modern Art Market Develops 112

7. New York Stories I: The Triumph of Abstract Expressionism 142

8. New York Stories II: From the Harlem Renaissance and the Civil Rights Movement to Just Above Midtown 168

9. New York Stories III: The Castelli-Sonnabend Model 184

10. Breaking the Rules: Damien Hirst's Auction *Beautiful Inside My Head Forever* 210

11. Blurring the Boundaries: The Rise of Blockbuster Museum Exhibitions in Commercial Galleries 220

12. The Rebirth of China's Art Market and Its Rising International Clout 234

13. The Art Market in a Global, Post-Pandemic, Turbulent Time 252

Acknowledgments 283
Index 284

Foreword

We often like to imagine the history of art as a silent procession of solitary geniuses working in a bubble of pure inspiration, far removed from the vulgarities of the counting house. We cling to the romantic myth of the artist as a recluse, or the masterpiece as a divine accident. But as Valentina Castellani reminds us in *Trading Beauty*, the history of art is, and has always been, a history of trade. From the blue of a Renaissance fresco to the chrome of a contemporary sculpture, every object we revere today was once a line item in a contract, a move in a geopolitical game, or a gamble on the future of taste.

In this book, Castellani performs a vital service for both the neophyte and the enthusiast: she maps the "operating system" of the visual world. She begins not in a gallery, but at the altar. In the Middle Ages and the Renaissance, art was a demand-driven industry. To look at Giotto's Scrovegni Chapel frescoes is to see not just the birth of modern painting, but also a sophisticated transaction of spiritual atonement. Value was measured in the tangible—the price of gold leaf or the rarity of lapis lazuli—and the artist was a skilled artisan bound by the specific whims of popes and bankers.

As we move through the centuries, Castellani traces the slow but dramatic transition from this patronage model to the "free market" of the Dutch Golden Age. Here, for the first time, we see the birth of the speculative artist—the creator who paints first and finds a buyer later. This evolution represents the true radical turn, where the dealer emerges as a crucial intermediary, a curator of desire who translates raw talent into cultural capital.

The narrative gains a thrilling momentum as it enters the nineteenth and twentieth centuries. Castellani details the heroic (and often desperate) efforts of Paul Durand-Ruel to invent a market for the Impressionists, a gambit that eventually shifted the center of the art world from the salons of Paris to the streets of New York. Through the "New York Stories" of Abstract Expressionism and the legendary Castelli-Sonnabend model, we see the gallery transform into something more than a shop—it becomes a laboratory where the very definition of art is negotiated and brand identities are forged: geniuses are discovered, sometimes twice a month.

What makes this book indispensable is Castellani's "insider-outsider" perspective. Having navigated the upper echelons of both the auction world and the mega-gallery, she understands the mechanics of the "blockbuster" era. She doesn't shy away from the complexities of the current moment: the rise of the Chinese market, the impact of the global pandemic, and the blurring of boundaries between commercial spaces and public institutions. Whether she is discussing the record-shattering sale of Leonardo's *Salvator Mundi* or Damien Hirst's rule-breaking auctions, she maintains a focus on how value is constructed and exchanged in an increasingly tumultuous world.

Trading Beauty is no mere chronicle of prices; it is a biography of the art object as a living entity. It teaches us that to understand a painting, we must understand the hands it has passed through and the systems that allowed it to survive. With Arnold Hauser on one side and Michael Baxandall on the other, Castellani navigates through art history, always reminding her readers that artworks are first and foremost traces of social relationships: she understands the art object as a node in a complex network of forces, not all necessarily disinterested. And yet she does not fall for conspiracy theories either, invariably providing a balanced overview, even amid the most unlikely financial speculations.

With such clarity of mind, Castellani's concise, informative guide proves that while beauty may be priceless, learning how prices are set will not spoil its mysteries; on the contrary, that knowledge helps us understand that art is a game in which we all together play a part—artists, dealers, collectors, and viewers. History belongs to everyone.

Massimiliano Gioni

1. Church, Royalty, Bankers: The Patronage Model from the Middle Ages through the Early Baroque Period

p. 14	p. 16	p. 17	p. 18
In the Name of the Church	Charlemagne	The Rebirth of the New Millennium	The Emergence of Private Patronage
p. 18	p. 19	p. 20	p. 21
Relics	Ultramarine Blue	Giotto's Scrovegni Chapel	The Medicis: The Epitome of Private Patronage
p. 22	p. 24	p. 25	p. 26
The Renaissance	Benozzo Gozzoli's Magi Chapel Frescoes (1459)	Female Patronage: Isabella d'Este	The Artist's Status
p. 28	p. 29	p. 32	p. 32
Raphael's *School of Athens* (1508–11)	Michelangelo, Julius II, and the Sistine Chapel	Leonardo da Vinci: Commissions Never Delivered	Rejected Commissions

One of the most forceful myths of the Renaissance is the idea that its artists freely explored their ideas and created their masterpieces for enlightened patrons eager to acquire these works of genius. . . . It was the patron who was the real initiator of the architecture, sculpture, and painting of the period, and that played a significant part in determining both form and content.

—Mary Hollingsworth, *Patronage in Renaissance Italy*

During the Middle Ages and the Renaissance, the production and acquisition of art followed a markedly different process compared to modern practices. Unlike today, when artists create based on personal inspiration and then seek buyers, all artworks of those earlier periods were commissioned. The driving force behind the art market was patronage, meaning that demand rather than supply determined its dynamics. The medieval and Renaissance art markets were shaped by the needs and tastes of patrons.

This patronage system significantly influenced both the status of artists and the valuation of their work. Instead of independent creators pursuing personal expression, artists were seen as skilled artisans tasked with executing specific works according to contractual agreements with their patrons. The value of artworks was primarily determined by factors such as the materials used—for example, gold or the costly ultramarine blue—dimensions, subject matter, and the amount of labor involved. In contrast to today's emphasis on artistic vision and originality, these practical considerations played a central role in pricing.

Following the fall of the Roman Empire in 476 CE, the Church emerged as the central spiritual, social, and cultural force in Europe, becoming the primary patron of art throughout the Middle Ages. As Europe's population expanded and economic activity shifted from rural to urban centers around the turn of the first millennium, a burgeoning urban bourgeoisie also gained considerable purchasing power. This newfound wealth enabled its members to commission artworks for private consumption, marking a notable shift in the dynamics of art patronage. During the Renaissance in Italy, a period marked by the division of the country into small city-states, influential ruling families such as the Medicis of Florence, the Gonzagas of Mantua, the Estes of Ferrara, the Sforzas of Milan, and the Montefeltros of Urbino, alongside the Republic of Venice and the Papal States, elevated patronage to unprecedented heights. These patrons recognized and effectively utilized art's prestige as a powerful tool for propaganda.

Despite the patriarchal constraints still prevailing in Renaissance society—imposing economic, social, and cultural limitations—female patronage began to ascend. Among these patrons, Isabella d'Este stands prominently above all others, her influence and legacy warranting deeper exploration.

Throughout the extensive medieval period, from approximately the fifth to the fourteenth century, the Church strongly influenced the content, function, and modes of producing art. This dominance stemmed from two events that shaped the social and economic landscape of Europe for centuries. First, the Edict of Milan, which Emperor Constantine (after 280?–337) issued in 313, granted Christians freedom of worship. From a persecuted sect originating in Galilee nearly three centuries earlier, the Christian faith rapidly spread across the Roman Empire. Second, in 476, the western part of the vast Roman Empire, which had spanned regions including not only what is now Italy but also present-day Great Britain, France, Germany, North Africa, Egypt, Syria, and Armenia, met its end with catastrophic repercussions.

Under its firm control, Rome had ensured peace and prosperity, a well-developed and extensive administrative system, and an efficient network of roads, facilitating safe trade. The empire promoted a certain amount of religious tolerance, boasted populous cities with magnificent public and private buildings, and nurtured the flourishing of the arts. Starting in the third century, however, waves of migrating populations, eventually turning into invasions, surged beyond the Roman border (known as the *limes*) and unleashed devastation and disorder across the empire. Rome attempted to manage and mitigate this phenomenon, without success. The once-unassailable capital of the empire, Rome, suffered a shocking siege and looting by Alaric's Visigoths in 410. By 476, the Western Roman Empire met its official end, when the last emperor of Roman descent, the sixteen-year-old Romulus Augustulus, was deposed by the Goth Odoacer. (After the eastern part of the empire had been administered separately for about a century, it split off entirely in 395 as the Eastern Roman Empire, with Constantinople, now Istanbul, as the capital. Regarding itself as the continuation of the Roman Empire, and centuries later more commonly called the Byzantine Empire, it survived until 1453.)

In the aftermath of devastating conflicts, the western territories that the Roman Empire once controlled saw the emergence of the so-called Roman-barbarian kingdoms, including the Vandals in Africa, Visigoths in Spain, Lombards in northern Italy, and Saxons in England. While modern scholarship has revisited and mitigated the negative assessment of the term "Dark Ages"—used to describe the period from approximately the fifth to the tenth century—it remains undeniable that the collapse of the Western Roman Empire had immediate and disastrous consequences. A demographic decline and the deterioration of urban safety and supply chains prompted a mass exodus from cities to rural areas. There, fortified structures offered security and facilitated direct production of essential goods, leading to a significant reduction in monetary transactions and a resurgence of barter.

As far as art production is concerned, the end of the western part of the Roman Empire also precipitated the dispersion of the skills and technical knowledge essential for constructing, sculpting, carving, and painting. The affluent and sophisticated public and private patrons who had previously fueled artistic commissions also disappeared.

Gradually, the Church stepped into the void left by the empire, assuming the role of spiritual unifier among ethnically diverse populations. Moreover, it became the primary—and practically the only—patron for art, dictating themes, styles, and purposes of all artworks created during this era. This overarching patronage not only preserved classical traditions but also laid the groundwork for the development of distinctive medieval artistic forms and practices.

Establishing venues where the communities of the faithful could gather and practice their religion was the most urgent goal of the Christians once Constantine's edict freed them from the need to worship clandestinely in catacombs or private homes. The first of these churches, including Santa Pudenziana, San Paolo fuori le mura (Saint Paul Outside the Walls), Santa Maria Maggiore, and Santa Sabina, all in Rome, adopted the longitudinal structure of Roman basilicas. Those basilicas originally served diverse civil and administrative purposes, distinct from the architectural model of pagan temples. While the medieval period was far from homogeneous, and indeed was marked by considerable diversity, the construction of church edifices stands out as the primary architectural endeavor across Europe. Even today, as the architect and author Christian Norberg-Schulz has noted, the majority of European towns are defined by a centrally positioned church, which imparts both visual structure and cultural significance to the urban landscape.[1]

Disseminating the divine word and ecclesiastical teachings to the predominantly illiterate masses was a paramount mission for the Church, and it became the primary purpose of art. Artists were tasked with translating written texts into visual images that served a precise didactic function, a concept that Pope Gregory the Great (c. 540–604) synthesized: "Words teach those who can read; pictures show the same to those who cannot read, but only see, so that even the ignorant can learn from pictures whom they should follow; pictures enable the illiterate to read."[2] Sculpture, initially confined to architectural elements such as capitals and portals before evolving into three-dimensional forms; cycles of frescoes; and magnificent stained-glass windows all shared a common purpose: to glorify God and the Church while spreading its teachings.

Starting in the sixth century, Benedictine abbeys emerged as the indefatigable custodians of Western culture and tradition. Founded by Benedict of Norcia (c. 480–547), who in 529 established the Montecassino Abbey in present-day Italy, these institutions adhered to the "Benedictine Rule," which emphasized the principles of *ora et labora*: prayer and work. Characterized by imposing fortified structures and extensive agricultural holdings, the abbeys wielded significant economic influence. Within their walls, libraries and scriptoria were centers of intellectual activity where sacred manuscripts were created and classical texts from antiquity were painstakingly transcribed and preserved for future generations.

On Christmas night in the year 800, Pope Leo III (750?–816) crowned Charlemagne (747?–814) emperor in Rome, in a deeply symbolic act that solidified the alliance between the Church and the Frankish kingdom. Charlemagne's grand ambition was to revive and embody the universal ideals of the Roman Empire, while positioning himself as the defender of Christianity. This aspiration led to the name "Holy Roman Empire," underscoring his dual role as both secular ruler and protector of the faith.

The Frankish realm under Charlemagne's rule encompassed a vast expanse, spanning much of present-day France and Germany, Belgium, northern Spain, and northern Italy. His victory in 774 over the Lombards, who posed a direct threat to the Church in Rome, solidified his dominion. Recognizing that the Christian faith served as the crucial cohesive force among diverse populations, Charlemagne understood the urgent need to establish doctrinal unity. To achieve this, he encouraged the creation of an educated clergy, ensuring a uniform doctrine and dogma across his empire.

Almost illiterate—he was able to read but not write—but culturally very curious, Charlemagne gathered in his court in Aachen the best scholars of the time, such as Alcuin of York and the historian Paulus Diaconus. He established a literary academy and an artists' workshop, creating what Arnold Hauser describes as the prototype of the European court—a haven for the Muses. This initiative marked a new departure. For the first time in the West since the second-century reigns of Roman emperors Hadrian and Marcus Aurelius, a ruler not only took an interest in learning, art, and literature but also implemented his own cultural program.[3]

The so-called Carolingian Renaissance (many Frankish kings were named Carolus, medieval Latin for Charles) was marked by a significant shift in which a powerful royal court emerged alongside the Church as a patron and commissioner. However, it is crucial to emphasize that the primary goal of the Renovatio Carolingia (Carolingian renovation), and its cultural and educational agenda, was the establishment of a unified liturgy, aiming at fostering cohesion among the community of believers. Intense building activity—including palaces, cathedrals, the Palatine Chapel with an octagonal plan in Aachen, monasteries, scriptoria both for copying ancient texts and for producing splendid illustrated manuscripts—also flourished during this time. In his palace, Charlemagne established a library, and—as Alessandro Barbero observes—because books were very expensive to produce, the emperor asked all his subjects who owned a manuscript either to gift it to him or to have it copied for him. During the Carolingian era, the production of texts dramatically increased.[4] In the first eight centuries of Christianity, approximately eighteen hundred Latin manuscripts had been created. One century later, this number surged to more than seven thousand. A distinguishing feature of Carolingian manuscripts was the incorporation of intricately carved ivory plaques into their covers, showcasing the craftsmanship of the period.

Although Charlemagne's heirs failed to keep the Carolingian Empire together, the concept of a Holy Roman Empire persisted. This idea was later revived by Otto of Saxony (912–973), who was crowned Emperor Otto I in 962, thereby continuing the legacy of Charlemagne's vision.

By the turn of the eleventh century, Europe's political and economic landscape began to stabilize. The relentless Viking raids from Scandinavia had subsided, and the expansionist ambitions of the Arabs had been halted earlier at the battle of Tours/Poitiers in 732 by Charles Martel, Charlemagne's grandfather.

When Otto assumed the title of emperor in 962, with a coronation by Pope John XII, the Holy Roman Empire was reborn in the Germanic region and northern Italy. In France, Hugh Capet (938–996) established a new dynasty in 987, replacing the Carolingians there. In 1066, William the Conqueror (c. 1028–1087), Duke of Normandy, invaded and asserted his rule over England. Concurrently, independent city-states began to thrive, particularly in Italy, where maritime republics such as Amalfi, Genoa, Pisa, and Venice dominated international trade routes.

The security and prosperity in Europe sparked a surge in construction, vividly captured by Rodulfus Glaber's evocative metaphor in his *Historiarum*: "It seemed that the earth itself, as if shaking and freeing itself from old age, covered itself entirely with a white mantle of churches."[5]

The Romanesque architectural style embodied the renewed constructive fervor during the eleventh and twelfth centuries. (It was retroactively named in the nineteenth century to highlight its connection with Roman heritage.) Despite numerous regional variations, Romanesque buildings across Europe shared common characteristics: a rectangular plan oriented west to east, internal spaces divided into naves defined by columns, and the use of semicircular arches, barrel vaults, heavy walls, and small windows. Over time, the architectural plans became more complex, incorporating side chapels, choirs, and ambulatories. Furthermore, sculptures began to adorn portals and capitals, adding to the distinctiveness of the style. In the area around Paris, Romanesque architecture gave way to the Gothic style during the twelfth century. The transformation was led by Abbot Suger (1081–1151) of Saint-Denis, who initiated the major renovation of the original seventh-century abbey church into a basilica. The distinctive elements of the new style were prominently displayed in Saint-Denis, including the extensive use of the pointed arch, which enabled greater vertical extension and reduced the weight of the heavy Romanesque walls. Light became a defining feature of Gothic architecture. Gothic walls seemed almost porous, allowing light to stream through majestic stained-glass windows and flood the entire space, creating a transformative effect.[6]

Suger's "invention" of the Gothic was a strategic tool in a precise political agenda: to establish a new architectural style that would result in grand and majestic cathedrals to assert the authority of the Capetian kings. Despite being nominal rulers of France, their actual power and influence were centered only around Paris. It was in this context that the magnificent Gothic cathedrals of Amiens, Reims, Rouen, and Chartres were constructed. No other artistic style has been as intimately intertwined with a political ideology and its historical manifestation.[7]

Over the course of the fourteenth and fifteenth centuries, Gothic architecture, with its varied local interpretations, spread across Europe and earned the designation "international."

THE EMERGENCE OF PRIVATE PATRONAGE

In the twelfth century, demographic growth, advances in agricultural techniques leading to surplus production, and improved security of roads for the safe travel of goods and people collectively contributed to a fundamental shift in the epicenter of social and economic life from the countryside to the city. Furthermore, the reintroduction of a monetary economy transformed every aspect of European society, reshaping its values and culture.[8]

The first universities were founded: Bologna in 1088, Oxford in 1096, Paris in 1208, Cambridge in 1209. Knowledge was no longer confined to abbeys and convents. In the reborn cities, an urban bourgeoisie with purchasing power emerged, capable of commissioning works of art for private use. While the subject and function of these commissioned artworks remained predominantly religious—such as sacred images for private devotion—new elements began to surface: the celebration of the patron, as well as the pleasure and prestige derived from owning precious and beautiful objects.

The patron became the fulcrum around which art production revolved. Contracts—or verbal agreements—between the patron and the artist detailed every aspect of the commissioned work: the subject to be represented, the figures to be included, the materials to be used, the timeline for completion, the artist's payment. For instance, the use of ultramarine blue,

RELICS

Skeletons, skulls, fragments of all kinds of bones, pieces of the true cross, the tunic in which the Virgin Mary allegedly gave birth: the sacred relics were an integral part of medieval religiosity. Ever since the edict issued by Emperor Constantine in 313 and another by Emperor Theodosius I (347–395) in 380 transformed Christianity from a persecuted cult into a tolerated and even encouraged community and then the official religion of the Roman Empire, the construction of cathedrals and churches proliferated across the expanding number of Christian domains. So did the competition to acquire the most precious relics, believed to perform miracles and healings. For example, Saint Mark's Basilica in Venice houses the remains of the eponymous evangelist, which two Venetian merchants stole in 828 from Alexandria in Egypt. Similarly, the Gothic jewel of the Sainte-Chapelle in Paris, consecrated in 1248, was built by King Louis IX (1214–1270) of France as a shrine to hold Christ's crown of thorns and fragments of the true cross, which he had acquired from Baldwin II, emperor of Constantinople. Beyond their religious significance, relics became formidable economic magnets for the cities that possessed them. Pilgrimage routes to devotional centers, such as Santiago de Compostela in Spain and Saint Peter's Basilica in Rome, crossed Europe, bringing both devotees and money.

derived from the semiprecious stone lapis lazuli, was costly, and its usage and quantity were specified precisely.

This patronage model would remain the dominant system of art production for centuries, particularly in Catholic countries.

Michael Baxandall explains in his seminal *Painting and Experience in Fifteenth-Century Italy*: "A fifteenth-century painting is the deposit of a social relationship. On one side there was a painter who made the picture, or at least supervised its making. On the other side there was somebody else who asked him to make it, provided funds for him to make it and, after he had made it, reckoned on using it in some way or other. Both parties worked within institutions and conventions—commercial, religious, perceptual, in the widest sense social—that were different from ours and influenced the forms of what they together made."[9]

The dependent relationship between artists and their patrons is evident in their written correspondence. For instance, Bram Kempers reports that Benozzo Gozzoli (c. 1421–1497), in a letter dated July 10, 1459, acknowledged Cosimo de' Medici's dissatisfaction with the inclusion of two angels in a painting for the family chapel.[10] Penalties were imposed when parties failed to meet their agreements. Mary Hollingsworth observes that when a statue of Saint John by Donatello (c. 1386–1466) was still unfinished in

ULTRAMARINE BLUE

"Ultramarine blue is a color illustrious, beautiful, and most perfect, beyond all other colors," wrote the medieval painter Cennino Cennini (c. 1370–c. 1440) in his *Treatise on Painting* (c. 1400).[11] Profusely used by Giotto in the Scrovegni Chapel—and probably applied dry, which would explain the areas of deterioration—ultramarine blue signaled a patron's wealth and prodigality. The pigment was in fact astronomically expensive. Victoria Finlay explains that the preciosity of the materials displayed in a work of art was the first aspect that the public of the time would have noticed and admired. An area of gold immediately signaled its preciousness. Likewise, another color that spoke of luxury and expense was ultramarine blue.[12] One ounce of it cost up to one-tenth of a contemporary craftsman's annual income in the seventeenth century.[13] Ultramarine pigment was obtained by grinding the semiprecious stone lapis lazuli, found for thousands of years only in the Sar-i-Sang mountains and nearby in what is now northeast Afghanistan (the word *ultramarine* means "beyond the sea"); despite modern mines in Russia, Chile, and other countries, including the southwestern United States, the original location is still the source of nearly all lapis lazuli. Extracting the blue pigment was a complex process, as the essential mineral lazurite (not to be confused with a different mineral called lazulite) had to be separated from the other minerals that composed the stone, then blended with various oils and wax. One kilogram of mineral produced only thirty grams of pigment. Lapis lazuli was known to ancient Egyptians and utilized in their jewelry, but as a pigment, its use did not emerge until much later, around the sixth century CE. An early example was the colossal Buddha sculptures in Bamiyan, Afghanistan, tragically destroyed by the Taliban in 2001.[14]

In the Western world, ultramarine blue arrived via the Silk Road during the Middle Ages and remained in use for centuries thereafter. A synthetic version was developed in 1826.

April 1415, the *opera*—a committee of guild members overseeing projects—threatened the artist with a penalty of 25 florins if he did not complete it by the end of May.[15] Artists indeed enjoyed limited freedom in their work, as they had to comply with their patrons' requests. In the numerous private chapels built and decorated in Florence during the Renaissance, for example, the patron's role in the design and execution of projects was central. The primary aim of a chapel was to celebrate the financial, political, and social prestige of its patron, rather than to showcase the artistic talents of its craftsmen, as Hollingsworth points out. It was the patron, not the artist, who was regarded by contemporaries as the creator of the project, and thus the patron sought to control its appearance.[16]

GIOTTO'S SCROVEGNI CHAPEL

A sin, or rather the desire to atone from it, led to one of the most remarkable achievements in Western art: the frescoes by Giotto (c. 1266–1337) in the Scrovegni Chapel at the church of Santa Maria della Carità in Padua. In 1302, Enrico Scrovegni, a wealthy banker and moneylender, commissioned Giotto—arguably the most renowned painter of his time—to adorn the chapel walls with scenes depicting the Life of Christ and the Life of the Virgin. Enrico's intention was to absolve his father's guilt of usury, a practice that the Church strongly condemned. Dante Alighieri had in fact placed Reginaldo Scrovegni in the Seventh Circle of Hell in his *Divine Comedy* for this offense. In Giotto's masterpiece, completed by 1305, Enrico Scrovegni is portrayed on the wall of the *Last Judgment*, depicted kneeling and offering a model of the chapel to the Virgin Mary. Positioned among the blessed on the right side of Christ, this representation symbolizes his quest for redemption through the patronage of this sacred artwork.

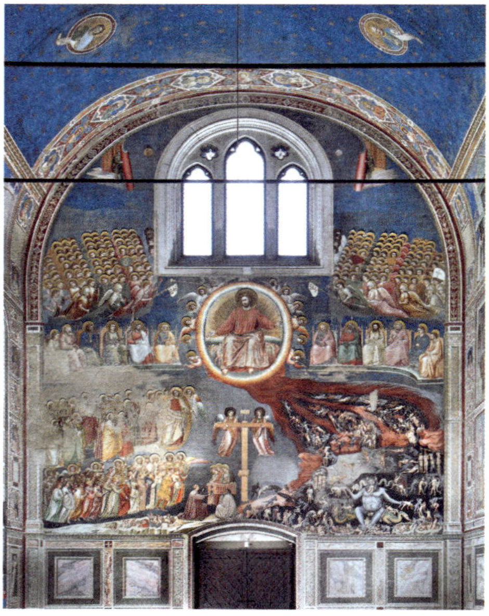

Giotto, *Last Judgment*, 1303–05, Scrovegni Chapel, Padua, Italy

The ruthless, influential, and controversial Medici family in Florence not only shaped the very nature of patronage but were instrumental in affecting the art and culture produced in their city.

As one of Europe's most prosperous trade, commercial, and banking centers, Florence stood as the sole Italian city-state besides Venice to maintain a republican form of government at the onset of the Renaissance. All the other small states in the Italian peninsula had evolved from medieval communal structures to absolute governments controlled by single families, where prominent dynasties emerged. The Sforzas in Milan, the Gonzagas in Mantua, the Estes in Ferrara, the Montefeltros in Urbino, and the Aragonese in Naples established magnificent and prosperous courts. These rulers competed among themselves in artistic and architectural achievements, contributing to the splendid flourishing of the arts across Renaissance Italy.

Progressive for its time, Florence was a republic with democratic elements—if not a full democracy: large segments of the population were totally excluded from its administration; slaves, women, salaried workers, and even aristocrats could not hold public office or vote. Instead, the executive body, the Signoria, composed of eight priors and presided over by the gonfalonier, was drawn from among the members of the guilds. Each prior served for two months and was then no longer eligible to hold the office again for three years.

Since the Middle Ages, great importance was placed on the appearance of cities through the construction and embellishment of public buildings. Guilds and affluent citizens in Florence were expected to contribute, and they competed with one another in lavishness. The Medici family participated in this long-standing tradition of private patronage in Florence. As their power and influence grew, so did their role as supporters of the arts and architecture in the city.[17]

The extraordinary rise of the Medici family, who by the fifteenth century were the wealthiest in Europe, began with Giovanni di Bicci de' Medici (1360–1429), founder of the Medici bank in 1397. He also initiated the family's long tradition of art patronage, participating in the 1401 committee to select and finance the sculptor to create *The Gates of Paradise*, two bronze doors with ten sculptural panels for the Baptistery of the city's cathedral. Lorenzo Ghiberti (1378–1455) was chosen over Filippo Brunelleschi (1377–1446). However, it was Giovanni's son Cosimo de' Medici (1389–1464) who oversaw the spectacular expansion of the bank. Establishing branches across Europe, the Medicis became principal lenders to monarchs and popes, thereby propelling the family's political ascent. Although Cosimo maintained a low profile, reflected even in his modest attire, and Florence retained its republican status, he became the de facto ruler of the city after his return in 1434 from an exile his adversaries forced upon him. With keen foresight, Cosimo directed the family's immense wealth toward patronage of the arts. According to Jean-Yves Boriaud, the Medicis' stroke of genius was to elevate their original identity as merchants and bankers into a far more prestigious cultural sphere in Italy: one centered around philosophy and the arts.[18]

Cosimo's patronage was unparalleled, matching the scale of the wealthiest guilds, as Hollingsworth notes. It visually represented not just his immense wealth but also his prominent position within the framework of Florentine politics.[19] Cosimo financed the restoration or construction of religious buildings: Brunelleschi's dome on the city's cathedral, known as the Duomo; the church of San Lorenzo; the Dominican convent of San Marco, where he always kept his own personal cell. He befriended contemporary artists, in particular Donatello, whose *David* (c. 1460) was the first freestanding male nude bronze statue executed after Roman times. Installed in the family's palace courtyard, the *David* sent a powerful message not unnoticed by the "image-conscious Florentines": the Medicis could afford the high costs of a bronze statue.[20] Another beneficiary of Cosimo's support, in the form of a house and a salary, was Marsilio Ficino (1433–1499), who translated from Greek into Latin the entire works of the philosopher Plato, enabling the wider Western world to read them for the first time. Cosimo also commissioned the architect Michelozzo di Bartolomeo (1396–1472) to design and build a palace for him; started in 1444 and finished in 1484, it was inspired by the classical tradition and became the prototype followed by all major families in Florence.

THE RENAISSANCE

The Renaissance, meaning "rebirth," sought to revive the greatness of classical antiquity. Traditionally believed to have begun in Florence in the early fifteenth century, it was preceded by a resurgence of interest in ancient Greek and Roman philosophy and literature. Central to this revival was the concept that unlike the Middle Ages, when God held center stage, man was now at the center of the world, with the freedom to shape his own destiny. This concept is embodied by the classical Roman idea expressed as "Homo faber suae quisque fortunae": man as the architect of his own fate.[21] The profound impact of this shift permeated every realm of knowledge and artistic expression. Scientific exploration of the natural world, grounded in observation, laid the groundwork for the experimental method. The invention of the movable-type printing press by the German Johannes Gutenberg (1395?–1468)—distinct in certain ways from older printing methods, especially in China and Korea, which are not known to have spread to Europe—made knowledge accessible at dramatically lower costs to an exponentially larger number of people, allowing ideas to circulate more easily. The Polish astronomer Nicolaus Copernicus (1473–1543) formulated the heliocentric theory, which Galileo Galilei (1564–1642) would later perfect, contradicting the long-held Church position that the universe, including the sun, revolves around Earth. The Renaissance's rational approach to knowledge and its renewed emphasis on mathematics also led to the invention of central-point perspective by Filippo Brunelleschi, which represented a transformative innovation in art.

It was in politically fragmented yet economically prosperous Italy that the Renaissance's new artistic language first flourished and later spread across Europe, displacing the previously dominant International Gothic style.

Under Lorenzo the Magnificent (1449–1492), grandson of Cosimo, the Medici influence extended beyond Florence, impacting the delicate balance of power across the Italian peninsula. Lorenzo's strategic marriage to Clarice Orsini, from a prominent Roman aristocratic family, signaled that his family's ambition now reached beyond the confines of the city walls. After he survived an assassination attempt during the infamous Pazzi conspiracy on April 26, 1478—named after the rival family who plotted against the Medicis—Lorenzo's control over Florence became unchallenged (though his brother Giuliano tragically lost his life in the attack).

Lorenzo, known for his refined culture and poetic talents, was not merely a patron but actively engaged in all facets of contemporary culture. He nurtured relationships with scholars, philosophers, and artists, personally contributing to them and enjoying their company.

In 1488, Lorenzo founded an academy in the garden of the family palace, providing a space for young artists to study and copy his extensive collection of classical statues. Among these apprentices was Michelangelo Buonarroti (1475–1564), who resided with Lorenzo's family for three years. Around 1480, to cultivate his leisurely pursuits, Lorenzo commissioned the architect Giuliano da Sangallo (c. 1443–1516) to design the villa at Poggio a Caiano, setting a precedent for aristocratic countryside retreats.

Arnold Hauser explains the profound difference between Cosimo and Lorenzo:

> Cosimo was still entirely a business man; it is true that he loved art and philosophy, had beautiful houses and villas built for himself, surrounded himself with artists and scholars . . . but the bank and the office were the real centre of his life. Lorenzo no longer takes any interest in the business of his grandfather and great-grandfathers, he neglects it and allows it to decline; he is only interested in state business, in his connections with the European dynasties, his court household, his role as intellectual leader, his Neoplatonic philosophers and his art academy, his experiments in poetry and his patronage of the arts.[22]

Lorenzo nurtured an entire generation of artists and facilitated their success by helping them secure commissions in various courts. In 1481, for example, he sent Sandro Botticelli (1444/45–1510) and Domenico Ghirlandaio (1449–1494) to Rome to paint frescoes on walls of the newly constructed Sistine Chapel at the Vatican. Under Lorenzo's patronage, Florence reached its pinnacle as a magnificent *fucina* (forge) of artistic innovation and production. As Hollingsworth points out, Lorenzo was the central figure in the portrayal of cultural superiority that fifteenth-century Florentines promoted as propaganda for their city's prestige.[23]

In 1494, two years after Lorenzo's death, Italy faced invasion by Charles VIII of France, leading to the exile of the Medicis from Florence. A "popular" republic was established, influenced by the fiery preaching of the Dominican friar Girolamo Savonarola (1452–1498), who vehemently denounced the vices of a corrupt society. Savonarola condemned all worldly luxuries, including the sophisticated culture epitomized by the Medicis, leading to the infamous "bonfires of the vanities" where books, perfumes, and works of art were burned. The following year, papal opposition led to Savonarola's death by hanging and the burning of his body. Ironically, during this period, a sculpture of David (1501–04), symbolizing the new Florentine republic's defiance against Medici tyranny, was commissioned to Michelangelo, who had been a young protégé of Lorenzo.

Restored to power in 1512, the Medicis extended their influence into the Church of Rome, ultimately producing two popes: Leo X (1475–1521), who was Lorenzo's second son, and Clement VII (1478–1534), the son of Giuliano, Lorenzo's brother. Leo X, known for his lavish patronage of the arts, commissioned Michelangelo in 1519 to create the Medici tombs in the church of San Lorenzo in Florence, to immortalize the family's glory for eternity.

BENOZZO GOZZOLI'S MAGI CHAPEL FRESCOES (1459)

On the piano nobile of the Medici palace, the frescoes by Benozzo Gozzoli in the Chapel of the Magi epitomize the family's celebration of the Epiphany; symbolically resonant in wealthy Florence, it was among the city's most significant public processions. These frescoes depict the wealthy and powerful paying homage to the baby Jesus. Two of the Magi are portrayed with the faces of Joseph II, patriarch of Constantinople, and John VIII Palaeologus, Eastern Roman emperor. Cosimo is depicted humbly on the back of a mule, to signify his modest demeanor, and the young Lorenzo, Cosimo's grandson, is also identifiable in the scene. The frescoes include representations of friends and political allies such as Galeazzo Maria Sforza from Milan and Sigismondo Pandolfo Malatesta, lord of Rimini. A confraternity named the Magi was established in 1417, and Cosimo was a member.

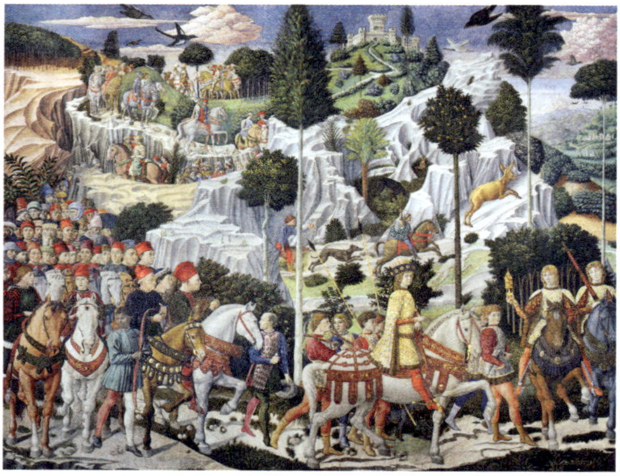

Benozzo Gozzoli, *Procession of the Magi* (detail), 1459, Chapel of the Magi, Palazzo Medici Riccardi, Florence, Italy

Despite the constraints of a patriarchal society, female patronage flourished during the Renaissance. Isabella d'Este (1474–1539), referred to as "the First Lady of the World" by the diplomat Niccolò da Correggio, was the most outstanding among them.

Her life unfolded between two sophisticated courts in the Pianura Padana, or Padan Plain (also known as the Po Valley), in northern Italy: Ferrara, where she was born—the daughter of Duke Ercole I d'Este and Eleanor of Naples—and Mantua, of which she became the marchioness by marrying, at the age of sixteen, Francesco Gonzaga. Enjoying a privileged status, Isabella was a participant in exciting but turbulent times, marked by the rise and fall of the Borgia family, that shook the fragile balance of the Italian peninsula.

Thanks to the approximately thirty thousand surviving letters written by and to Isabella throughout her lifetime, we have insights into her extensive interactions. She encountered popes—Julius II, Leo X, and Clement VII—and was in Rome during the devastating sack of the city on May 6, 1527; she met with rulers such as Duke Ludovico Sforza, "il Moro"; kings like Louis XII of France; and others including Charles V, the Holy Roman emperor. Isabella actively supported literary figures such as Matteo Maria Boiardo, Baldassare Castiglione, and Ludovico Ariosto, as well as renowned artists like Andrea Mantegna, Titian, and Leonardo da Vinci, among others.

In the sophisticated Este court of Ferrara, Isabella received a humanistic education. She mastered Latin, Greek, and Roman history, along with learning to play multiple musical instruments and developing skills in singing and dance. Upon entering the Gonzaga court through her marriage—a union intended to solidify the alliance between the strategically vital city-states of Ferrara and Mantua—Isabella immediately assumed a substantial role in the administration of the marquisate. Francesco, like many Renaissance rulers of city-states, served as a condottiere—an experienced military leader. As captain general of the armies of the Republic of Venice, he frequently had to leave Mantua. During his extended absences, Isabella assumed the role of ruler. In Italian city-states, it was not uncommon for wives to assist in public administration. In 1509, when Francesco was imprisoned in Venice after serving in another army, Isabella temporarily governed the marquisate, demonstrating exceptional diplomatic skills and political acumen.

Isabella was renowned for her strong, determined, and authoritative temperament. Upon arriving in Mantua, she clashed with the court painter Andrea Mantegna (c. 1431–1506) over a portrait he painted of her, which she found unflattering. (The portrait has been lost.) As a patron, Isabella exercised tight control, providing detailed instructions to artists regarding the subjects and styles she expected from them. She commissioned allegorical and mythological paintings from some of the era's most celebrated masters, including Mantegna, Pietro Perugino, and Lorenzo Costa. An avid and passionate collector, Isabella was the only Renaissance woman to have her own *studiolo*, a private study and true expression of the Renaissance spirit, a place to meditate and contemplate beauty, which the owner would fill with artistic treasures. In hers, in the Palazzo Ducale in Mantua, Isabella gathered antique busts, fine bronzes, coins, cameos, vases, and paintings that her agents in Venice and Rome chased down for her. Isabella's passion and unwavering determination are exemplified in several anecdotes from her life. One notable instance involves Michelangelo's marble of *Venus and Cupid*, created in 1491 for the Duke of Urbino. Isabella acquired this sculpture through Cesare Borgia when he conquered Urbino. Despite the legitimate duke reclaiming his possessions later on, Isabella refused to return the bust and instead wrote a shrewd and diplomatic letter to justify her possession. She also compelled the court painter Mantegna to sell her a Roman bust of Faustina, a second-century empress, as compensation for his debts.

Isabella's *studiolo*, a sanctuary for her collection and intellectual pursuits, was disbanded after her death. Only an inventory code remains, and its contents have been dispersed among various museum collections worldwide, including the Musée du Louvre in Paris, the Victoria and Albert Museum in London, and the Castello Sforzesco in Milan.

A preparatory drawing now housed in the Louvre represents Isabella's unfulfilled desire to be portrayed by Leonardo da Vinci (1452–1519). After encountering Leonardo's painting *Lady with an Ermine* (c. 1489) in Milan, which depicts Ludovico il Moro's mistress Cecilia Gallerani, Isabella actively sought to commission her own portrait from the artist. However, despite her persistent attempts, she could only humbly ask, albeit unsuccessfully, "to have something we have longed for, something of your hand."[24]

Isabella's sisters-in-law Elisabetta Gonzaga (1471–1526), Duchess of Urbino, and Lucrezia Borgia (1480–1519) were also influential art patrons in Renaissance Italy.

THE ARTIST'S STATUS

In the Middle Ages and early Renaissance, artists were regarded as artisans, skilled laborers. Their work as painters and sculptors fell under the category of mechanical arts, which were deemed less noble compared to the liberal arts, such as philosophy, rhetoric, and mathematics.

In the construction sites of medieval churches, abbeys, and cathedrals, techniques and artistic skills evolved, giving rise to distinct professional roles: stonecutters, sculptors, painters, and glassmakers. A master builder organized the workforce, assigning tasks and coordinating the project's execution. During this period, the concept of the "architect" as the primary designer of a project had not yet emerged. The Romanesque site remained relatively anonymous, with knowledge transmitted orally rather than through written records.[25] Over time, the role of the architect began to be distinguished from that of the master builder, and their names started to be recorded alongside those of sculptors and painters.

During the early Middle Ages, workshops had an itinerant nature, moving to wherever work was needed. For instance, the renowned comacine (stonemason) masters—possibly named for their origins around Italy's

Lake Como or from the Latin *cum machinis*, indicating their use of certain structures like wooden scaffolds—were documented as active across different parts of Europe.

A significant transformation in the status of artists occurred with the resurgence of urban life toward the end of the twelfth century. As the urban bourgeoisie flourished, there emerged a steady demand for artistic creations, liberating artists from what were little more than construction sites. Establishing themselves as independent masters and recognizing their own professionalism, artists began to maintain stable workshops with apprentices. Painters and sculptors started signing their works, marking a departure from anonymity. Treatises and instructional books, such as Cennino Cennini's renowned *Treatise on Painting*, were written to transmit and celebrate an accumulated knowledge to be proud of.[26]

In order to practice their profession, artists had to be members of guilds, associations that originated in the Middle Ages to safeguard the collective interests of workers practicing the same craft. A member would pay a certain fee to join the guild, and usually artists were not permitted to work if they were not members. The guild established norms for training, determined the number of apprentices allowed to enter the trade every year, defined days and hours of work, and set quality standards for the various objects that its members made. In Florence, painters belonged to the guild of the Arte dei Medici e Speziali (Doctors and Apothecaries), because they bought their pigments from the apothecaries; sculptors were members of the Maestri di Pietra e Legname (Masters of Stone and Wood) guild.

The guild usually imposed sanctions on foreign artists. For instance, in Venice, even if an artist had become a permanent resident and was thus eligible to join the painters' guild, the entrance fee would have been double that of a native artist, and permission to sell works came with limitations. The German painter Albrecht Dürer (1471–1528) was invited to Venice by the Scuola dei Tedeschi (School of the Germans)—the *scuole* were religious confraternities of merchants from foreign countries operating in the lagoonal city. Commissioned to paint the *Feast of the Rosary* (1506) for the altar of the church of San Bartolomeo in the Rialto, Dürer created a masterpiece that offered a unique synthesis of German and Venetian aesthetic values. However, he constantly complained about the hostile treatment from the local painters and guild, reporting that he was summoned three times before the local magistrates and forced to pay a fine. Guild rules also often prohibited women from learning or practicing certain trades, thereby institutionalizing the patriarchal system that was reflected in the labor market and broader society at that time.[27]

Due to the artist's status as an artisan, the factors determining the value of an artwork differed greatly from contemporary standards. The use of precious materials such as gold or costly ultramarine, the dimensions of the artwork, the subject matter, the complexity of the composition, and the hours of labor were considered more valuable than the artist's creativity and originality. Jonathan K. Nelson and Richard J. Zeckhauser observe that until the sixteenth century, even for renowned artists, materials for a large altarpiece cost more than their labor.[28]

RAPHAEL'S *SCHOOL OF ATHENS* (1508–11)

In 1508, Pope Julius II commissioned Raphael to decorate the Stanze, the pope's personal apartments, which are now part of the Vatican Museums. In the Stanza della Segnatura (Room of the Signature), the four branches of human knowledge are depicted: Theology, Philosophy, Poetry, and Justice. Philosophy is represented by the fresco *The School of Athens*. In a Roman-inspired setting, Raphael included the most important philosophers of ancient times, centering the composition on Plato and Aristotle. Heraclitus, portrayed as sitting alone and deep in thought, bears the features of Michelangelo, who was working on the Sistine Chapel frescoes while Raphael painted the Stanze. Euclid is modeled after the architect Donato Bramante, who was overseeing the reconstruction of Saint Peter's Basilica. Raphael's work boldly asserts the elevated status of the artist, claiming intellectual value and recognition on par with the most revered ancient philosophers and thinkers.

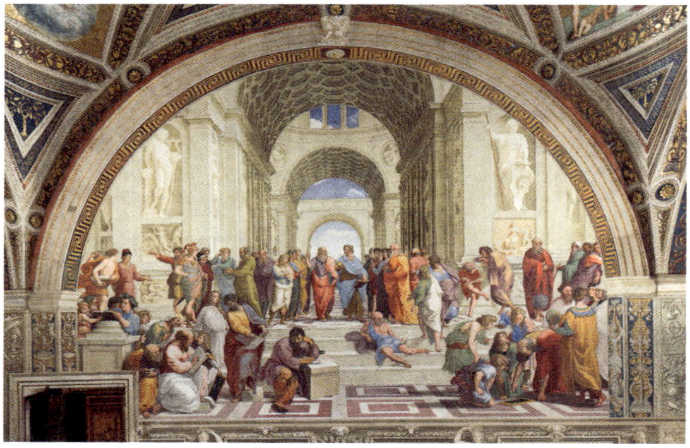

Raphael, *The School of Athens*, 1508–11, Apostolic Palace, Vatican City

By the end of the 1400s, the status of artists began to undergo a transformation. As Hauser points out, although artists still relied on commissions for their work, they started to receive better pay. Toward the late fifteenth century, some artists accrued wealth and gradually gained independence from their guilds, whose protection became less crucial as their personal reputations soared. Furthermore, artists began to be viewed as subjects of interest in their own right. Biographies of artists were emerging, with the first known one being that of Brunelleschi. Ghiberti even penned his own autobiography, signaling a significant shift in which the artist was recognized as a noteworthy figure deserving of literary attention.[29]

Critical to the recognition of artists was the publication of Giorgio Vasari's *The Lives of the Most Excellent Painters, Sculptors, and Architects* in 1550. Chronicling artistic development from Cimabue (c. 1240–before 1302) to his contemporaries, Vasari introduced the concept of "genius," whereby the work of art becomes the expression of an original personality.

This perspective shifted the focus of artistic appreciation from the subject matter itself to the unique and creative choices that the artist made in representing that subject. In their introduction to an edition of the *Lives* that they translated, Julia Conaway Bondanella and Peter Bondanella observe that Vasari did not employ the word *artista* (artist) in his text, nor did he consistently use the term *artigiano* (artisan), but instead he referred to an artist as an *artefice* (artificer), from the Latin *artifex*, usually utilized in theological writings to refer to God the Creator.[30]

The changed status of the artist was reflected in the payments and in the relationship with patrons. Raphael (1483–1520) had his own palace in Rome; Titian (c. 1488–1576) was named a count by the Holy Roman emperor, Charles V, and admitted to the imperial court; Michelangelo was the highest-paid artist of the era, and he had personal relationships with various popes. Federico II Gonzaga (1500–1540), Duke of Mantua, wrote to his agent instructing him to obtain a work by Michelangelo: "And should he per chance ask what subject we prefer, tell him that we merely wish and hope for a work of his genius."[31]

The establishment of the first academies in cities such as Rome, Bologna, Paris, and Antwerp, beginning with the Florentine Accademia del Disegno in 1563, marked a significant milestone in the emancipation of artists from the guild system. These academies provided artists with education that went beyond technical skills, encompassing philosophy, history, literature, and theology. This development reflected a newfound recognition and awareness of artists' status and intellectual needs within society.

MICHELANGELO, JULIUS II, AND THE SISTINE CHAPEL

Michelangelo's frescoes for the ceiling of the Sistine Chapel (1508–12), depicting scenes from the Old Testament interspersed with figures of the Sibyls, are among the most astounding and revolutionary accomplishments of Western art. The story behind their commission is equally fascinating, highlighting the tempestuous relationship between Michelangelo and his patron, Pope Julius II (1443–1513).

In 1505, Julius II (who had become pope two years earlier) lured Michelangelo to Rome from his native Florence with the grandiose project of designing and sculpting the pontiff's marble tomb in Saint Peter's Basilica. The monument was envisioned on an unprecedented scale, featuring more than forty full-figure statues across three stories. It was intended to embody Julius II's immense power and, in the words of Bram Kempers, to surpass not only the achievements of his predecessors Sixtus IV and Innocent VIII but also those of most princes.[32]

The project thrilled the ambitious Michelangelo, whose major accomplishments at the time were primarily sculptures. These included the *Pietà* (1498–99) now in Saint Peter's Basilica, for Jean Bilhères de Lagraulas, a French cardinal in Rome; the *David* (1501–04) for the Republic of Florence; and a *Madonna and Child* (*Madonna of Bruges*, 1501–04) for the Bruges

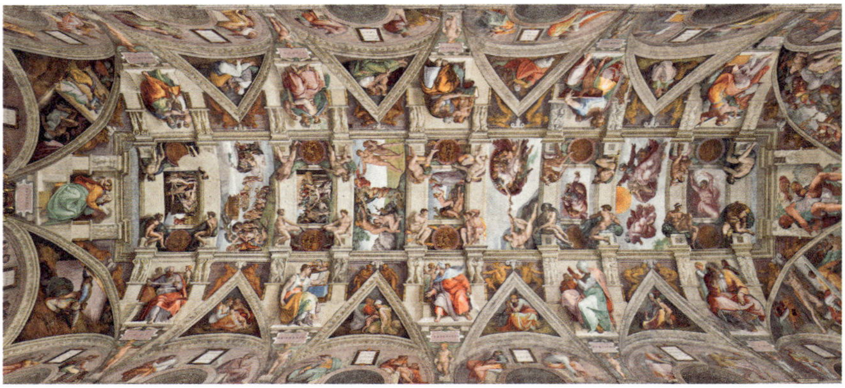

Michelangelo's frescoes for the Sistine Chapel (detail), 1508–12, Apostolic Palace, Vatican City

merchants Giovanni and Alessandro Moscheroni. Julius II's tomb promised to be of a grander magnitude than any of Michelangelo's previous works.

In 1505, he spent five months in the Carrara quarries searching for the perfect pieces of marble. However, upon the artist's return to Rome in 1506, Julius II decided to postpone the tomb project and instead commissioned Michelangelo to paint the vault of the Sistine Chapel. Vasari writes: "Michelangelo, who wished to finish the tomb and saw that painting the vault would be an enormous and difficult task, considering his lack of experience with colors, tried in every way possible to remove this burden from his shoulders, recommending Raphael instead. But the more he refused, the more persistent he made the pope, who was an impetuous man in his undertakings."[33]

The Sistine Chapel ceiling, frescoed—with gold stars on a blue background—between 1477 and 1480 by Piermatteo d'Amelia (c. 1450–1508) during the pontificate of Sixtus IV, was in desperate need of restoration due to irreparable cracks. Reluctantly, as he considered himself primarily a sculptor, Michelangelo accepted Julius II's commission to paint the vault. A contract for the project was drafted by Cardinal Francesco Alidosi, promising Michelangelo the substantial sum of 3,000 ducats. The artist embarked on this four-year enterprise, confronting and overcoming numerous technical challenges. Unfamiliar with the fresco technique, he initially faced significant difficulties, including the appearance of mold on the surface of *The Deluge* during the early phase of the decoration.

Vasari reported:

> When a third of the chapel had been completed, certain spots of mould started to appear one winter as the north wind was blowing. This was caused by the fact that Roman lime, which is white and made from travertine, does not dry very quickly, and when mixed with pozzolana, which is tan in colour, it makes a dark mixture that is watery when it is in a liquid state, and when the wall is well moistened, it often develops a

powdery crust while drying: here, in this case, the salty secretion popped up in many places but was worn away by the air with the passage of time. Michelangelo was in despair over this and did not want to continue.[34]

But continue he did, and to extraordinary results.

The Sistine Chapel was just one of Julius II's ambitious undertakings. The pontiff dedicated all his efforts to bolstering the power and splendor of the Papal States. Known as "the Warrior Pope," Julius II not only expanded the territory of the papacy and personally led troops in battle but also transformed Rome into an exceptional center of artistic and architectural patronage, challenging the dominance of Florence and Venice. He summoned the foremost artists of the era, and in the ensuing decades, Rome would cultivate a solemn and majestic artistic style to manifest the authority of the Church.

Pope Julius II's ambitious projects in the early 1500s marked the culmination of nearly a century of efforts to reinvigorate both the papacy and the city, after more than a century of earlier crises triggered by factionalism in the Church and conflicts with the French king. Seven popes had abandoned Rome, residing in Avignon, France, from 1309 to 1377, and that was soon followed by a complete split, with competing claimants to the papacy in the two cities (and even a third, in Pisa, for a few years). The Western Schism ended in 1417 when the Church rejected the so-called antipopes and united in Rome behind Pope Martin V.

By then, Rome was in a state of economic decline and urban decay. Its population, numbering several hundred thousand at the peak of the Roman Empire, had plummeted to seventeen thousand inhabitants; its churches, palaces, roads, and bridges were dilapidated and in ruins. Restoring the unimpressive city's appearance and urban structure became a top priority. As Hollingsworth explains, Pope Martin V's initial motivation for urban and artistic revitalization was propaganda.[35] He and his successors initiated a program to reinstate papal authority, with the restoration and enhancement of Rome's monuments and churches as a cornerstone.

It was not until the election of Giuliano della Rovere as Pope Julius II in 1503 that Rome truly became a thriving and independent artistic center. During this time, while Michelangelo painted the Sistine Chapel, the architect Donato Bramante (c. 1444–1514) designed the new Saint Peter's Basilica project. The original fourth-century building, founded by Emperor Constantine, had become inadequate for Julius II's ambitions. Young Raphael was also summoned to Rome to decorate the Stanze, the pope's private rooms. Concurrently, existing churches were being renovated, roads and aqueducts were undergoing repairs, and Castel Sant'Angelo (which had evolved from an ancient Roman imperial mausoleum to a fortress and papal castle) was being fortified.

In addition to the pontiff's support, a flourishing private patronage emerged from wealthy cardinals, merchants, and bankers. Figures such as the banker Agostino Chigi and the influential Cardinal Scipione Borghese played significant roles in supporting and commissioning art.

LEONARDO DA VINCI: COMMISSIONS NEVER DELIVERED

Leonardo da Vinci was renowned among his contemporaries not only for his extraordinary talents as a painter, engineer, and scientist but also for his frequent tendency to fail to deliver commissioned works of art. Never completely satisfied with his creations, Leonardo often made revisions and sometimes retained pieces for himself.

One of the most famous examples of Leonardo's unfulfilled commissions is the universally admired *Mona Lisa*, which he began in 1503. According to Giorgio Vasari, Leonardo undertook the portrait of Lisa Gherardini, the wife of Francesco del Giocondo. After laboring over it for four years, Leonardo left the work incomplete and brought it with him to France when summoned in 1516 by King Francis I (1494–1547), who provided the artist with a generous allowance and a residence at the Château du Cloux (later renamed Clos Lucé), near Amboise.

Following Leonardo's death, the *Mona Lisa* was listed in the inventory of his estate and likely purchased by Francis I. The painting remained in the royal collections and eventually found its place in the Musée du Louvre, where it continues to be housed today.

Another of Leonardo's paintings, *The Virgin of the Rocks*, depicting the Virgin Mary with the infants Jesus and Saint John the Baptist as well as an angel, exists in two versions: one in the Louvre and the other in the National Gallery in London. In the early 1480s, while residing in Milan, Leonardo received a joint commission with the painters Ambrogio and Evangelista de Predis from the Confraternity of the Immaculate Conception in Milan for an altarpiece intended for the church of San Francesco Grande. The first version, completed between 1483 and 1486 and now in the Louvre, reportedly led to a dispute over payment with the confraternity, as Walter Isaacson suggests in his biography of the artist. Subsequently, this version was either sold or relocated. Its presence in the French royal collections is documented from 1627, but evidence suggests it may have been acquired much earlier, possibly during Louis XII's time in Milan around 1500–1503. Around 1495, Leonardo collaborated with Ambrogio de Predis for the same confraternity on another version of *The Virgin of the Rocks*, finally completed in 1508 and now in London.[36]

REJECTED COMMISSIONS

Commissions could, and sometimes did, face rejection if they failed to meet the patron's expectations. This was the fate of two significant works by Michelangelo Merisi, known as Caravaggio (1571–1610): *Saint Matthew and the Angel*, painted in 1602 and unfortunately destroyed during World War II, and *The Death of the Virgin* (1601–06), now considered one of his masterpieces.

Saint Matthew and the Angel was commissioned for the Contarelli Chapel in the church of San Luigi dei Francesi in Rome, following his earlier successful works, *The Martyrdom of Saint Matthew* and *The Calling of Saint Matthew*, both completed in 1599-1600. These paintings marked Caravaggio's first major commission to be displayed prominently in a public space. While *The Martyrdom of Saint Matthew* and *The Calling of Saint Matthew* pleased their patrons, the third painting, depicting Saint Matthew writing his Gospel, did not.

According to Andrew Graham-Dixon in his biography of the artist, the dissatisfaction stemmed from the realistic and somewhat unflattering portrayal of Saint Matthew. Caravaggio's initial depiction showed Matthew with balding head, gnarled hands, bare legs, and heavy feet—a starkly realistic, proletarian figure that was deemed disrespectful. As a result, Caravaggio had to paint a revised version, *The Inspiration of Saint Matthew* (1602), which portrays the saint in a more dignified manner. This revised painting was ultimately approved by his patrons and, with the first two portraits of Saint Matthew, is still in the Contarelli Chapel.[37]

Even more scandalous at the time of its creation was *The Death of the Virgin*, which Laerzio Cherubini commissioned for his chapel in the church of Santa Maria della Scala in the Trastevere section of Rome. Caravaggio allegedly used the body of a woman drowned in the Tiber, likely a prostitute, as the model for the Virgin Mary. The composition lacks any glorification of Christ's mother, portraying her with swollen feet and in the stark abandonment of death.

The fathers of Santa Maria della Scala were deeply displeased and rejected the painting, subsequently commissioning Carlo Saraceni (c. 1579–1620) to replace it. However, *The Death of the Virgin* later found its way into the collection of the Duke of Mantua, Vincenzo Gonzaga, thanks to Peter Paul Rubens's recommendation. King Charles I of England acquired it in 1627 as part of the Gonzaga collection. Following Charles I's execution in 1649, the painting entered another royal collection, that of Louis XIV of France. It is now in the Louvre.

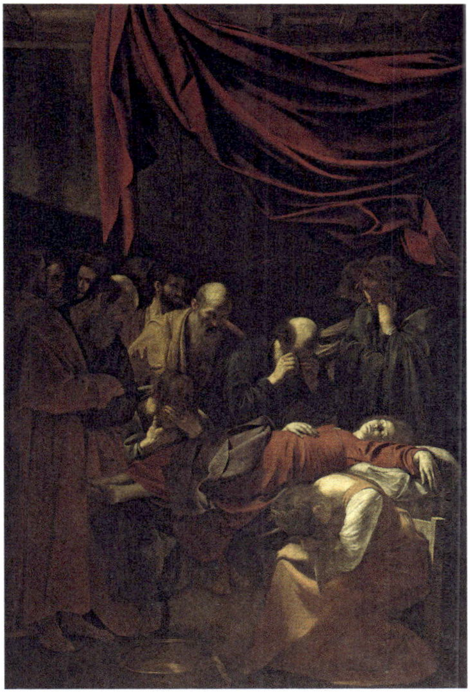

Caravaggio, *The Death of the Virgin*, 1601–06, Musée du Louvre, Paris

NOTES

1 Christian Norberg-Schultz, *Meaning in Western Architecture* (New York: Rizzoli International, 1980), 58.

2 Saint Gregory the Great, *Dialogues*, trans. Odo John Zimmerman, Fathers of the Church (Washington, DC: Catholic University of America Press, 2022), 223.

3 Arnold Hauser, *The Social History of Art*, vol. 1, *From Prehistoric Times to the Middle Ages* (New York: Vintage Books, 1957), 152–53.

4 Alessandro Barbero, *Carlo Magno: Un padre dell'Europa* (Rome: Economica Laterza, 2000), 259.

5 *The Chronicle of Rudolf the Glaber*, trans. Ernest H. McCarthy (Washington, DC: Catholic University of America Press, 1955), 119.

6 Otto von Simson, *The Gothic Cathedral: Origins of Gothic Architecture and the Medieval Concept of Order* (Princeton, NJ: Princeton University Press, 1956), 3.

7 Simson, *Gothic Cathedral*, 62.

8 Colin B. Bailey, director's foreword to *Medieval Money, Merchants, and Morality*, by Diane Wolfthal et al., exh. cat. (New York: Morgan Library & Museum in association with D. Giles, 2023), 6.

9 Michael Baxandall, *Painting and Experience in Fifteenth-Century Italy: A Primer in the Social History of Pictorial Style*, 2nd ed. (Oxford, UK: Oxford University Press, 1988), 1.

10 Bram Kempers, *Painting, Power and Patronage: The Rise of the Professional Artist in Renaissance Italy*, trans. Beverley Jackson (London: Allen Lane, an imprint of Penguin Press, 1992), 187.

11 Cennino d'Andrea Cennini, *The Craftsman's Handbook: The Italian "Il libro dell'arte,"* trans. Daniel V. Thompson Jr. (1933; repr., Garden City, NY: Dover, 1954), 37.

12 Victoria Finlay, *The Brilliant History of Color in Art* (Los Angeles: Getty Publications, 2014), 44–46.

13 E. Melanie Gifford and Lisha Deming Glinsman, "Collective Style and Personal Manner: Materials and Techniques of High-Life Genre Painting," in *Vermeer and the Masters of Genre Painting: Inspiration and Rivalry*, ed. Adriaan E. Waiboer, with Arthur K. Wheelock Jr. and Blaise Ducos, exh. cat. (Dublin: National Gallery of Ireland; Washington, DC: National Gallery of Art; Paris: Musée du Louvre, in association with Yale University Press, 2017), 68.

14 Finlay, *Brilliant History of Color*, 44–46.

15 Mary Hollingsworth, *Patronage in Renaissance Italy: From 1400 to the Early Sixteenth Century* (Baltimore: Johns Hopkins University Press, 1994), 34.

16 Hollingsworth, *Patronage in Renaissance Italy*, 10, 52.

17 Hollingsworth, *Patronage in Renaissance Italy*, 28–30.

18 Jean-Yves Boriaud, *La Fortune des Médicis: Le Siècle d'or de Florence* (Paris: Perrin, 2019), 150.

19 Hollingsworth, *Patronage in Renaissance Italy*, 63.

20 Hollingsworth, *Patronage in Renaissance Italy*, 85.

21 A maxim by Appius Claudius (who had Caecus, or "the Blind," appended to his name later in life), a Roman censor, or magistrate, who flourished before and after 300 BCE.

22 Arnold Hauser, *The Social History of Art*, vol. 2, *Renaissance, Mannerism, Baroque* (New York: Vintage Books, 1957), 35.

23 Hollingsworth, *Patronage in Renaissance Italy*, 97.

24 Isabella d'Este to Leonardo da Vinci, October 31, 1504, in David S. Chambers, *Patrons and Artists in the Italian Renaissance* (Columbia: University of South Carolina Press, 1971), 147–48.

25 Francesca Prina, *The Story of Romanesque Architecture* (Munich: Prestel, 2011), 9.

26 Hauser, *Social History of Art*, vol. 1.

27 Steven A. Epstein, "The European Economy, 1200–1500," in Wolfthal et al., *Medieval Money, Merchants and Morality*, 25.

28 Jonathan K. Nelson and Richard J. Zeckhauser, *The Patron's Payoff: Conspicuous Commissions in Italian Renaissance Art* (Princeton, NJ: Princeton University Press, 2008), 51.

29 Hauser, *Social History of Art*, 2:65.

30 Giorgio Vasari, *The Lives of the Artists*, trans. with an introduction and notes by Julia Conaway Bondanella and Peter Bondanella, Oxford World's Classics (Oxford, UK: Oxford University Press, 1998), xii.

31 Federico II Gonzaga to his agent in Florence, Giovanni Borromeo, 1527, in Anna Tummers, "'By His Hand': The Paradox of Seventeenth-Century Connoisseurship," in *Art Market and Connoisseurship: A Closer Look at Paintings by Rembrandt, Rubens and Their Contemporaries*, ed. Anna Tummers and Koenraad Jonckheere (Amsterdam: Amsterdam University Press, 2008), 60n30.

32 Kempers, *Painting, Power and Patronage*, 249.

33 Vasari, *Lives of the Artists*, 439.

34 Vasari, *Lives of the Artists*, 441.

35 Hollingsworth, *Patronage in Renaissance Italy*, 267.

36 Walter Isaacson, *Leonardo da Vinci* (New York: Simon & Schuster, 2017), 224.

37 Andrew Graham-Dixon, *Caravaggio: A Life Sacred and Profane* (New York: W. W. Norton, 2010), 234–37.

2. The Dutch Golden Age and the First Free Market

p. 37 The Birth of the Dutch Republic

p. 39 A New Art for New Buyers

p. 39 Portraiture

p. 40 Landscape

p. 41 Rembrandt

p. 43 Still Life

p. 44 Peter Paul Rubens

p. 46 Johannes Vermeer

p. 47 Genre Painting and Interior Scenes

p. 48 Artists' Status, Dealers, Prices

p. 50 The Decline of the Dutch Golden Age

This surge in both demand and supply created a dynamic Dutch art market that differed fundamentally from the art markets of previous periods, especially in Italy, which had been dominated by patronage.

—Titia Hulst, ed., *A History of the Western Art Market*

In the seventeenth-century Dutch Republic, an open art market developed for the first time in history. A combination of political, economic, religious, and social changes spurred this development.

Holland and its neighboring provinces, after a decades-long struggle against Spanish rule, had finally been recognized as a Protestant state and a republic, which meant that artists could no longer depend on the patronage of the Church and the court. This shift had profound and immediate repercussions on the art system. Dutch artists had to reinvent themselves to adapt to the preferences of the burgeoning bourgeoisie, who were their primary clients.

New genres were created, such as the landscape, the still life, and interior scenes; existing genres, like portraiture, were reinterpreted in order to satisfy the tastes and aspirations of the mercantile classes.

In the prosperous Dutch Republic, wealth was much more widely distributed than in the rest of Europe, and this was accompanied by significant social mobility and the highest literacy rate. This meant that even the middle and working classes became art buyers, and their demand prompted an unprecedented mass production, created not on commission but for an anonymous open art market.

THE BIRTH OF THE DUTCH REPUBLIC

When Martin Luther (1483–1546), an Augustinian monk and professor of moral theology at the University of Wittenberg, posted his Ninety-Five Theses on the door of Wittenberg's Castle Church on October 31, 1517, he could have not foreseen that he was igniting a profound upheaval that would ultimately divide the Christian world. The theses criticized the Catholic Church's practice of selling indulgences, or the remission of sins through monetary payment. In Rome, under the pontificate of Leo X (1513–21), the activity had escalated to unparalleled levels. The pope intended to use the money raised in the form of the so-called plenary indulgence—full removal of all temporal penalty for sins—to finance the reconstruction of Saint Peter's Basilica.

The Counter-Reformation of the Church of Rome against Luther's attempt to "reform" the Church led to devastating religious wars in a Christian world eventually split between Protestant and Catholic countries.

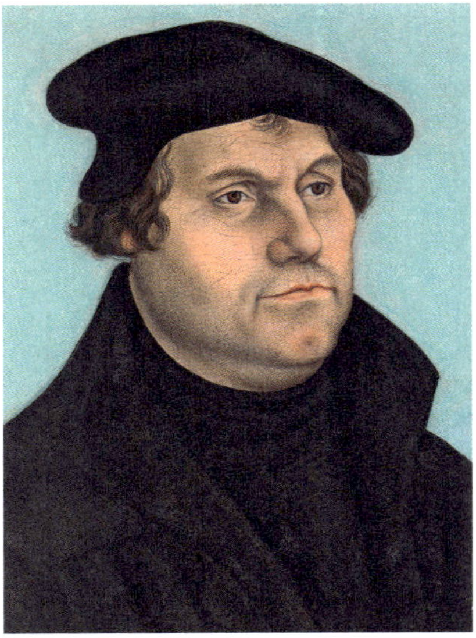

Workshop of Lucas Cranach the Elder, *Martin Luther*, probably 1532, Metropolitan Museum of Art, New York

The political and economic structure of Europe would be dramatically shaken and forever changed, and these transformations would also deeply affect the role and function of art.

Starting in 1556, the seven northern provinces of the Low Countries (most of what is today the Netherlands) were part of the Spanish Empire. Having embraced Protestant reforms as primarily developed by the French theologian John Calvin (1509–1564), then living in Switzerland, what came to be known as the Seven United Provinces soon entered into an open conflict with the ruling Catholic king of Spain, Philip II, which in 1568 turned into what was later called the Eighty Years' War. In 1648, in the Peace of Münster, Spain formally recognized the independence of the Protestant northern provinces as the Dutch Republic. The southern provinces (essentially, present-day Belgium and Luxembourg) remained under Spanish control and Catholic.

The new Dutch Republic, a confederation but widely seen as led by the economic and maritime power of Holland, quickly became the most prosperous and urbanized nation in Europe, with half of its population living in cities. Trade, industry, sciences, and arts thrived; it was the "Dutch Golden Age." Improved agriculture, along with flourishing fishing, shipping, and trading industries, propelled this small nation of only two million people to the status of an economic world power.

The Dutch East India Company, established in 1602, would expand and monopolize the trade routes to the Far East for the next two centuries, building outposts—the first one in what is now Indonesia—and even employing its own army. It was also the first company in history to be publicly traded, meaning that private citizens were allowed to buy public shares.

Also worth mentioning is the tulip mania bubble, often cited as one of the first recorded financial bubbles in history. Tulips, newly introduced in the Dutch Republic from the Ottoman Empire, became a luxury item and status symbol, and their prices reached extraordinary highs. People invested heavily, often paying the equivalent of a skilled worker's annual salary for a single bulb. When the speculative frenzy burst in 1637, prices plummeted, causing the financial ruin of many investors.

A NEW ART FOR NEW BUYERS

Without commissions from the Catholic Church or an aristocratic court, Dutch art had to reinvent itself to meet the bourgeoisie's demands: content, style, and methods of production were profoundly impacted. Furthermore, wealth distribution meant widespread ownership of paintings. Titia Hulst cites an estimate that in the mid-seventeenth century, two-thirds of the population of the town of Delft lived in a household with at least one painting on the wall—eleven on average—and small paintings were even listed in the personal inventories of simple artisans.[1]

The new buyers desired paintings that resonated with them, featuring subjects that reflected their own aspirations and lifestyles. Grand mythological and historical scenes were declined in favor of new genres, or already existing ones that acquired a different meaning and impulse. Portraits, landscapes, still lifes, and interior scenes became the most coveted genres, and their production dramatically increased. According to Michael North, seventeenth-century Dutch painting is the most evident manifestation of all the changes that occurred during the Golden Age.[2]

PORTRAITURE

Although portraiture was not a new genre, Dutch painters imbued it with new and original interpretations. Portraits were still commissioned, but the patrons belonged to the mercantile classes and their civic organizations. Bob Haak notes that the number of portraits painted in Holland during the seventeenth century was enormous. Besides individual ones, there were portraits of couples, whole families, and groups, especially of civic organizations such as the militia and guilds, to show their collective identity and camaraderie. In the booming economy of the Dutch Golden Age, portraits became the favorite form of interior decoration.[3]

A combination of realism, attention to detail, and a focus on the individuality and social status of the subjects characterized the portraits produced during this time. Artists like Rembrandt van Rijn (1606–1669), Frans Hals (1580–1666), Johannes Vermeer (1632–1675), and Judith Leyster (1609–1660) employed techniques such as chiaroscuro (the contrast of light and dark) to create greater dimensionality, giving their subjects a lifelike presence. Rembrandt was renowned for his ability to capture the psychological depth and nuanced expressions of his sitters, often using a warm, golden light to enhance their features.

The composition was carefully considered to reflect the sitter's social status and personality. Clothing, accessories, and backgrounds were meticulously detailed to convey wealth, profession, and personal taste. The use of symbolism was prevalent, with objects included in the paintings to hint at the subject's virtues, achievements, or interests. Indeed, Golden Age portraits not only documented the appearances of individuals but also provided a window into society and the values it expressed.

LANDSCAPE

Landscape had previously functioned in European painting only as the setting for religious or historical scenes. In the Dutch Republic, the depiction of the national landscape flourished as an independent subject, with Haarlem in the 1620s as its most important production center. According to Haak, the landscape was first accepted as an independent genre in the Flanders region, where certain artists at the beginning of the sixteenth century were already known as landscape painters. The first among them was Joachim Patinir (c. 1485–1524), who painted biblical scenes in mountain settings.

Landscape was favored by the middle classes, and it rapidly became the most common type of painting. Between 1610 and 1679, the market share of landscape painting jumped from 25 percent to 40 percent, while history painting dropped from 46 percent to just 17 percent. Marine, winter, and pastoral scenes abounded; the Dutch painters were interested in exploring and recording the world around them.[4]

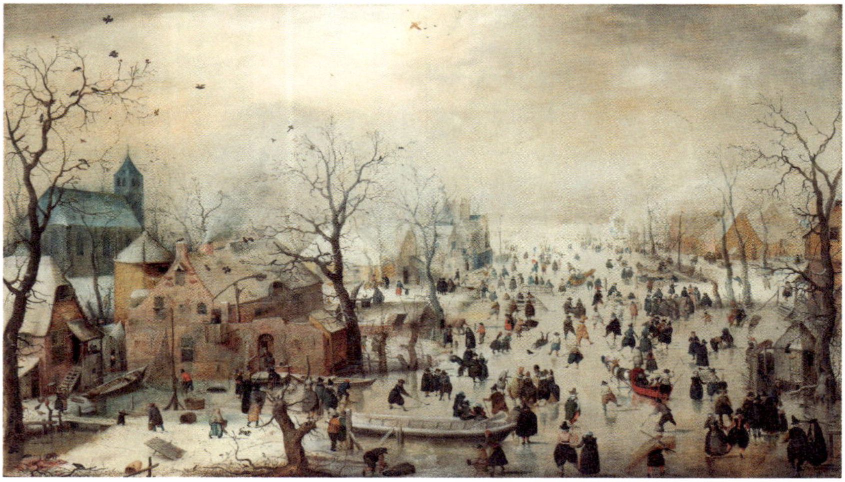

Hendrick Avercamp, *Winter Landscape with Ice Skaters*, c. 1608, Rijksmuseum, Amsterdam

As the Netherlands experienced economic prosperity and a sense of national pride, artists celebrated the country's varied landscape, capturing it with unprecedented realism and emotional depth. Artists such as Jacob van Ruisdael (1628/29–1682), Aelbert Cuyp (1620–1691), and Jan van Goyen (1596–1656) rendered the subtleties of light, weather, and atmosphere, which they conveyed through painstaking brushwork and a refined color palette. The Dutch landscape was often depicted with low horizons and expansive skies, emphasizing the flatness of the terrain and the vastness of the heavens. Artists like Ruisdael also introduced dramatic elements, such as stormy skies and turbulent seas, adding a sense of movement and dynamism.

Scenes of everyday rural life, maritime views, and urban panoramas were common subjects. The depiction of windmills, canals, and farms symbolized the ingenuity and industriousness of the Dutch. A recurring theme was the integration of human activity within the natural environment, which reflected the harmonious relationship between people and nature.

REMBRANDT

The Night Watch, executed in 1642, marked the apogee of Rembrandt's fame. It is one of three group portraits that a company of the Amsterdam civic guard commissioned from different artists for the banquet hall in its new headquarters, called the Kloveniersdoelen, to be hung in a row on a single wall. These paintings would be the largest in Amsterdam at the time.[5] The importance of the commission is reflected in the high price of as much as 4,000 guilders paid to Rembrandt. The result is a masterpiece that revolutionized the group portrait, one of the most typical genres created during the Dutch Golden Age, in part by showing the usually static, posed figures in motion. The originality and novelty of the painting were recognized by Rembrandt's contemporaries. Samuel van Hoogstraten, one of his former pupils, wrote that "this picture . . . will in my opinion outlast all its competitors, being so painterly in concept, so daring in invention and so powerful that, as some people feel, all the other pieces stand there beside it like playing cards."[6]

Rembrandt could not enjoy the enormous admiration that *The Night Watch* generated. The tragic death of his beloved wife, Saskia, on June 14, 1642, combined with the accumulation of debts resulting from his uncontrolled spending, initiated the steep fall that followed the similar rise in his career. On July 14, 1656, Rembrandt had to apply for *cessio bonorum* (surrender of goods), meaning that he had to hand over all his property to the civil authorities to be sold at auction, except the tools of his trade and personal items.

Fame and financial success had come early for the artist. Rembrandt Harmenszoon van Rijn was the son of a wealthy miller from Leiden, the second-largest city in Holland, with a population of forty-five thousand inhabitants in the 1620s. After an apprenticeship with a local artist, followed by six months in Amsterdam with Pieter Lastman, a renowned painter of biblical scenes, Rembrandt set up his own studio in Leiden at the age of only nineteen. Likely encouraged by the dealer Hendrick van Uylenburgh, Rembrandt settled in Amsterdam by 1632. By then, with Van Uylenburgh's help, he had obtained his first commissions: a portrait, *Nicolaes Ruts* (1631), and *The Anatomy Lesson of Dr. Nicolaes Tulp* (1632). As Jonathan Bikker writes, "With these two paintings Rembrandt not only joined the ranks of the best Amsterdam portrait painters, but indeed left them behind."[7] Rembrandt's innovative use of light, his

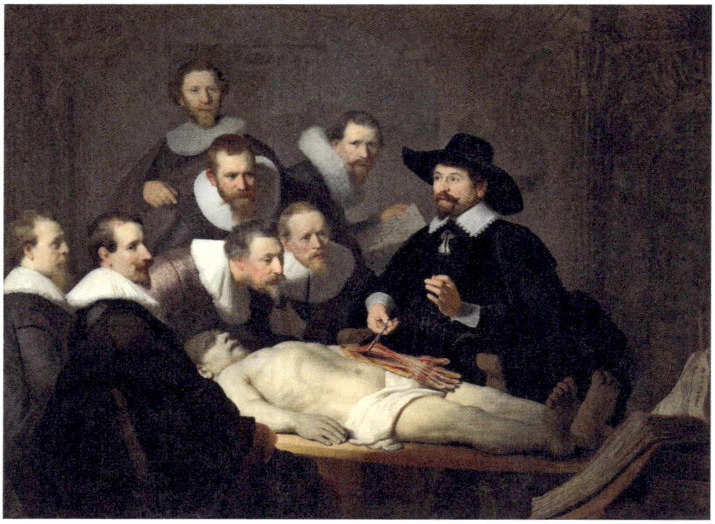

Rembrandt van Rijn, *The Anatomy Lesson of Dr. Nicolaes Tulp*, 1632, Mauritshuis, The Hague, Netherlands

virtuosic rendering of details, and his unique ability to capture emotions and facial expressions were so extraordinary that the demand for his works exploded. The artist was well aware of his success. He changed his signature to his first name, Rembrandt, which, as Bikker notes, was unprecedented in the Netherlands. Only the great Italian artists such as Raphael, Michelangelo, and Titian used just their Christian names.[8]

His association with Van Uylenburgh, whose cousin Saskia became Rembrandt's wife, lasted until 1634 and was very rewarding, both in the number of portraits he produced and in the amounts he was paid for them. (As Svetlana Alpers observes, Rembrandt's production reached an apex twice in his career: in 1634, when he was associated with Van Uylenburgh, and in 1661, not long after he declared bankruptcy.)[9] After establishing his own Amsterdam studio in 1635, the ambitious painter mainly dedicated himself to large and important historical and biblical commissions.

Rembrandt's aspirations were not limited to his professional career. In 1639, he decided to buy a house in the new, fashionable "Breestraat" area, to reflect his increased social status. He paid the huge price of 13,000 guilders, which required him to take out a substantial mortgage. The house allowed him to have many pupils and a shop to sell his works, but before long, it would also be the beginning of his future financial downfall.

As Rembrandt underwent a profound personal and professional crisis after the death of Saskia in 1642, his creativity and fame dramatically declined. He was no longer everyone's artist of choice.[10] When a new city hall was inaugurated in 1655, the commissions went not to Rembrandt but to his pupils. A shift in taste had also occurred: as Bikker remarks, what had become fashionable was the bright and elegant style that Peter Paul Rubens (1577–1640) and his followers had used in many European courts. This style appealed to the Amsterdam chief magistrates, who were responsible for selecting the artists, because it associated them with Europe's monarchs.[11]

Rembrandt died in poverty on October 4, 1669, and was buried in a common grave in Amsterdam.

Representations of fruits, flowers, and various other objects had been present in Western art since Greek and Roman times. The theme did not become an autonomous genre, however, until the end of the Renaissance, both in Italy and in the Dutch Republic. Caravaggio's *Basket of Fruit* (c. 1599), painted as a gift from Cardinal Francesco Maria del Monte to Archbishop Federico Borromeo of Milan, marked the rise of the *natura morta* (still life; literally, "dead nature") in Rome. It was in the Dutch Republic, though, that the production of still lifes exploded. The myriad variations on the theme—which Haak grouped into the categories of "floral," "kitchen paintings and market scenes," "little banquets," "breakfasts and tobaccos," "vanitas," and "fish and birds"[12]—were meant to express and celebrate the dynamism, sophistication, and luxury of the bourgeois classes' way of life. Meticulous attention to detail, rich symbolism, and masterful use of light were employed to depict everyday objects with extraordinary realism and complexity. Artists challenged themselves with virtuosic renderings of the sheen of metal, the translucence of glass, the softness of fabric, and the freshness of fruits and flowers. The advancement of science—for

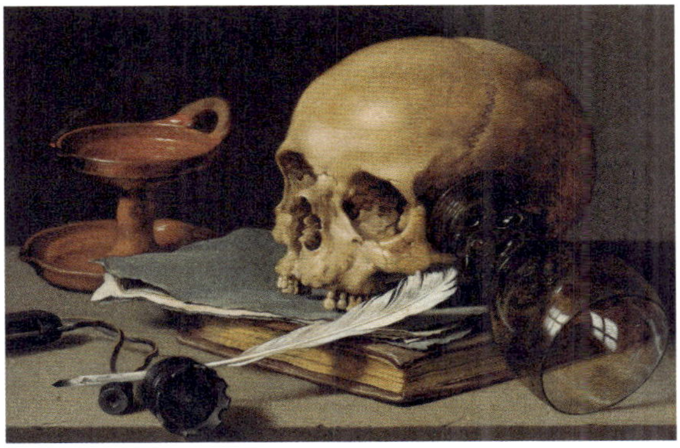

Pieter Claesz, *Still Life with a Skull and a Writing Quill*, 1628, Metropolitan Museum of Art, New York

instance, the discovery of the microscope—allowed a deeper knowledge and understanding of the natural world, and painters often collaborated with scientists. Skulls, wilting flowers, butterflies, watches, and hourglasses were symbolically introduced as *memento mori* ("remember you must die") to add a moral message about the transience of life and the inevitability of death. Compositions were carefully arranged to guide the viewer's eye through the scene, and the skillful use of light and shadow added depth and drama, highlighting the texture and form of each object.

Luxury items such as imported fruits, fine china, and exotic spices reflected the wealth and global trade connections of the Dutch Republic, not only celebrating the material abundance but also conveying a sense of pride in the country's economic achievements. It is worth noting that still life was also the genre that the few women painters usually practiced. Rachel Ruysch (1664–1750) and Clara Peeters (1594–1636) excelled in it (see "Women of the Dutch Golden Age," p. 85).

PETER PAUL RUBENS

Peter Paul Rubens, one of the most successful and prolific artists of his era, thrived in Catholic Antwerp, epitomizing the aristocratic and religious patronage model. While art in the neighboring Dutch Republic was in the process of adapting to the tastes and needs of a bourgeois public, Rubens was sought after by popes, kings, and the aristocracy of all Europe.

His style was rooted in the Flemish tradition, but it was also influenced by the masters of the Italian Renaissance, in particular Titian and Michelangelo, whose lessons Rubens carefully studied during his long stay in Italy. The new, revolutionary language of Caravaggio also impressed him, and he recommended that the Duke of Mantua acquire Caravaggio's *The Death of the Virgin* (1601–06) after officials of the church for which it was commissioned rejected the painting.

Born in 1577 in Siegen, in what is now Germany, where his Calvinist family had fled from Catholic Antwerp, Rubens was the son of a disgraced magistrate and a mother from an affluent family. The details of his life have been recorded and handed down by his nephew Philip, who wrote a biography of the artist, the *Vita Petri Pauli Rubenii* (first published in its original Latin in 1837, with an English translation in 1946). Not long after his father died, the family was allowed to return to Antwerp, and the young Rubens was admitted, at his mother's request, as a page at the court of the wife of the governor of Tournai, in present-day Belgium. However, and to the surprise of his family, Rubens quite early manifested his desire to be an artist. After an initial apprenticeship with Tobias Verhaecht, a mediocre painter who specialized in religious themes, Rubens was eventually accepted in the workshop of Otto van Veen, a renowned painter in Antwerp. Convinced that his artistic training could not be complete without a trip to Italy, Rubens traveled there in 1600, spending time in Padua and Venice before being hired by Vincenzo Gonzaga (1562–1612), duke of the small but sophisticated court of Mantua. There, Rubens had the opportunity to directly admire works by Titian, Raphael, Correggio, Veronese, and Tintoretto that were part of the duke's collection. Additionally, he accompanied the duke on diplomatic expeditions, honing the political negotiation skills that would be invaluable throughout his career. In Rome in 1601–02, Rubens was deeply impressed by the art of Michelangelo. A 1603 diplomatic mission to Spain on behalf of Vincenzo Gonzaga turned into a yearlong stay in that country. After returning to Italy, Rubens spent time in Genoa, where he produced many portraits for the local aristocracy, and in Rome, where he received his first major commission, for the high altar of Santa Maria in Vallicella.

Due to his mother's illness, Rubens hastily returned to Antwerp in 1609 (but she died before his arrival) and decided to settle and set up his studio there. His first important commission in that city came in 1610: he was asked by the Antwerp Church Council to paint a triptych for the altar of the church of Saint Walburga, titled *The Raising of the Cross* (also called the *Elevation of the Cross*); it was soon followed by *The Descent from the Cross* for the Cathedral of Our Lady. The artist's fame was already growing, and during the final stages of the first painting, the church was filled with great crowds. A huge screen had to be constructed to shield the painter and his work from his admirers.[13]

After his marriage in 1609 to Isabella Brandt, with whom he had three children and many years of happiness, Rubens's professional and social rise became unstoppable, and commissions multiplied. Noel B. Gerson writes that by 1620, the artist had become so famous and had earned so much money that it was no longer necessary for him to seek commissions, no matter what their source, and that he was able to accept only a limited number of the ones that came to him.[14]

Rubens's workshop grew to employ many painters and apprentices. His association with Jan Brueghel the Elder (1568–1625) is worthy of notice, as is that with Anthony van Dyck (1599–1641), who trained with Rubens for three years. The workshop was operating as a powerful manufacturer that produced not only paintings but also tapestry cartoons, engravings, and smaller replicas of his works to be exported all over Europe. It was an innovative model, and Alpers remarks that as far as production went, it was Rubens, not Rembrandt, who was the prime innovator in Northern Europe at the time. Rubens promoted a division of labor and developed a painting factory, with assistants who specialized in certain skills—landscapes, animals, and so on—while the master devised a mode of creation employing a clever combination of preparatory oil sketches and drawings. Thus, Rubens's works could be executed by others, with the master himself applying only the final touches to hands and faces.[15]

Among Rubens's most notable commissions are the twenty-four largely allegorical canvases depicting the life of Maria de' Medici (in France, Marie), including her marriage to King Henry IV, for her Palais de Luxembourg (1621–30; now in the Musée du Louvre, Paris); and the huge ceiling decoration (1629–34) of the Banqueting House, part of the Palace of Whitehall, London, for King Charles I of England.

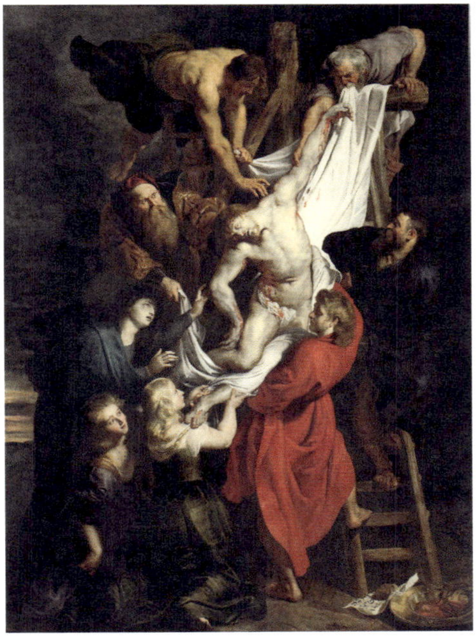

Peter Paul Rubens, *The Descent from the Cross*, 1611–14, Cathedral of Our Lady, Antwerp, Belgium

Scant information survives about the life of Johannes Vermeer, now universally considered one of the most talented Dutch painters of all time.

The artist spent his entire existence in Delft, where he was born in 1632. His father owned an inn, where he also sold paintings. The name of the teacher with whom Vermeer completed his apprenticeship is unknown. He might have been from Utrecht, and, given the subjects of Vermeer's earliest works—*Diana and Her Companions* (c. 1655–56), *Christ in the House of Martha and Mary* (c. 1655), and *The Procuress* (1656)—it is likely that he was a painter of biblical and historical scenes. Vermeer's marriage to Catharina Bolnes, who belonged to a wealthier and Catholic family, and his conversion to Catholicism, both in 1653, are certain. Late that same year, the artist joined the Guild of Saint Luke in Delft. In 1672, as a member of the guild, he testified as an expert witness in an affair involving Gerrit van Uylenburgh (son of Hendrick) over the authenticity of some Italian paintings that the dealer had sold to the elector of Brandenburg, who then claimed they were fake.[16] Vermeer died in 1675, leaving his wife and eight minor children in a dire financial situation.

Thirty-five paintings are now considered authentic works by Vermeer; only three are dated. The majority of them belong to the genre of the domestic interior scene, which was dominant in Holland in the third quarter of the seventeenth century. Small in size, they have a recurring compositional scheme with the unseen light source at the top left. The limited production indicates, according to Haak, that Vermeer probably painted very slowly.[17]

During Vermeer's lifetime, his market was local, meaning that his paintings ended up in collections in Delft. We know that he had a major buyer, Pieter Claesz. van Ruijven (though his wife, Maria Simonsdr. de Knuijt, had more money, and some scholars now believe she was Vermeer's main patron); an auction of Van Ruijven's art possessions in 1696 listed twenty-one works by the painter. In 1669, the aristocrat Pieter Teding van Berckhout of The Hague wrote in his diary that on May 14, he had visited "an excellent painter by the name of Vermeer," who showed him several works. More interesting is what the French nobleman Balthasar de Monconys noted in his journal about a visit to Delft in the summer of 1663. He had seen a painting by Vermeer, in the house of a banker, that had cost 600 livres even though it contained only one figure. Not much more is known about Vermeer's prices. As reported by Bakker, after Vermeer's death in 1675, his widow paid a debt of 617 guilders by selling two works, probably *Lady Writing a Letter with Her Maid* (c. 1670) and *The Guitar Player* (c. 1672).[18]

Posthumously, Vermeer rapidly fell into oblivion, and a half century after his death, his work was known by only a small group of amateurs. The catalyst for Vermeer emerging from obscurity was Jean-Baptiste Pierre Le Brun (1748–1813). The French scholar, in his *Galerie des peintres flamands, hollandais et allemands* (1792–96), invited art historians to pay particular attention to Vermeer, underlining his ability to render the effects of sunlight.[19]

Other authors echoed Le Brun's positive review, and slowly Vermeer's reputation grew, although he was not included in the Gallery of Honor of the Rijksmuseum when it opened in its current building in 1885. Crucial to Vermeer's fame was the dedication of the French journalist, scholar, and collector Étienne-Joseph-Théophile Thoré-Bürger (1807–1869). Impressed by the *View of Delft* (c. 1660–61), which he had seen in the Mauritshuis in The Hague, he began searching for and acquiring all the paintings by Vermeer that he could find, and eventually he drafted the first catalogue of the painter's work. Marcel Proust (1871–1922) was another of Vermeer's first admirers, in particular of the *View of Delft*, of which he speaks in the fifth volume of the *Recherche*. The writer had the opportunity to admire it from life in the 1921 exhibition, at the Jeu de Paume in Paris, dedicated to Dutch painting, together with *The Milkmaid* (c. 1657–61) and *Girl with a Pearl Earring* (c. 1665–67).

Before the 2023 retrospective at the Rijksmuseum in Amsterdam, only one other survey of Vermeer's work had been organized, in 1995–96 at the National Gallery of Art in Washington, DC, and the Mauritshuis.

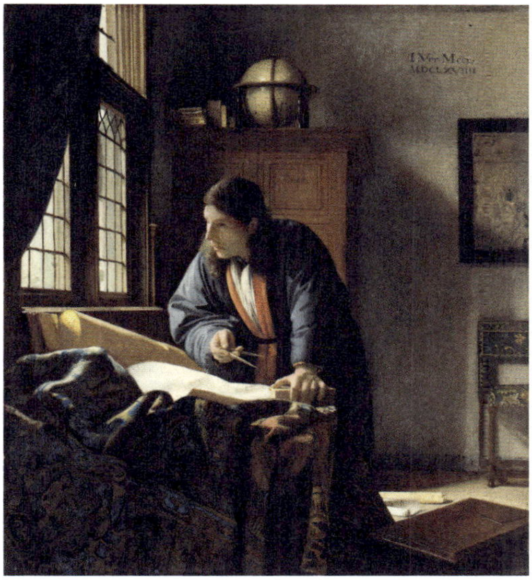

Johannes Vermeer, *The Geographer*, 1669, Städel Museum, Frankfurt, Germany

GENRE PAINTING AND INTERIOR SCENES

The seventeenth-century collectors in the Netherlands favored paintings depicting simple episodes from contemporary daily life, rather than grandiose historical or mythological narratives. It was a way for the ruling bourgeoisie to celebrate themselves and immortalize their lifestyle through art. Interior scenes exalted the virtues of domestic life and imparted the moral values cherished by Dutch society at the time. Arnold Hauser writes that "the more direct, obvious, and commonplace a motif is, the greater is its value for this art. The attitude to the world which is expressed here is without aloofness and based on everyday experience—it regards reality as something that has been conquered and is, therefore, familiar. . . . What art is most interested in is the possessions of the individual, the family, the community, and the nation: rooms and courtyards, the town and its environs, the local landscape and the liberated, regained countryside."[20]

Painting captured the essence of Dutch people like never before. The canvas turned into a vibrant tapestry of their lives, portraying the care of households, the leisure pursuits of the prosperous such as music lessons, the tender intricacies of courtship. From the graceful exchange of letters—a testament to the nation's high literacy rate—to scenes of jubilant wedding feasts and lively tavern encounters, every facet of society found its place in the artful strokes of the Dutch masters.

Claudio Strinati intriguingly compares the function of interior painting during the Dutch Golden Age to that played by the television in the twentieth century. Paintings of domestic interior scenes were a true mirror of society, a realistic but in some way idealizing mirror, in which people could retrace the various activities, private and public, of their lives.[21]

By the end of the seventeenth century, domestic interior scenes had become the most sought-after and expensive genre of painting in the Dutch Republic.

ARTISTS' STATUS, DEALERS, PRICES

Hulst reports an estimate that Dutch artists created more than five million paintings during the seventeenth century.[22] This unprecedented output was mainly not on commission but for an anonymous open art market, and its volume had deep repercussions on the artistic production system. First of all, the increased demand meant that the number of active artists rose to unparalleled levels. North reports that in Dutch cities around 1650, there was one painter to every two to three thousand inhabitants, whereas in Italy during the Renaissance, there was one painter to every ten thousand inhabitants.[23] The careers of the painters were regulated and controlled by the Guild of Saint Luke, founded in the Middle Ages. After 1640, though, artists in various cities began to push for their own independent organizations.[24]

Another significant aspect of the huge demand for paintings was extreme specialization: many artists limited their production to just one genre, and this was utterly new. Maarten Prak reports, for example, that Jan van Goyen created only landscapes in quite a small format, executed with rapid brushstrokes in predominantly yellow and brown hues. Pieter Jansz. Saenredam (1597–1665) concentrated exclusively on the rendering of precisely measured church interiors and exteriors. Willem van de Velde the Elder (1611–1693) made extremely accurate depictions of sea battles observed firsthand. Frans Hals confined himself to portraiture, Simon de Vlieger (1601–1653) to seascapes, and Frans van Mieris (1635–1681) to so-called merry companies—interiors with a group of figures engaged in activities such as making music. Hendrick Avercamp (1585–1634) devoted himself to winter scenes.[25]

How were all these paintings sold? North lists various ways: directly from the artists' studios, through the exhibitions and sales that the Guild of Saint Luke organized, by lotteries and auctions, and from tavern keepers who would display the paintings on their walls.[26]

It is in this context that the figure of the professional dealer started to emerge. There were those who served a high-class clientele, including travel from city to city in search of particular works on request. Some dealers also began to collaborate with artists, directing their production according to the demand and helping them financially if, for example, they did not have the means to buy work tools. Philip Hook notes that when Rembrandt started to be handled by the dealer Hendrick van Uylenburgh (c. 1587–1661) in 1631, he painted many more portraits: half of the approximately one hundred he produced during his whole life date to the four years of this association.[27]

Art also started to be sold in fairs, the first of which began as part of larger trade fairs and markets, where merchants and craftsmen gathered to sell their goods. Artists and art dealers took advantage of these bustling events to show and sell their works to a wider audience. The informal nature of these fairs allowed for a diverse range of artworks to be displayed, from paintings and sculptures to prints and drawings. One of the earliest and most notable art fairs was the Pand market in the cloister of the Church of Our Lady in Antwerp, operating since 1460; though not in the Netherlands, it greatly influenced similar events in Dutch cities.

The mass production of paintings meant that, in general, prices were quite low. Hauser reports that one could buy a painting for a mere 2 or 3 guilders, and even a good portrait cost 60 guilders, when the price of an ox was 90.[28]

Several artists had another job—Vermeer ran a tavern, where he also sold paintings—and only successful artists earned enough to be considered middle or upper middle class. Haak writes that, with few exceptions, living masters in the seventeenth century did not receive very high prices for their paintings, and that only a few of them became wealthy.[29] Hauser goes even further and affirms that the Dutch Golden Age was the first time in the history of Western art that saw an abundance of masters and the existence of an "artistic proletariat."[30]

Prices were determined, first of all, by the subject, as there was a hierarchy among them. Initially, history and architectural paintings were the most highly priced, followed by portraits, then genre scenes and still lifes. However, North reports that in the last quarter of the seventeenth century, the order changed: genre paintings became the most expensive, followed by history, religious, and landscape paintings, still lifes, and portraits.[31] The increasing importance of interior paintings is emphasized by Eric Jan Sluijter, who notes that during the third quarter of the seventeenth century, the most ambitious and talented painters in the Dutch Republic did not pursue history painting as earlier generations had. Instead, they specialized in depicting beautifully dressed young women and men in opulent interiors.[32]

Technical skills, the fame of the artist, the size of the painting, the complexity of the composition, details, labor, and a client's wealth were also elements that conditioned prices. As receipts of transactions rarely survived, the most important historical sources of art prices are the estate inventories drawn at a person's death or in case of bankruptcy.[33]

While Dutch artists primarily catered to patrons within their own urban centers, the allure of Dutch art transcended national boundaries. Before the advent of the eighteenth-century "Grand Tour" of Italy, a "Tour of

Holland" emerged as a fashionable pilgrimage for art devotees and collectors. Cosimo III de' Medici (1642–1723), not long before he became the Grand Duke of Tuscany, went to Holland twice, in 1667 and 1669, visiting collections in Amsterdam, Delft, The Hague, Rotterdam, and Leiden. He is reported to have met Rembrandt.

THE DECLINE OF THE DUTCH GOLDEN AGE

Weakened by a series of costly wars that drained its finances, particularly against England (1652–54), for the domination of maritime routes, and France (1672–78), which initially defeated it and occupied its territory, the Dutch Republic began its downturn toward the end of the seventeenth century. The loss of political and economic relevance corresponded to the decline of the Golden Age of painting. The predominant artistic style changed toward a banal and cold classicism favored by the wealthiest patrons, who became more Francophile in their tastes. The art that was produced, in the words of Haak, "gained in refinement but lost in originality."[34]

NOTES

1 Titia Hulst, ed., *A History of the Western Art Market: A Sourcebook of Writings on Artists, Dealers, and Markets* (Oakland: University of California Press, 2017), 158.

2 Michael North, introduction to *Art and Commerce in the Dutch Golden Age*, trans. Catherine Hill (New Haven, CT: Yale University Press, 1997).

3 Bob Haak, *The Golden Age: Dutch Painters of the Seventeenth Century* (New York: Harry N. Abrams, 1984), 274.

4 Haak, *Golden Age*, 134–61.

5 Jonathan Bikker, *Rembrandt: Biography of a Rebel* (Amsterdam: Rijksmuseum, 2019), 77.

6 Haak, *Golden Age*, 296.

7 Bikker, *Rembrandt*, 274.

8 Bikker, *Rembrandt*, 61.

9 Svetlana Alpers, *Rembrandt's Enterprise: The Studio and the Market* (Chicago: University of Chicago Press, 1988), 91.

10 Bikker, *Rembrandt*, 10.

11 Bikker, *Rembrandt*, 175.

12 Haak, *Golden Age*, 115.

13 Noel B. Gerson, *Peter Paul Rubens: A Biography of the Flemish Baroque Genius* (Leeds, UK: Sapere Books, 1973), 135.

14 Gerson, *Peter Paul Rubens*, 165.

15 Svetlana Alpers, "Freedom, Art, and Money," in Hulst, *History of the Western Art Market*, 173–74.

16 Haak, *Golden Age*, 446.

17 Haak, *Golden Age*, 451.

18 Bakker, "Painters of and for the Elite," 91.

19 Pieter Roelofs, "Johannes Vermeer (Delft 1632–1675)," in *Vermeer*, ed. Gregor J. M. Weber and Pieter Roelofs, exh. cat. (Amsterdam: Rijksmuseum, 2023), 26.

20 Arnold Hauser, *The Social History of Art*, vol. 2, *Renaissance, Mannerism, Baroque* (New York: Vintage Books, 1957), 212–13.

21 Claudio Strinati, *Caravaggio e Vermeer: L'ombra e la luce* (Turin, Italy: Einaudi, 2021), 133–34.

22 Hulst, *History of the Western Art Market*, 158.

23 North, *Art and Commerce*, 79.

24 Haak, *Golden Age*, 310.

25 Maarten Prak, *The Dutch Republic in the Seventeenth Century: The Golden Age*, trans. Diane Webb (Cambridge, UK: Cambridge University Press, 2005), 239.

26 North, *Art and Commerce*, 87, 93.

27 Philip Hook, *Rogues' Gallery: A History of Art and Its Dealers* (London: Profile Books, 2017), 18.

28 Hauser, *Social History of Art*, 2:221.

29 Haak, *Golden Age*, 35.

30 Hauser, *Social History of Art*, 2:218.

31 North, *Art and Commerce*, 99.

32 Eric Jan Sluijter, "Emulative Imitation among High-Life Genre Painters," in *Vermeer and the Masters of Genre Painting: Inspiration and Rivalry*, ed. Adriaan Waiboer, exh. cat. (New Haven, CT: Yale University Press), 37.

33 Piet Bakker, "Painters of and for the Elite: Relationships, Prices and Familiarity with Each Other's Work," in *Vermeer and the Masters*, 87.

34 Haak, *Golden Age*, 352.

3. At His Majesty's Service: The Monopsony Model under Louis XIV of France

p. 54
The Creation of the Royal Manufactories

p. 55
Controlling the Academies

p. 56
Louis XIV

p. 58
Versailles: The Residence of the Sun King

p. 60
Nicolas Fouquet: The Fall of an Art Patron

Art is nothing but an instrument of state government with the special function of raising the prestige of the monarch. . . . Artists are purely the creatures of the state educational system.

—Arnold Hauser, *The Social History of Art, vol. 2*

The establishment of the absolute monarchy in seventeenth-century France under Louis XIV (1638–1715), known as "the Sun King," shaped the purpose, content, style, and production of all art forms. This era marked France's supremacy in Europe, not just in military, economic, and political realms but also in culture and customs. French became the lingua franca spoken by European aristocracy, and French tastes inspired and dictated fashion, art, table manners, and all other aspects of cultural life.

Moreover, when France developed the most innovative political structure of the age—the absolute monarchy—this provided art production with nearly unlimited resources. Arnold Hauser argues that this shift prompted the art world's center to move from Italy, which was plagued by foreign occupation, wars, and economic decline, to France.[1]

The recognition of art's formidable power as a propaganda tool did not emerge solely during the reign of Louis XIV. In the fifth century BCE, Athenian democracy utilized the sculptural program of the Parthenon, conceived by Phidias, to celebrate Greece's victorious values of civilization and freedom against the "barbaric" Persian Empire. Similarly, during the Renaissance, art in all its forms flourished and was championed by the ruling families of the Italian city-states. Pope Julius II, for example, entrusted Michelangelo, Bramante, and Raphael with glorifying the splendor of Rome (see "Church, Royalty, Bankers," p. 12). A century later, the royal houses of Europe competed to secure the best artists of their time to decorate their palaces. In the seventeenth-century Dutch Republic, being portrayed by renowned painters was a way to affirm one's social position and prestige (see "The Dutch Golden Age and the First Free Market," p. 36). In our time, the possession of trophy artworks is perceived as one of the most potent status symbols. In 2017, when the Japanese billionaire Yusaku Maezawa bought Jean-Michel Basquiat's *Untitled* (1982) at auction for the record price of $110.5 million, he immediately posted the acquisition on his Instagram account.

However, during the reign of Louis XIV, the understanding of the fundamental role of art in the sovereign's glorification evolved into strict control over every form of art production. The Crown effectively became the primary and almost exclusive patron of the arts. It was a monopsony: a market structure in which a single buyer becomes the major or even the sole purchaser of goods and services offered by sellers.

The protagonist and orchestrator of France's cultural policy during the reign of Louis XIV was Jean-Baptiste Colbert (1619–1683). The son of a merchant, he was chosen by the king as his finance minister in 1661.

Colbert's program to transform France into the most advanced country in Europe included reform of the fiscal system, improvement of the postal service and the road network, abolition of local taxes to facilitate internal trade, and commercial expansion overseas with the creation in 1664 of the French East India Company to compete with the English and Dutch companies operating in other parts of the world.[2]

From 1664, Colbert was also named "superintendent of the king's buildings"—equivalent to a minister of culture. The pillar of his vision was the glorification of the sovereign himself, to which every form of art had to contribute. It was a question of the state; as Thierry Sarmant explains, finance, commerce, manufactories, and royal houses were all held together for the same goal: the exaltation of the king and hence the consolidation of his absolute power.[3] Colbert's cultural strategy relied both on the control and subsidy of the production of all luxury products—tapestries, furniture, carpets, cabinetry, silver—achieved through the creation of royal manufactories, and on the firm guidance exercised on all the academies, in particular that of the fine arts.

Manufactories that the government subsidized through protectionist laws and tax-relief measures already existed in France; for example, the Savonnerie in Paris and the Aubusson in the Creuse valley were both dedicated to the production of luxury tapestries. Colbert's plan, though, was of a higher scale and ambition: to produce directly in France all luxury products, which until then had been imported at extremely expensive prices—tapestries from Flanders, marquetry from Italy, carpets from the Middle East. Creating a local manufacturing excellence would dramatically cut costs, while at the same time allow Colbert to control and dictate the content and style of the products. Furthermore, as Sarmant points out, the royal house would serve as a showcase for French creativity.[4]

In 1662, Colbert decided to acquire for the Crown the dyeing and tapestry workshops of the Gobelins family, located in boulevard Saint-Marcel in Paris, on the banks of the river Bièvre. Transformed into the Manufactures Royales des Meubles de la Couronne (Royal Manufactories of Furniture of the Crown), commonly called the Gobelins, they had the duty, by statute, to exalt the grandeur and splendor of the Crown. This reflected what Sarmant refers to as a "global approach to decorative arts," encompassing all the artists involved in enhancing the royal residences.[5] The Gobelins' atelier, which at its maximum expansion counted eight hundred employees, became a small, autonomous town for artists, with courtyards and gardens, a chaplain, and even a doctor. Craftsmen from all over Europe were employed there. In 1668, for example, Colbert invited a team of Florentine lapidaries who specialized in hard stone marquetry—the brothers Orazio and Ferdinando Megliorini, Gian Ambrogio Giacchetti, and Filippo Branchi—to work and reside at the Gobelins.

Though they were engaged in the production of all luxury products, it was in the area of tapestries that the Gobelins excelled and established their unmatched reputation. A complex organization relying on teams of craftsmen with different skills was led by the painter Charles Le Brun (1619–1690), who was named director of the Gobelins. In this capacity, Le Brun provided the designs for the tapestries and directed their production, supervised directly by Colbert and the king himself. Among the masterpieces executed at least in part during Le Brun's tenure were the *History of the King* (1654–68) and the *History of Alexander* (1660–73).

Indeed, as Antoine Maës observes, it was the activity of the Gobelins manufactories in the two decades following their foundation that best exemplified the degree of perfection associated with the arts during the reign of Louis XIV.[6]

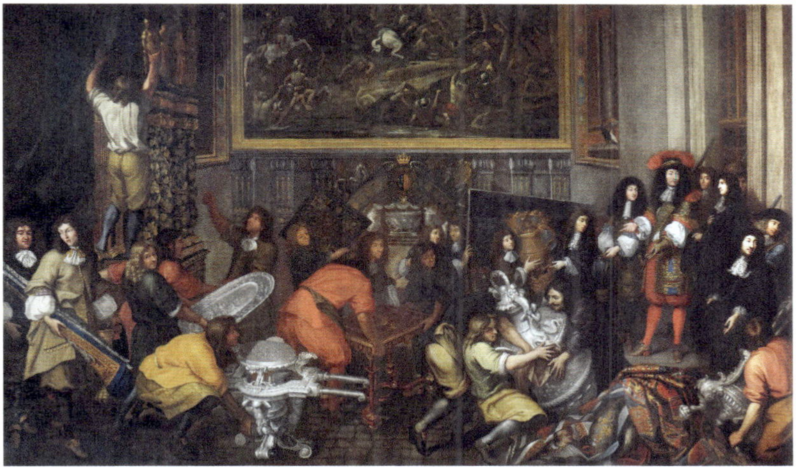

Simon Renard de Saint-André, *Louis XIV visite la Manufacture des Gobelins, 15 octobre 1667*, 1667–77, Château de Versailles, France

CONTROLLING THE ACADEMIES

Complementary to the creation of the royal manufactories was the subjection of the fine arts academy to the needs of the Crown.

The Académie Royale de Peinture et de Sculpture (Royal Academy of Painting and Sculpture) had been founded in 1648 under the patronage of the king's first minister of state for two decades, Cardinal Mazarin (1602–1661), born Giulio Mazzarino (among other spellings) in what is now Italy. It is worth remembering that the aim of the first academies, instituted during the late Renaissance in Rome, Bologna, Paris, and Antwerp, was the emancipation of artists from the restrictive and controlling guilds. This reflected the evolution of the artist's status: no longer a simple craftsman; in the academies, his training was not limited to technical and practical skills but also included a knowledge of literature, history, and philosophy.

In this spirit, the Royal Academy of Painting and Sculpture was born as a free association of painters with no limits in number or hierarchy of members. It changed radically in 1663, however, when Colbert named Charles Le Brun—who by the early 1660s was also running the Gobelins and was honored as *premier peintre du roi* (first painter to the king)—to be director of the academy for life, under the patronage of Louis XIV. The purpose of the academy then became to professionalize and control the artists working for the court, by establishing strict rules regarding content and style. And the state needed artists in large numbers, to be employed in the decoration of the new royal residences, in particular that of Versailles, which was to be unprecedented in scale and splendor. Thus, the academy was intended to supply as well as educate artists, whereas the court itself provided the guiding principles for the creation of a *grande manière*, or "grand manner," a solemn and resplendent style, which would set the standard for official art in the whole of Europe.[7]

From the mid-seventeenth to the end of the nineteenth century, the academy dominated French art. Aside from everything else, it assigned scholarships, decided the winner of the prestigious Prix de Rome (which, starting in 1666, fully funded three to five years of study at the newly created Académie de France in the Italian capital), and organized the official exhibitions, called Salons. Until the 1863 Salon des Refusés and the Impressionists' revolution beginning a decade later, the academy dictated the accepted taste and aesthetic doctrine in France (see "Paul Durand-Ruel and the Birth of the Impressionist Market," p. 94). In the words of Hauser: "From 1661 onwards political imperialism is paralleled by an intellectual imperialism. No department of public life is spared from the intervention of the State.... For the arts Le Brun and [the French poet and critic known as] Boileau are the legislators, the academies are the courts, and the protectors are the King and Colbert."[8]

The academy in Paris and the one in Rome were part of a growing system that began with the Académie de Poésie et de Musique (Academy of Poetry and Music), founded in 1570 under the auspices of King Charles IX; among the others were the Académie Française (French Academy), established in 1635 by Cardinal Richelieu, chief minister to King Louis XIII (1601–1643), to oversee the French language; the Académie Royale de Danse (Royal Academy of Dance), in 1661; and the Académie Royale d'Architecture (Royal Academy of Architecture), in 1671.

LOUIS XIV

In 1701, the painter Hyacinthe Rigaud (1659–1743) immortalized Louis XIV as the personification of the divine right of monarchs. Commissioned by Louis's grandson Philip, Duke of Anjou, the painting remained in Versailles, where it was installed above the fireplace in the throne room. A copy still hangs there, while the original is now at the Musée du Louvre.

Louis XIV was nearing sixty-three at the time of the portrait, for which Rigaud was bestowed the honor of a few sittings. Every detail of the painting—the majestic pose, the regal clothing, the preciousness of the fabrics, the scepter, the sword—was meant to express the grandeur and splendor of Louis XIV's absolute power.

King at the age of four—under the regency of his mother, Anne of Austria, and the powerful Cardinal Mazarin, until he reached what was considered adult age, which for a monarch was thirteen—Louis XIV reigned for more than seventy-two years.

His was an epoch of contradictions, which saw the apogee of France's power but also planted the seed of his nation's destitution, eventually leading to the French Revolution. Protracted expansionist wars, sustained by increased taxation and huge losses of human lives, along with the king's politics of magnificence, ultimately left France impoverished and weakened. Furthermore, the reckless revocation in 1685 of the Edict of Nantes, which had guaranteed freedom of worship to Protestants since 1598, not only unleashed new waves of religious persecution but also pushed a class of affluent and enterprising merchants out of France. Philip Mansel wonders:

> Louis XIV was both King of France and a global ruler with global ambitions. He founded colonies in America, Africa and India, tried to seize Siam (as Thailand was then known), sent missionaries and mathematicians to the Emperor of China and launched the struggle for France's global markets which continues to this day. . . .Louis was a man in pursuit of glory, a king devoted to dynastic aggrandizement and a leader bent on national expansion. . . . Did he leave France stronger or weaker? He dominated his age and, since he chose the sun as his symbol, later became known as *le roi soleil*—the Sun King. Did he deserve the name?[9]

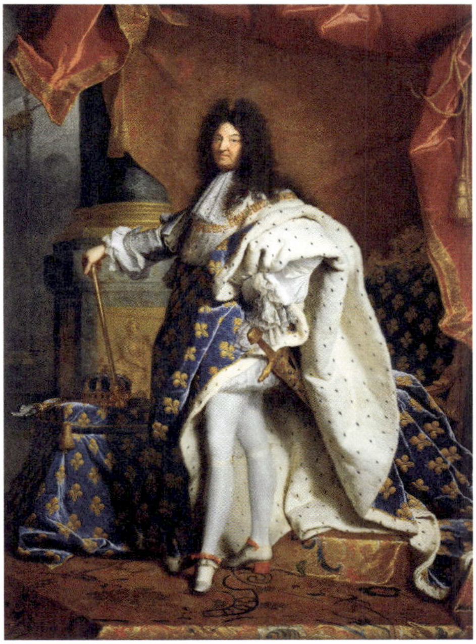

Hyacinthe Rigaud, *Louis XIV*, 1701, Musée du Louvre, Paris

The Palais de Versailles, which Louis XIV selected in 1682 as his main residence and effectively the seat of government, became the physical embodiment of the centralization of power and absorbed in large measure the art production of its time.

When Louis XIV ascended to the throne, Versailles, situated about ten miles southwest of Paris, was still a modest château, which his father, Louis XIII, had expanded in 1631–34 from the simple hunting lodge built for the king a decade earlier.

From 1546, under Francis I, the main residence of the French monarchs had been the Louvre, in Paris, which evolved over the centuries and through various transformations into a palace, from a fortress built at the turn of the twelfth century by Philip II, also known as Philip Augustus.

During the reign of Louis XIV, the Louvre was going through a substantial renovation, for which the most renowned architects of the time were consulted, including the pope's favorite sculptor and architect, Gian Lorenzo Bernini (1598–1680). In France from June to October 1665, Bernini did not win the commission, but during his stay he sculpted a famous bust of the French king.

In Colbert's vision, the Louvre, located in the center of Paris, was intended to be the ideal main residence and the core of royal power. However, after the design by a three-man French committee was chosen, with a colonnade that would become a distinctive feature of French architecture, Louis XIV's attention shifted toward a different building, that of Versailles. Colbert was not in favor, as he was concerned by the astronomical costs he envisaged. However, despite Colbert's objection, Versailles became a construction site—which would continue uninterrupted until the king's death in 1715, and then off and on, including changes in the interior, until the French Revolution in 1789. Louis Le Vau (c. 1612–1670), since 1654 the first architect to the king, was appointed for the monumental enterprise.

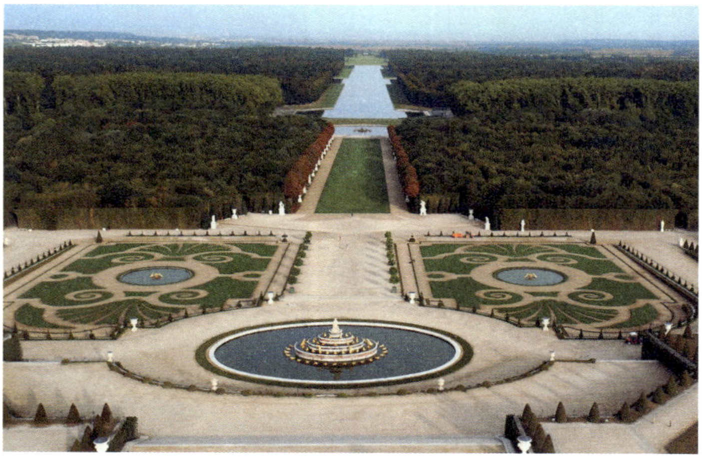

Gardens at the Château de Versailles, France

The project featured an extension of Louis XIII's original brick-and-stone palace. The new building, called "the Envelope," would include two symmetrical corner wings around the forecourt for the king's and queen's apartments, connected by a central hall. Two structures for stables and service rooms were also to be added, as well as an Orangerie and a Menagerie in the park. The architect Jules Hardouin-Mansart (1646–1708) would continue the direction of the works from 1675, five years after Le Vau died, until his own death.

The enormous task of the interior decoration of the Palais de Versailles was assigned to Le Brun, supervised by Colbert and the king. For the state apartment, a solar theme was chosen, and each room was assigned a planet, represented by the image of the corresponding ancient deity painted on the ceiling.[10]

By employing ancient history, mythology, and complex symbolism elaborated on during the Renaissance, mottoes, themes, and models were created that associated Louis XIV with Alexander the Great and Apollo. The latter was the sun god, who reigned over the world of the arts, and Louis XIV had adopted the sun as his emblem since 1662. In addition to Versailles's elaborated iconography, the luxuriousness of the materials employed and the outstanding skills of the French artisans contributed to the glorification of the king, while at the same time stating the supremacy of France's creativity in every field. For example, as Tony Spawforth points out, the seventeen arcades filled with blown glass in the Hall of Mirrors showed the mastery of the French craftsmen in a luxury sector that had been the tightly guarded monopoly of the Venetians until Colbert successfully set up a state-sponsored French manufactory in 1665.[11]

In this absolute monarchy, the palace gardens were also part of a system aimed at celebrating the power of the king. The landscape designer André Le Nôtre (1613–1700) created in Versailles the prototype of what is called the "French garden." Characterized by a geometric organization of the space, with axial paths, low hedges, and an abundance of water in every form, from fountains to channels to small lakes, it was admired and imitated all over Europe.

The construction of the Versailles gardens proved to be a particularly difficult enterprise due to the irregularity of the ground, in part occupied by swamps. Ponds and streams were turned into ornamental sheets of water, while a vast amount of soil was shifted to create a terrace in front of the château, where the ground naturally slopes. Even villages that blocked Le Nôtre's new vistas were relocated.[12]

By 1689, the entire government was installed at Versailles, which provided the perfect representation of the centrality of the sovereign, while at the same time allowing the king to directly control the aristocracy. Required to spend at least some part of the year in Versailles and ensnared in court rituals, noblemen were offered wealth, security, and privileges in exchange for loyalty. The palace became a city in itself, with five thousand people living there. If Versailles, in Mansel's words, "was a bid for global fame,"[13] its exact cost is not known, as the monarchy at the time did not publish accounts. Spawforth also reminds us of the high human costs, which were for a long time ignored: fatalities and injuries during the construction of Versailles, compensated with very meager indemnities to the families of the deceased.[14]

The last years of the Sun King's reign were marked by a contraction of the royal patronage in favor of a revival of private commissions to artists from aristocrats and wealthy financiers.

And the imposing and majestic royal Baroque style was gradually replaced by the exuberant Rococo, more suited to the urban nobility's tastes.

NICOLAS FOUQUET: THE FALL OF AN ART PATRON

The Palais de Versailles consecrated the names of the architect Louis Le Vau, the painter Charles Le Brun, and the garden designer André Le Nôtre for posterity. However, it was at the château of Vaux-le-Vicomte, the splendid residence of Nicolas Fouquet (1615–1680), that these three artists proved their talents before the king employed them. Coming from a wealthy family of the *noblesse de robe* (nobility of the robe), referring to a class of hereditary aristocrats who held governmental positions, Fouquet was named superintendent of finances in 1653 by Mazarin and the queen. His extraordinary rise and sudden and disastrous fall and imprisonment have been the subject of numerous studies and speculations.[15]

The circumstances of Fouquet's disgrace seem like fiction. On August 17, 1661, he threw a sumptuous party in honor of Louis XIV in his residence at Vaux-le-Vicomte—and he was arrested shortly afterward on the orders of the king himself. With a little poetic license, Voltaire wrote much later: "On August 17, at six in the evening Fouquet was King of France, at two in the morning, he was nobody."

It was allegedly the grandeur of Fouquet's castle and the ostentatious party that aroused the sovereign's envy and consequent decision to arrest him. In reality, both Louis XIV and especially Colbert had been plotting for some time to get rid of Fouquet, who had become too powerful and was considered uncontrollable. Furthermore, Colbert coveted Fouquet's position as controller of finances, and he would eventually obtain it.

Accused of having used public funds for personal purposes and of high treason, Fouquet was ultimately—after a trial that dragged on for three years—sentenced to life imprisonment, and all his assets were confiscated. Imprisoned in a remote fortress in the Alps, he lived until 1680.

Fouquet was the last of the great private art patrons in France, and Vaux-le-Vicomte the most sumptuous residence ever built before Versailles, with a remarkable collection of paintings, other art objects, and manuscripts. It was after the conclusion of Fouquet's case that Louis XIV and Colbert created a "state patronage": all artists would be considered the property of the king, whose will they had to obey. Anyone who did not adhere to this model was cut off from every role, deprived of their pension, disgraced, and often forced into exile.[16]

NOTES

1 Arnold Hauser, *The Social History of Art*, vol. 2, *Renaissance, Mannerism, Baroque* (New York: Vintage Books, 1957), 187.

2 Josephine Wilkinson, *Louis XIV: The Power and the Glory* (New York: Pegasus Books, 2019), 292.

3 Thierry Sarmant, "Louis XIV, Colbert, Le Brun et les manufactures de la Couronne," in *Créer pour Louis XIV: Les Manufactures de la Couronne sous Colbert et Le Brun*, ed. Thierry Sarmant, exh. cat. (Paris: Mobilier national; Milan: Silvana Editoriale, 2019), 22.

4 Sarmant, "Louis XIV, Colbert, Le Brun," 22.

5 Thierry Sarmant, "Avant-Provos," in *Créer pour Louis XIV*, 17.

6 Antoine Maës. "La Vie dans l'enclos des Gobelins sous le directorat de Charles Le Brun (1663–1690)," in *Créer pour Louis XIV*, 41.

7 Hauser, *Social History of Art*, 2:190.

8 Hauser, *Social History of Art*, 2:191.

9 Philip Mansel, *King of the World: The Life of Louis XIV* (Chicago: University of Chicago Press, 2019), 1.

10 Tony Spawforth, *Versailles: A Biography of a Palace* (New York: St. Martin's Press, 2008), 29.

11 Spawforth, *Versailles*, 33.

12 Spawforth, *Versailles*.

13 Mansel, *King of the World*, 2.

14 Spawforth, *Versailles*, 40–41.

15 Alessandra Necci gives a compelling account of Fouquet's fall in *Re Sole e lo Scoiattolo: Nicolas Fouquet e la vendetta di Luigi XIV* (Venice: Marsilio Edizioni, 2013).

16 Necci, *Re Sole e lo Scoiattolo*, 340.

4. Leonardo's *Salvator Mundi* and Aspects of the Old Masters Market

p. 63 What Is *Salvator Mundi*?

p. 64 Debated Authenticity

p. 65 A Royal Provenance?

p. 66 A Substantial Restoration

p. 67 Attribution to Leonardo

p. 67 Looking for a Buyer

p. 68 Exceptional Discoveries of Paintings by Caravaggio and Cimabue

p. 69 Christie's Auction, November 15, 2017

p. 70 The Old Masters Market in the United States during the Gilded Age

p. 70 Contradictions of the Gilded Age: Economic Growth, Urbanization, Inequality, and Racism

p. 72 Joseph Duveen

p. 73 Henry Clay Frick: The Embodiment of the Gilded Age Collector

p. 75 Women Collect: Isabella Stewart Gardner

p. 77 Women Collect: Louisine Havemeyer

p. 78 A Market for Women Old Masters in Their Time?

p. 79 Andrew Mellon and the Founding of the National Gallery of Art

p. 80 Nuns, Professionals, and Noblewomen

p. 81 The Market for Women Old Masters Now

p. 83 The Unrivaled Artemisia

p. 85 Women of the Dutch Golden Age

p. 86 The Professionalization of Women Artists during the Eighteenth and Nineteenth Centuries

p. 88 Rosa Bonheur

Mystery is the defining quality of Leonardo's art. . . . Our understanding of Leonardo's life and work rarely becomes more than a pool of theories, surrounded by a tangle of conjecture, suspended from a geometry of clues. Amidst this network of possibilities, the *Salvator* presents the most fundamental mystery of them all.

—Ben Lewis, *The Last Leonardo: The Secret Lives of the World's Most Expensive Painting*

Leonardo da Vinci's *Salvator Mundi* (Savior of the World) sold at a Christie's auction in New York on November 15, 2017, for $450 million—the highest price ever achieved by a work of art. The sale not only shattered previous records but also disrupted traditional marketing and promotion norms for paintings by old masters. Furthermore, it sparked intense debate over attribution criteria, museum validation, permissible restoration practices, and the art market's inherent opacity.[1]

Salvator Mundi had been discovered and purchased for $1,175 by the dealer Robert Simon, in partnership with Alex Parish, in April 2005 at the St. Charles Gallery, a small auction house in New Orleans. Listed as lot 664, it was described as "After Leonardo da Vinci (1452–1519)," with an estimated value of $1,200 to $1,800. The remarkable events that followed the purchase transformed the painting into one of the greatest discoveries in the art market—or, as many believe, one of the biggest frauds and financial schemes in history.

The *Salvator Mundi* case study will serve as a gateway to explore the expansion of the old masters market during America's Gilded Age, as well as the market for works by female old masters during their time.

WHAT IS *SALVATOR MUNDI*?

The existence of a Leonardo painting depicting the "Savior of the World" has been debated for centuries, because there are approximately twenty works believed to be copies of the master's original. A 1650 print by Wenceslaus Hollar (1607–1677) featuring the Savior includes a Latin caption stating that it was engraved from an original by Leonardo. The subject, derived from the Gospels, portrays Christ symbolically holding a transparent globe in his left hand.

The *Salvator Mundi* that sold at Christie's is a painting on a walnut panel in the standard size for a devotional work: 25 ⅞ × 18 inches (65.7 × 45.7 cm). Christ is depicted frontally, wearing a blue tunic, with a beard and long hair, and making a gesture of blessing.

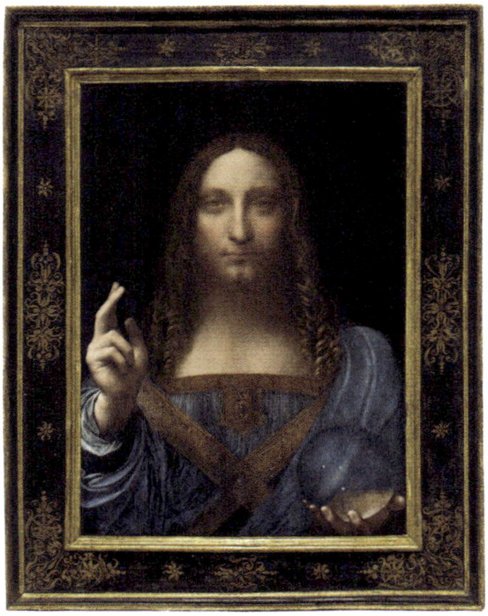

Leonardo da Vinci, *Salvator Mundi*, c. 1500

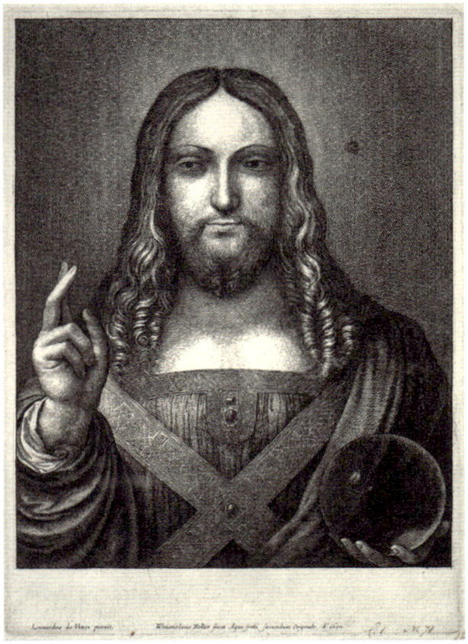

Wenceslaus Hollar, *Salvator Mundi*, 1650

DEBATED AUTHENTICITY

The attribution of *Salvator Mundi* to Leonardo has been hotly debated by scholars and in the media. Ben Lewis succinctly summarizes the key points of the dispute:

1. There is no record during the artist's lifetime, or for a further hundred years, of a Leonardo painting of a *Salvator Mundi*; all the paintings Leonardo executed after 1496, given his fame, are referred to in contemporary sources.
2. The panel on which the painting was executed, pieced together, and restored has a knot in the lower center, and it is odd that Leonardo would have accepted such a flawed surface to paint on; panels were usually cut as a single piece of wood.
3. *Salvator Mundi* vanished from sight from a total of 184 of its estimated first 500 years of existence—between 1763 and 1900, then between 1958 and 2005.
4. The last time a new painting by Leonardo was widely accepted as original was almost a century ago: the *Benois Madonna* (1478), soon after it entered the collection of the State Hermitage Museum in St. Petersburg, Russia.[2]

In his essay "Apparition ou disparition" in the catalogue for the acclaimed 2019 Leonardo da Vinci exhibition at the Musée du Louvre—where *Salvator Mundi* was expected but ultimately not included—Vincent Delieuvin also outlines some key facts about the painting. He notes, for example, that *Salvator Mundi* is not mentioned in any documents from

Leonardo's time, although this is not unusual given its intended use for private devotion. Delieuvin suggests that the earliest reference to the painting could be found in a 1525 inventory by Leonardo's pupil known as Salai, listing "A Christ in the manner of God the Father." Although undated, the painting was likely created during Leonardo's second stay in Milan, around 1507. This Milanese origin is supported by the use of walnut for the panel, rather than the poplar typically employed in Florence.

Delieuvin notes as well that in 1935, the art historian Kenneth Clark published his two-volume catalogue of Leonardo's drawings in the British Royal Collection at Windsor Castle, including two works on paper that he interpreted as preparatory sketches for Leonardo's *Salvator Mundi*. Clark believed these drawings were also connected to the aforementioned Hollar engraving. Together, the two drawings and the engraving seemed to confirm the existence of a *Salvator Mundi* painting by Leonardo, which historians had long endeavored to identify.[3]

A ROYAL PROVENANCE?

In the Christie's auction catalogue, the provenance for *Salvator Mundi* begins as follows: "(Possibly) Commissioned after 1500 by King Louis XII of France (1462–1515) and his wife, Anne of Brittany (1477–1514), following the conquest of Milan and Genoa, and possibly by descent to Henrietta Maria of France (1609–1669), by whom possibly brought to England in 1625 upon her marriage to King Charles I."[4]

The painting is said to have spent part of the seventeenth century in the court of Charles I (1600–1649). However, it is not listed in the inventory of the Royal Collection that Abraham van der Doort compiled at the request of the king, nor does it have the typical royal stamp of Charles I. Another inventory, called the Commonwealth Sale, was drawn up ten years later, in 1649–51, after Charles I was beheaded. The inventory mentioned a painting that could be the *Salvator Mundi*: "a peece of Christ done by Leonardo," with a low price of 30 pounds (maybe because of poor condition).

Based on the Christie's provenance, *Salvator Mundi* passed to Charles II (son of the beheaded king and restorer of the monarchy) and then, probably by inheritance, to his brother, King James II. From James II it possibly went to his mistress Catherine Sedley, Countess of Dorchester; thence to her daughter and son-in-law, John Sheffield, Duke of Buckingham and Normanby; and later to his illegitimate son, Sir Charles Herbert Sheffield. Sir Charles sold the original residence that later became Buckingham Palace to King George III in 1761, and two years later he consigned much of his art collection to Prestage auction house.

The Prestage auction on February 24, 1763, included lot 53, "L. Da Vinci A head of our Saviour," which sold for 2.10 pounds. After that, the painting vanished from view for 137 years, to resurface in 1900 in the English collection of Sir Francis Cook, as "Milanese School (circa 1520)."

In June 1958, the Cook heirs sold *Salvator Mundi*, which was bought for 45 pounds by Warren E. Kuntz, a collector from New Orleans, whose widow later bequeathed it to her nephew.

Salvator Mundi eventually ended up, in 2005, in an online catalogue of an obscure auction house in New Orleans, the St. Charles Gallery: "Lot 664. After Leonardo da Vinci," priced at $1,200–1,800.

A SUBSTANTIAL RESTORATION

Two weeks after Robert Simon purchased *Salvator Mundi* at auction in 2005, he enlisted Dianne Modestini, one of the most renowned conservators of Renaissance paintings, to analyze and restore it. The painting was in poor condition: the face had been entirely repainted, the background had been repainted at least twice, and a significant crack ran down the center of the panel. Overall, according to Lewis, up to 60 percent of the painting might have lost Leonardo's top layer of paint.[5] After studying Leonardo's *Mona Lisa* for comparison, Modestini became convinced that *Salvator Mundi* was created by Leonardo. Her conviction was bolstered by the discovery of a pentimento, or earlier draft, where the thumb of the blessing hand was initially painted straight rather than curved. This detail was deemed crucial evidence that the painting was an original, not a copy. The first phase of the restoration took two years, followed by a second phase in 2011, involving work on the orb, the eyes, and the original black background, which had been repainted brown sometime later.

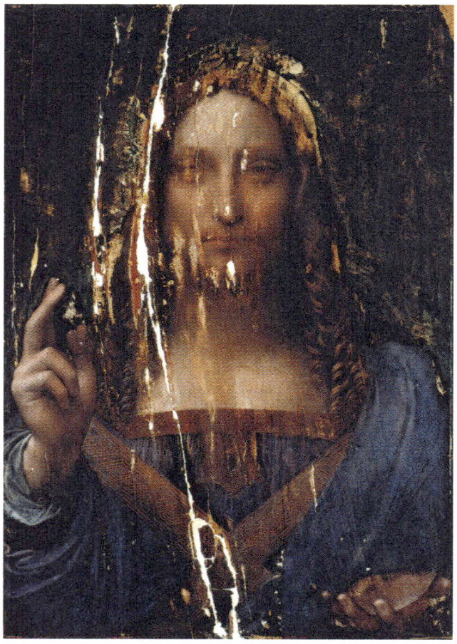

Leonardo da Vinci, *Salvator Mundi*, c. 1500, prior to restoration

Simon writes that after Modestini's revelation about the potential attribution of the painting to Leonardo, he felt confident enough to present his discovery to scholars of the artist. Nicholas Penny, who had just been appointed director of the National Gallery in London, viewed *Salvator Mundi* in New York in 2008 and supported its attribution to Leonardo. However, he acknowledged that acceptance of this attribution would necessitate a consensus among scholars.[6]

Penny therefore suggested that Simon bring the painting to London for examination alongside Leonardo's *Virgin of the Rocks* (1495–1508), in the National Gallery's collection. Penny also organized a meeting with Leonardo scholars Carmen Bambach, David Alan Brown, Maria Teresa Fiorio, Martin Kemp, and Pietro Marani, as well as conservators and curators from the National Gallery. Franck Zöllner, the author of Leonardo's catalogue raisonné, was not invited. The scholars' opinions were conveyed privately to Penny and to the National Gallery's curator of Italian paintings, Luke Syson. No minutes were taken during this meeting—a highly unusual practice, as Lewis points out—and no formal declarations were signed by those present. Syson, who attended the meeting, simply informed Penny, who was not present, that the experts had agreed the painting was indeed by Leonardo.[7]

In July 2010, the National Gallery announced its upcoming 2011 exhibition, *Leonardo da Vinci: Painter at the Court of Milan*, and that it would feature *Salvator Mundi*. This decision marked a significant endorsement of the painting's attribution to Leonardo. Lewis highlights the highly unorthodox and unprecedented nature of including a recently discovered and still-unconfirmed work by a renowned artist like Leonardo in an exhibition at such a prestigious institution as the National Gallery. Moreover, *Salvator Mundi* was still on the market at the time of the exhibition.[8] As stated in the 2017 Christie's catalogue, "The dramatic public unveiling of *Christ as Salvator Mundi* ("Savior of the World") in the exhibition *Leonardo da Vinci: Painter at the Court of Milan* at The National Gallery, London, in 2011, caused a worldwide media sensation."[9]

LOOKING FOR A BUYER

After the National Gallery exhibition, Simon and Parish, joined by dealer Warren Adelson, attempted to sell *Salvator Mundi* to major museums. Institutions such as the Museum of Fine Arts, Boston; the Gemäldegalerie in Berlin; the Dallas Museum of Art (which had borrowed the painting for months in 2012 for examination only by staff, donors, and some others); and the J. Paul Getty Museum in Los Angeles, as well as members of the royal family in Qatar, all declined the opportunity.

In May 2013, the Swiss art dealer Yves Bouvier purchased the painting for $83 million, in a private sale brokered by Sotheby's, and then immediately sold it to the Russian billionaire Dmitry Rybolovlev for $127.5

Equally remarkable, though receiving less media attention than *Salvator Mundi*, was the discovery of *Judith and Holofernes* (c. 1607) by Michelangelo Merisi, known as Caravaggio (1571–1610), in the attic of a house in Toulouse, France, in 2014. A dramatic depiction of the biblical story of Judith beheading the Assyrian general Holofernes, the painting exemplifies Caravaggio's use of chiaroscuro, heightening the emotional impact of the action. An earlier version—from about 1602—of the same subject by Caravaggio was already known; it is held in the collection of the Galleria Nazionale d'Arte Antica in Rome. The newly discovered *Judith and Holofernes* was privately sold in June 2019 by Marc Labarbe, head of a Toulouse auction house, and acquired by the American collector J. Tomilson Hill for an undisclosed amount thought to be close to $170 million.

Similarly astonishing was the discovery of a work by Cimabue (c. 1240–before 1302), *The Mocking of Christ* (c. 1280), a small tempera on a poplar panel, during a routine valuation in the kitchen of an elderly woman in Compiègne, France. The first artist in the seminal *Lives of the Most Excellent Painters, Sculptors, and Architects* (1550), by Giorgio Vasari (1511–1574), Cimabue broke away from the rigid, stylized forms of Byzantine art, introducing a more naturalistic depiction of reality and emotional expression. His work influenced later artists, including Giotto, allegedly his pupil. Only around fifteen works by Cimabue are known, which makes the discovery of *The Mocking of Christ* even more exceptional. The painting was auctioned in October 2019 and achieved a record price for pre-Renaissance art at $26.6 million. However, the French government did not authorize its export and eventually bought it for the collection of the Louvre. This painting is believed to be part of the same late thirteenth-century altarpiece series as Cimabue's *The Flagellation of Christ*, now housed in the Frick Collection in New York, and *The Virgin and Child with Two Angels*, in the National Gallery in London. The provenance of *The Mocking of Christ* remains largely unknown.

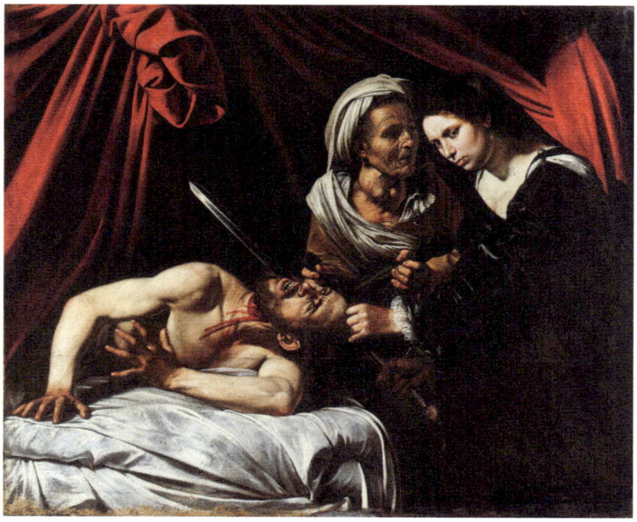

Caravaggio, *Judith and Holofernes*, c. 1607

million. This astonishing $44.5 million markup in the prearranged transaction led Rybolovlev to sue Bouvier—from whom he had bought several masterpieces by such artists as Pablo Picasso, Amedeo Modigliani, and Gustav Klimt—with accusations of fraud, manipulation, breach of trust, and inflated pricing. Rybolovlev argued that Bouvier had deceived him by presenting himself as a neutral intermediary rather than a dealer profiting from the sales. Bouvier, in his defense, contended that his role was that of an independent art dealer, free to set his prices. The contentious legal battle, which sparked numerous lawsuits across multiple jurisdictions including Monaco, Switzerland, and Singapore, drew widespread attention to some opaque practices of the high-end art market and the role of intermediaries before it eventually ended with a private settlement. In January 2024, Rybolovlev also sued Sotheby's for its involvement in several disputed sales. However, the lawsuit against Sotheby's was unsuccessful.

CHRISTIE'S AUCTION, NOVEMBER 15, 2017

In 2017, Rybolovlev entrusted *Salvator Mundi* to Christie's to be sold at auction. Rather than placing it in a sale of old masters, Christie's opted to include the work in its auction of postwar and contemporary art in New York in November—a decision that was unprecedented but strategically sound. This move aimed to expose *Salvator Mundi* to the world's wealthiest collectors, those purchasing modern and contemporary art.[10]

Christie's employed an extensive array of marketing strategies to promote *Salvator Mundi*, which included traveling exhibitions to San Francisco, Tokyo, and London; a dedicated catalogue; and a promotional video capturing emotional reactions from viewers, including the actor Leonardo DiCaprio, in front of the painting, some moved to tears. Central to the campaign's success was the creation of a nearly sacred aura around *Salvator Mundi*, portraying it as a unique and irreplaceable opportunity to acquire an original work by Leonardo, which it dubbed "the male *Mona Lisa*." In a significant move, Christie's secured a third-party guarantee for *Salvator Mundi* (meaning there was a definite buyer if the work did not reach the set price; if it did, the buyer would share in the profit). On the evening of November 15, 2017, the painting was auctioned with bidding starting at $75 million and soaring to a staggering hammer price of $400 million, totaling $450 million including the buyer's premium paid to the auction house.

On December 6, the *New York Times* revealed that the "Mystery Buyer" of *Salvator Mundi* was Prince Mohammed bin Salman of Saudi Arabia.[11] Although the painting was initially supposed to be displayed at the Louvre Abu Dhabi, it never appeared there. It was also announced as part of the Leonardo da Vinci quincentenary exhibition at the Louvre in Paris in 2019, but it was ultimately excluded. Reports later surfaced that the painting was withheld because the owner insisted that it be displayed next to the *Mona Lisa*, a request the Louvre declined. The current whereabouts of *Salvator Mundi* remain unknown.

THE OLD MASTERS MARKET IN THE UNITED STATES DURING THE GILDED AGE

Around the end of the nineteenth century, a significant and extensive migration of masterpieces from Europe to the United States unfolded, spurred by the emergence of immensely wealthy American buyers during the Gilded Age. This influx of cash injected into the art market propelled the purchase of old masters to unprecedented heights. This dominance persisted until 1987, when Vincent van Gogh's *Vase with Fifteen Sunflowers* fetched $39.9 million at Christie's London.

Dynasties of dealers such as the Knoedlers, Colnaghis, Agnews, Wildensteins, Seligmanns, and notably Joseph Duveen supplied American collectors with sought-after treasures. They not only facilitated transactions but also shaped the tastes of these new buyers, many of whom were self-made businessmen lacking formal art education. Few museums existed in the United States at the time, so there was also a scarcity of established models to emulate.

Prominent figures such as the Rockefellers, Huntingtons, Havemeyers, Benjamin Altman, and Samuel H. Kress amassed exceptional collections, many of which were eventually donated to museums or transformed into museums of their own. Examples include the Isabella Stewart Gardner Museum in Boston and the Frick Collection and the Morgan Library & Museum in New York. The extensive collection of Andrew Mellon (1855–1937) formed the foundation for the establishment of the National Gallery of Art in Washington, DC.

CONTRADICTIONS OF THE GILDED AGE: ECONOMIC GROWTH, URBANIZATION, INEQUALITY, AND RACISM

The term "Gilded Age" refers to the period from shortly after the end of the Civil War (1861–65) until the onset of World War I (1914–18). Coined from Mark Twain's satirical 1873 novel of the same name, "gilded" rather than "golden" suggests that the era appeared prosperous and shiny on the surface but concealed an unpleasant reality underneath.

During this time, the United States emerged as a dominant economic power. By 1914, the national income had surged to $37 billion, more than triple the income of either Germany or Britain—the next two largest economies.[12] The remarkable economic expansion and industrial development were driven by significant technological and scientific advancements. As Gail Feigenbaum observes, "The American economy was on fire in the decades after the Civil War. Fortunes were made in steel mills, breweries, railroads, streetcars and subways, oil refineries, agriculture, department stores, mining, and the stock markets and banking needed to finance these ventures. American millionaires, some even billionaires, had more money than they knew how to spend."[13]

Simultaneously, a significant demographic surge occurred, driven by waves of immigration from Europe and China. Major cities, particularly in the North, expanded rapidly, transforming the United States from a primarily agricultural nation before the Civil War into an increasingly urbanized society. However, these advancements were accompanied by deepening and lacerating contradictions. A widening wealth gap, pervasive corruption, systemic racism, and the tragic decimation of the Native American population, who were denied citizenship and confined to reservations, underscored the stark realities beneath the surface prosperity of the Gilded Age.

Central to the economic development of the Gilded Age was the expansion of the railroad system, which revolutionized both travel and commerce. By 1880, the Pacific Railroad, linking the East and West Coasts of the United States and comprising the Union Pacific and Central Pacific, was transporting a dramatically increasing amount of goods annually.

Cornelius Vanderbilt (1794–1877) was a pioneering entrepreneur who foresaw and capitalized on the potential of the railroad industry. Alongside such figures as John D. Rockefeller, J. P. Morgan, Henry Clay Frick, and Andrew Mellon, Vanderbilt was part of a powerful group of business leaders who strategically invested in transportation, steel, oil, and banking. Their dominance led to the creation of monopolies, resulting in a massive concentration of wealth among a few individuals. By 1890, as Alan Axelrod points out, 73 percent of America's wealth was controlled by the top 10 percent of the population.[14] As it happens, according to the World Inequality Database, in 2023 (the latest data at the time of writing), the richest 10 percent in America owned nearly 70 percent of the total wealth.[15]

Derisively labeled "robber barons," these immensely wealthy Gilded Age businessmen spared no expense in constructing opulent residences. One notable example is the Biltmore House in Asheville, North Carolina, boasting 250 rooms and modeled after the grandeur of French Renaissance châteaux. The extravagant lifestyles of these nouveaux riches were exemplified by the legendary costume ball hosted by Alva Vanderbilt (married to Cornelius's grandson) on March 26, 1883. Held at her newly erected mansion, "the Petit Château," located at 660 Fifth Avenue in New York, the event featured 1,200 guests and cost $250,000—the equivalent of approximately $6 million now.

The industrialists and financiers of the Gilded Age turned into the most aggressive and consistent art buyers in the world, driving prices to unprecedented heights. According to Cynthia Saltzman, a painting by Rembrandt van Rijn (1606–1669) fetched $25,000 in the early 1880s. By 1911, his landscape *The Mill* (1645–48) was acquired by the Philadelphia philanthropist and tycoon Peter Arrell Brown Widener (1834–1915) for the then-record price of $500,000. On the eve of World War I, Czar Nicholas II (1868–1918) spent the astronomical, and for many decades unmatched, price of $1.5 million for Leonardo's *Benois Madonna* after an initial authentication.[16]

JOSEPH DUVEEN

Towering above all the dealers operating in America during the Gilded Age was the legendary British merchant Joseph Duveen (1869–1939).

The biographies devoted to him, from the first one published in 1952 by S. N. Behrman to the one by Meryle Secrest in 2004, abound with anecdotes showing Duveen's business inventiveness and his readiness to do anything to achieve his goals. One of the most memorable episodes is Duveen's meeting with the Pittsburgh banker and collector Andrew Mellon, whom he had been after for years. When Duveen found out that Mellon was staying at the same hotel in London, Claridge's, he bribed Mellon's valet to inform him of the collector's movements, so that he could "casually" bump into Mellon in the elevator.[17]

Duveen was the son of a Dutch Jew who had immigrated to England and in 1868 opened a gallery of decorative arts. The enterprise flourished, and in the 1870s his brother Henry set up a branch in New York. Duveen Brothers established fruitful relationships with all the most important collectors of the time, selling them precious porcelains, furniture, and tapestries.

When, at the age of seventeen, Joseph was sent by his father to New York, he soon realized that the big money was to be made in selling pictures, not tapestries or porcelain. On his famous quote "Europe has a great deal of art, and America has a great deal of money," Duveen built his spectacular career, expanding the family business from decorative to fine arts.

Secrest explains why many British aristocratic families were forced to sell the contents of their mansions in the last two decades of the nineteenth century. The basis of the aristocracy's livelihood had always been the agricultural proceeds from their vast estates. However, when these products, thanks to the new railway system and refrigerated ships, began to be imported to England from the United States, Canada, Argentina, Australia, and New Zealand, where production on a much larger scale allowed much lower prices, domestic prices dramatically fell. Whereas in the mid-Victorian years, wheat sold for 50 to 55 shillings a quarter, in the 1880s and 1890s the flood from overseas forced prices down to 27 shillings, reaching a catastrophic low of 22 shillings and 10 pence by 1894. The English aristocracy had no other way to meet their expenses than selling their pictures, furniture, and tapestries.[18] Duveen secured many of these precious heirlooms and sold them to his American clients, both nurturing and exploiting their desire to own artworks that not only were remarkable but had a prestigious provenance. In the words of Don Thompson, "He was the first to sell social status in the guise of selling art."[19]

The turning point of Duveen's ascent in the old masters market was the purchase of the collection of the German banker Rodolphe Kann in 1907: a hundred paintings by Italian, English, French, and Flemish masters, including masterpieces such as *A Maid Asleep* (c. 1656–57) by Johannes Vermeer (1632–1675) and Rembrandt's *Aristotle with a Bust of Homer* (1653), both now in the collection of the Metropolitan Museum of Art in New York.

At the peak of his career, Duveen strategically partnered with Bernard Berenson (1865–1959), a scholar of Lithuanian descent renowned for his expertise in Italian Renaissance art. This collaboration was marked by Duveen's innovative decision to offer Berenson an exceptionally high fee of as much as 25 percent for each painting he authenticated. This move proved prescient: as explained by Secrest, Italian Renaissance paintings were at the time among the most speculative items in the market. Unlike their English and Flemish counterparts, these artworks often suffered from poor condition and lacked signatures, thus allowing for considerable conjecture.[20]

Duveen dealt with, sold to, and advised all the major collectors of his time, shaping American taste in art. Feigenbaum writes that "Duveen's genius was to inflame his collector's desire for the superlative, and often the most expensive, art."[21] The numbers, as reported by Behrman in a 1951 *New Yorker* profile, are staggering: 95 of the 115 pictures in the Mellon Collection, now in the National Gallery of Art in Washington, DC, came to Mellon through Duveen. Of the 700 paintings in the Kress Collection, also in the National Gallery of Art, more than 150 were supplied by Duveen as well.[22]

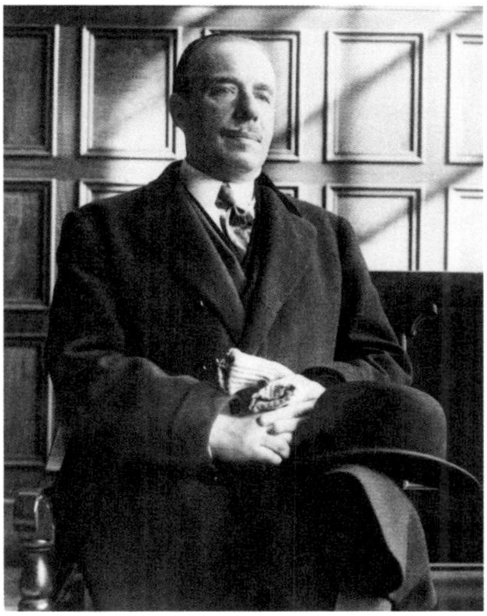

Joseph Duveen, c. 1929

HENRY CLAY FRICK: THE EMBODIMENT OF THE GILDED AGE COLLECTOR

Henry Clay Frick (1849–1919), of humble origins and with only a year of college, epitomized the contradictions of the Gilded Age. By his thirties, he had amassed a fortune, and he later put together one of America's finest art collections.

Frick's economic ascent began in 1871 at just twenty-one years old with the founding of the Frick Coke Company, which specialized in the production of coke—a vital fuel derived from coal and used extensively in the steel industry. A prosperous alliance with Andrew Carnegie (1835–1919), a prominent Pittsburgh steel magnate, soon followed. Frick supplied Carnegie's steel empire with the essential coke it required.

As a key partner and manager within the Carnegie Steel Company, Frick became embroiled in one of the era's most notorious and violent labor disputes: the Homestead massacre of 1892. The workers were protesting against deplorable conditions, advocating for better pay and shorter hours. Frick, resolute in dismantling the union, adamantly refused negotiations, closed the factory, and enlisted a private militia—the Pinkertons—when workers picketed the plant. The conflict intensified into violence: ten lives were lost and more than seventy individuals were injured. Ultimately, the Pennsylvania state militia was dispatched to quell the strike. Frick endured harsh scrutiny from the local media and narrowly survived an assassination attempt in Pittsburgh.

New business ventures, combined with his strained relationship with Carnegie, who had blamed Frick for the turmoil at Homestead, prompted Frick to depart Pittsburgh in 1905 and establish himself in New York. This transition marked the mature phase in Frick's life as a collector. After acquiring works by local artists in Pittsburgh and later showing interest in the mid-nineteenth-century French Barbizon school painters, Frick now gravitated toward collecting old masters. Rembrandt's *Portrait of a Young Artist* (c. 1650) was his first important purchase. Frick would eventually also own the Dutch painter's *The Polish Rider* (c. 1655) and a *Self-Portrait* (1658), with an early portrait, *Nicolaes Ruts* (1631), added to the collection much later.

In New York, Frick finally met Duveen, whose advances he had inexplicably rebuffed for years, opting instead to purchase from other dealers. The pivotal moment came with the opportunity to acquire the renowned late eighteenth-century suite *The Progress of Love* by Jean-Honoré Fragonard (1732–1806), previously owned by J. P. Morgan. Following Morgan's passing in 1913, his son chose to sell the paintings. They were briefly exhibited at the Metropolitan Museum of Art, possibly with the hope of an institutional acquisition, which did not materialize. Brokered by Duveen, the Fragonard purchase could not have been better timed. Frick was building a grand new residence on a block on Fifth Avenue between Seventieth and Seventy-First Streets and needed a lot of things to put in it.[23] Duveen was directly involved in the choice of architect for Frick's mansion, the Beaux Arts master Thomas Hastings (1860–1929) of the prominent firm Carrère and Hastings, which also designed the Main Branch of the New York Public Library (inaugurated in 1911). Sir Charles Allom (1865–1947) was in charge of the interior decoration and worked closely with Frick on the installation of his eclectic collection, which included Renaissance bronzes, porcelains, tapestries, and period furniture as well as paintings.

Frick enjoyed the house for only a few years, until he died in 1919. When his residence was transformed into a museum in 1935, a few years after his wife's death, the architect John Russell Pope (1874–1937) oversaw the renovation, which included the addition of an entrance hall, a reception area, and a library. Nearly ninety years later, the Frick Collection, as the museum is known, underwent a new expansion led by Selldorf Architects.

WOMEN COLLECT: ISABELLA STEWART GARDNER

The unique trajectory of Isabella Stewart Gardner (1840–1924) as a collector is epitomized by her Boston palace, Fenway Court, now a museum. Constructed between 1899 and 1901, the building was commissioned from architect Willard T. Sears (1837–1920) to replicate the ambience of the Palazzo Barbaro in Venice, where Gardner and her husband had enjoyed numerous summers. Organized around a courtyard with a Roman mosaic floor, Fenway Court was inaugurated with a concert on January 1, 1903. The museum harbors a very eclectic collection that Gardner put together: Renaissance masterpieces by Raphael (1483–1520), Piero della Francesca (c. 1416–1492), Fra Angelico (1395–1455), Sandro Botticelli (1444/45–1510), and Titian (c. 1488–1576) alongside works by then-contemporary artists

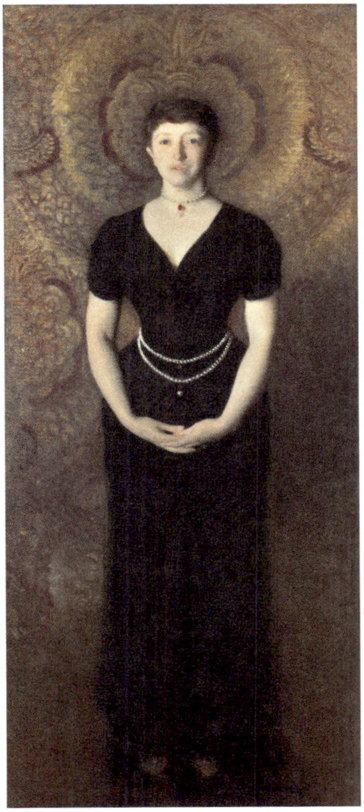

John Singer Sargent, *Isabella Stewart Gardner*, 1888, Isabella Stewart Gardner Museum, Boston

whom Gardner befriended, such as John Singer Sargent (1856–1925) and James McNeill Whistler (1834–1903); antique tapestries in the vicinity of stained glass from a French cathedral; and porcelains near historical architectural elements incorporated into the walls of the new building. Although Gardner was not the only wealthy American of her time amassing an exceptional collection, she was the only one—as Natalie Dykstra has pointed out—to design and build a new structure to house her collection for public view.[24]

Isabella Stewart was from New York, where she was born into a wealthy family of Scottish origin. She relocated to Boston in 1860 after marrying John Lowell "Jack" Gardner Jr. (1837–1898) and soon became a shining protagonist of the city's social and cultural scene. Gardner's personal life was marked by a terrible tragedy, though—the loss of her son at less than two years old. A trip to Europe in 1867, which her husband organized to bring her out of the deep depression into which she had fallen, was the first of many and planted the seed of her passion for art.

The inheritance in 1891 of the considerable sum of $2 million from her father allowed Gardner to direct her artistic interests into the building of an astounding collection. Morris Carter, author of the first biography of Gardner, notes that in collecting, Isabella finally found her life-absorbing purpose.[25] Commenting on Gardner's role in the American environment of her time, Dykstra writes: "What was there of cultural value in a country so relatively new? American literature and history would not merit their own disciplines of study until the twentieth century. In this context, Isabella Stewart Gardner occupied an interesting position. She was on the cutting edge, supporting American artists and, more radically, doing so as a woman."[26]

The new course of Gardner's collecting was inaugurated at an 1892 auction in Paris by the purchase of Vermeer's *The Concert* (1663–66), for 29,000 francs (around $6,000). With the acquisition, as Saltzman observes, she showed her independence of mind and her ambition, at a time when the number of Americans buying old masters was still small.[27] Sadly, the Vermeer masterpiece and twelve other works, including five by Edgar Degas (1834–1917), three by Rembrandt, and one by Édouard Manet (1832–1883), were stolen from the museum on March 18, 1990, and none have ever been recovered.

Gardner expanded her interests under the guidance of the abovementioned Bernard Berenson, whom she had met in Boston while he was still a student at Harvard, and who had later turned into one of the most erudite scholars of the Italian Renaissance. [28] *The Death of Lucretia* (1496), bought in 1894, was the first painting by the Italian Renaissance master Botticelli to enter America. With that, in the words of Saltzman, "Isabella Gardner took American collecting in a new direction, and her collaboration with Bernard Berenson began."[29]

One of Gardner's coups, through Berenson, was the acquisition in 1896 of a late masterpiece by Titian, *The Rape of Europa* (1559–62), which is part of a group of six canvases known as "Poesie." Inspired by the *Metamorphoses* of the Latin poet Ovid (43 BCE–17 CE), the mythological paintings commissioned by King Philip II of Spain are considered among the most significant of the artist's oeuvre. They were reunited for the first time in centuries in the Isabella Stewart Gardner Museum's temporary exhibition *Titian: Women, Myth & Power* in 2021.

WOMEN COLLECT: LOUISINE HAVEMEYER

When, in 1929, a substantial part of the Havemeyer art collection was donated to the Metropolitan Museum of Art in New York, it transformed the institution, as noted in 1993 by Gary Tinterow, former longtime chair of the museum's Department of Nineteenth-Century, Modern, and Contemporary Art.[30] Donations were also made to the National Gallery of Art, Washington, DC; Brooklyn Museum; Denver Art Museum; J. Paul Getty Museum; and Nelson-Atkins Museum of Art, Kansas City. Comprising old master and Impressionist paintings, ceramics, textiles, and bronzes, the eclectic collection was the result of fifty years of a shared passion between Louisine Waldron Elder Havemeyer (1855–1929) and Henry Osborne "Harry" Havemeyer (1847–1907).

Each of them started buying art independently before marrying. Louisine left an account of her journey in *Sixteen to Sixty: Memoirs of a Collector*, published posthumously. She was not yet eighteen when she was introduced to the American painter Mary Cassatt (1844–1926), who became her mentor. Under Cassatt's guidance, she made her first art purchase within a few years: the pastel *Ballet Rehearsal* (c. 1875) by Edgar Degas, for 500 francs—a large sum for Louisine at the time, the result of "many little economies and even some privations."[31] Cassatt, who came from a wealthy background and lived mostly in Paris, was, with Berthe Morisot (1841–1895), a rare female member of the original Impressionist circle (see "Paul Durand-Ruel and the Birth of the Impressionist Market," p. 94). After that first acquisition and especially after Louisine married Harry in 1883, Cassatt acted as a "godmother" of the Havemeyers' collection, inspiring and guiding their choices. She ignited their interest in the Impressionists, of whom they would become among the first consistent buyers, amassing one of the best groups of works by Degas and Impressionist precursor Édouard Manet in the United States. Cassatt also triggered in Harry and Louisine an unusual passion for Spanish painting. Old masters, mainly Dutch, were already part of the Havemeyer collection, but after an extensive trip to Italy and Spain in 1901, organized by Cassatt, the Havemeyers focused their attention on Spanish artists, still an uncharted territory for American collectors. At the turn of the century, as Saltzman remarks, Spain was considered exotic and off the beaten path. As such, due in part to the country's relative isolation, Spanish painting had not yet attracted the same degree of scholarly attention—along with higher prices—as the Italian and Dutch schools.[32]

The hunt for works by Francisco de Goya (1746–1828) resulted in fifteen acquisitions—of which, unfortunately, only four turned out to be authentic. In addition, the Havemeyers bought two masterpieces by El Greco (1541–1614), *Portrait of a Cardinal* (c. 1600) and *View of Toledo* (c. 1599–1600), both now in the collection of the Metropolitan Museum of Art. Louisine was aware of their pioneering role and wrote in her memoir that "we were, so to speak, to open the market for Grecos and Goyas, at least in the United States."[33]

The Havemeyers' residence, at 1 East Sixty-Sixth Street, built by the architect Charles Coolidge Haight (1841–1917) in a Romanesque Revival style and, regrettably, destroyed in 1930, was also testimony to the couple's independent and original choices. Instead of importing European furniture and decor, as the majority of wealthy Americans did, the Havemeyers hired as interior designers the Americans Louis Comfort Tiffany (1848–1933) and Samuel Colman (1832–1920). Thus, as Alice Cooney Frelinghuysen points out, they moved away from traditional, conservative tastes to embrace original American solutions.[34]

Also worthy of notice is Louisine's commitment to the suffragist cause. In April 1915, she lent almost half of the fifty-nine works in the *Loan Exhibition of Masterpieces by Old and Modern Painters* at the galleries of M. Knoedler & Co. in New York to raise money for the cause, and she participated in a march up Fifth Avenue in May 1915.[35]

A MARKET FOR WOMEN OLD MASTERS IN THEIR TIME?

The market for female artists in historical periods is intricately tied to their presence and societal standing within a predominantly male-dominated art world. This environment imposed stringent constraints on their learning, apprenticeship, and career opportunities. Linda Nochlin's groundbreaking essay "Why Have There Been No Great Women Artists?," published in the January 1971 issue of *ARTnews*, ignited a crucial debate. By exploring the numerous cultural and social barriers that historically hindered women from pursuing artistic careers, Nochlin provocatively asserted that "there *are* no women equivalents for Michelangelo or Rembrandt, Delacroix or Cézanne, Picasso or Matisse, or even, in very recent times, for de Kooning or Warhol." She also critiqued the pervasive "white Western male viewpoint" entrenched in art historical narratives, highlighting its limitations not only on moral and ethical grounds but also on intellectual ones.

Nochlin's essay had the merit of encouraging further studies devoted to past female artists, which were followed by important exhibitions. *Women Artists: 1550–1950*, curated by Nochlin herself with Ann Sutherland Harris for the Los Angeles County Museum of Art in 1976 (before it traveled to the University of Texas at Austin; the Museum of Art, Carnegie Institute, in Pittsburgh; and the Brooklyn Museum by late 1977), was one of the first.

Awareness of women's contributions to the history of art has grown since, nurtured by outstanding monographic and group shows.[36] In 2023, Katy Hessel even published an art history volume that cut men out completely: *The Story of Art without Men*.[37]

ANDREW MELLON AND THE FOUNDING OF THE NATIONAL GALLERY OF ART

Andrew Mellon was a banker and businessman, philanthropist and art collector, and the US secretary of the treasury from 1921 to 1932. Intrigued, in part due to his friendship with Henry Clay Frick, by the works of British artists Thomas Gainsborough (1727–1788) and Joshua Reynolds (1723–1792), Mellon embarked on a journey of artistic exploration by acquiring works to decorate his Washington, DC, estate. As his interest in art grew, Mellon added to his collection masterpieces such as Goya's *Marquesa de Pontejos* (c. 1786) and—among twenty-one works from the State Hermitage Museum treasures that the Soviet government sold in 1930–31—*Alba Madonna* (c. 1510) by Raphael, *The Annunciation* (c. 1434–36) by Jan van Eyck (c. 1390–1441), and *Philip, Lord Wharton* (1632) by Anthony van Dyck (1599–1641).

Recognizing the absence of a world-class art museum in the nation's capital that could rival European institutions, Mellon conceived of that visionary project. His choice set him apart from his contemporaries like Frick and Gardner, who had preferred to establish private museums for their collections. Instead, Mellon decided to lead the initiative that would ultimately give birth to the National Gallery of Art in Washington, DC.

In 1930, he established a trust to be the legal owner of the works he planned to donate, and five years later, Mellon asked the architect John Russell Pope to plan the museum's structure. In 1936, Mellon formally offered in a letter to President Franklin D. Roosevelt (1842–1945) to build the National Gallery of Art and donate his art collection. On March 24, 1937, Congress passed legislation to accept the donation and approve the construction of the museum. Tragically, however, in August of that year, within twenty-four hours of each other, both Mellon and Pope passed away. Nevertheless, construction proceeded following Russell's Neoclassical plans.

What is now the West Building of the museum was finished and dedicated on March 17, 1941, including Mellon's 126 paintings and 26 sculptures. The opening ceremony was attended by nearly nine thousand guests, including President Roosevelt, who declared the National Gallery of Art's duty to serve the people of the United States. In order to fulfill this mission, it established a lending program to make its collection accessible to museums across the country. Mellon's vision inspired the donation of other remarkable collections, including those of Samuel H. Kress, Joseph E. Widener, Lessing J. Rosenwald, Chester Dale, Paul Mellon, and Ailsa Mellon Bruce.

Highlighting the profound impact of Mellon's vision was the historic exhibition of Leonardo da Vinci's *Mona Lisa* in 1963. The loan of the Louvre's iconic painting was unprecedented and has been repeated only once since then, in Tokyo and Moscow in 1974. During its twenty-six-day display, more than half a million visitors flocked to Washington to view the masterpiece, before it traveled to the Metropolitan Museum of Art for viewing by another million people in a month. Among the visitors was Andy Warhol (1928–1987), who would subsequently capture the popularity of the artwork as a Pop icon in his 1963 *Mona Lisa* silkscreen series.

The National Gallery of Art was expanded with the East Building, designed by I. M. Pei (1917–2019), which President Jimmy Carter (1924–2024) dedicated and opened on June 1, 1978. Already hanging in the building's atrium was the *Untitled* mobile (1976) by Alexander Calder (1898–1976), a site-specific commission installed a year after his death.

Today, the National Gallery of Art houses an impressive collection of more than 150,000 works, welcomes millions of visitors a year—with no admission charge—and remains one of the world's largest public art museums.

History has preserved the names of a few remarkable women artists who not only earned recognition during their lifetimes but also achieved notable commercial success.

Six female artists were mentioned by the ancient Roman historian Pliny the Elder (23–79 CE) in his *Historia naturalis*.

Centuries later, the Renaissance painter and writer Vasari included only one woman in the first edition of his *Lives*. She was the sculptor Properzia de' Rossi (c. 1490–1530), who received a public commission—and this was indeed exceptional—in Bologna for the marble relief *Joseph and Potiphar's Wife* (c. 1526). Vasari wrote: "It is extraordinary that in all the skills and pursuits in which women in any period whatever have with some preparation become involved, they have always succeeded most admirably and have become more than famous, as countless examples could easily demonstrate."[38]

A contrasting judgment was vehemently expressed by the Venetian painter Paolo Pino (active 1534–65), Vasari's contemporary, in his *Dialogo di pittura* (Dialogue on painting), published in 1548: "It does not please me to hear women equaled to the excellence of men in this virtue; and it seems to me that the art is debased by this, and the female species drawn outside of what is proper to it, for nothing suits women save the distaff [used to hold wool or other material] and the spindle."[39]

NUNS, PROFESSIONALS, AND NOBLEWOMEN

In her essay "Art as Women's Work: The Professionalization of Women Artists in Italy, 1350–1800," Sheila Barker begins by exploring the distinct social status of the three female painters included in Vasari's second edition of his *Lives* (1568). Plautilla Nelli (1524–1588) was a nun, Sofonisba Anguissola (c. 1532–1625) a professional painter, and Lucrezia Quistelli (1541–1594) an aristocrat. Barker therefore identifies three categories of women artists: the professionals, whose career path, despite the difficulties and limitations imposed on their gender at the time, was similar to that of their male colleagues; and what she calls "the alternative scene": members of a religious order and noblewomen.[40]

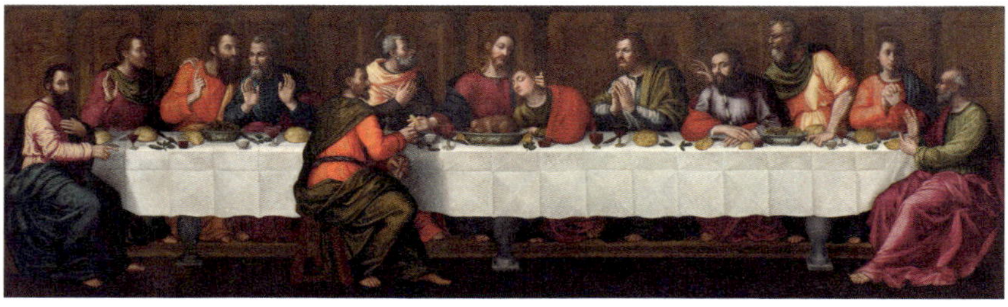

Plautilla Nelli, *The Last Supper*, c. 1568, Museum of Santa Maria Novella, Florence, Italy

In the religious category, one who excelled was Nelli, of whom Vasari significantly wrote that "she would have done wonderful things if she had only studied as men do."[41] A self-taught nun in the Dominican convent of Santa Caterina di Cafaggio, in Florence, she is the author of the only *Last Supper* (c. 1568) painted and signed by a woman, which was restored in 2015–19 thanks to Advancing Women Artists, a nonprofit organization based in Florence. It is worth highlighting the market model that Nelli pioneered: she established an all-women painting workshop within her convent, allowing the nuns to achieve financial independence.

Anguissola, born in Cremona (northern Italy) into a family of the local minor nobility, turned the artistic education that was part of the upbringing of aristocratic girls into a long and successful career. Vasari praised her: "She has worked with deeper study and greater grace than any woman of our times."[42] Trained with the locally renowned master Bernardino Campi (1522–1595), Anguissola became an accomplished painter, specializing in portraiture. In Rome, she caught the eye of Michelangelo (1475–1564), and he provided advice. In 1559, Anguissola was called to the Spanish court as lady-in-waiting to Elisabeth of Valois, third wife of King Philip II. Anguissola's portraits, although adhering to the dominant Mannerist style of her time, are characterized by a remarkable freedom and lively way

THE MARKET FOR WOMEN OLD MASTERS NOW

Recent market interest in women artists has expanded beyond young rising stars to include female old masters. In my final chapter, I explore how compelling personal narratives, such as that of the Baroque master Artemisia Gentileschi (1593–1654 or later) or Surrealist female painters like Leonora Carrington (1917–2011) resonate profoundly with contemporary audiences (see "The Art Market in a Global, Post-Pandemic, Turbulent Time," p. 252). Additionally, the realm of women old masters represents an untapped niche, where exceptional works of art can still be acquired at relatively modest prices. Despite notable auction records being shattered, the prices and overall market activity for female old masters remain significantly lower compared to their male counterparts, accounting for only roughly 5 percent of the entire old masters market. Moreover, the disparity in prices between female and male artists in this sector appears insurmountable.

The auction of Gentileschi's *Self-Portrait as Saint Catherine of Alexandria* (c. 1614–15), for instance, set a record price of $5,687,000 for her work, at Christie's New York, on February 4, 2026—compared to $30,490,000 for *Danaë* (c. 1621) by her father, Orazio Gentileschi (1563–1639), at Sotheby's New York in January 2016. Élisabeth Louise Vigée Le Brun (1755–1842), one of the most expensive female old masters, holds a record of $7,185,900 for her 1788 portrait of Muhammad Dervish Khan, established at Sotheby's New York in January 2019. But the highest price for a work by Angelica Kauffman (1741–1807) is only $1,110,000 for *Cornelia, Mother of the Gracchi* (1788), which sold at Christie's New York in October 2021. On the male side, the record price for a Rembrandt, *Portrait of a Man with Arms Akimbo* (1658), is $33,258,562 (Christie's London, December 2009); and for a Peter Paul Rubens, *The Massacre of the Innocents* (1609–11), is $76,529,056 (Sotheby's London, July 2002).

of positioning her subjects and capturing their personalities. Among her several self-portraits, *Self-Portrait at the Easel* (1554–55) is the first depicting a woman in the act of painting, fiercely staring at the viewer. The religious painting in the background served as Anguissola's way of advertising her skills in a genre typically dominated by male artists.[43]

Vasari refers to Quistelli as "Madonna Lucrezia," specifying that she was the wife of Count Clemente Pietra and that she "learned from Alessandro Allori, the pupil of [Agnolo] Bronzino." He adds that her many paintings and portraits "are worthy of being praised by everyone."[44]

In addition to these specific women, the city of Bologna appears to have fostered an unusually supportive environment for women artists. Babette Bohn, who extensively studied this phenomenon, documents the presence of sixty-eight women artists active in the city from the fifteenth to the eighteenth century, a significantly higher number than is known in any other location in Italy or Europe. What sets Bologna apart is not only the quantity but also the diversity of roles these women undertook, including as sculptors—a medium at the time rarely pursued by women—as well as printmakers and creators of drawings. Furthermore, thirty-five women painters received public commissions during the seventeenth century. Bohn attributes the significant yet relative flourishing of female artists in Bologna to several factors. One crucial element was the patronage from university scholars, particularly noteworthy given that Bologna's university, established in 1088 as the first in Europe, included women among its faculty. Additionally, Bologna's unique patronage system distinguished itself from those in other cities by including women as commissioners of artworks.[45]

One of the artists active in Bologna was Lavinia Fontana (1552–1614), often regarded as the first woman to successfully build a commercial career in art. Born into a middle-class family in Bologna, she received her artistic education in the workshop of her father, who was an established painter himself. Nochlin observes in her 1971 *ARTnews* essay that, historically, the

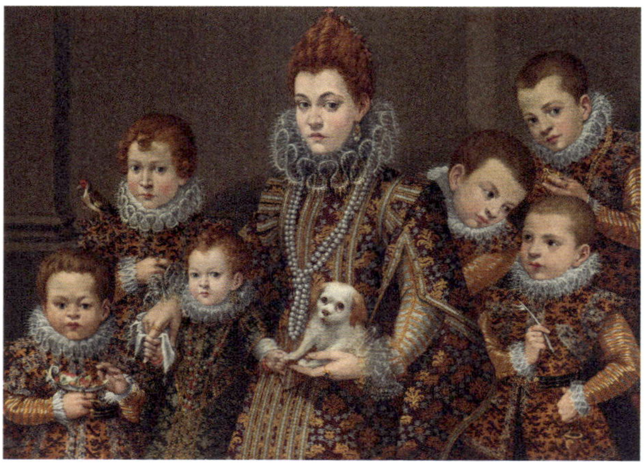

Lavinia Fontana, *Portrait of Bianca degli Utili Maselli and Her Children*, c. 1604–05, Fine Arts Museums of San Francisco

majority of women artists were daughters of painters who trained them, as a formal apprenticeship was usually inaccessible. Fontana expanded her artistic repertoire beyond the conventional genres typically open to women—portraits and small devotional paintings—and received numerous commissions for large-scale altarpieces depicting mythical and biblical subjects. She is also credited as the first woman to paint female nudes. Aoife Brady observes that the scale and complexity of Fontana's works indicate that she oversaw a busy studio. However, detailed records about its structure are sparse, largely because societal norms limited women's ability to maintain stable teams of assistants. Despite these constraints, Fontana likely enlisted occasional helpers for specific projects as needed.[46] Fontana also worked for the Vatican, and she was the first woman elected to the prestigious Accademia di San Luca in Rome.

From Bologna also emerged Elisabetta Sirani (1638–1665),[47] whose inclusions by Count Carlo Cesare Malvasia in his 1678 book, *Felsina pittrice: Vite de' pittori bolognesi* (Lives of the Bolognese painters)—Felsina is the Etruscan name for Bologna—is testament to the reputation she enjoyed in her time. Adelina Modesti states in her biography that Sirani represented a pioneering figure in "a new, gendered concept of womanhood" and was a role model: she was a "single, independent professional woman" who prioritized a successful career as an artist over traditional roles of marriage and motherhood.[48] Despite her tragically short life—she died at the age of twenty-seven—Sirani left behind an impressive body of works, including prestigious and lucrative commissions for altarpieces and other public artworks, usually reserved for male artists. Her subjects varied widely, from Madonnas influenced by the classicism of the Carracci family to more complex historical and religious compositions such as *Judith and Holofernes* (1658). Unlike Gentileschi's depiction of the same subject, Sirani portrayed Judith as triumphant rather than engaged in the act of decapitating her adversary.

Outside of Italy, Luisa Ignacia Roldán (1652–1706), called "La Roldana," was the only woman to be named royal sculptor by two Spanish kings, in 1692 by Charles II (1661–1700) and in 1701 by Philip V (1683–1746). After training in her father's workshop in Seville, Roldán moved to Madrid, where she began working for the court. She specialized in painted terra-cottas of religious subjects and in a small format aimed for private devotion, not seen before in Spain. Around twenty of her sculptures have survived.

THE UNRIVALED ARTEMISIA

Artemisia Gentileschi (1593–1654 or later) towers above all other female artists of her era and ranks among the most accomplished Baroque painters. However, for too long, Gentileschi's artistic achievements have been overshadowed by the dramatic events of her life. The rape by Agostino Tassi, a collaborator in the workshop of her father, Orazio Gentileschi, and the ensuing trial have elevated Artemisia to the status of a feminist icon, inspiring numerous books and films. Yet this focus has detracted from recognition of her exceptional artistic contributions.[49]

Significant exhibitions, including at the National Gallery of London in 2020, along with the discovery of her love letters about her affair with a wealthy nobleman, in the family archives of the Marchesi Frescobaldi in Florence, have provided fresh insights into Gentileschi's life and the formidable challenges she faced and triumphed over throughout her illustrious career.

She was successful indeed, thanks to her precocious and indisputable talent, which her father was the first to recognize and nurture. Her career spanned forty years and five cities. By her twenties, as Barker points out, Gentileschi had established her own customized workshop and was able to hire assistants and procure painting materials. Upon her admission to the Florentine artists' guild in 1616, she assumed full fiscal and legal autonomy over her business operations. Gentileschi's entrepreneurial approach allowed her to adeptly navigate the patronage system, utilizing brokers and agents to enhance her reputation throughout Europe.[50]

After the rape trial, Gentileschi left Rome for Florence with the painter Pierantonio Stiattesi (1584–?), whom she had just married. There she set up an independent studio, was supported by the Medici family, and was the first woman admitted to the prestigious Accademia del Disegno (Academy of Drawing). When Gentileschi returned to Rome in 1620, her fame preceded her, and numerous commissions arrived. After three years in Venice, Artemisia moved to Naples in 1630. By this time, as Whitney Chadwick points out, she had become a celebrity, sought-after by patrons and

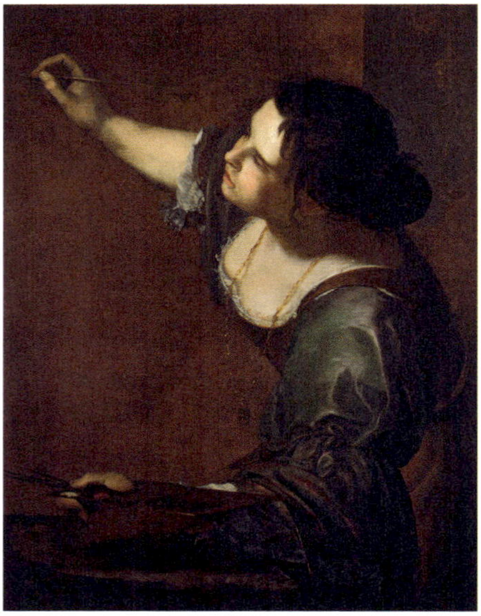

Artemisia Gentileschi, *Self-Portrait as the Allegory of Painting (La Pittura)*, c. 1638–39, Royal Collection Trust, London

protected by the aristocracy.[51] In 1638, she decided to join her father in London, where Orazio was court painter for Charles I of England. Together, they worked on the decoration of a ceiling in the Queen's House in Greenwich, *An Allegory of Peace and the Arts* (c. 1635–38).

What made Artemisia Gentileschi so successful all over Europe? From her first known painting, *Susanna and the Elders* (1610), executed when she was only seventeen, Gentileschi displayed an interest in portraying violent biblical themes involving women, which she interpreted with a unique and new sensibility, highlighting the defiant strength of her heroines. Aware of her growing fame and importance—"You will find the spirit (*animo*) of Caesar in this soul (*anima*) of a woman," she wrote in a letter[52]—she strategically used her own image as a promotional tool. As Letizia Treves, curator of the acclaimed 2020 London exhibition, explains, the allure of Gentileschi's self-portraits—especially those depicting such figures as Susanna, Judith, or Cleopatra in full or partial nudity—was enhanced by their dual role as both a representation of the artist herself and an embodiment of feminine power.[53]

WOMEN OF THE DUTCH GOLDEN AGE

In the seventeenth century, women painters in the Dutch Republic typically specialized in the still life genre. This choice was a practical necessity due to limited access to lessons with nude models and restrictions on traveling alone to paint landscapes.

Of Clara Peeters (1594–1636), born in Antwerp, scant biographical details are known, but her surviving still life paintings attest to her successful and esteemed career. Approximately forty of her paintings are extant, each distinguished by her distinctive touch, often featuring hidden miniature portraits within the compositions. In a historic milestone, the Museo Nacional del Prado in Madrid honored Peeters in 2016 with its first-ever exhibition dedicated to a female artist.

Judith Leyster (1609–1660), the sole female member of Haarlem's Guild of Saint Luke, operated her own workshop, where she mentored three male apprentices. In a daring move, recounted by Jennifer Higgie, she took legal action against the influential and highly successful artist Frans Hals (1580–1666) when one of her apprentices defected to his studio.[54] Leyster's narrative, as detailed by Chadwick, is emblematic of her era. To meet market demands, she consciously modeled her style after Hals's. Consequently, when Leyster fell into obscurity after her death, many of her paintings were misattributed to Hals or others. Only after the scholar Cornelis Hofstede de Groot credited to Leyster *The Happy Couple*, painted in 1630 and in the Louvre collection, were seven additional paintings by her identified.[55]

Rachel Ruysch (1664–1750) enjoyed a remarkable sixty-year career that is meticulously documented, and she was the first woman in the Netherlands to be admitted to an artists' society, that of The Hague. Born to a distinguished scientist, anatomist, and botanist in that city, Ruysch was raised

Rachel Ruysch, *Still Life with Flowers in a Vase on a Ledge with a Dragonfly, Caterpillar, and Butterfly*, 1698

in a cultured and intellectually stimulating environment. She excelled in compositions featuring asymmetrical spirals of flowers. Her works were highly coveted by contemporary collectors, evidenced by the documented substantial prices they commanded.

THE PROFESSIONALIZATION OF WOMEN ARTISTS DURING THE EIGHTEENTH AND NINETEENTH CENTURIES

During the eighteenth century, the notion of a woman as an artist began to gain traction in the popular imagination, mirroring a broader awakening among women regarding their rights. While this shift in awareness did not immediately lead to tangible changes, it is significant that in 1791, amid the French Revolution, Olympe de Gouges wrote a pamphlet titled *The Declaration of the Rights of Woman* (1791) as a response to the Declaration of the Rights of Man and of the Citizen, which the French Assemblée Nationale adopted in August 1789. The latter document proclaimed universal principles such as liberty, equality, and fraternity—but largely excluded women.

The Académie Royale de Peinture et de Sculpture in France began admitting female members in 1783, with Élisabeth Vigée Le Brun and Adélaïde Labille-Guiard among the first to be accepted. However, this acceptance came with restrictions: only four women could be admitted each year, and they were prohibited from participating in classes that involved working with nude models.

The 2021 exhibition *Peintres Femmes, 1780–1830: Naissance d'un combat* (*Women Painters, 1780–1830: The Birth of a Battle*) in Paris at the Musée du Luxembourg shed light on the significant contributions of women to the French artistic scene and market during that era. As Martine Lacas notes, the growing trend of providing girls with artistic education, initially seen as a valuable asset in the marriage market, led to the establishment of numerous *ateliers de demoiselles* (girls' studios), ultimately transforming many of these young women into professional artists. Moreover, the rise of a capitalist market system that evaluated artists based on the quality of their work rather than on their gender further benefited women. While few female artists ventured into the historical and mythological genres, which the academy favored and which generated the public commissions, women excelled in portraiture. And portraiture was the most commercially viable genre at the time, with portraits becoming "must-have" items.[56]

It is as a portraitist that Élisabeth Vigée Le Brun established her reputation, built a solid clientele, and became one of the best-paid painters in eighteenth-century Paris.

The daughter of a middle-class artist from whom she received her first art lessons, Élisabeth Vigée (her maiden name) was a child prodigy. Orphaned at the age of twelve, by fourteen she was supporting her family. "My father had left us penniless. But I was earning a deal of money, as I was already painting many portraits," she recalled in her memoirs.[57] Talent, independence, and resourcefulness characterized Vigée Le Brun's life and career. Her unstoppable rise followed an invitation to court to portray the king's brother. Soon after, she became Marie Antoinette's official painter, producing more than twenty portraits of the queen.

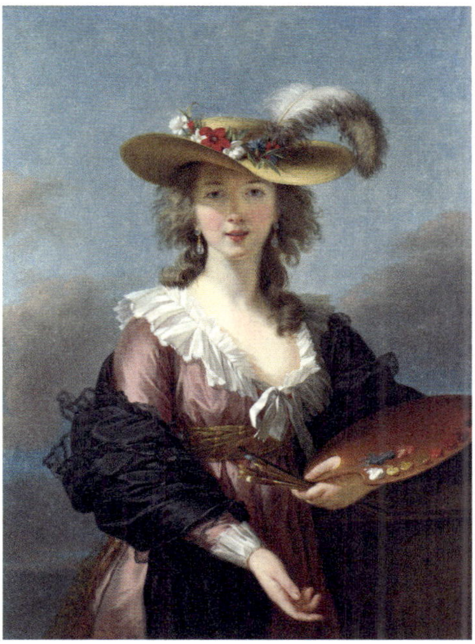

Élisabeth Louise Vigée Le Brun, *Self Portrait in a Straw Hat*, 1782, National Gallery, London

"Only a few women painters have made a name for themselves in the history of French art. . . . Mlle Rosa Bonheur is the first among them to distinguish herself by a touch which is completely virile," wrote the French critic Henri Delaborde.[58] Famous and wealthy during her lifetime, Rosa Bonheur (1822–1899) achieved various international honors, including the prestigious Officier de la Légion d'Honneur, yet today remains relatively unknown to many. Hewitt's comprehensive biography published in 2020 and a retrospective at the Musée d'Orsay in Paris in the fall of 2022 have brought renewed attention to the artist, whose unconventional life represents a beacon of female emancipation. Specializing in pastoral and animal scenes, Bonheur ventured into animal markets and slaughterhouses, dressed in men's clothing—a guise for which she obtained a special permit from the French police. She lived openly with her longtime companion and lover, Nathalie Micas, and then with Anna Klumpke. With her earnings, Bonheur purchased a château in By-Thomery, south of Paris, where she maintained a menagerie.

Her artistic output, exemplified by *The Horse Fair* (1852–55), her most famous painting, outwardly appeared more conventional than her lifestyle. However, Bonheur's use of monumental canvases to depict animals in particular—when they were traditionally reserved for mythological, historical, or religious subjects—was groundbreaking. Hewitt notes that Bonheur was not focused on subverting artistic conventions of her time, yet her unparalleled success as a painter surpassed that of many of her male counterparts.[59]

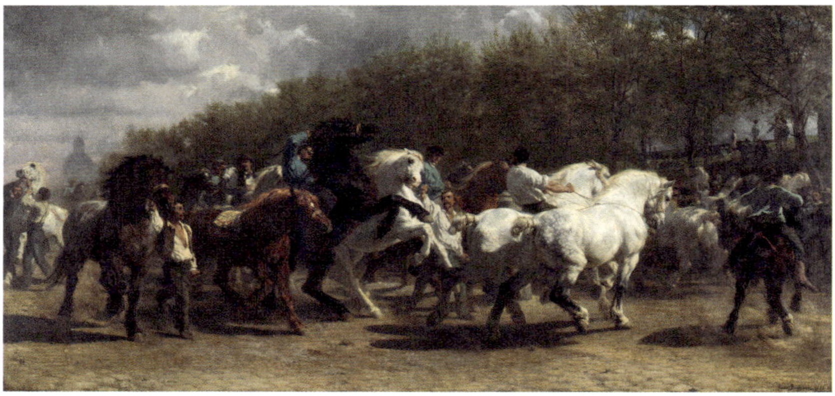

Rosa Bonheur, *The Horse Fair*, 1852–55, Metropolitan Museum of Art, New York

It is noteworthy that the court of Marie Antoinette generally provided a supportive environment for women. Chadwick also highlights the significance of the literary salons that flourished in Paris, which served as crucial spaces where artists—often from middle-class backgrounds like Vigée Le Brun's—could connect with upper-class patrons. Social class distinctions were somewhat softened in these salons, allowing for greater interaction and opportunity for women artists to gain visibility and support.[60]

Rejecting the rigidity of Neoclassicism and the excess of Rococo, Vigée Le Brun introduced a fresher, more naturalistic portrayal of her subjects, offering a more authentic image of the female body. Soon she was one of the most sought-after portraitists of her time. In 1776, she married Jean-Baptiste-Pierre Le Brun (1748–1813), an artist of minor talent and a dealer, who gambled away much of her earnings.

Among the most famous portraits Vigée Le Brun executed is that of Muhammad Dervish Khan (1788). It is fascinating to read the artist's account about the genesis of the work: "In 1788 some envoys were sent to Paris by the Emperor Tippoo Sahib. I saw these Indians at the opera and they appeared to me so remarkably picturesque that I thought I should like to paint them. But as they communicated to their interpreter that they would never allow themselves to be painted unless the request came from the King, I managed to secure that favour from His Majesty."[61]

The outbreak of the French Revolution in 1789 forced Vigée Le Brun, whose status as a protégée of Marie Antoinette was particularly risky, to hastily leave France with her young daughter. Wandering around Europe—Florence, Rome, Naples, Venice, Vienna, St. Petersburg—Vigée Le Brun depicted aristocrats and notables, men and women, also excelling in the nascent market for child portraits. She finally returned in early 1802, after twelve years of exile, to a very changed France.

While in Rome, Vigée Le Brun met another successful painter, the Swiss-born Angelica Kauffman. Like the French artist, Kauffman was a child prodigy and daughter of a painter, who traveled through Europe with her family at an early age. In England, where Kauffman settled in 1767, she was—along with Mary Moser (1744–1819)—one of only two women among the founding members of the Royal Academy of Arts in 1768. The status brought by belonging to the prestigious institution was crucial to Kauffman's decision to stay in London for the next ten years, Annette Wickham says, and to the artist's confidence in setting her fees in line with those of her flourishing peers such as Joshua Reynolds.[62] The solid clientele that Kauffman developed in London included emancipated women from privileged backgrounds, such as the sculptor Anne Seymour Damer (1748–1828).[63] After marrying the Italian painter Antonio Zucchi (1726–1795), Kauffman moved to Rome, where she set up her own workshop specializing in historical paintings, the most valued of all the genres and usually produced only by men.

The Royal Academy would not accept another woman as a member until 1922, when Annie Swynnerton (1844–1933) was allowed to join. In fact, during Queen Victoria's lengthy reign (1837–1901), marked by economic expansion and bourgeois ascendancy but also moral conservatism, women still faced significant challenges in being accepted as professional artists. While some level of art education for women was tolerated, and even encouraged, the prevailing stereotype cast all women artists as mere amateurs. Tabitha Barber points out that some women participating in public shows defied this stereotype by prominently listing their names and addresses in the exhibition catalogues, signaling their professionalism and availability for commissions. Others, however, opted to exhibit their work anonymously, using the designation "a Lady," as it was deemed improper for women of a certain social class to engage in commercial activities.[64] Elizabeth Thompson (1846–1933), known in later years as Lady Butler, excelled as a historical painter of military campaigns and battles, a subject traditionally depicted by men. When *The Roll Call* (1874), a large canvas representing a scene from the Crimean War, was exhibited at the Royal Academy in 1874, it attracted such large crowds that guards had to be stationed to manage them. Even the Prince of Wales expressed interest in purchasing the painting. Despite this success, when some members of the Royal Academy proposed Lady Butler as an associate, she encountered rejection twice, in 1875 and 1879.

It was mainly the emergence of a market system in late nineteenth-century London, centered around art dealers and commercial galleries, that proved advantageous for women artists. Art forms traditionally regarded as "feminine"—such as flower paintings, watercolors, still lifes, and travel landscapes—were well suited to the tastes of the burgeoning middle-class buyers, in terms of both size and subject matter.[65]

During the nineteenth century in France, women artists' slow and arduous path toward recognition continued. Chadwick reports that in the Paris Salon of 1801, 14.6 percent of the artists were women; by 1835, the percentage of women exhibiting had grown to 22.2 percent.[66] And whereas for female artists, access to the Académie des Beaux-Arts (created in 1816) continued to be limited, private academies flourished. A few of them, like the Académie Julian, established in Paris in 1868, admitted students without discriminating on the basis of gender.

The fabric of society was also undergoing gradual changes. Catherine Hewitt highlights the crucial role of the rising middle class in advancing women's emancipation. Unlike their counterparts in the aristocracy or the lower social strata, middle-class women were not pressured to marry solely to secure estates or titles, or to escape poverty. This shift provided them with greater autonomy and freedom to make choices in their lives, such as embracing an artistic career.[67]

On a broader scale, the French feminist Hubertine Auclert (1848–1914) founded the Société le Droit des Femmes (Society for the Rights of Women) in 1876, to advocate for women's suffrage. However, the right of women to vote would be granted in France only in 1944. Finland was the first European country to approve women's suffrage, in 1906, while the United States did not grant women the right to vote until 1920.

NOTES

1 See Ben Lewis, *The Last Leonardo: The Secret Lives of the World's Most Expensive Painting* (Glasgow, UK: William Collins, 2019); Margaret Dalivalle, Martin Kemp, and Robert B. Simon, *Leonardo's "Salvator Mundi" and the Collecting of Leonardo in the Stuart Courts* (Oxford, UK: Oxford University Press, 2019); *The Savior for Sale*, directed by Antoine Vitkine (2021), film; and *The Lost Leonardo*, directed by Andreas Koefoed (2021), film. In addition, innumerable articles have been dedicated to the compelling affair of the painting.

2 Lewis, *Last Leonardo*, 17.

3 Vincent Delieuvin, "Apparition ou disparition," in *Léonard de Vinci*, exh. cat. (Paris: Musée du Louvre, 2019), 302–08.

4 *Post-War & Contemporary Art Evening Sale*, sale cat. (Christie's New York, November 15, 2017), lot 9 B. Subsequent information about the work's provenance is from this catalogue.

5 Lewis, *Last Leonardo*, 121.

6 Dalivalle, Kemp, and Simon, *Leonardo's "Salvator Mundi,"* 40.

7 Lewis, *Last Leonardo*, 161.

8 Lewis, *Last Leonardo*, 8–9.

9 Christie's New York, *Post-War & Contemporary Art Evening Sale.*

10 Similarly, a *Tyrannosaurus rex* would be included in the Christie's New York sale of twentieth-century art in October 2020, selling for a record price of $31.8 million. Again, the aim was to capitalize on the rare specimen and expose it to the wealthiest collectors in the world, who typically purchased modern and contemporary art.

11 David D. Kirkpatrick, "Mystery Buyer of $450 Million 'Salvator Mundi' Was a Saudi Prince," *New York Times*, December 6, 2017.

12 Cynthia Saltzman, *Old Masters, New World: America's Raid on Europe's Great Pictures* (London: Penguin Books, 2008), 215.

13 Gail Feigenbaum, "The Art Market Sets Sail: An Introduction," in *Money in the Air: Art Dealers and the Making of a Transatlantic Market, 1880–1930*, ed. Gail Feigenbaum, Sandra van Ginhoven, and Edward Sterrett (Los Angeles: Getty Research Institute Publications Program, 2024), 7.

14 Alan Axelrod, *The Gilded Age, 1876–1912: Overture to the American Century* (New York: Sterling, 2017), 2.

15 World Inequality Database, https://wid.world/country/usa/.

16 Saltzman, *Old Masters, New World*, 4.

17 Meryle Secrest, *Duveen: A Life in Art* (Chicago: University of Chicago Press, 2004), 299.

18 Secrest, *Duveen*, 43–44. A quarter is a unit of dry volume equaling eight bushels; one bushel equals thirty-two quarts, or eight gallons.

19 Don Thompson, *The $12 Million Stuffed Shark: The Curious Economics of Contemporary Art* (New York: St. Martin's, 2008), 31.

20 Secrest, *Duveen*, 88.

21 Feigenbaum, "Art Market Sets Sail," 29.

22 S. N. Behrman, "Profiles: The Days of Duveen," *New Yorker*, September 22, 1951.

23 Secrest, *Duveen*, 147.

24 Natalie Dykstra, *Chasing Beauty: The Life of Isabella Stewart Gardner* (New York: Mariner Books, 2024), 127.

25 Morris Carter, *Isabella Stewart Gardner and Fenway Court* (Boston: Houghton Mifflin, 1925), 125.

26 Dykstra, *Chasing Beauty*, 127.

27 Saltzman, *Old Masters, New World*, 46.

28 Among Berenson's publications are *The Venetian Painters of the Renaissance* (1894), *Lorenzo Lotto* (1895), *The Florentine Painters of the Renaissance* (1896), *The Central Italian Painters of the Renaissance* (1897), *The Drawings of the Florentine Painters* (1903), and *North Italian Painters of the Renaissance* (1907).

29 Saltzman, *Old Masters, New World*, 57.

30 Gary Tinterow, "The Havemeyer Pictures," in Alice Cooney Frelinghuysen et al., *Splendid Legacy: The Havemeyer Collection*, exh. cat. (New York: Ursus Press, 1993), 3.

31 Louisine W. Havemeyer, *Sixteen to Sixty: Memoirs of a Collector*, ed. Susan Alyson Stein (1961; repr., New York: Ursus Press, 1993), 250.

32 Saltzman, *Old Masters, New World*, 109–10.

33 Havemeyer, *Sixteen to Sixty*, 135.

34 Alice Cooney Frelinghuysen, "The Havemeyer House," in *Splendid Legacy*, 174.

35 Rebecca A. Rabinow, "The Suffrage Exhibition of 1915," in *Splendid Legacy*, 89.

36 Just to name a few, the retrospective dedicated to Élisabeth Vigée Le Brun at the Grand Palais, Paris, in 2016; *A Tale of Two Women Painters: Sofonisba Anguissola and Lavinia Fontana* at the Museo Nacional del Prado, Madrid, in 2020; *Artemisia*, curated by Letizia Treves, at the National Gallery, London, in 2020; *By Her Hand: Artemisia Gentileschi and Women Artists in Italy, 1500–1800* at the Wadsworth Atheneum Museum of Art, Hartford, Connecticut, and Detroit Institute of Arts, in 2021–22; and *Angelica Kauffman* at the Royal Academy of Arts, London, in 2024.

37 Katy Hessel, *The Story of Art without Men* (New York: W. W. Norton, 2023).

38 Giorgio Vasari, *The Lives of the Artists*, trans. with an introduction and notes by Julia Conaway Bondanella and Peter Bondanella, Oxford World's Classics (Oxford, UK: Oxford University Press, 1998), 339.

39 Mary Pardo, "Paolo Pino's 'Dialogo di pittura': A Translation with Commentary" (PhD diss., University of Pittsburgh, 1984), 322.

40 Sheila Barker, "Art as Women's Work: The Professionalization of Women Artists in Italy, 1350–1800," in *By Her Hand: Artemisia Gentileschi and Women Artists in Italy, 1500–1800*, ed. Eve Straussman-Pflanzer and Oliver Tostmann, exh. cat. (Detroit: Detroit Institute of Arts, 2021), 43–48.

41 Vasari, *Lives of the Artists*, 342.

42 Vasari, *Lives of the Artists*, 343.

43 Oliver Tostmann, "*Self-Portrait at the Easel*" (cat. entry), in Straussman-Pflanzer and Tostmann, *By Her Hand*, 58.

44 Vasari, *Lives of the Artists*, 343.

45 Babette Bohn, "Introduction: The Bolognese Phenomenon," in *Women Artists, Their Patrons, and Their Publics in Early Modern Bologna* (University Park, PA: Penn State University Press, 2021), 1–8.

46 Aoife Brady, "Lavinia Fontana: The Workshop of a Woman Artist," in *Lavinia Fontana: Trailblazer, Rule Breaker*, exh. cat. (Dublin: National Gallery of Ireland, 2003), 20–33.

47 A solo exhibition at the Gallerie degli Uffizi, Florence, was dedicated to Sirani in 2018, followed by a biography by Adelina Modesti in 2023.

48 Adelina Modesti, "Bologna: 'A Paradise of Women,'" in *Elisabetta Sirani* (Los Angeles: Getty Publications, 2023), 13.

49 Roberto Longhi's essay "Gentileschi, Father and Daughter," published in Italian (as "Gentileschi, padre e figlia") in 1916 in *L'arte: Rivista di storia dell'arte medieval e moderna*, was the first attempt to examine and assess Artemisia Gentileschi's value as an artist.

50 Barker, "Art as Women's Work," 43–44.

51 Whitney Chadwick, *Women, Art, and Society* (London: Thames & Hudson, 1990), 115.

52 Artemisia Gentileschi to Don Antonio Ruffo (a Sicilian patron), November 13, 1649, quoted in Mary D. Garrard, *Artemisia Gentileschi: The Image of the Female Hero in Italian Baroque Art* (Princeton, NJ: Princeton University Press, 1989), 136.

53 Letizia Treves, "Artemisia Portraying Herself," in *Artemisia*, ed. Letizia Treves, exh. cat. (London: National Gallery, 2020–21), 64.

54 Jennifer Higgie, *The Mirror and the Palette: Rebellion, Revolution, and Resilience; Five Hundred Years of Women's Self Portraits* (New York: Pegasus Books, 2021), 57.

55 Chadwick, *Women, Art, and Society*, 26–27.

56 Martine Lacas, "Naissance d'un combat," in *Peintres Femmes, 1780–1830: Naissance d'un combat*, exh. cat. (Paris: Musée du Luxembourg, 2021), 154 and 19.

57 *Memoirs of Madame Vigée Lebrun* (New York: Doubleday, 1903), 9.

58 Catherine Hewitt, *Art Is a Tyrant: The Unconventional Life of Rosa Bonheur* (London: Icon Books, 2020), 152.

59 Hewitt, *Art Is a Tyrant*, 411–12.

60 Chadwick, *Women, Art, and Society*, 146–48.

61 *Memoirs of Madame Vigée Lebrun*, 24.

62 Annette Wickham, "Angelica Kauffman and the Royal Academy," in *Angelica Kauffman*, exh. cat. (London: Royal Academy of Arts, 2024), 29.

63 Bettina Baumgärtel, "She Was of Her Time and Her Time Was Made for Her," in *Angelica Kauffman*, 18.

64 Tabitha Barber, "The First Exhibitors," in *Now You See Us: Women Artists in Britain, 1520–1920*, by Tabitha Barber and Tim Batchelor, exh. cat. (London: Tate Britain, 2024), 49.

65 Maria Quirk, *Women, Art and Money in Late Victorian and Edwardian England: The Hustle and the Scramble* (New York: Bloomsbury Visual Arts, 2019), 6.

66 Chadwick, *Women, Art, and Society*, 179.

67 Hewitt, *Art Is a Tyrant*, 152.

5. Paul Durand-Ruel and the Birth of the Impressionist Market

p. 95	p. 96	p. 96	p. 97
The Dictatorship of the Académie des Beaux-Arts	Gustave Courbet and the Pavilion of Realism	Shaking Up the System: The Salons des Refusés (1863)	The Birth of Impressionism
p. 98	p. 100	p. 102	p. 103
Édouard Manet's *Le Déjeuner sur l'herbe* (1863)	Alexandre Cabanel's *Birth of Venus* (1863) and Édouard Manet's *Olympia* (1863)	Baron Haussmann: Shaping the New Capital	Paul Durand-Ruel
p. 104	p. 106	p. 107	p. 109
Claude Monet's Series	Gustave Caillebotte's Bequest	Pierre-Auguste Renoir's *Bal du moulin de la Galette* (1876)	Models Turned Artists

Without Paul Durand-Ruel, art history might be different.

—Philip Hook, *Rogues' Gallery: A History of Art and Its Dealers*

Impressionism, which emerged in the final three decades of the nineteenth century in Paris—the heart of the Western art world at the time—marked the beginning of a transformative shift in artistic expression.

Preceded by the disruptive Gustave Courbet's 1855 Pavilion of Realism and the 1863 Salon des Refusés, Impressionism not only challenged the established artistic norms dictated by the Académie des Beaux-Arts (Academy of Fine Arts), it triggered the development of a new commercial and critical system. For the first time, an artist's success was determined by the market rather than the academy. A model that revolved around the central role of the gallerist—embodied most of all by Paul Durand-Ruel—was responsible for the promotion of the new and radical Impressionist language. Furthermore, Durand-Ruel pioneered strategies crucial to building critical acceptance and commercial success for the Impressionists, which would define the role of the modern gallerist. Essential to this vision was international expansion, exemplified by the landmark exhibition organized in New York in 1886. The show not only introduced American audiences to Impressionism but consolidated critical and public acclaim of the movement, sealing its ascendance in the market.

THE DICTATORSHIP OF THE ACADÉMIE DES BEAUX-ARTS

Until the mid-nineteenth century, it was the Académie des Beaux-Arts that determined an artist's success in France. As examined earlier (see "At His Majesty's Service," p. 52), the Académie de Peinture et de Sculpture (which in 1816 merged with the Académie de Musique and the Académie d'Architecture to form the Académie des Beaux-Arts) had been founded in 1648 as a free association of painters. By 1663, it had come under the patronage of King Louis XIV and the direct control of his finance minister, Jean-Baptiste Colbert, with the court painter Charles Le Brun named director for life. The academy's purpose became to educate and guide artists working for the court, establishing strict guidelines for content and style. Grand historical, mythological, and religious themes were the most valued, with a preference for carefully constructed compositions executed in a realistic and precise manner.

Under its various names, the Académie des Beaux-Arts governed and influenced French art for nearly three centuries, acting as the strict guardian of tradition. It regularly organized official art exhibitions known as "Salons," with the most prestigious being the Salon de Paris, established in 1667 and held in the Salon Carré of the Louvre. Participation in these official Salons was crucial for artists because, as Sue Roe explains, before the advent of art dealers and small galleries, the Salons were the primary venue for artists to exhibit their work, gain a reputation, and attract aristocrats, other collectors, and museums looking for art to buy.[1]

GUSTAVE COURBET AND THE PAVILION OF REALISM

Despite a promising start—with some of his paintings successfully exhibited at the 1849 Salon and the French state purchasing *After Dinner at Ornans* in 1849—the fortunes of Gustave Courbet (1819–1877) changed as he developed his mature, realistic style. Emperor Napoleon III (1808–1873) allegedly struck *The Bathers* (1853) with his whip, irritated by its crude rendering of the female nude. Courbet's commitment to depicting reality, rather than an idealized version of it, was central to his artistic belief.

In 1855, when the jury of the Exposition Universelle rejected several of his paintings including *The Painter's Studio* (1854–55), Courbet decided to set up his own pavilion, called the "Pavillon du Réalisme" (Pavilion of Realism)—within sight of the Salon. The accompanying catalogue, which the artist wrote, became his Manifesto of Realism in painting.

Courbet was revolutionary not only in his art but also in his actions. He actively participated in the Paris Commune, the rebellious government that citizens of Paris proclaimed in March 1871 during the insurrection following France's defeat by Prussia—a tragic end to the disastrous war declared by Napoleon III. The Commune was violently suppressed, resulting in a massacre of as many as twenty thousand people. In the aftermath, Courbet was accused of instigating the demolition of the Colonne Vendôme, a symbol of Napoleon I's victories. Despite his defense that he only advocated for the column to be relocated rather than destroyed, Courbet was condemned to pay 300,000 francs for its restoration. To avoid this crippling debt, he went into voluntary exile in Switzerland, where he died in 1877 at the age of fifty-eight.

SHAKING UP THE SYSTEM: THE SALONS DES REFUSÉS (1863)

In 1863, the jury of the official annual art Salon organized by the Académie des Beaux-Arts rejected thousands of paintings—an unprecedented number. Vehement protests by the artists who had been turned down prompted Napoleon III to intervene. He sanctioned the establishment of an alternative exhibition, the "Salon des Refusés" (Salon of the Refused), to show the works rejected for the official Salon. As Pierre Assouline points out, this would allow the public to judge for themselves whether the controversy that the rejected artists stirred up was warranted. The participants were given the freedom to show their works, and the public had the liberty to view and assess them.[2]

Among the "refusés" were Paul Cézanne, Édouard Manet, and Camille Pissarro. More than forty of them were women. A catalogue was put together, which provided an incomplete list of about seven hundred exhibited works.

The Salon des Refusés, held in a separate gallery in the Palais de l'Industrie on the Champs-Élysées, next door to the official Salon, marked a turning point in the French art system. It signaled a shift in which the arts could no longer be judged solely by an elite of aristocrats and enlightened amateurs. This democratization of art criticism allowed the broader public to engage directly with contemporary works and form their own opinions.[3] After this event, artists began to establish their own alternative salons, which became popular venues in which to see avant-garde art, such as the Salon des Indépendants (Salon of the Independents), founded in Paris in 1884. Another was the Salon d'Automne (Autumn Salon), started in 1903; in 1905, it would exhibit together for the first time works by the disparagingly named *fauves*, or "wild beasts," avant-garde painters such as Henri Matisse, André Derain, Maurice de Vlaminck, Georges Braque, Raoul Dufy, Albert Marquet, and Kees van Dongen, known for their bold and expressive use of color. Organized by the artists themselves, who usually had to pay an annual fee in order to exhibit their works, these salons were part of a new capital system of the art market, as Claire Maingon discusses. They served not only as exhibition spaces but also as hubs for sales, with an office that retained a percentage of the final price in case of a transaction.[4]

In 1863, participating in the Salons des Refusés presented a difficult decision for artists, who risked exposure to ridicule from both the public and critics. It is also noteworthy that the majority of the "refused" artists continued to submit their work to the official Salon in the years following 1863. This persistence underscores their desire for recognition within the established system, despite the innovative implications of the Salon des Refusés.

THE BIRTH OF IMPRESSIONISM

Intolerance toward the dominant subjects and style imposed by the academy and eagerness to explore new paths brought four young artists in Paris of the 1860s to share their interest in and love for painting *en plein air* ("in the open air").

Claude Monet, Pierre-Auguste Renoir, Alfred Sisley, and Frédéric Bazille met as students in Paris, at the studio of the Swiss painter Charles Gleyre (1806–1874), who ran one of the many "free academies" for those who had not been accepted, or could not afford the official training, at the Académie des Beaux-Arts. The four painters came from different social backgrounds: Claude Monet (1840–1926), born in Paris, grew up in Le Havre, where his father was a grocer and supplier of goods to ships. Pierre-Auguste Renoir (1841–1919), the sixth of seven children of a modest family from Limoges—his father was a tailor and his mother a seamstress—decorated porcelains before turning to the canvas. Alfred Sisley (1839–1899) belonged to a family of English merchants living in Paris. Frédéric Bazille (1841–1870), who tragically died during the Franco-Prussian War just

"But one painting completely stole the show. . . . Everyone stared in horror at *Le Déjeuner sur l'herbe*."[5] The infamous painting was by Édouard Manet (1832–1883), a Parisian artist from an affluent family. He had received traditional training under the history painter Thomas Couture (1815–1879) and spent countless hours at the Musée du Louvre studying and copying the works of the masters. The critics of the time who ferociously attacked *Le Déjeuner sur l'herbe* failed to understand, or deliberately ignored, how deeply the painting was rooted in the pictorial tradition. The depiction of two women (one bathing in the background) and two men having a picnic in the countryside was inspired by classical works such as Titian's *Pastoral Concert* (c. 1509) and Raphael's *Judgment of Paris* (c. 1510–20), a drawing known through an engraving by Marcantonio Raimondi. Manet sought to translate a classic subject into a modern context, adhering to the recommendation in an essay by the poet and art critic Charles Baudelaire (1821–1867)—best known for his 1857 poetry collection, *Les Fleurs du mal* (*The Flowers of Evil*)—that artists should capture "the heroism of modern life."[6] Baudelaire wrote further on this subject in a later essay, "Le Peintre de la vie moderne" ("The Painter of Modern Life"), first published in three parts in the French newspaper *Le Figaro* in late 1863, a few months after the Salon des Refusés.

Contemporary critics saw *Le Déjeuner sur l'herbe* as an obscene attack on decency and tradition. They were scandalized by the presence of a naked woman who, unlike idealized nudes of the past, has discarded her clothes on the grass and is sitting with two fully dressed men. Her direct, defiant gaze at the viewer further provoked outrage. The woman was a real, recognizable person: the model Victorine Meurent. As Assouline observes, "By penetrating reality, the nude had become flesh and blood."[7] And that was unacceptable. Furthermore, *Le Déjeuner sur l'herbe* was criticized for its seemingly incoherent composition and unclear narrative. Manet's technique, characterized by flat brushstrokes, was deemed as unattractive as the subject itself. The painting, which is now part of the Musée d'Orsay's collection in Paris, never found a buyer during Manet's lifetime.

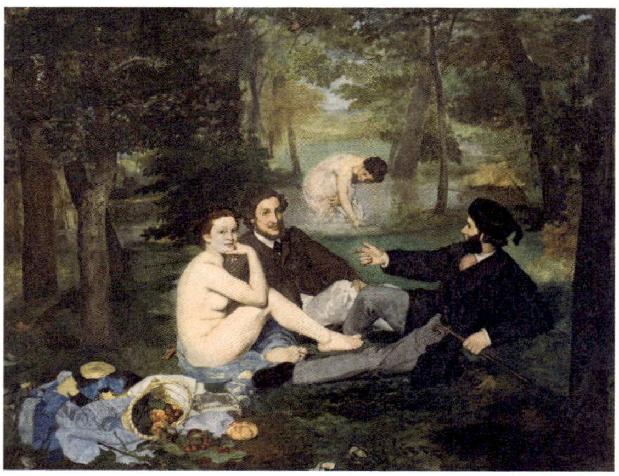

Édouard Manet, *Le Déjeuner sur l'herbe* (*Luncheon on the Grass*), 1863, Musée d'Orsay, Paris short of his twenty-ninth birthday, came from a family of means, and he often generously helped his peers by sharing his studio and offering financial assistance.

Rejection and scorn were the response of the official Salon to the group's artistic innovations, whose dire consequence was the impossibility to receive state commissions or generate public and private acquisitions. Not only the taste but also the market was indeed still dictated by the academy.

The first exhibition of what would be recognized as the Impressionist movement was therefore organized in 1874 by the artists themselves, who had to pay a fee in order to be included. It opened in the Paris studio of the photographer known as Nadar (1820–1910) on April 15, two weeks before the official Salon; the entrance fee was 1 franc, and the catalogue cost 50 centimes. The artists did not initially adopt for themselves the term "impressionism," which the critic Louis Leroy coined to ridicule the unfinished look of Monet's painting *Impression, soleil levant* (*Impression, Sunrise*) (1872) in the exhibition; participating artists called themselves the "Société Anonyme des Artistes Peintres, Sculpteurs, Graveurs, etc." (Anonymous Society of Painters, Sculptors, Engravers, etc.).

Liesbeth de Strooper and Erwin Dekker point out that the painters who would been identified collectively as "Impressionists" were not interested in the recognition of a shared aesthetic program. The eight exhibitions traditionally associated with Impressionism were organized to contest the monopoly of the Paris academy and its associated Salons by providing more opportunities for artists to exhibit different works. Developing a collective identity at the expense of their individual reputations was not a goal for the artists taking part in these exhibitions.[8] Catherine Méneux also states that the "Société Anonyme" had as its objective not the defense of a common aesthetic but simply a liberal and economic purpose: to organize exhibitions without a jury or reward, sell the exhibited works, and, its members hoped, publish an art journal.[9]

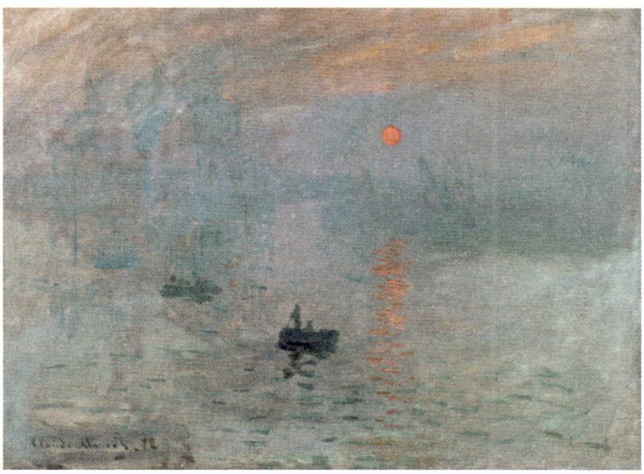

Claude Monet, *Impression, soleil levant* (*Impression, Sunrise*), 1872, Musée Marmottan Monet, Paris

ALEXANDRE CABANEL'S *BIRTH OF VENUS* (1863) AND ÉDOUARD MANET'S *OLYMPIA* (1863)

Alexandre Cabanel (1823–1889) epitomized the successful academic painter. His *Naissance de Vénus* (*Birth of Venus*), exhibited to great acclaim at the official Salon of 1863, was purchased by Napoleon III for his personal collection. In stark contrast, Manet's *Olympia*, accepted in the 1865 Salon, prompted such anger that it had to be hung high on the wall to prevent viewers from physically attacking it.

Cabanel's and Manet's depictions of the female nude could not be more different. Cabanel's *Venus* belongs to a mythological realm, floating on the sea foam from which she was born. In contrast, *Olympia* presents a real, contemporary woman—in fact, a prostitute. The model, Victorine Meurent, who also posed for Manet's *Déjeuner sur l'herbe*, is shown receiving flowers from her maid, likely a tribute from a client. Manet intended to offer a modern interpretation of the classical theme of the reclining female nude, drawing from illustrious precedents such as Titian's *Venus of Urbino* (1534) and Diego Velázquez's *Rokeby Venus* (c. 1647–51). However, his contemporaries perceived it only as a provocative challenge to tradition and convention. Unlike Cabanel's *Venus*, *Olympia* never found a buyer during Manet's lifetime. Today, both paintings reside in the Musée d'Orsay.

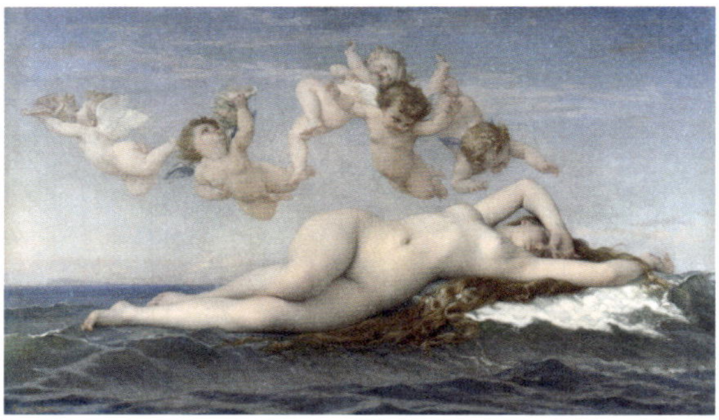

Alexandre Cabanel, *Naissance de Vénus* (*Birth of Venus*), 1863, Musée d'Orsay, Paris

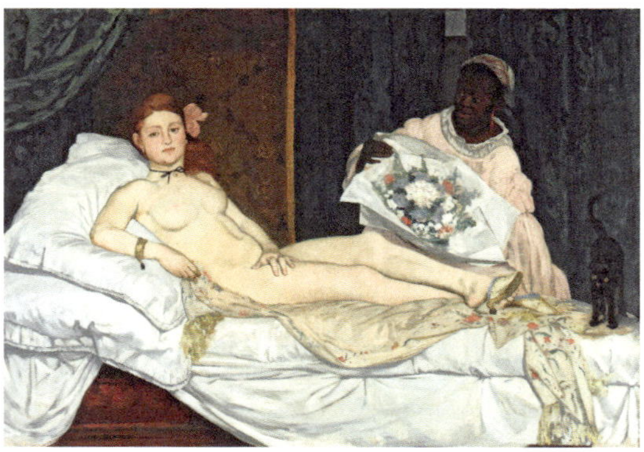

Édouard Manet, *Olympia*, 1863, Musée d'Orsay, Paris

A total of 165 works by 31 artists were included in the 1874 exhibition. It was a heterogeneous group, which—as Anne Robbins points out—included not only those who would be identified as Impressionists, but also artists who had already exhibited in established official Salons, such as Eugène Boudin and Félix Bracquemond, and artists who would not be well remembered, like Ludovic Napoléon Lepic and Édouard Brandon.[10]

Besides Monet and Renoir, as well as Sisley, another of the leading figures who would come to be identified as Impressionists was Camille Pissarro (1830–1903), a few years older than the others and born on the Caribbean island of St. Thomas; he had met and befriended Monet at the Académie Suisse, which both attended in the early 1860s, before Monet studied with Gleyre. Associated with them but displaying distinct artistic styles were Edgar Degas (1834–1917), descended from a wealthy and aristocratic Neapolitan family, whose interests were subjects taken from the modern life of Paris, such as dance classes, horse races, and nightlife scenes, investigated with a curious eye and unusual and inventive composition cuts; and Paul Cézanne (1839–1906), a shy and reclusive artist from Aix-en-Provence, whose explorations would eventually move beyond the Impressionists' tenets and open the path to Cubism. Berthe Morisot (1841–1895) and the American Mary Cassatt (1844–1926) were the only women in the original group. They privileged more intimate subjects, such as domestic interiors and mother and child, depicted with emotional participation. This was a forced choice deriving from the numerous obstacles faced by women artists, particularly of the upper classes like Cassatt and Morisot: they were barred from academy classes that utilized male nude models and hindered from freely exploring the countryside for plein air painting and from participating in the vibrant cultural discussions happening in cafés, spaces their male counterparts typically dominated. As for Édouard Manet, whom the Impressionists revered as their inspiration and the epitome of the modern artist, he refused to participate in any of the seven exhibitions that the group organized before his death in 1883, instead continuing to submit his works to the official Salons.

Visitors to the monthlong 1874 show—two hundred on the opening day and one hundred on average each of the following days—were drawn by curiosity, and their negative reactions were practically a repeat performance of the 1863 Salon des Refusés, as Roe observes.[11] The exhibited works were perceived by critics and the public alike, with few exceptions, as extremely radical, both in content and in style. Abandoning the grand historical, mythological, and literary themes the academy favored, the Impressionists focused on landscape, painted en plein air, and without preparatory sketches, but with rapid and small brushstrokes directly onto the canvas, in order to capture the luminous optical sensation, the fleeting atmosphere. "For me, a landscape doesn't exist in its own right. . . . The surrounding atmosphere brings it to life," declared Monet.[12]

The discovery of Japanese prints was a significant influence on the Impressionists. First introduced to France following the forced opening by the United States of Japanese trade with the West starting in 1853, the prints offered a different kind of perspective and flat surfaces. And

BARON HAUSSMANN: SHAPING THE NEW CAPITAL

The Paris that the Impressionists were living in and experiencing represented the prototype of the modern European capital. It was the result of the radical transformation conceived by Georges-Eugène Haussmann (1809–1891), prefect of the Seine and commonly known as Baron Haussmann. In 1853, Napoleon III charged him with the very ambitious project of redesigning Paris in the middle of a population boom—from 1 million in 1841 to 1.7 million in 1861. But it was still in many aspects a medieval city, with narrow streets—the widest being about sixteen feet, the narrowest less than seven—that were badly lit, no public parks, and an inadequate sewer system. Inspired by London, where he had spent years in exile (1846–48), Napoleon III dreamed of an organized and healthy city, with avenues and wide boulevards to connect its different poles, where even the poorest could live in decent conditions, and commerce and industry could flourish.

Haussmann's genius was to envisage the city as a whole, and not as a sum of districts, hence the long arteries crossing Paris from one side to another. About one hundred miles of new roads were realized by 1870, as well as twenty-four new squares, and new train stations. Splendid public parks were created: the already existing Bois de Boulogne and the Bois de Vincennes were reorganized, the gardens of the Champs-Elysées and the Parc Monceau redesigned, and the Parc des Buttes Chaumont and Parc Montsouris created from scratch. A new opera house was built by the architect Charles Garnier (1825–1898) and is still in use. A strict regulation to standardize the apartment blocks was put in place, and an extensive new system of streetlights installed. The Paris of today is still very much the result of Haussmann's plan.[13]

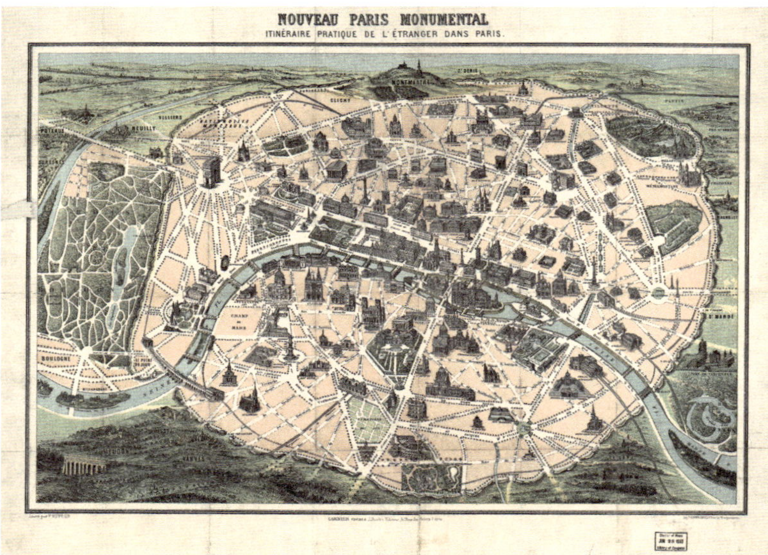

Map of Paris published by Garnier Frères, c. 1878

Courbet's and Manet's embrace of realism constituted a seminal reference in the development of Impressionism's language. Also worth noting is that painting outdoors had become more practical thanks to the introduction in 1841 of premixed colors in tubes, which were easily transportable. Besides landscape, the city itself, with its train stations and boulevards, and the various aspects of urban life and activities of the rising bourgeois classes were the subjects the Impressionists favored.

As Roe reports, the results of the Société Anonyme's first exhibition were very disappointing. Only a few paintings sold, including Monet's *Impression, Sunrise*. The liabilities amounted to 3,713 francs, the cash in hand to 278 francs. Each exhibitor owed 184 francs and 50 centimes. The society was unanimously liquidated.[14] Despite the financial failure, David W. Galenson points out that the 1874 exhibition marked the beginning of a new era, in which the reputations of artists would no longer be created and decided in the Salon, but instead in independent group exhibitions.[15]

PAUL DURAND-RUEL

Paul Durand-Ruel (1831–1922) was instrumental in establishing the market for the Impressionists and securing their critical recognition.[16]

Between 1870 and 1922, the dealer organized about 200 exhibitions in Paris and 130 in New York. He acquired approximately a thousand works by Monet, fifteen hundred by Renoir, eight hundred by Pissarro, two hundred by Manet, and four hundred each by Degas, Sisley, and Cassatt. Beyond these staggering numbers, it was Durand-Ruel's intelligence and courage that for the first time embodied the visionary gallerist in the modern sense of the word. In the mid-nineteenth century, as Assouline notes, a dealer-entrepreneur like Durand-Ruel was a novel phenomenon. He

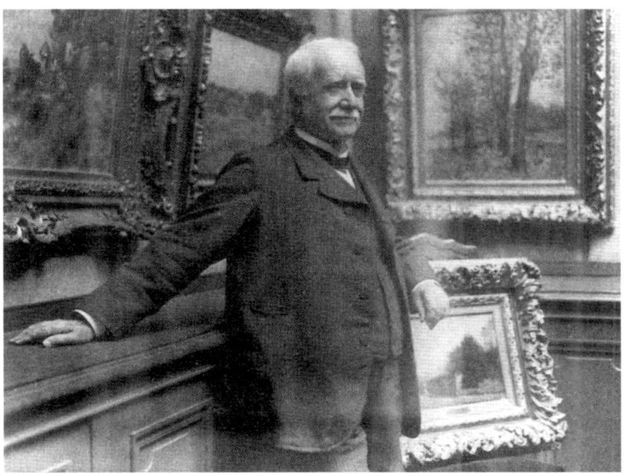

Paul Durand-Ruel in his gallery, Paris, c. 1910

uniquely combined the roles of sponsor, organizer, and exclusive intermediary between artists and their collectors.[17]

Born in Paris in 1831, Durand-Ruel was the son of a stationer turned art dealer, who promoted and sold works by the generation of artists preceding Impressionism, such as Jean-Baptiste-Camille Corot (1796–1875) and the Barbizon school. It was not Durand-Ruel's intention to be involved in the family business; he wished instead to pursue a military career and in 1851 was admitted to the military academy at Saint-Cyr. However, after encountering and being transfixed—by his own confession—by the paintings of Eugène Delacroix (1798–1863) at the Exposition Universelle in 1855—he would later buy more than sixty works by the artist, including the masterpiece *Death of Sardanapalus* (1827), now in the Louvre, for the record price of 96,000 francs—the young Durand-Ruel took over the family business, and in 1867 he moved the gallery to a street in the center of the Paris art scene.

In his later memoirs, he writes that it was in London—where he had escaped during the Franco-Prussian War of 1870–71 and opened a gallery in Bond Street—that his fateful encounters with Monet and Pissarro took place, forever changing his trajectory as a dealer and the futures of the artists who would be known as the Impressionists. Durand-Ruel immediately recognized the potential of the new art and began "to slip a few paintings by these two artists into my exhibitions and manage with difficulty to sell a few of them."[18] Back in Paris, he was introduced to other members of the Impressionist group, including Sisley and Renoir, as well as to Manet.

Embarking on the promotion and support of the new artists was not an easy journey. "Everybody agreed that I had gone mad and lost all sense of taste. All my clients were quickly alienated from me," he recalls. He defiantly adds: "I confess I always enjoyed the struggle, despite the sorrow and torment it caused me. The easy trade of buying whatever is fashionable and immediately reselling it at a profit, always following the current trend, is a business similar to selling stylish items of clothing. I could never become interested in that."[19]

CLAUDE MONET'S SERIES

The two highest prices at auction for works by Monet—*Nymphéas en fleur* (*Water Lilies in Bloom*) (c. 1914–17), sold at Christie's New York in May 2018 for $84,687,504; and *Meules* (*Haystacks*) (1890–91), sold at Sotheby's New York in May 2019 for $110,747,000—were achieved by paintings that were each conceived as part of a series.

Monet inaugurated the practice of producing series of a single subject depicted in different light and atmospheric conditions, at different times of day, across the seasons, and in many types of weather, with the *Haystacks* in 1890–91. Presented to the public by Durand-Ruel at his gallery in 1891, they sold out. *Rouen Cathedral*, *Poplars*, and *Houses of Parliament* followed, along with many variations on his *Water Lilies*.

In 1883, Monet settled with his large family—two children with his first wife, Camille, who died in 1879, and the six children of his companion and later second wife, Alice Hoschedé, from her previous marriage—in Giverny, a small village in Normandy. There, not without controversy and aversion from the villagers, he deviated the course of the river Ru to create his own water garden and embarked on his most famous investigation, the *Water Lilies*, which would dominate the artist's production for the last decades of his life. In 1909, he successfully exhibited forty-eight paintings of water lilies at Durand-Ruel's gallery.

By 1914, afflicted by cataracts and grieving over the deaths of his elder son, Jean, early that year and his beloved second wife in 1911, Monet was hardly painting anymore. But he was encouraged to work again by his longtime friend Georges Clemenceau (1841–1929), a journalist, publisher, and former French prime minister who would regain that office in 1917. Monet decided to create a "great decoration," a circular series of *Water Lilies*—a project that would occupy him until his death in 1926. He offered the first two panels to the French state on November 12, 1918, the day after the Armistice ended World War I, and eventually he agreed to donate the entire series. In huge canvases for which a new studio had to be built, Monet pushed his language to uncharted territories. The brushstrokes dissolved, becoming almost abstract, with results that would have a profound influence in the 1950s on American Abstract Expressionists Jackson Pollock and Mark Rothko. Ultimately, eight majestic *Water Lilies* canvases were given to the French state, installed in two purposefully designed oval rooms in the newly created Musée de l'Orangerie, where they still are.

In Simon Kelly's research into Monet's account books, an interesting discovery emerges: the artist's strategic shift to creating series of paintings, starting with his exhibition of *Haystacks* at Durand-Ruel's gallery in 1891, proved instrumental in his ascent to financial success. An examination of Monet's career from the 1890s, supported by entries in the account books from 1898, vividly illustrates the substantial rise in his prices following his adoption of the series approach in making his art.[20]

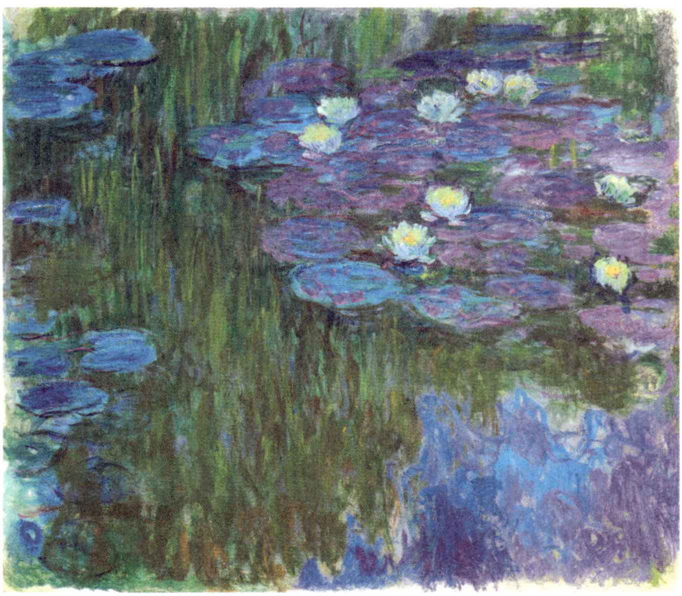

Claude Monet, *Nymphéas en fleur* (*Water Lilies in Bloom*), c. 1914–17

Durand-Ruel's strategy as an art dealer—as summarized by his descendants Paul-Louis Durand-Ruel and Flavie Durand-Ruel—relied on "seven entirely new principles: the protection of the art first and foremost; the exclusivity of the artists' work; the founding of art reviews; the marriage of the worlds of art and finance; the staging of solo rather than group exhibitions; a network of international galleries; and regular unrestricted access to his galleries and apartment."[21]

In order to build and develop a market for the new artists, with critical and public acceptance, Durand-Ruel first of all effectively created monopolies controlling their works, a tactic that began to pay off only after 1886 but was initially fraught with significant risk. Jennifer A. Thompson notes that Durand-Ruel typically purchased ten to thirty paintings a year from each artist he represented. Given that these artists were relatively unknown at the time, this approach left him vulnerable to economic downturns.[22]

GUSTAVE CAILLEBOTTE'S BEQUEST

Raboteurs de parquet (*The Floor Scrapers*) (1875) was one of the seven canvases by Gustave Caillebotte (1848–1894) shown in the second Impressionist exhibition, at Durand-Ruel's gallery in 1876. Its author was a talented portrayer of the Parisian urban life who, thanks to his family's means, became a key supporter of the Impressionist movement. Caillebotte offered his friends money when in need and financial support to organize shows. Upon inheriting a small fortune after the death of his parents, he also became one of the first consistent buyers of Impressionist works. At his premature death in 1894, Caillebotte bequeathed sixty-seven paintings from his collection to the French state, to be exhibited in the Musée du Luxembourg with works by other living artists. However, his generous gift triggered a heated and controversial debate, and it took Renoir—the executor of Caillebotte's will—two years of negotiations to obtain the right for thirty-eight paintings to be exhibited at the Luxembourg. It was the first display of Impressionist works in a public venue. The remaining twenty-nine were offered but refused twice by the French state, and Caillebotte's family eventually sold them.

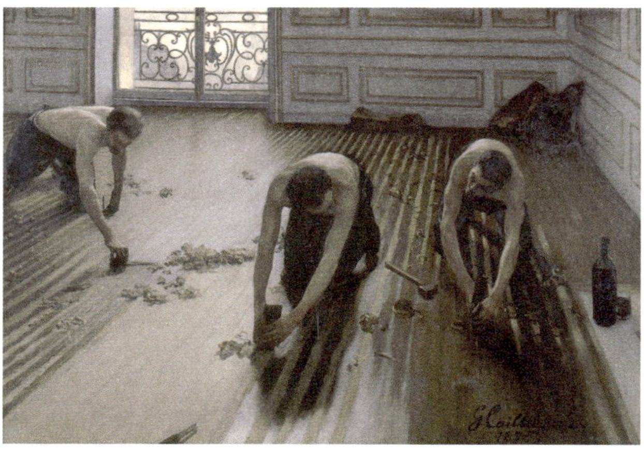

Gustave Caillebotte, *Raboteurs de parquet* (*The Floor Scrapers*), 1875, Musée d'Orsay, Paris

A notable instance in which he used the bulk-purchase method is Manet. After encountering two of Manet's paintings at the home of Belgian-born painter Alfred Stevens in January 1872, Durand-Ruel rushed to Manet's studio and bought every painting available, acquiring twenty-three works. A few days later, he made another substantial purchase, ultimately amassing nearly fifty of Manet's paintings.

Giving artists monthly stipends and more generally supporting them in every aspect of their lives, developing a sincere friendship with many, was another pillar of Durand-Ruel's practice. John Rewald states that he was not just a dealer of the Impressionists; he was their defender and friend. He was among the first to grasp the revolutionary nature of their art, and for many years, he displayed unparalleled courage by investing heavily, often jeopardizing his financial stability, to support their work. This commitment sometimes brought him perilously close to bankruptcy.[23]

PIERRE-AUGUSTE RENOIR'S *BAL DU MOULIN DE LA GALETTE* (1876)

Considered one of Renoir's masterpieces, *Bal du moulin de la Galette* (*Dance at the Moulin de la Galette*) was shown in the second Impressionist exhibition, in 1876. It depicts a joyous moment of leisure in a fashionable venue of the middle class—of whom the Impressionists were the interpreters. The canvas, totally executed en plein air, vibrates with color and light. The larger version of the painting hangs in the Musée d'Orsay; a smaller one was catapulted into the world's attention on May 15, 1990, when it was auctioned at Sotheby's in New York for the record price of $78.1 million. The buyer was the Japanese Ryoei Saito (1916–1996), who two days before had also purchased Vincent van Gogh's *Portrait of Dr. Gachet* (1890) at Christie's for $82.5 million. Both paintings have since disappeared from public view. Although Saito had declared that he wanted to be cremated with them, the smaller *Bal du moulin de la Galette* is allegedly now in a private collection in Switzerland.

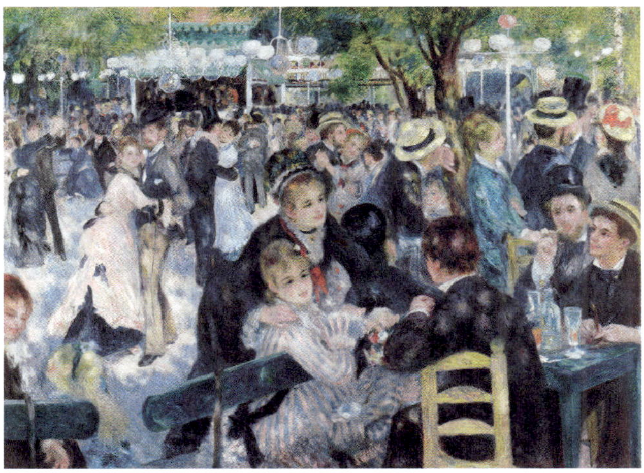

Pierre-Auguste Renoir, *Bal du moulin de la Galette* (*Dance at the Moulin de la Galette*), 1876, Musée d'Orsay, Paris

By organizing a series of seminal exhibitions, Durand-Ruel linked showing and selling, which was not common practice at the time. In addition to hosting group shows like the second Impressionist exhibition in 1876, Durand-Ruel's gallery also staged groundbreaking solo exhibitions in 1883 that lasted one month each, dedicated to Eugène Boudin (1824–1898), Monet, Renoir, Sisley, and Pissarro. Sylvie Patry highlights the historical significance of these presentations, explaining that they represented a first in the history of exhibitions.[24]

In order to educate the public, Durand-Ruel produced publications and opened up to visitors his own Paris apartment, at 35, rue de Rome, which he turned into a small museum of Impressionism. At the time, the only public venue in Paris devoted to living artists was the Musée du Luxembourg, which opened in 1818, but it did not feature any work by the Impressionists.

Durand-Ruel also operated on the auction front, by setting up high-quality sales of Impressionist artists at the Hôtel Drouot, like that of the atelier of Manet, which took place over two days in 1884 (the year after he died), and where *A Bar at the Folies-Bergère* (1882) was sold for 5,850 francs. Furthermore, Durand-Ruel defended the prices of his artists at auction, bidding on works himself to help them achieve higher levels.[25]

Central to his strategy was the conquest of new international markets, particularly the American one. As he recalls: "In the midst of the countless difficulties I had been struggling with for years, I had the felicitous inspiration to think that in America, where I had many friends, I would encounter less hostility."[26] The intuition that prompted Durand-Ruel to accept the 1885 invitation from the American Art Association to organize an exhibition in New York represents indeed the turning point for the Impressionists' market and critical and public acceptance. The association's inducements included payment of all shipping, insurance, and advertising expenses—and, even more significantly, removal of the import tax on the works that would be sold (with Durand-Ruel receiving a percentage of each sale).

On March 13, 1886, the show, titled *Works in Oil and Pastel by the Impressionists of Paris*, opened at 6 East Twenty-Third Street in New York. On display were 289 paintings, among them 48 by Monet, 42 by Pissarro, 38 by Renoir, and 23 by Degas. It was received with interest and approval by critics and the public; more importantly, 49 paintings found buyers. Philip Hook asserts that the exhibition Durand-Ruel brought to New York in 1886 is not only a milestone in the history of Impressionism but also a transformative moment in the evolution of art dealing.[27] Durand-Ruel immediately understood that expansion into the American market was the key to success. The positive outcome inspired him to agree to organize a second exhibition for the following year and eventually, in 1888, establish a permanent gallery in New York, operated in partnership with his children and known as Durand-Ruel & Sons. The favorable outcome within the American market in turn propelled the Impressionists' acceptance and commercial affirmation in Europe. Thus, it was on the far side of the Atlantic, in the New World—as Assouline emphatically writes—that the

Impressionists finally vanquished their old enemy, the conventionalism of their contemporaries.[28]

Motivated by necessity, as Thompson notes, Durand-Ruel's turn to international markets reinvented his business and transformed it with the introduction of new practices.[29] His collaborations with German dealers, especially with Paul and Bruno Cassirer, based in Berlin, were also intense and fruitful. Together, they organized exhibitions and successfully sold Impressionist works to collectors and museums. In 1905, Durand-Ruel orchestrated the largest Impressionist exhibition in London, at the Grafton Galleries. However, the English market was initially hesitant to embrace this new art form.

MODELS TURNED ARTISTS

The Museum of Fine Arts, Boston, owns both Manet's *Portrait of Victorine Meurent* (1862) and a *Self-Portrait* (c. 1876) by Meurent herself. The young woman modeled at least nine times for Manet, lending her features to the scandalous *Olympia* and to the naked woman at the center of the controversial *Déjeuner sur l'herbe*. Meurent's own activity as a painter, though, might come as a surprise to most.

It is worth repeatedly emphasizing the significant challenges women have had to face in pursuing careers as professional artists. Coming from an affluent background certainly helped, as was the case with Berthe Morisot and Mary Cassatt, contemporaries of Meurent. It was not uncommon for girls from a poor background to model from a young age for famous painters, and later to become artists themselves.

Victorine Meurent (1844–1927) came from a working-class family; her mother was a seamstress and her father an artisan. She started modeling at the age of sixteen for the atelier of Thomas Couture, and she later posed for Manet and Degas before facing the canvas herself. In her new field, Meurent enjoyed some success, and her paintings were accepted in the official Salons of 1876 (from which the jury rejected Manet's work), 1879, and 1885. She became a member of the Société des Artistes Français in 1903.

If Meurent's style remained somewhat traditional, though, much more innovative was the work of Suzanne Valadon (1865–1938), who started as a model too. The daughter of an indigent single mother, Valadon was born Marie-Clémentine; it was the artist Henri de Toulouse-Lautrec (1864–1901) who renamed her Suzanne. After an attempt at a career as a horsewoman at the Cirque Fernando in Montmartre, an accident forced Valadon to give up that path, and she started modeling for painters. A fixed figure in the cafés and nightclubs of Montmartre, she was bored by conventions, and Jennifer Higgie recounts an occasion when Valadon entered the Moulin de la Galette dressed in nothing but a mask.[30]

Self-taught, Valadon was respected by her peers; her work was included in several independent Salons and regularly shown at the Galerie Bernheim-Jeune. Her subjects were primarily working-class women—young and old—engaged in everyday activities such as bathing, resting, or combing their hair. There is nothing titillating or idealized in these depictions, as Higgie observes; while the women and girls might occasionally be shown undressed, they are also portrayed as exhausted, their skin a natural part of their lived experience.[31] Valadon also produced several nude self-portraits and—highly unusual for a woman of her time—male nudes. Her admission to the Société Nationale des Beaux-Arts in 1894 made Valadon the first woman to achieve that recognition.

Other models turned artists include Jeanne Hébuterne (1898–1920), companion of Amedeo Modigliani (1884–1920), who tragically ended her life when her lover died; and Fernande Olivier (1881–1966), who lived with Pablo Picasso (1881–1973) during several of his early years in Paris and modeled for many of his most famous Cubist paintings and sculptures.

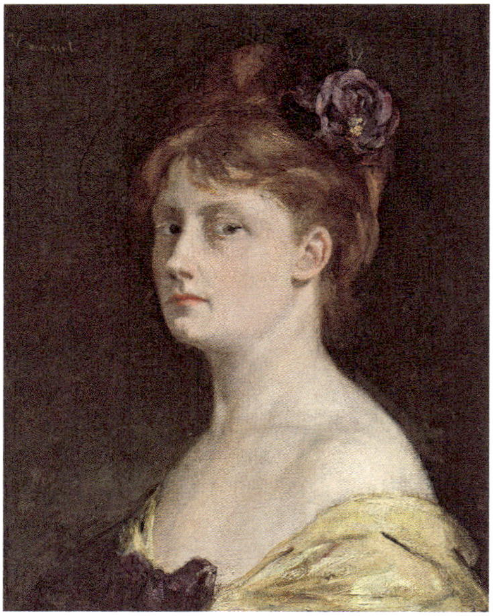

Victorine Meurent, *Self-Portrait*, c. 1876, Museum of Fine Arts, Boston

NOTES

1 Sue Roe, *The Private Lives of the Impressionists* (New York: Harper Perennial, 2007), 8.

2 Pierre Assouline, *Discovering Impressionism: The Life of Paul Durand-Ruel* (New York: Vendôme Press, 2004), 71.

3 Assouline, *Discovering Impressionism*, 73.

4 Claire Maingon, "Les Salons, au coeur de l'echiquier artistique," in *Le Paris de la modernité, 1905–1925*, exh. cat. (Paris: Paris Musées, 2023), 62.

5 Roe, *Private Lives*, 28.

6 Charles Baudelaire, "De l'héroïsme de la vie moderne," in *Salon de 1846* (Paris: Michel Lévy Frères, 1846).

7 Assouline, *Discovering Impressionism*, 73.

8 Liesbeth de Strooper and Erwin Dekker, "Why the Impressionists Did Not Create Impressionism," *Journal of Cultural Economics* 48, no. 2 (June 2024): 171–98.

9 Catherine Méneux, "Une société coopérative pour une exposition indépendante," in *Paris 1874: Inventer l'impressionnisme*, ed. Sylvie Patry and Anne Robbins, exh. cat. (Paris: Musée d'Orsay, 2024), 102.

10 Anne Robbins, "15 avril 1874: Une exposition impressioniste ou 'éclectique,'" in Patry and Robbins, *Paris 1874*, 108.

11 Roe, *Private Lives*, 126.

12 *Artists: Their Lives and Works* (New York: DK, 2017), 239.

13 Patrice de Moncan and Claude Heurteux, *Le Paris d'Haussmann* (Paris: Les Éditions du Mécène, 2009), 37.

14 Roe, *Private Lives*, 135.

15 David W. Galenson, *Conceptual Revolutions in Twentieth-Century Art* (Cambridge, UK: Cambridge University Press, 2009), 18.

16 Philip Hook, *Rogues' Gallery: A History of Art and Its Dealers* (London: Profile Books, 2017), 108.

17 Assouline, *Discovering Impressionism*, 86.

18 Flavie Durand-Ruel and Paul-Louis Durand-Ruel, *Paul Durand-Ruel: Memoirs of the First Impressionist Art Dealer (1831–1922)* (Paris: Flammarion, 2014), 80.

19 Durand-Ruel and Durand-Ruel, *Paul Durand-Ruel*, 103.

20 Simon Kelly, "How Monet Became a Millionaire: The Importance of the Artist's Account Books," *Journal of Cultural Economics* 47, no. 3 (September 2023): 437–60.

21 Paul-Louis Durand-Ruel and Flavie Durand-Ruel, "Paul Durand-Ruel (1831–1922): A Portrait," in *Inventing Impressionism: Paul Durand-Ruel and the Modern Art Market*, ed. Sylvie Patry, exh. cat. (London: National Gallery, 2015), 41.

22 Jennifer A. Thompson, "Old and New Worlds: Durand-Ruel and the International Market for Impressionism," in *Pioneers of the Global Art Market: Paris-Based Dealer Networks, 1850–1950*, ed. Christel H. Force (New York: Bloomsbury Visual Arts, 2022), 44.

23 John Rewald, *The History of Impressionism* (New York: Museum of Modern Art, 1946).

24 Sylvie Patry, "Durand-Ruel and the Impressionists' Solo Exhibitions of 1883," in *Inventing Impressionism*, 100.

25 Judith Benhamou, "Paul Durand-Ruel: L'Inventeur du marché de l'art moderne," in *Histoires extraordinaires de l'art à l'hôtel Drouot: De Vermeer à Louise Bourgeois* (Paris: Flammarion, 2023), 81.

26 Durand-Ruel and Durand-Ruel, *Paul Durand-Ruel*, 155.

27 Hook, *Rogues' Gallery*, 118.

28 Assouline, *Discovering Impressionism*, 201.

29 Thompson, "Old and New Worlds," 44.

30 Jennifer Higgie, *The Mirror and the Palette: Rebellion, Revolution, and Resilience; Five Hundred Years of Women's Self Portraits* (New York: Pegasus Books, 2021), 244.

31 Higgie, *Mirror and the Palette*, 246–47.

6. From Cézanne to Picasso: The Modern Art Market Develops

p. 113 New Art, New Dealers

p. 114 Ambroise Vollard and the Creation of Cézanne's Market

p. 116 The Goldschmidt Auction

p. 117 Vollard Explores: Van Gogh, Gauguin, and Picasso

p. 118 Johanna van Gogh-Bonger and Vincent van Gogh's Legacy and Market

p. 120 Berthe Weill

p. 122 Gertrude and Leo Stein's Role in the Early Promotion of Matisse and Picasso

p. 124 Pablo Picasso's *Les Demoiselles d'Avignon* (1907)

p. 125 Gertrude Stein

p. 127 Daniel-Henry Kahnweiler: The Cubist Promoter

p. 128 The Skin of the Bear

p. 129 Paul Guillaume and African Art

p. 131 Paul Rosenberg and Georges Wildenstein: A New Take on the Promotion of Picasso

p. 133 Sergei Shchukin and the Morozov Brothers

p. 134 Picasso and America

p. 137 The Barnes Collection in Philadelphia

Modernism was not merely shaped by artists; the market played a key part in this scenario.

—Christel H. Force, ed., *Pioneers of the Global Art Market*

The market model that was centered on the predominant role of the dealer, pioneered by Paul Durand-Ruel to promote the Impressionists (see “Paul Durand-Ruel and the Birth of the Impressionist Market,” p. 94), reached its full development in Paris during the first half of the twentieth century. Paris strengthened its status as the Western capital of the arts, radiating an international commercial network that extended into new territories.[1]

As artists diverged from the tenets of Impressionism and delved into other explorations, a new wave of dealers emerged to support and build their markets: Ambroise Vollard, who created Paul Cézanne's market; Daniel-Henry Kahnweiler, the indefatigable promoter of Cubism and the first dealer to exclusively represent Pablo Picasso; and Paul Rosenberg, who, in collaboration with Georges Wildenstein, consolidated and expanded the reach of Picasso's market in America.

Integral to this dynamic market model were courageous collectors such as Gertrude and Leo Stein, American expatriates residing in Paris, and the Russians Sergei Shchukin and the Morozov brothers.

In 1914, the avant-garde was publicly put to the test by the auction of the works belonging to “La Peau de l'Ours” (the Skin of the Bear), the first example of an art investment fund. The astonishing success of the sale marked a turning point in the trajectory of the art market, demonstrating—just months before Europe plunged into one of the deadliest and most destructive conflicts in history—that contemporary art could indeed be a lucrative investment.

In the 1920s, with Europe's economy rebounding from the devastation of war, the market for modernism solidified and expanded internationally.

NEW ART, NEW DEALERS

Dissatisfied with the Impressionists' approach to painting, artists toward the turn of the century began exploring new artistic frontiers. Their groundbreaking styles attracted a new generation of dealers who courageously supported and cultivated their markets.

Georges Seurat (1859–1891) and Paul Signac (1863–1935) provided a scientific foundation to their variation on the Impressionists' luminous sensations on canvas: precisely placing colors in tiny dots, or points, rather than short, horizontal brushstrokes. Paul Gauguin (1848–1903), pursuing the utopia of a primitive style first in Pont-Aven in Brittany and then in Polynesia, used flat and uniform large fields of color to turn the real into a personal and symbolistic language. Vincent van Gogh (1853–1890) produced, in only a few years, astonishing paintings characterized by powerful brushstrokes and dazzling, unnatural color that would influence the Expressionism movement to come. Paul Cézanne (1839–1906) restored volume to the Impressionists' fleeting sensations, proposing a way of representing objects in space from multiple viewpoints that would pave the way to Cubism.

The challenge that the dealers promoting the avant-garde artists were facing was huge, as Christel H. Force stresses. They had to create a demand for unwanted art forms, and this required vision and dedication as well as business savvy, in order to turn avant-garde works initially perceived as worthless into desirable commodities.[2]

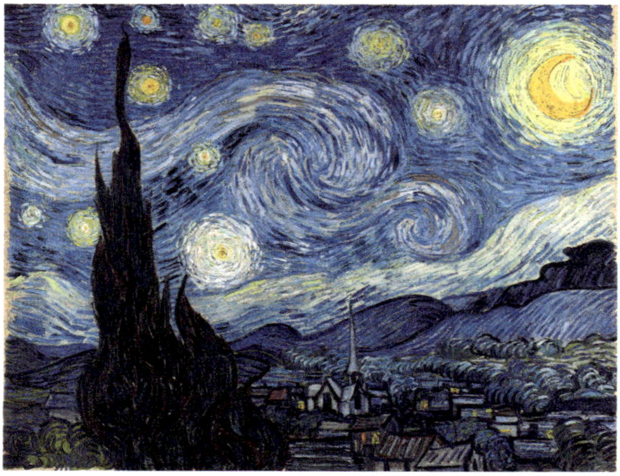

Vincent van Gogh, *The Starry Night*, 1889, Museum of Modern Art, New York

AMBROISE VOLLARD AND THE CREATION OF CÉZANNE'S MARKET

At the dawn of the twentieth century, Ambroise Vollard (1866–1939) emerged as a pivotal figure in the Parisian art scene. His most notable achievement was promoting and creating a market for the work of Paul Cézanne. Vollard's strategic support was crucial to the artist's rise in both critical and public spheres, transforming him from an overlooked talent into a foundational figure of modern art.

Enigmatic and controversial, Vollard left an account of his life in *Recollections of a Picture Dealer*, first published in 1936. Born in the French island colony of La Réunion (in the Indian Ocean east of Madagascar), where his father was a notary public, the young Vollard was sent to France in 1885 to study law, first in Montpellier and then in Paris. In the capital, Vollard came to a decision to pursue a career in art dealing, which led to his father cutting off his allowance in disapproval.

After renting two modest rooms on the rue des Apennins in Montmartre, where he lived and worked from 1887, Vollard was able to open his own small gallery in 1893 at 37, rue Laffitte, known at the time as the *rue des tableaux* (the street of paintings). While his inaugural exhibition, *Dessins et croquis de Manet provenant de son atelier*, drawings and sketches purchased directly from Édouard Manet's widow, was not particularly innovative, Vollard quickly realized that to succeed, he needed to shift his focus elsewhere. Most of the Impressionists were already established, represented by other dealers and financially out of reach for him. It was an encounter with the work of Cézanne, first seen in the window of the little art supply shop of Père Tanguy, that would determine the subsequent developments of Vollard's activity. As he wrote: "As soon as I had a shop, it was my ambition to arrange an exhibition of Cézanne's works."[3]

Although Cézanne participated in the first Impressionist exhibition in 1874, his work remained largely unknown in Paris and had not been exhibited there since the third Impressionist show, in 1877. Withdrawing to his hometown of Aix-en-Provence, Cézanne embraced solitude, devoting himself to new artistic exploration and finding inspiration in the surrounding landscapes, particularly Mont Sainte-Victoire and the Bibémus quarries. Deepening his experimentation with form and color, Cézanne gradually broke away from the Impressionist vocabulary, by emphasizing structure over the transient effects of light, and by layering brushstrokes to create depth and solidity, in order to capture the underlying essence of his subjects.

In late 1895, not long after moving from 37, rue Laffitte, to no. 39, Vollard orchestrated a retrospective in collaboration with Cézanne's son,

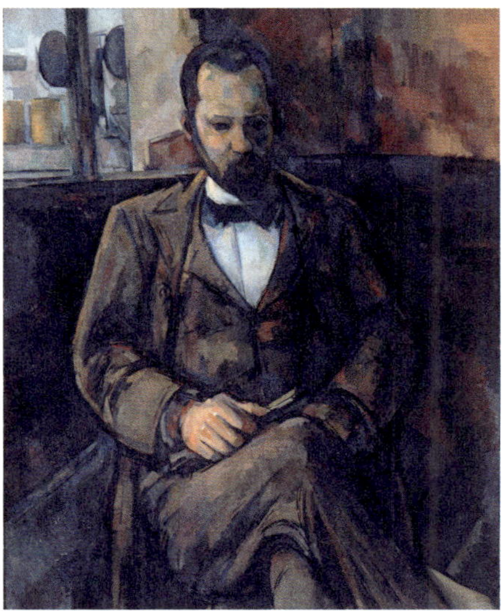

Paul Cézanne, *Portrait of Ambroise Vollard*, 1899, Petit Palais, Paris

Paul Cézanne's *Garçon au gilet rouge* (*Boy in a Red Waistcoat*) (1888–90) was the main character of a defining sale in the history of the Impressionist and modern art markets. On October 15, 1958, Sotheby's London hosted an unprecedented auction of a selection of paintings from the Goldschmidt Collection—just seven masterworks assembled by the late German Jewish banker Jakob Goldschmidt (1882–1955), much of whose pre–World War II acquisitions had been seized and sold by the Nazis. The seven lots in the Sotheby's auction went for £781,000—at the time the highest total for a single auction. The group included three paintings by Manet and one each by Renoir and Van Gogh—but it was one of two works by Cézanne that commanded the spotlight. The painting shattered records, selling for an astounding £220,000 ($616,000) to dealer Georges Keller on behalf of the American collector Paul Mellon. Today, *Boy in a Red Waistcoat* is in the National Gallery of Art in Washington, DC.

Aside from the astonishing price, the event marked a pivotal turning point in the evolution of the art market. Sotheby's introduced an innovative auction format—an exclusive, black-tie evening sale—that set the standard for future high-profile art transactions. The carefully staged atmosphere attracted a powerful audience of collectors, dealers, museum representatives, and celebrities, turning the auction into a spectacle of prestige and influence—even though the actual bidding lasted only twenty-one minutes. Furthermore, the sale of the Cézanne painting—for the highest price achieved until then by a painting at auction—marked a shift in the global art trade. Previously, major works were usually quietly exchanged within a tight-knit circle of European dealers, but the Goldschmidt auction signaled the rise of public sales as the new battleground for acquiring masterpieces. As James Stourton notes: "The grand London dealers at once realized that a new power had been unleashed."[4] It was the beginning of a new era, in which auctions would become theatrical, highly publicized events, capable of setting trends and breaking records.

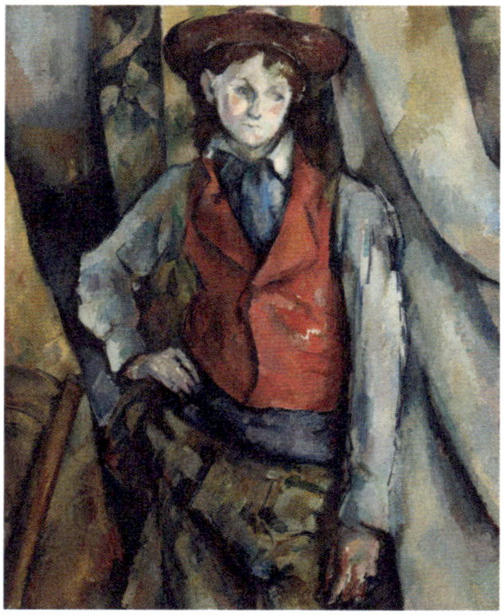

Paul Cézanne, *Garçon au gilet rouge* (*Boy in a Red Waistcoat*), 1888–90, National Gallery of Art, Washington, DC also named Paul, despite never having met the artist in person. Ann Dumas highlights Vollard's unwavering belief in Cézanne's artistic potential. He astutely recognized that Cézanne was the only major figure of the Impressionist generation without a dealer, as others were represented by Durand-Ruel. Showing both opportunism and courage, with the November 1895 exhibition Vollard became the first in Paris to present a solo show of Cézanne's work, solidifying his role as a key promoter of the artist.[5] Vollard bet big on Cézanne, not only by showing his work at all, but also by buying 150 canvases from him, following a strategy that Dumas calls "stockpiling," rather than simple representation.[6]

The 1895 exhibition, to be followed by a second one in 1898 and a third in 1899, was an astounding revelation for the public, critics, and artists. The success of the first show allowed Vollard to move to a larger space at 6, rue Laffitte, and to develop an international clientele. Furthermore, he started to establish international collaborations with the dealers Paul and Bruno Cassirer in Berlin, of whose gallery he said that "it might be a prolongation of the rue Laffitte,"[7] and with Heinrich Thannhauser in Munich.

According to Isabelle Cahn, in the years following the initial exhibition, nearly seven hundred works by Cézanne flowed through Vollard's hands, granting him a near monopoly over the artist's production, despite the absence of a formal contract between them.[8] One year after Cézanne's death, Vollard's efforts culminated in triumph with the *Exposition rétrospective d'oeuvres de Cézanne*, held in October 1907 as part of the Salon d'Automne in Paris.

VOLLARD EXPLORES: VAN GOGH, GAUGUIN, AND PICASSO

In June 1895, before his initial Cézanne exhibition, Vollard was the first dealer to dedicate a solo exhibition to Van Gogh, with which he inaugurated his new gallery at no. 39. The artist had died five years earlier, his work had very little exposure before or since then, and a market hardly existed for it. Vollard borrowed works from the collection of the painter Émile Schuffenecker, from the dealer Père Tanguy, and from Paul Gauguin. The works lent by Johanna van Gogh-Bonger (1862–1925), the widow of Vincent's brother Theo (1857–1891)—who had died only six months after Vincent—did not arrive in time to be included in the show. Vollard recalled that "except for the young painters, the public showed little enthusiasm. The time was not ripe."[9] A few sales, though, encouraged the dealer to organize a second exhibition the following year, with paintings from the estate. The prices that Van Gogh-Bonger set for this body of work, however, were too high. Nevertheless, Hans Luijten reports that between 1896 and 1899, Vollard sold around twenty-five works from her collection, and that he later acknowledged it was a great mistake for him to abandon Van Gogh's market.[10] After Vollard's disengagement, the task of administering and promoting Van Gogh's legacy and market was brought forward by Van Gogh-Bonger.

The architect behind Vincent van Gogh's rise to critical acclaim and market success was his sister-in-law, Johanna van Gogh-Bonger. Hans Luijten states that the artist's posthumous fame owes much to her unwavering dedication and efforts, not solely to the quality of his works. Over thirty-five years, navigating a predominantly male-dominated domain with resilience, she tenaciously pursued her mission to establish recognition for Van Gogh's artistic legacy worldwide.[11] Van Gogh-Bonger was married to Theo van Gogh, who throughout his brother Vincent's short and tragic life had served as the artist's devoted confidant and unwavering champion, offering relentless financial and moral support. Vincent shot himself in Auvers-sur-Oise on July 27, 1890, and died a little more than a full day later. Theo passed away after only six months, during which he tried unsuccessfully to organize an exhibition of his brother's works with Durand-Ruel. The twenty-eight-year-old Van Gogh-Bonger thus inherited approximately four hundred paintings and hundreds of drawings by Vincent, at the time of little commercial value. The daunting responsibility of managing this legacy rested solely on her shoulders, despite having been married to Theo for less than two years and having met Vincent on just a few occasions.

It is now accepted that Van Gogh enjoyed some appreciation at least from his peers while alive. Theo had presented a few of Vincent's works at the Salon des Indépendants in 1886, 1888, and 1889, and in early 1890, at the seventh annual show of the Brussels avant-garde group Les XX (Les Vingt), the only reported sale of a Van Gogh painting during his lifetime took place: *Red Vineyard at Arles, Montmajour* (1888). Bregje Gerritse and Sara Tas write that Van Gogh died just when his work was finally arousing some interest and being recognized in artistic environments.[12] However, the painter was still virtually unknown to a larger public, and a market for his work did not exist.

In 1891, Van Gogh-Bonger sent ten of Van Gogh's works to the Salon des Indépendants, which took place in Paris from March 20 to April 27. After this effort, however, she decided to leave the French capital and settle back in her native Netherlands, in the small village of Bussum. From there, she devised her promotional strategy on two fronts. First, she cultivated a network of relationships with merchants and museum directors, with the goal of expanding Van Gogh's presence in exhibitions of various types. Crucial was an alliance with Bruno and Paul Cassirer in Germany, who started early on to show and sell Van Gogh works. In 1891, exhibitions were mounted in Rotterdam, The Hague, and Antwerp; in December 1892, the largest show to date was put together at the Panorama gallery in Amsterdam. Vollard, as mentioned above, ventured into the Van Gogh market and organized the artist's first solo exhibition in Paris, in 1895, but he soon abandoned the enterprise. Therefore, in the French capital, Van Gogh-Bonger relied on a collaboration with another dealer, Gaston Bernheim. In every exhibition, in order to create demand and not flood the market, Luijten states, she interspersed works for sale with others not available for purchase. The latter represented the core of her own collection and would eventually end up in the Van Gogh Museum in Amsterdam.[13]

The second cornerstone of Van Gogh-Bonger's strategy involved publishing the poignant correspondence between Vincent and Theo, comprising more than eight hundred letters. With great acumen, she realized that the contents of the correspondence would be essential for the public to learn and understand who Van Gogh was, and to appreciate his artistic vision. It was a meticulous and time-consuming undertaking, as the letters needed to be transcribed and then placed in order. The letters would first be published, mainly in Dutch and French as written, in three volumes in 1914; a two-volume edition that Van Gogh-Bonger translated from the Dutch volumes into English was published posthumously in 1927.

In 1905, the Stedelijk Museum in Amsterdam opened the first comprehensive retrospective devoted to Van Gogh, organized and paid for by Van Gogh-Bonger, with about five hundred works. Visited by critics and dealers coming from all over Europe, the show deeply impacted the artist's market, pushing his prices to unprecedented levels.

In the United States, where Van Gogh-Bonger lived between 1915 and 1919, the American public first saw work by Van Gogh at the Armory Show of 1913. The artist would eventually find an ardent champion in Alfred H. Barr Jr. (1902–1981), the first director of the Museum of Modern Art in New York. Barr's tireless efforts to promote Van Gogh's work culminated in a landmark retrospective at MoMA from November 4, 1935, to January 5, 1936, which was vital in securing the artist's reputation as a modern art icon. About 125 works were shown, and more than one hundred thousand visitors saw the exhibition in New York before it traveled to Philadelphia, Boston, Cleveland, and San Francisco, among other cities.

At her death in 1925, Van Gogh-Bonger bequeathed around two hundred works to her son, Vincent, who in 1962 channeled them into the recently created Van Gogh Foundation. The opening in 1973 of the Van Gogh Museum in Amsterdam, commissioned by the Dutch government and designed by the architect Gerrit Rietveld, with a new wing by Kisho Kurokawa completed in 1999, marked the coronation of Van Gogh-Bonger's efforts.

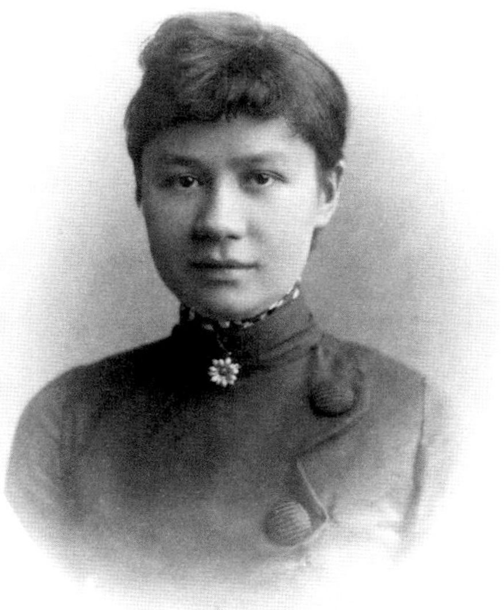

Johanna van Gogh-Bonger, 1889

It was Berthe Weill (1865–1951), owner of a small gallery in Montmartre, who sold Picasso's first works in Paris: three bullfighting pastels, obtained through the mediation of the Catalan Pere Mañach. They were bought by Adolphe Brisson, editor of the magazine *Les Annales politiques et littéraires.*

Born in Paris, the fifth of seven children in a modest Jewish family of Alsatian origin, Weill developed her passion for art during an apprenticeship with an antique dealer named Salvator Mayer, perhaps a cousin of the family. Pledging the modest 50-franc capital of her dowry, Weill subsequently opened a small space on the rue Victor Massé in Montmartre, dealing at the beginning in rare books and prints, before moving to contemporary art.[14] These were the years of the infamous Dreyfus Affair and of growing anti-Semitism in France. Alfred Dreyfus (1859–1935), a Jewish army officer, was falsely accused of treason and in 1894 sent to Devil's Island, a penal colony in French Guiana. His wrongful conviction deeply divided the nation. Weill, despite being Jewish and of limited financial means, persevered in her mission, and her gallery became the first venue in Paris dedicated exclusively to young artists.

The list of those who debuted at Weill's is impressive: Picasso, with works from his Blue Period, in a group display in 1902; Raoul Dufy and Georges Rouault (1871–1958) in 1906. In 1917, Weill organized the only solo exhibition dedicated to Amedeo Modigliani during the artist's lifetime, though the police censored it for the presence of nude paintings considered scandalous. In 1933, Weill published her autobiography, featuring a frontispiece portrait of her painted by Picasso in 1920. Weill's gallery, which moved from Montmartre to rue Taitbout, then in 1920 to rue Laffitte, and in 1934 to rue Saint-Dominique, was shut down in 1939, when Paris was on the brink of World War II.

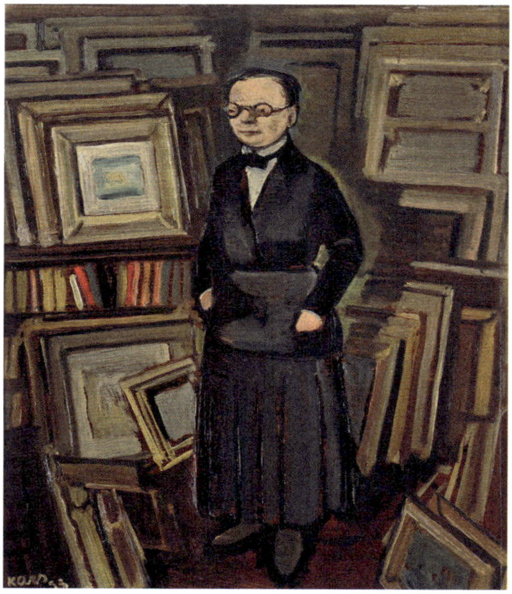

Georges Kars, *Portrait of Mme. Berthe Weill, Art Dealer*, 1927

Paul Gauguin was the focus of an 1896 exhibition at Vollard's gallery. At the time of the opening, Gauguin was living in Tahiti, struggling with severe financial difficulties, and lacked stable representation in Paris. His earlier exhibition in 1893 at Durand-Ruel's gallery had been met with indifference, resulting in few, if any, sales. In 1895, before returning to Polynesia, Gauguin attempted an unsuccessful auction at the Hôtel Drouot. He also sold Vollard several paintings and ceramics, along with works by Van Gogh from his personal collection. Unfortunately, Vollard's exhibition did not achieve the success Gauguin had hoped for.

During his time in Tahiti, Gauguin entrusted his works to his friend and fellow painter Georges-Daniel de Monfreid, hoping that he would secure better opportunities and a new dealer for him. Gauguin had a distaste for Vollard, and their relationship, as documented by their letters, was always fraught with difficulty and tinged with mutual suspicion.[15] To Gauguin's dismay, his second solo exhibition in Paris, held in 1898 at Vollard's gallery and showcasing his latest works from Tahiti, also met with little success. Despite this, Gauguin and Vollard reached a financial agreement in 1900 that would remain in place until the artist's death. According to Douglas Druick, the agreement provided Gauguin with a monthly payment of 300 francs, along with coverage for materials, and set prices at 200 francs each for up to twenty-five paintings a year.[16]

Only after Gauguin's death was his reputation solidified. The retrospectives held at the Salon d'Automne in 1903 and 1906 were essential in establishing his legacy and significantly boosting his market presence.

It was Vollard who gave the nineteen-year-old Pablo Picasso (1881–1973) his first exhibition in Paris, in June 1901. The show was organized through

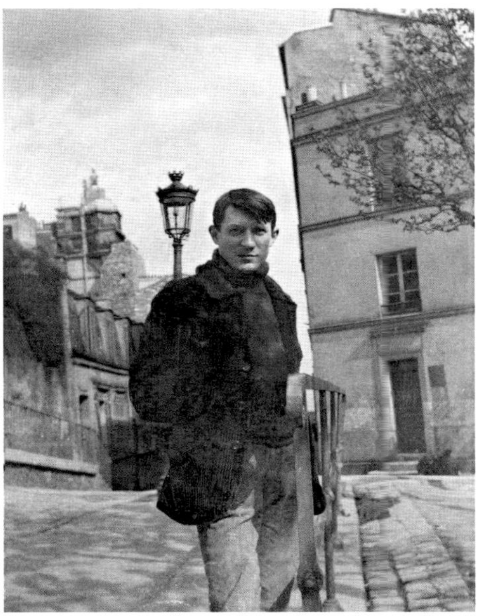

Pablo Picasso at Place Ravignan, Paris, 1904

the mediation of Pedro "Pere" Mañach, a Catalan middleman with whom Picasso had been put in touch by other Spanish painters.

In his memoirs, Vollard recounts his first encounter with Picasso: "Towards 1901 I received a visit from a young Spaniard, dressed with the most studied elegance. He was brought to me by one of his countrymen whom I knew slightly, a manufacturer from Barcelona called Manache, I fancy, or something like it."[17] Depicting mainly Parisian scenes, Picasso's paintings in Vollard's exhibition, as pointed out by Michael FitzGerald,[18] revealed the young artist's attempt at presenting himself as the successor to the Post-Impressionists, particularly Henri de Toulouse-Lautrec (1864–1901), the interpreter of Parisian nightlife. Cunningly, the young Picasso also included portraits of the three backers of the exhibitions: Mañach, the art critic Gustave Coquiot, and Ambroise Vollard. The latter considered that the exhibition was "not a success, and for a long time after Picasso got no better reception from the public."[19] On the contrary, John Richardson writes that the exhibition "was not only a succès d'estime; it was, in a modest way, a financial success. Well over half the items sold."[20] Regardless, the show did not turn into a stable commercial relationship between Picasso and Vollard, although the dealer would occasionally buy and sell works from the artist's studio and much later commission him to do a series of etchings, the famous *Vollard Suite* (1930–37). But early on, Vollard did not grasp Picasso's potential; he saw and passed on the artist's early Blue Period works, which were instead shown at Galerie Berthe Weill in 1902. As FitzGerald remarks, Picasso—and Henri Matisse—represented experimental forays beyond Vollard's main focus on Impressionism and Post-Impressionism.[21]

However, the association of Picasso's art with that of Cézanne, which Vollard facilitated, played a significant role in solidifying Picasso's reputation among French, American, Russian, and German art connoisseurs, as Gary Tinterow has stated.[22]

GERTRUDE AND LEO STEIN'S ROLE IN THE EARLY PROMOTION OF MATISSE AND PICASSO

Emily Braun writes that "it is no exaggeration" to state that Gertrude and Leo Stein "did more to support avant-garde painting" in the first decade of the twentieth century "than any other collectors or institutions" worldwide. Within the small space of the weekly salons in the siblings' Paris apartment, avant-garde artists found both comfort and economic support, their reputations were bolstered by in-house competition, and their careers were advanced through introductions to collectors. Critics and art historians also soaked up emerging ideas during these gatherings.[23]

For Picasso, who eventually settled in Paris from his native Spain in 1904, stable representation would not be achieved until 1912, when he was finally signed up by Daniel-Henry Kahnweiler. Until then, the support of the Steins was crucial. Another avant-garde artist, Henri Matisse (1869–1954), had exhibited in several independent venues. At the 1905 Salon d'Automne, he shocked the art world with his bold, unnatural, flat fields of color, for which he and his fellow artists were disparagingly called *fauves* (wild beasts)—and buyers and representation were lacking for him too.

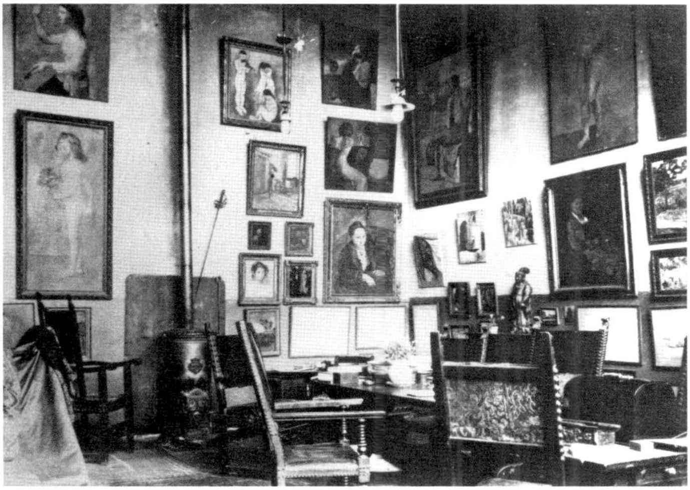

Gertrude Stein's apartment in Paris, c. 1915

Leo Stein (1872–1947) and his sister Gertrude (1874–1946) had moved to Paris in 1903 and soon after started buying works by young and avant-garde artists. Rebecca Rabinow writes that whereas it was common for rich Americans to purchase art in Paris to send back to the States, the Steins were different. Despite not being particularly wealthy and not initially intending to assemble a collection, when they began acquiring contemporary art, they chose not to send the works to America. Instead, they opened their Paris apartment to anyone interested in viewing the artwork. Therefore, their discovery of modern art—especially the work of Matisse and Picasso—had an indelible impact on its development.[24] Their interest in contemporary art was triggered by a visit to the 1904 Salon d'Automne, which included retrospectives of Paul Cézanne, Henri de Toulouse-Lautrec, Pierre-Auguste Renoir (1841–1919), Pierre Puvis de Chavannes (1824–1898), and Odilon Redon (1840–1916) Immediately after, the siblings rushed to Vollard's gallery to buy two works by Cézanne, two by Gauguin, two by Renoir, and one by Maurice Denis (1870–1943). Rabinow notes that the turning point in their collecting occurred in 1905 with the acquisition of Matisse's *Femme au chapeau* (*Woman with a Hat*) (1905), a striking portrait of the artist's wife featuring green skin. From that moment on, the Steins' interests and choices shifted from modern French masters to young contemporaries.[25] Two other masterpieces by Matisse to enter the Steins' collection were *Le Bonheur de vivre* (*The Joy of Life*) (1905–06), subsequently sold to Albert C. Barnes, and *Blue Nude: Memory of Biskra* (1907), now in the collection of the Baltimore Museum of Art after the sisters Claribel and Etta Cone acquired it.

It was Leo who boasted in a letter to a friend about the purchase of two pictures "by a young Spaniard named Picasso whom I consider a genius of very considerable magnitude and one of the most notable draughtsmen living."[26] Both works were bought from the dealer Clovis Sagot: the gouache *The Acrobat's Family with a Monkey* (1905) and the oil painting *Fillette à la corbeille fleurie* (*Young Girl with a Basket of Flowers*) (1905), which later ended up in the collection of David and Peggy Rockefeller and was subsequently sold at Christie's New York in May 2018 for $115 million. The Steins' support and interest in Picasso eventually resulted in their gathering together a substantial and exceptional group of works, among which were masterpieces of the Blue Period such as *Two Women Seated at a Bar* (1902) and *Young Acrobat on a Ball* (1905), and early Cubist works such as *Three Women* (1907–08), later sold to Sergei Shchukin and currently in the State Hermitage Museum, St. Petersburg.

The Steins' apartment at 27, rue de Fleurus, near the Jardin du Luxembourg, was open to the public on Saturdays and became the salon where visitors could admire the more daring productions of the avant-garde, as well as a rendezvous for collectors and critics. It was there, where masterpieces by Picasso and Matisse hung side by side, that the rivalry between the two artists was born. The result is a duality that has been used as a lens to read the art development of the first half of the twentieth century, as Sebastian Smee points out: Matisse the artist of color, Picasso the artist of line and form.[27] The Steins' extraordinary collection was split up in 1913–14, with the Matisses going to Leo and the Picassos to Gertrude, before Leo moved out in 1914.

FitzGerald very interestingly establishes a direct relationship between the financial security that Picasso achieved around 1906, thanks to substantial purchases by the Steins, Shchukin, Vollard, and André Level, and the artist's audacity to embark on the revolutionary explorations that would result in *Les Demoiselles d'Avignon* (1907) and the invention of Cubism.[28]

When Picasso and Matisse were finally able to secure stable commercial representation, the support of the Steins became less crucial to them, and their presence in the rue de Fleurus salon decreased.

PABLO PICASSO'S *LES DEMOISELLES D'AVIGNON* (1907)

The painting that would revolutionize the course of Western art and initiate Cubism was for a long time kept away from the public's eye, and it was never handled by Picasso's primary dealers. After the artist painted it in 1907, friends flocked to see it in his studio, with varied reactions. Kahnweiler, who would become Cubism's paladin and a few years later write that the painting was the beginning of the movement, did not try to buy it, and he considered it a "failure," an attempt to do something that was not reached. Apollinaire thought it contained "a wonderful new language"; however, Braque's shocked, famous reaction was (among a few variations), "With your paintings it is as though you wanted us to eat tow [loose fibers used for yarn, twine, or stuffing] or drink kerosene."[29]

Les Demoiselles d'Avignon was not exhibited in Paris until the 1916 Salon d'Antin, one of the few exhibitions taking place during the years of World War I. Organized by André Salmon, who allegedly invented the name for Picasso's painting, the show gathered works by fifty-two French and foreign artists. After that first public display, *Les Demoiselles* remained in the artist's studio until 1924, when Picasso agreed to sell it—through the mediation of André Breton—to the designer Jacques Doucet for 25,000 francs, payable in monthly installments of 2,000 francs. The reason for Picasso's decision to part with *Les Demoiselles d'Avignon* remains unclear. In 1917, his market had taken off, and he had no financial concerns. Richardson suggests that Doucet had promised to donate his collection to the Musée du Louvre: "Surprising as it is that Picasso sold the *Demoiselles*, it is even more surprising that he sold it for so little. In 1916, when his work was nothing like as valuable, he had refused an offer of 20,000 francs. A few months after the sale to Doucet, [Henri-Pierre] Roché would appraise the painting at 200,000–300,000 francs. The explanation: Doucet had deceived Picasso with a false promise."[30] The donation to the Louvre never happened, and *Les Demoiselles* was dispersed like the rest of Doucet's collection after his death in 1929. The painting ended up with the dealer Jacques Seligmann & Co. in New York and was included in its November 1937 exhibition *20 Years in the Evolution of Picasso, 1903–1923*. Eventually, Barr acquired *Les Demoiselles* for the Museum of Modern Art's collection, for $24,000. In order to finance the acquisition, he had to deaccession a painting by Edgar Degas.

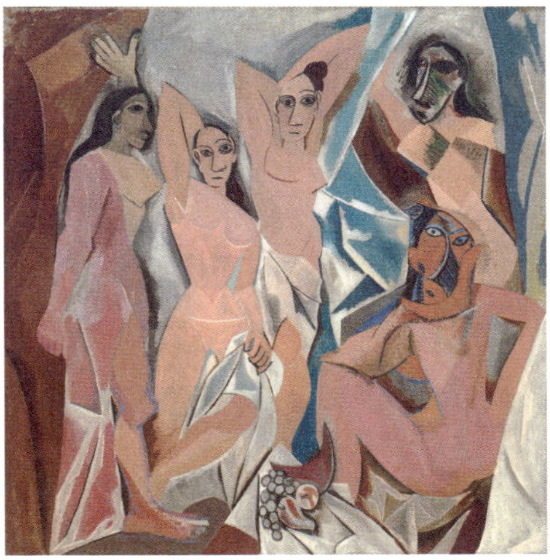

Pablo Picasso, *Les Demoiselles d'Avignon*, 1907, Museum of Modern Art, New York

GERTRUDE STEIN

Picasso's portrait of Gertrude Stein, completed in 1906, sealed the intimate friendship between two kindred spirits. For it, Stein allegedly had to sit about ninety times. Hélène Klein writes that Picasso was struck by her massive body, her sculpted features, and her masculine side.[31] He translated her into juxtaposed volumes, inspired by Iberian sculptures. (Stein bequeathed her portrait in 1946 to the Metropolitan Museum of Art in New York, the first work by Picasso to enter its collection.)

The relationship between Picasso and Stein transcended that of an ambitious young painter and his patron. The two were united by experimentation aimed at the decomposition of language, pictorial and literary. "Pablo is doing abstract portraits in painting. I am trying to do abstract portraits in *my* medium, *words*," declared Stein.[32]

While Picasso was pioneering Cubism and exploring its potential, alongside Georges Braque, Stein began dissecting and reassembling the elements and structure of language—as highlighted in the revealing exhibition at the Musée du Luxembourg in Paris in 2023–24, *Gertrude Stein and Pablo Picasso: The Invention of Language*.

Writer, patron of the avant-garde, feminist, and gay icon: Stein was born into a wealthy Jewish merchant family in Allegheny, Pennsylvania. After residing in Europe, the Steins settled in Oakland, California. Growing up in a cultivated and open environment, she enrolled at Radcliffe College in Cambridge, Massachusetts, and then at Johns Hopkins School of Medicine in Baltimore. However, Stein decided to quit without attaining her medical degree and joined her brother Leo in Paris in 1903.

The apartment at 27, rue de Fleurus, near the Jardin du Luxembourg, that Gertrude shared first with Leo and later with her life companion, Alice B. Toklas (1877–1967), became the most active and avant-garde cultural salon in the city. It was a place where writers, collectors, critics, and artists met, surrounded by works of new art hanging on the walls. Picasso and Matisse, and later the young American writers Ernest Hemingway and F. Scott Fitzgerald, were among the frequent visitors.

A generous supporter of others, Stein had to struggle to be recognized as a writer herself. Commercial success came only in 1933 with the publication of her own memoir, *The Autobiography of Alice B. Toklas*, written as if by her companion. An invitation to tour the States in a series of conferences followed in 1934–35.

Stein's previous *The Making of Americans* (1925), a novel that deals with American identity by following four generations of two families, was not published until more than a decade after she finished writing it.

After finding refuge with Toklas from Nazi persecution in their country house in Bilignin, near the Swiss border, Stein resettled in Paris in 1944.

She died on July 27, 1946, in Neuilly-sur-Seine, near Paris, and is buried at the Père Lachaise Cemetery in the French capital.

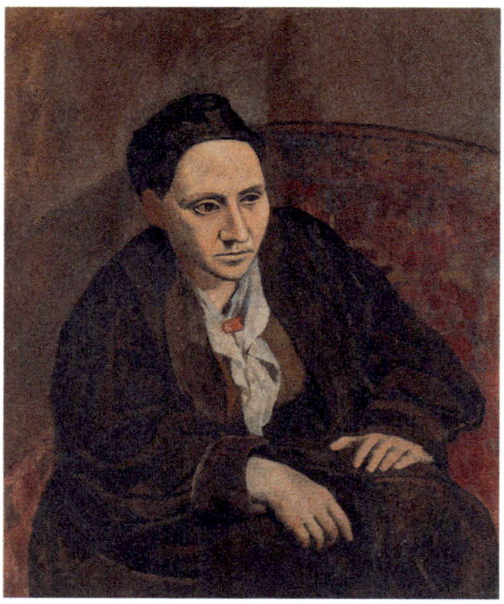

Pablo Picasso, *Portrait of Gertrude Stein*, 1905–06, Metropolitan Museum of Art, New York

Daniel-Henry Kahnweiler (1884–1979) was distinctive as a dealer in his intellectual embrace and staunch support of a singular artistic movement: Cubism. The most revolutionary language of the century, it was invented in 1907–08 by Picasso and Georges Braque (1882–1963). By breaking away from the Renaissance perspective on which Western painting was based, Cubism presented on the flat surface of the painting simultaneous different views of the same subject. The resulting fragmented rendering, reminiscent of small cubes, inspired the name "Cubism," given by the critic Louis Vauxcelles in 1908.

A sophisticated intellectual, Kahnweiler championed Cubism from the very beginning, making it his mission to educate the public and arouse collectors' interest in it.

Kahnweiler came from a wealthy German Jewish family of bankers from Mannheim, where he was born. Not interested in the family business, he embarked in his twenties on a career as an art dealer in Paris. From his first purchase at the Salon des Indépendants in 1907, Kahnweiler's goal was to identify a new generation of young artists to believe in, and to which to devote himself, uncompromisingly. After opening a tiny space on the rue Vignon in 1907, he dedicated his efforts and time to exploring the work of avant-garde artists in depth, visiting their studios—he was one of the first to see Picasso's *Les Demoiselles d'Avignon*. At the same time, Kahnweiler started to build a select and loyal client base. Among them were André Level, Roger Dutilleul, André Lefèvre, Paul Poiret, Jacques Doucet, the Russians Sergei Shchukin and Ivan Morozov, the art historian Vincenc Kramář from Prague, and the Germans Wilhelm Uhde and Hermann Rupf. Richardson writes: "Kahnweiler was unquestionably the most intelligent, farsighted, and scrupulous dealer of his generation. He had an intuitive eye and an instinctive understanding of modernism. . . . He also had the courage to support his artists in the face of attacks by chauvinists and cubist hacks and devise strategies to counter them."[33]

In 1912, Kahnweiler was able to put under contract Braque, André Derain (1880–1954), and Picasso, followed in 1913 by Juan Gris (1887–1927), Maurice de Vlaminck (1876–1958), and Fernand Léger (1881–1955). The agreement with Picasso, as described by Pierre Assouline,[34] committed the artist to sell exclusively to Kahnweiler, and the dealer to buy Picasso's whole production for three years at a fixed scale of prices: 100 francs per drawing, 200 francs each for gouaches, and 250 to 3,000 francs for paintings, depending on their size. Not included in the agreement were older works belonging to Picasso and portraits and large-scale decorative commissions.

As unconventional as it may seem now, Kahnweiler's strategy did not revolve around hosting exhibitions in his gallery for the artists he represented, apart from a Braque show in 1908, controversially received. Newly produced works and those that Kahnweiler acquired would be privately shown to individual collectors, or he would send photographs of them to his clients abroad. He was one of the pioneers in utilizing photography as a systematic tool to document the production of his artists.

Like Durand-Ruel before him, Kahnweiler also applied his skills to establish a network of profitable international collaborations. As Vérane Tasseau explains, Kahnweiler opted for working closely with other galleries instead of opening his own branches in other countries. His partners in Germany, the United States, Britain, and Scandinavia represented the largest contingents of the gallery's buyers. The collaborations with them allowed Kahnweiler to consign and exhibit artworks in their venues, increase the circle of collectors, and widen his and his artists' reputations beyond French borders.[35]

Heinrich Thannhauser in Munich and Alfred Flechtheim in Düsseldorf and other cities were key to building a solid clientele for Picasso and Cubism in Germany. Unfortunately, as Richardson writes, because of Nazi confiscations in the 1930s, details about the pioneering role of the German collectors in Picasso's early promotion have been lost.[36] In order to expand his reach in the United States, Kahnweiler set up an agreement with Robert J. Coady and Michael Brenner, founders of the Washington Square Gallery in New York. It stipulated the consignments of paintings to the gallery, with payments every three months for all sales. Furthermore, the two American dealers committed to buy 2,500 francs' worth of works up front. Before the end of 1914, the gallery held an exhibition of works by Picasso.[37]

After only two years of successes, when "he was enjoying his first taste of victory,"[38] the outbreak of World War I in mid-1914 put an abrupt stop to Kahnweiler's activities. Being German, hence regarded as an enemy, the dealer had to flee Paris; he spent the war years in Switzerland. The French government confiscated all his possessions, to be auctioned at the Hôtel Drouot in 1921–23.

Kahnweiler would resume his activity as a dealer in Paris in 1920, but never under his own name. He operated first as Galerie Simon, and during and after World War II as Galerie Louise Leiris, named for his stepdaughter.

THE SKIN OF THE BEAR

On March 2, 1914, the Hôtel Drouot in Paris hosted the auction of the collection of contemporary works gathered by André Level (1863–1946), a young businessman, and his twelve partners over the previous ten years. The collection was named "La Peau de l'Ours" (the Skin of the Bear), from a fable by the French writer Jean de La Fontaine (1621–1695) that tells of two hunters who sell a bear's skin to a furrier before going off to try—unsuccessfully—to kill the beast (the moral: do not sell the bear's skin before you have killed it). With this enterprising initiative, Level created what can be considered the first art investment fund in history.

In 1904, after being deeply impressed by the works shown in the previous year's first Salon d'Automne, Level convinced a group of young investors to each contribute 250 francs annually to the purchase of works of art to be sold after ten years. Level's initiative was courageous and unprecedented. The structure of the enterprise established that in the event of a profit, each member of the Skin of the Bear would receive the amount invested plus 3.5 percent interest. Any additional profit would be distributed to Level (20 percent) and the artists (20 percent). Meanwhile, investors would also have access to the fund's artworks to decorate their homes. Level, as the sole director of the fund, decided on the purchases, supported by a two-member committee with the right of veto. Over the next decade, the group spent 27,500 francs for the purchase of 145 works, the vast majority by contemporary artists. "The experience was daring," writes Judith Benhamou. "Nothing similar had been done until then. In addition to its speculative aspect, the operation had the advantage of providing money to a population that really needed it: young artists. . . . They would receive 20 percent of the profit made. This was the invention of the resale right, sixteen years before its introduction into French legislation in 1920."[39]

The Skin of the Bear's auction, consisting of the group's 145 lots mainly by avant-garde artists, was preceded by an advertising campaign, an exhibition open to the public, and an accompanying illustrated catalogue—all common practices today but unusual at the time. The result was extraordinary. FitzGerald reports that the initial investment was more than quadrupled: 116,545 francs against 27,500 spent. Picasso's *Family of Saltimbanques* (1905), one of the masterpieces of his Rose Period (now in the collection of the National Gallery of Art in Washington, DC), was sold for 12,650 francs, twelve times the price Level had paid.[40]

Beyond the innovative investment formula, the auction of the Skin of the Bear was indeed a turning point in the course of the modern art market. For the first time, the art of the avant-garde was publicly put to the test, which it passed brilliantly, demonstrating that contemporary art could be a fruitful investment.

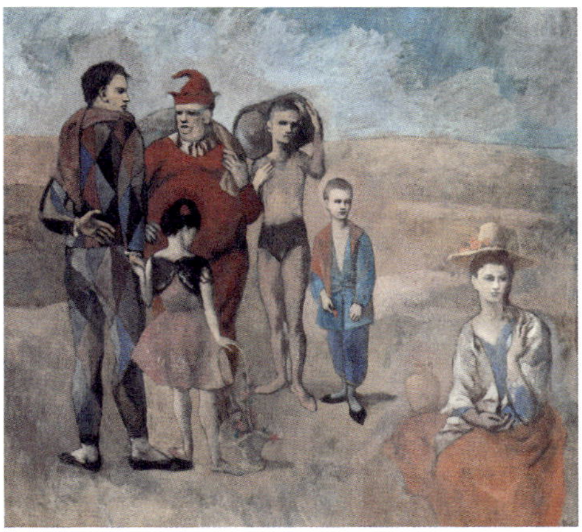

Pablo Picasso, *Family of Saltimbanques*, 1905, National Gallery of Art, Washington, DC

PAUL GUILLAUME AND AFRICAN ART

Paul Guillaume (1891–1934) holds a special position among Parisian dealers of the early twentieth century. Alongside his early engagement and commercial promotion of some of the most prominent figures of the École de Paris (School of Paris, a loose grouping of French and émigré artists there in the early twentieth century), such as Chaïm Soutine (1893–1943) and Amedeo Modigliani (1884–1920), Guillaume was also the first to exhibit, sell, and establish a market for African art. While other merchants of the time would discover African sculpture through their interest in modern art, for Guillaume it was the other way round. As emphasized by Yaëlle Biro, African art was the trigger in his career.[41]

Of a modest background and fatherless since an early age, Guillaume was working in a luxury car garage on the avenue de la Grande Armée when his first fortuitous encounter with an African sculpture happened, as recounted by his biographer Sylphide de Daranyi. The manufacture of tires required rubber, imported at the time from the French colonies in Africa. It is likely that Guillaume discovered African objects added to the caoutchouc chests. Deeply impressed, he placed some of them in the garage window, where they caught the attention of Guillaume Apollinaire (1880–1918). Curious, the poet and avant-garde promoter entered the garage and spoke to Guillaume. A friendship soon developed, and Apollinaire introduced Guillaume to the artistic circles of Paris, acting as his mentor.[42]

Guillaume opened his first gallery in February 1914 on the rue de Miromesnil, with a selection of works by Francis Picabia (1879–1953), Giorgio de Chirico (1888–1978), and Pierre Roy (1880–1950), together with a group of African sculptures. Presenting contemporary art with African sculptures was an absolute novelty, and it would remain a feature that accompanied Guillaume's whole exhibition activity.

It is important to remember, though, as Biro has pointed out, that Guillaume's admiration for and commitment to African art were stained by the weight of history, linked to a colonized Africa from which objects were extracted in an often violent context. Guillaume addressed the colonial administrators directly with publications and articles in specialized magazines, asking them to refer works to him. Furthermore, if the role of African sculpture was fundamental in the renewed language of European avant-garde artists at the beginning of the twentieth century, their approach was indeed purely aesthetic, concentrated on the forms of the objects and never interested in who made them or in their intended cultural uses.[43]

World War I pushed Guillaume to explore new business opportunities by establishing a collaboration with the Mexican artist and dealer Marius de Zayas in New York. Guillaume entrusted him with fifteen sculptures from Gabon and Côte d'Ivoire (Ivory Coast), to be presented at Alfred Stieglitz's gallery, commonly known as 291 from its address on Fifth Avenue, in the fall of 1914 under the title *Statuary in Wood by African Savages: The Root of Modern Art*.[44]

In 1918 in Paris, Guillaume mounted the exhibition *Matisse et Picasso*, which

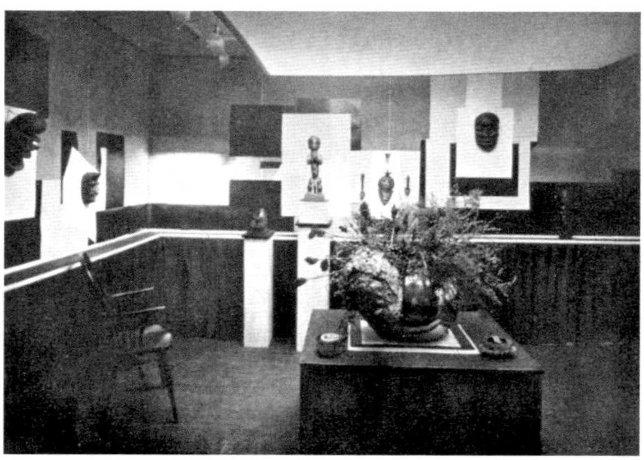

Edward Steichen, installation view, *Statuary in Wood by African Savages: The Root of Modern Art*, 291, New York, November 3–December 8, 1914

paired the two giants of the avant-garde, although he never managed to represent either of them. In the same year, in collaboration with Apollinaire, the dealer launched his own magazine, *Les Arts à Paris*, which not only published a variety of essays on contemporary and African art but also became a tool to promote his artists.

Crucial for Guillaume's expansion in the United States was his association with Albert C. Barnes (1872–1951). After the collector's first purchase, which, according to Daranyi, was probably Soutine's *Le Pâtissier* (*The Pastry Chef*) (c. 1919),[45] an intense relationship between Guillaume and Barnes developed. The dealer would both sell works directly to Barnes from his inventory and act as his adviser—he introduced Barnes to African art—and broker, with an agreed commission of 5 percent on purchases from other dealers or collectors. The collaboration, which lasted seven years, was also cemented by common intellectual interests. For example, Guillaume published an essay by Barnes, "L'Art Nègre en Amerique," in the ninth issue of *Les Arts à Paris*. The breakup between dealer and collector in 1929 happened, Daranyi explains, because in also publishing Barnes's article "French Primitive Negro Sculpture," Guillaume modified and reworked Barnes's text, which the collector found outrageous and unacceptable.[46]

After Guillaume's death, his widow sold more than 200 works from his collection, including all the Cubist Picassos and the de Chiricos, Modigliani portraits, works by Matisse, and all the African art; the French state acquired a total of 146 works in 1959 and 1963, and they are now permanently at the Musée de l'Orangerie in Paris.

PAUL ROSENBERG AND GEORGES WILDENSTEIN: A NEW TAKE ON THE PROMOTION OF PICASSO

Kahnweiler's forced departure from Paris in 1914, with the consequent abrupt lack of representation for his artists, was just one of the dire repercussions of the outbreak of World War I on the artistic community. Most of the salons stopped operating, exhibition opportunities became rare, and the market in general weakened considerably. For Picasso, who had chosen to remain in the capital during the war years, Kahnweiler's absence forced him to seek out another dealer. After an unfruitful stint with Léonce Rosenberg, who was dedicated to the cause of Cubism but lacked effective salesmanship—despite his bold declaration to Picasso, "Together we will be invincible. You will be the creator, I will be the action"[47]—the artist decided in 1918 to ally himself with Léonce's brother Paul.

Children of the Impressionist and Post-Impressionist dealer Alexandre Rosenberg, Léonce (1879–1947) and Paul (1881–1959), after an apprenticeship with their father, had founded two distinct galleries in 1911. Avant-garde art, Cubism in particular, was the focus of Léonce's Galerie de l'Effort Moderne, while Paul's venue, on the elegant rue La Boétie, concentrated on more established and traditional art. Richardson claims that Picasso would have preferred to sign up with Vollard—who had closed his gallery in 1914—but recognizes that the artist's decision to appoint Paul Rosenberg as his representative was pragmatic, despite Rosenberg's lacking the distinctive qualities of Picasso's prewar dealer, Kahnweiler. Rosenberg proved to be an immensely successful dealer, wholly dedicated to the art market, tirelessly industrious, driven by profit, and deeply loyal to his artists—as long as their work sold well.[48]

The new alliance was a strategic change for Picasso. Until the meeting with him, Rosenberg had promoted and sold recognized masters of the past, such as Jean-Auguste-Dominique Ingres (1780–1867), Jean-Baptiste-Camille Corot (1796–1875), and Eugène Delacroix (1798–1863). Therefore, while Picasso represented for the dealer the challenge of expanding his market into the contemporary field, for Picasso the association meant being shown side by side with major earlier artists. "It was Paul's mission to move Picasso from his position in the avant-garde to that of a master of modern painting," writes Anne Sinclair, Rosenberg's granddaughter.[49] Picasso's transition from the militant intellectual Kahnweiler, a champion of Cubism—the most revolutionary art movement of the early twentieth century—to Rosenberg coincided with a dramatic shift in his artistic direction. Picasso was moving away from Cubism to explore classicism and figuration, and in Rosenberg he found a dealer who both understood and supported his evolving artistic vision. The agreement between Picasso and Rosenberg also included collaboration with the New York–based gallerist Georges Wildenstein (1892–1963). Sinclair observes that Rosenberg quickly developed a strong belief that the United States would surpass Europe in both the art market and cultural excitement. Beginning in 1922, he therefore dedicated himself to awakening Americans to the exhilaration of modern art.[50] This resulted in the strategic alliance with Wildenstein in New York.

For his first exhibition at the Rosenberg gallery in Paris, in the fall of 1919, Picasso selected classicist-style drawings and watercolors: harlequins, circuses, bullfights, landscapes, still lifes. The critics and public responded positively.

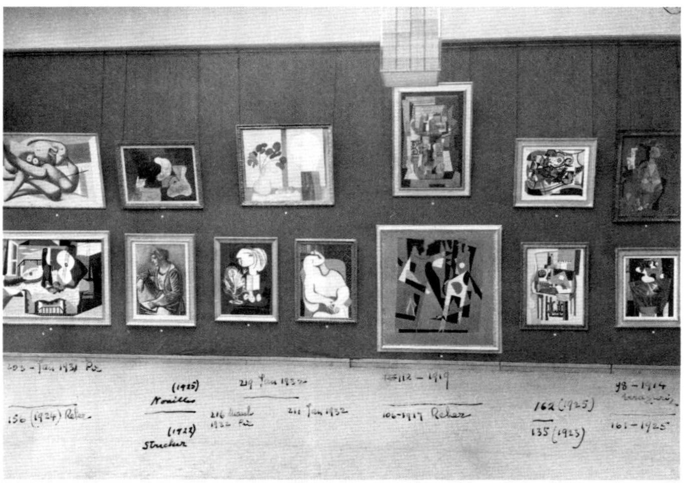

Installation view, *Exposition Picasso*, Galeries Georges Petit, Paris, June 16–July 30, 1932. Photograph annotated by Margaret Scolari Barr and Alfred H. Barr, Jr. Museum of Modern Art Archives, New York

Wildenstein's first Picasso presentation in New York opened on November 17, 1923, and was a critical, public, and market success; it then traveled in December to the Arts Club of Chicago.

The collaboration between Picasso and Rosenberg, which lasted until the outbreak of World War II, would prove to be extremely profitable, and it consolidated the artist's market internationally.

Its coronation was the 1932 retrospective held at the Galeries Georges Petit—whose spaces after the owner's financial decline and death had been taken over by a consortium of dealers. With 225 paintings, 7 sculptures, and 6 illustrated books, the exhibition was the first complete display of Picasso's developments from 1900 on. It was Picasso himself, Richardson noted, who had insisted on a full-scale retrospective, and on control over the selection and the catalogue. *Les Demoiselles d'Avignon* was missing, though, and no loan from the Shchukin or Morozov collection was possible as they had been nationalized by the Soviet government in Russia. Nothing was officially for sale, but at least one-third of the loans were available at the right price, according to Richardson, who also remarks that the vernissage, which Picasso deserted, was a mundane success.[51] After Paris, the exhibition traveled to the Kunsthaus in Zurich.

The year 1932 saw another cornerstone in Picasso's promotion: publication of the first volume of the artist's catalogue raisonné by Christian Zervos (1889–1970). A Greek émigré living in Paris, Zervos had launched *Cahiers d'art*, an art and literary journal, in 1926; it was followed by monographs dedicated to contemporary living masters. Called *Les Maîtres de la peinture contemporaine* (Masters of Contemporary Painting), they would feature Picasso, Léger, Henri Rousseau (1844–1910), and Raoul Dufy (1877–1953).

SERGEI SHCHUKIN AND THE MOROZOV BROTHERS

Two of the most remarkable collections of Impressionist and Post-Impressionist art—each comprising more than two hundred works—were put together by the Moscow textile industrialists Sergei Shchukin and the brothers Mikhail and Ivan Morozov.

Belonging to a solid and active group of international buyers gravitating to Paris, Shchukin and the Morozovs were the product of a renovated Moscow society, as Anna Poznanskaya and Alexey Petukhov point out. During the final third of the nineteenth century, the city had become a major center of industrial and cultural innovation, with the trading and industrial elites forging firm bonds with modern European culture.[52] A precursor to the two collectors' interest in Western art was the establishment in 1892 of the Moscow City Gallery of Pavel and Sergei Tretyakov, now the State Tretyakov Gallery in Moscow.

Shchukin (1854–1936) built his collection between 1897 and 1917, for a total of 258 paintings, acquiring them from all the major Parisian dealers, with whom he developed strong ties. Durand-Ruel nurtured Shchukin's initial passion for Claude Monet, whereas through Vollard and later Kahnweiler, Shchukin extended his interests and acquisitions to Degas, Cézanne, Van Gogh, Gauguin, and Picasso, whom he met in 1908. Inspired by Gertrude and Leo Stein, whose Parisian apartment he frequented and from whom he purchased Picasso's *Three Women*, Shchukin decided to open his Moscow mansion, the Trubetskoy Palace, to the public one day a week. It was there that a young generation of Russian artists, among them Kazimir Malevich, Alexander Rodchenko, and Mikhail Larionov, were exposed for the first time to the achievements of the French avant-garde.

Mikhail Morozov (1870–1903), a generation younger than Shchukin, initiated his family's collection. After his premature death at the age of thirty-three, the task was carried forward by his brother Ivan (1871–1921), whose first purchase was Alfred Sisley's *Frost at Louveciennes* (c. 1874).

Anne Baldassari curated the *Icons of Modern Art* exhibitions for the Fondation Louis Vuitton in Paris, featuring in two separate displays the collections of Sergei Shchukin (2016–17) and the Morozov brothers (2021–22). For the first time, these gatherings of exceptional art were seen in their entirety, attesting to the pioneering vision of their founders. Ivan Morozov and Shchukin shared a dream of creating an ideal museum of French art in Moscow, and they often coordinated their acquisitions. For instance, while Shchukin owned fifty-four works by Picasso, Morozov deliberately acquired only three, including the famous portrait of Vollard. Not only are the depth and vastness of the two Russian collections remarkable, but so are the passion and involvement of their creators with living artists. In 1909, Shchukin commissioned Matisse to create *The Dance* and *The Music* for his Moscow residence; for the installation, the artist traveled to Moscow. Similarly, Pierre Bonnard (1867–1947) painted the monumental canvases of the *Four Seasons* for Ivan Morozov's palace in 1910–12.

After the 1917 Russian Revolution, the Soviet government confiscated both Shchukin's and Morozov's artworks. They would eventually (in 1948) be split between the Pushkin State Museum of Fine Arts in Moscow and the Hermitage in St. Petersburg, where they still are.

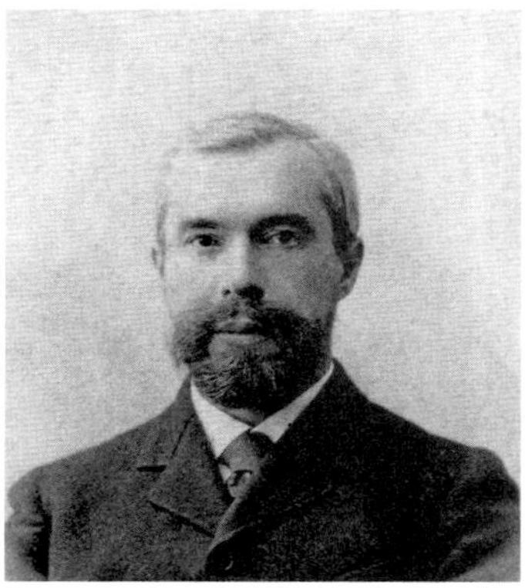

Sergei Shchukin, c. 1890

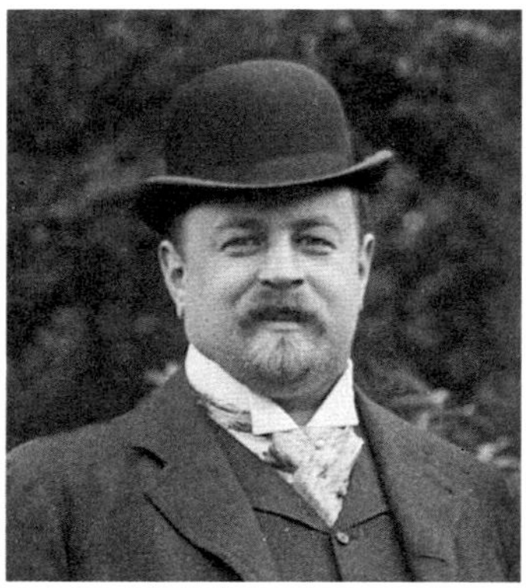

Ivan Abramovich Morozov, c. 1908

PICASSO AND AMERICA

While the alliance between Paul Rosenberg and Georges Wildenstein would be crucial for promoting Picasso in the United States, the artist was not previously entirely unknown in the country. Occasional presentations in small galleries and the interest of a few early collectors had already garnered some attention for his work.

Alfred Stieglitz (1864–1946), the photographer and founder of the legendary gallery 291 in New York, had introduced Picasso's work to America in March 1911, showing eighty-three drawings and watercolors. According to Richardson, only one drawing found a buyer.[53] He was Hamilton Easter Field (1873–1922), collector, artist, and art critic, who had previously met Picasso in Paris and would soon commission him to create eleven panels for his library in Brooklyn. Anna Jozefacka emphasizes in her catalogue for a 2023–24 Metropolitan Museum of Art exhibition, which introduced the library project to the public for the first time, that the commission challenged the artist to transcend easel painting and create a cohesive ensemble of individual Cubist works, envisioned as an all-encompassing aesthetic whole. Furthermore, the project would have allowed Picasso to branch out into private decorative commissions, thus gaining independence from his dealers.[54] The artist never completed the commission, though, and its story was forgotten for decades.

In the 1913 Armory Show in New York, which offered a comprehensive survey of European modernism and profoundly impacted a wider audience, Picasso was represented by eight works. In the winter of 1915, Stieglitz organized a second exhibition dedicated to Picasso, also featuring paintings by Braque alongside Mexican pottery. In between these two exhibitions, as previously mentioned, Kahnweiler had initiated a collaboration with the Washington Square Gallery in 1914 to promote Picasso and Cubism. However, this partnership was cut short by the outbreak of World War I before it could demonstrate its potential.

It was the indefatigable promotion of the Museum of Modern Art in New York, and in particular its first director, Alfred H. Barr Jr., that broadened the acceptance and understanding of Picasso and modernism on a larger scale in the United States. At the time of the museum's founding in 1929, on the initiative of three visionary women—Abby Aldrich Rockefeller (1874–1948), Lillie P. Bliss (1864–1931), and Mary Quinn Sullivan (1877–1939)—modern art was known to only a few wealthy collectors, as remarked by Alice Goldfarb Marquis, and the general public ignored even the notion of it.[55] Among these collectors were Maud and Chester Dale and John Quinn in New York, Louise and Walter Arensberg and Albert C. Barnes in Philadelphia, Claribel and Etta Cone in Baltimore, and John Spaulding in Boston. As a young professor at Wellesley College, where he taught the first course in America on twentieth-century art to the women-only student body, Barr had dedicated himself to educating the public about the essence and significance of modern art. With the fervor of a missionary, he pursued his objective as director of MoMA, conceiving the museum as a laboratory, innovatively structured in different departments ranging from visual arts to architecture, design, and film. Besides the creation of a permanent collection through acquisitions and donations, cornerstones of Barr's program were groundbreaking exhibitions dedicated to modern masters and movements, such as the Matisse retrospective in 1931, Van Gogh's in 1935–36, *Cubism and Abstract Art* in 1936, and *Fantastic Art, Dada, Surrealism* in 1936–37. These shows were far more ambitious than anything presented in Europe. Furthermore, they

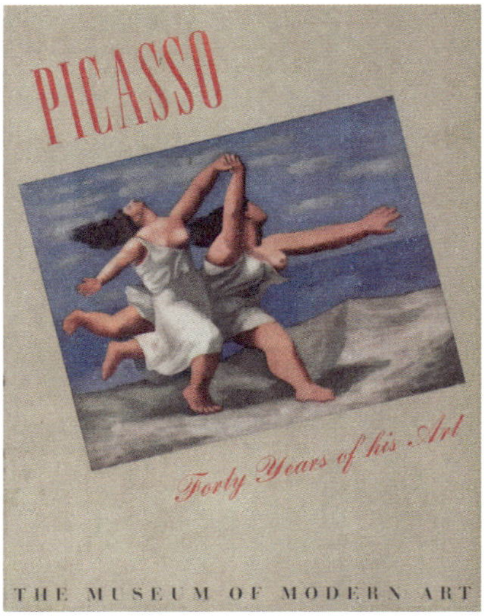

Cover of the catalogue for the 1939–40 Museum of Modern Art exhibition *Picasso: Forty Years of His Art*

helped shape the very idea of modernism and its development, as observed by Marquis.[56]

The first paintings by Picasso to enter the museum's collection were through the bequest of Lillie P. Bliss in 1934. Four years later, Barr was able to buy the masterpiece *Girl before a Mirror* (1932), followed in 1939 by the landmark *Les Demoiselles d'Avignon* from three decades earlier.

From late 1939, MoMA, which was called by its enemies a "Picasso museum,"[57] also benefited from the presence of the artist's masterpiece *Guernica* (1937), though it traveled extensively in the United States and Europe until 1956. Commissioned by the Spanish Republic for its pavilion in the 1937 Exposition internationale des arts et techniques dans la vie moderne (International Exposition of Arts and Techniques in Modern Life) in Paris, the monumental painting commemorated the brutal bombing of the Basque town of Guernica, perpetuated by German allies of Generalísimo Francisco Franco during the Spanish Civil War. Picasso had pledged that *Guernica*, a symbol of freedom and pacifism, should not return to Spain until a democratic government was restored. Only in 1981 was *Guernica* permanently moved to Madrid, where it has been at the Museo Nacional Centro de Arte Reina Sofía since 1992.

Barr's ultimate ambition was to mount the most comprehensive Picasso retrospective ever seen. It would be *Picasso: Forty Years of His Art*, which opened at the Museum of Modern Art on November 15, 1939, not long after Europe's entry into the most devastating conflict in its history. The museum's press release stated that the exhibition was "six months in the making," but FitzGerald reports that, in fact, Barr had pursued it for almost a decade with unwavering determination.[58] Several obstacles forced the postponement of the project, including the lack of support from

Rosenberg and Picasso himself. As Hugh Eakin explains, Rosenberg, in theory, should have embraced Barr's Picasso project. After all, he had been striving for nearly a decade to send the artist's work across the Atlantic to prominent American museums. However, by the time the project was taking shape, Rosenberg had shifted his focus away from the United States. His attention was now firmly fixed on his life in Paris, where his endeavors had become remarkably lucrative.[59] Preparations for Picasso's first retrospective, at the Galeries Georges Petit in 1932, had also absorbed the artist's and Rosenberg's interests and efforts until then. After that, obtaining loans from Europe had become increasingly difficult, if not impossible. Italy, Germany, and then Spain were in the clutches of fascist dictators; in addition, the Soviet government in Russia had confiscated Shchukin's and Morozov's collections.

Despite the organizational difficulties, *Picasso: Forty Years of His Art*, with more than 350 paintings, drawings, prints, and sculptures, was the biggest and most influential display of the artist's production ever put together. The press release counted forty-four American private lenders and eighteen museums providing about 145 works, while the rest came from European lenders, including 95 from Picasso himself. By the time it closed on January 7, 1940, before moving to the Art Institute of Chicago for about a month, attendance totaled 100,670 visitors, exceeded only by MoMA's Van Gogh retrospective, which—a press release noted—was open six days longer, among other factors.

FitzGerald points out that the retrospective also established a model for all blockbuster shows to come, while offering Barr's own interpretation of Picasso's career, which highlighted the achievements of Cubism, linking *Les Demoiselles d'Avignon* to *Guernica*, and de-emphasized classicism and the Rose and Blue periods.[60]

THE BARNES COLLECTION IN PHILADELPHIA

The Barnes Collection contains 181 Renoirs; 69 Cézannes, including *Boy in a Red Vest* (1888–90); 59 Matisses; 46 Picassos, including *The Ascetic* (1903) from his Blue Period and the Rose Period masterpiece *Acrobat and Young Harlequin* (1905); more than 50 Soutines, including *The Pastry Chef*; Modigliani nudes; metaphysical paintings by de Chirico; El Greco's *Apparition of the Virgin and Child to Saint Hyacinth* (c. 1605–10)—and also Tang dynasty and African sculptures, as well as so much more.

It is not only the staggering quantity and quality that make the Barnes Collection unique, but the very concept it was founded on: to be an educational center, not a museum. Its creator was Albert C. Barnes from Philadelphia. Of modest origins—his father was a butcher—Barnes went to the prestigious Central High School on a scholarship; there he met William James Glackens (1870–1938), an artist who would play an important role in introducing him to collecting. A graduate of the medical school at the University of Pennsylvania, Barnes practiced the profession only briefly. In 1899, he and the German chemist Hermann Hille invented Argyrol, a silver nitrate antiseptic drug used to prevent or treat eye infections, including those in newborns caused by gonorrhea. The resulting

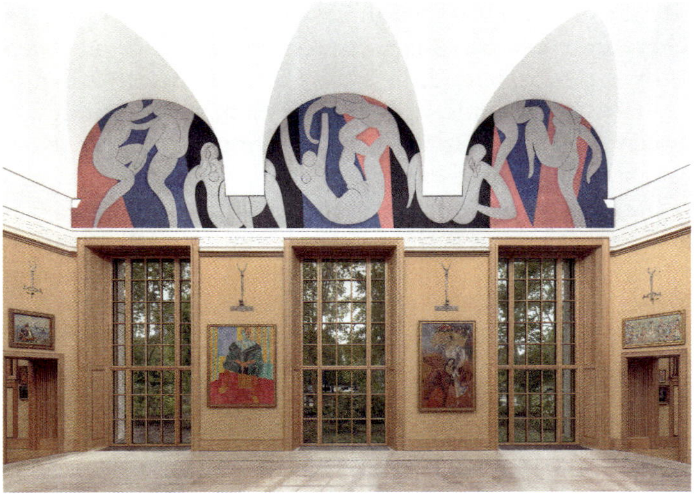

The main room of the Barnes Collection, Marion, Pennsylvania, 2006. Installation view, featuring Henri Matisse's *The Dance* (1932–33) and *Seated Riffian* (*Le Rifain assis*) (1912), and Pablo Picasso's *Composition: The Peasants* (1906)

economic success—in 1907, Barnes made his first million dollars—provided him with the capital to start buying art. For his first purchases, Barnes instructed Glackens in early 1912 to travel to Paris on his behalf. Glackens came back with a trove of thirty-two paintings, watercolors, and prints, including Cézanne's *Toward Mont Sainte-Victoire* (1878–79), Picasso's *Young Woman Holding a Cigarette* (1901), and Van Gogh's *The Postman* (1889).[61]

Later, Barnes himself would visit the French capital, meeting the Steins at the end of 1912 and purchasing from them Matisse's Fauvist *Le Bonheur de vivre*. Introduced to Durand-Ruel and Vollard, he was quickly one of their major buyers. Guillaume became Barnes's trusted adviser soon after they met and initiated him into an appreciation of African sculpture and the artists Soutine and Modigliani, by whom he would purchase numerous and exceptional works.

Snubbed by the Philadelphia cultural circles and dismissed as an eccentric misanthropist, Barnes—for whom art had become his life's main interest and passion—decided to turn his collection into a foundation. Housed in a nineteenth-century mansion in Merion, a suburb of Philadelphia, the foundation opened in 1925, with strict and unusual regulations. It did not have the status of a museum, so access had to be requested with a letter of motivation—and was not guaranteed; reproduction of images of the artworks was not allowed, and neither were loans.

In 1930, Barnes commissioned Matisse to paint *The Dance* (1932–33) for three lunettes in the foundation's main room. Barnes already owned forty-seven paintings by Matisse, and he would continue to buy more.

Upon Barnes's sudden death in a car accident in 1951, his will dictated that the works in the foundation would not be physically moved from the display he had conceived, which was informed by his personal aesthetic and thematic resonances, not by art movements or chronological order.

However, serious financial problems and controversial judicial vicissitudes eventually led to the decision—which split public opinion and triggered a heated debate—to move the foundation from Merion to the center of Philadelphia. The new headquarters, opened in 2012 and designed by the architects Tod Williams and Billie Tsien, respects the original location of the works in the Barnes residence, but displays them in more airy and accessible spaces.

In July 2023, a Pennsylvania judge also ruled in favor of allowing selected works from the collection to be loaned to other institutions—until then, the collection had traveled only once, to seven far-flung venues in 1993–95, to raise funds for the Barnes Foundation while the Merion galleries were closed for renovation.

NOTES

1 Christel H. Force, introduction to *Pioneers of the Global Art Market: Paris-Based Dealer Networks, 1850–1950*, ed. Christel H. Force (London: Bloomsbury Visual Arts, 2020), 1.

2 Force, *Pioneers of the Global Art Market*, 6–7.

3 Ambroise Vollard, *Recollections of a Picture Dealer*, trans. Violet M. MacDonald (1936; repr., Mineola, NY: Dover Publications, 2003), 60.

4 James Stourton, *Rogues and Scholars: A History of the London Art World, 1945–2000* (New York: Pegasus Books, 2025), 22.

5 Ann Dumas, "Ambroise Vollard, Patron of the Avant-Garde," in *Cézanne to Picasso: Ambroise Vollard, Patron of the Avant-Garde*, ed. Rebecca A. Rabinow, exh. cat. (New York: Metropolitan Museum of Art, 2006), 9.

6 Dumas, "Ambroise Vollard," 9, 12.

7 Vollard, *Recollections of a Picture Dealer*, 145.

8 Isabelle Cahn, *Vollard: Un marchant d'art et ses trésors* (Paris: Gallimard, 2007), 49.

9 Vollard, *Recollections of a Picture Dealer*, 62.

10 Hans Luijten, *Jo van Gogh-Bonger: The Woman Who Made Vincent Famous*, trans. Lynne Richards (London: Bloomsbury Visual Arts, 2022), 163.

11 Luijten, *Jo van Gogh-Bonger*, 3.

12 Bregje Gerritse and Sara Tas, "Les Premiers Signes de reconnaissance de l'artiste," in *Van Gogh à Auvers-sur-Oise: Les Derniers Mois*, exh. cat. (Paris: Éditions Hazan, 2023), 191.

13 Luijten, *Jo van Gogh-Bonger*, 150.

14 Marianne Le Morvan, *Berthe Weill, 1865–1951: La Petite Galeriste des grands artistes* (Paris: L'Écarlate, 2011), 20.

15 Douglas Druick, "Vollard and Gauguin: Fictions and Facts," in Rabinow, *Cézanne to Picasso*, 73.

16 Druick, "Vollard and Gauguin," 73.

17 Vollard, *Recollections of a Picture Dealer*, 219.

18 Michael C. FitzGerald, *Making Modernism: Picasso and the Creation of the Market for Twentieth-Century Art* (Berkeley: University of California Press, 1996), 28.

19 Vollard, *Recollections of a Picture Dealer*, 220.

20 John Richardson, *A Life of Picasso*, vol. 1, *1881–1906*, with the collaboration of Marilyn McCully (New York: Random House, 1991), 199.

21 FitzGerald, *Making Modernism*, 23.

22 Gary Tinterow, "Vollard and Picasso," in Rabinow, *Cézanne to Picasso*, 101.

23 Emily Braun, "Saturday Evenings at the Steins," in *The Steins Collect: Matisse, Picasso, and the Parisian Avant-Garde*, ed. Janet Bishop, Cecile Debray, and Rebecca Rabinow, exh. cat. (San Francisco: San Francisco Museum of Modern Art, 2011), 49.

24 Rebecca Rabinow. "Discovering Modern Art: The Steins' Early Years in Paris, 1903–1907," in *The Steins Collect*, 21.

25 Rabinow, "Discovering Modern Art," 32.

26 Leo Stein to Mabel Weeks, November 29, 1905, box 3, folder 52, YCAL MSS 78, Beinecke Rare Book and Manuscript Library, Yale University.

27 Sebastian Smee, *Side by Side: Picasso v. Matisse* (Potts Point, Australia: Duffy & Snellgrove, 2002), 20.

28 FitzGerald, *Making Modernism*, 29–30.

29 William Rubin, *Picasso and Braque: Pioneering Cubism* (New York: Museum of Modern Art, 1989), 348. In another version Rubin mentions right after, Kahnweiler recalled Braque saying, "It is as if someone had drunk kerosene to spit fire."

30 Richardson, *Life of Picasso*, 3:244.

31 Hélène Klein, "Gertrude Stein and Pablo Picasso: In Their Own Words," in *The Steins Collect*, 49, 244.

32 Arnold Rönnebeck, "Gertrude Was Always Giggling," *Books Abroad* (Board of Regents of the University of Oklahoma) 19, no. 1 (Winter 1945): 3.

33 John Richardson, *A Life of Picasso*, vol. 3, *The Triumphant Years, 1917–1932*, with the collaboration of Marilyn McCully (New York: Alfred A. Knopf, 2007), 107–8.

34 Pierre Assouline, *An Artful Life: A Biography of D. H. Kahnweiler, 1884–1979*, trans. Charles Ruas (New York: Grove Weidenfeld, 1990), 97.

35 Vérane Tasseau, "Daniel-Henry Kahnweiler's International Partnerships, 1907–1937," trans. Celia Abele, in Force, *Pioneers of the Global Art Market*, 75–80.

36 John Richardson, *A Life of Picasso*, vol. 2, *1907–1917: The Painter of Modern Life*, with the collaboration of Marilyn McCully (New York: Random House, 1996), 325.

37 Tasseau, "Kahnweiler's International Partnerships," 76–80.

38 Richardson, *Life of Picasso,* 2:345.

39 Judith Benhamou, "L'Opération 'La Peau de l'Ours' ou les grands débuts de la spéculation dans l'art moderne," in *Histoires extraordinaires de l'art à l'hôtel Drouot: De Vermeer à Louise Bourgeois* (Paris: Flammarion, 2023), 137–38.

40 FitzGerald, *Making Modernism*, 40.

41 Yaëlle Biro, "Amedeo Modigliani, Paul Guillaume et les arts de l'Afrique," in *Modigliani: Un peintre et son marchand*, ed. Simonetta Fraquelli and Cécile Girardeau (Paris: Flammarion, 2023), 49.

42 Sylphide de Daranyi, *Paul Guillaume: Marchand d'art et collectionneur (1891–1934)* (Paris: Flammarion, 2023), 14–15.

43 Biro, "Amedeo Modigliani, Paul Guillaume," 49–51.

44 Daranyi, *Paul Guillaume*, 38–39.

45 Daranyi, *Paul Guillaume*, 102.

46 Daranyi, *Paul Guillaume*, 193–94.

47 FitzGerald, *Making Modernism*, 66.

48 Richardson, *Life of Picasso*, 3:107–8.

49 Anne Sinclair, *My Grandfather's Gallery: A Family Memoir of Art and War*, trans. Shaun Whiteside (New York: Farrar, Straus and Giroux, 2014), 112.

50 Sinclair, *My Grandfather's Gallery*, 72.

51 Richardson, *Life of Picasso,* 3:475–79.

52 Anna Poznanskaya and Alexey Petukhov, "Sergei Shchukin: an Outstanding Muscovite Collector," in *Icons of Modern Art*, ed. Anne Baldassari, exh. cat. (Paris: Gallimard, 2016), 44.

53 Richardson, *Life of Picasso,* 3:312.

54 Anna Jozefacka, *Picasso: A Cubist Commission in Brooklyn*, with Lauren Rosati, exh. cat. (New York: Metropolitan Museum of Art, 2023), 11–15.

55 Alice Goldfarb Marquis, *Alfred H. Barr Jr.: Missionary for the Modern* (Chicago: Contemporary Books, 1989), 1.

56 Marquis, *Alfred H. Barr Jr.*, 149.

57 Sybil Gordon Kantor, *Alfred H. Barr, Jr. and the Intellectual Origins of the Museum of Modern Art* (Cambridge, MA: MIT Press, 2002), 241.

58 FitzGerald, *Making Modernism*, 245.

59 Hugh Eakin, *Picasso's War: How Modern Art Came to America* (New York: Crown, 2022), 227.

60 FitzGerald, *Making Modernism*, 261.

61 Judith F. Dolkart and Martha Lucy, *Masterworks: The Barnes Foundation* (New York: Skira Rizzoli, 2012), 11.

7. New York Stories I: The Triumph of Abstract Expressionism

p. 143
The Dawn of the American Art Scene

p. 145
The Great Depression and the Federal Art Project

p. 147
Abstract Expressionism Takes Shape

p. 150
Peggy Guggenheim

p. 151
Promoting the New Art

p. 156
Mark Rothko's Commissions

p. 157
Clement Greenberg and Harold Rosenberg: The Militant Critics

p. 158
Institutional Recognition

p. 160
The Irascibles

p. 161
Women of the Abstract Expressionist Era

p. 165
American Artists in Postwar France

The decades following World War II were unique in the history of American art. . . . Beginning with Abstract Expressionism, New York City became the acknowledged center of the avant-garde art world, disseminating styles that were widely imitated by foreign artists and producing artworks that were purchased in substantial numbers by foreign collectors and museums.

—Diana Crane, introduction to *The Transformation of the Avant-Garde*

After World War II, New York emerged as the epicenter of the international Western art world, supplanting Paris. This shift was marked by the rise of Abstract Expressionism, a revolutionary and distinctly American style pioneered by a young generation of artists who matured during the Great Depression of the 1930s. Drawing inspiration from various sources, including earlier European movements—particularly Surrealism—as well as Mexican Muralism and Native American art, the Abstract Expressionists created an innovative artistic language that marked a radical new beginning, liberating American art from its subservience to the Old World.

The rise and ultimate success of Abstract Expressionism were driven by the unwavering efforts of influential gallerists such as Peggy Guggenheim, Betty Parsons, Charles Egan, and Sidney Janis, alongside the critical voices of Clement Greenberg and Harold Rosenberg. The Museum of Modern Art, under the visionary leadership of director Alfred H. Barr Jr. and curator Dorothy C. Miller, contributed significantly to the promotion of the movement, in the forms of early acquisitions for its collection and inclusion of the new artists in seminal group exhibitions.

Despite the very important participation of women in the birth and development of Abstract Expressionism, critical recognition of them has occurred only recently. The narrative that traditionally identified the movement as white and male is finally being revised, leading to a dramatic increase in the market value of female artists from that era.

THE DAWN OF THE AMERICAN ART SCENE

The quest for a national identity had always been intertwined with the artistic production of the young American nation as it struggled to break free from European models. The Hudson River School (1825–70), epitomized by Thomas Cole (1801–1848), captured the essence of American identity through the sublime beauty of the vast, untouched landscape. A few decades later, Thomas Eakins (1844–1916) pioneered a realistic style, focusing his keen eye on advancements in science, as evidenced by his masterpieces depicting surgical operations, *The Gross Clinic* (1875) and *The Agnew Clinic* (1889).

James McNeill Whistler (1834–1903), Mary Cassatt (1844–1926), and John Singer Sargent (1856–1925) spent much of their lives in Europe, immersing themselves in, and contributing to, the Parisian avant-garde. Whistler's *Symphony in White, No. 1: The White Girl* (1861–62) was shown at the 1863 Salon des Refusés in Paris, and Cassatt participated in several of the major Impressionist exhibitions (see "Paul Durand-Ruel and the Birth of the Impressionist Market," p. 94). Sargent, one of the most sought-after portraitists of his time, captured the elegance and character of his subjects with striking realism and luminous brushstrokes, influenced by the Impressionists' technique.

Art had been produced in America long before the Europeans' arrival, by the Indigenous populations. However, the diversity and richness of their achievements were never considered part of the national identity, much like the Native Americans themselves, who were denied US citizenship until 1924.

Similarly, the artistic contributions of people of African descent, who had been creatively active for hundreds of years despite the appalling conditions of slavery and segregation, were generally ignored or marginalized. Robert S. Duncanson (c. 1821–1872), Henry Ossawa Tanner (1859–1937), and Edmonia Lewis (1844–1907) were among the few who achieved significant recognition as artists during their lifetimes. Duncanson, despite lacking formal training, infused his landscapes with Romantic inspiration and mythological references. Tanner, who studied in Paris at the renowned Académie Julian, developed a distinctive style that incorporated the innovations of the French avant-garde. Lewis, who was born near Albany, New York, to a mixed Black and Ojibwe Indian mother and an African American father, and grew up near Niagara Falls after being orphaned at about nine, was one of the first acknowledged American women sculptors. After studying in Boston, she moved to Italy in 1865 and established a thriving practice in Rome the following year. Decades later, the artists of the Harlem Renaissance (see "New York Stories II," p. 168) forged a unique visual language that delved into the origins of their identity, blending African influences with aspects of everyday Black life. Despite their inventive creations, they faced substantial neglect from both art institutions and the market.

As for white American artists, they were trained primarily in England during the colonial period. Formal art education became available not long after the establishment of the nation. In the early nineteenth century, the first academies were founded in New York and Philadelphia.[1] Art museums also opened during the century—among them, the New-York Historical Society in 1804, as a repository of books and documents as well as art; the Wadsworth Atheneum in Hartford, Connecticut, in 1842; and the Metropolitan Museum of Art, founded in New York in 1870 and open to the public two years later.

Slowly, a New York gallery scene began to emerge. A few years after the success of his two temporary Impressionist exhibitions in New York in 1886 and 1887, the dealer Paul Durand-Ruel (1831–1922) established a permanent presence in the city (see "Paul Durand-Ruel and the Birth of the Impressionist Market," p. 94). Alfred Stieglitz (1864–1946) opened the Little Galleries of the Photo-Secession in 1905; known as 291 after its Fifth

Avenue address, it was the first venue—and for many years, the only one—where visitors could see the work of Paul Cézanne (1839–1906), Auguste Rodin (1840–1917), Henri de Toulouse-Lautrec (1864–1901), Georges Braque (1882–1963), Pablo Picasso (1881–1973), and Henri Matisse (1869–1954), along with that of young American artists such as Georgia O'Keeffe (1887–1986), John Marin (1870–1953), and Arthur Dove (1880–1946).

In February and March 1913, the *International Exhibition of Modern Art* at the 69th Regiment Armory in New York—commonly known as the Armory Show—presented, for the first time, a comprehensive survey of European modernism to a broad American audience, including former president Theodore Roosevelt, who was among its 87,000 visitors. The exhibition featured 1,300 works by 300 artists, about one-third of them Europeans, from the Neoclassical master Jean-Auguste-Dominique Ingres (1780–1867) to Cubists Picasso and Braque. Despite mixed reactions ranging from outrage to enthusiasm, 174 works were sold (123 by Europeans and 51 by Americans) by the time the exhibition ended following different versions in Chicago and Boston, signifying a definitive turning point in American art history.

The Downtown Gallery, which Edith Halpert (1900–1970) opened in New York's Greenwich Village in 1926, was the only commercial venue dedicated solely to promoting contemporary American artists then. A. Deirdre Robson highlights that Halpert's choice was both courageous and visionary. In the 1920s, institutional and market support for contemporary American art was rare, largely limited to a few private dealers, while New York's Metropolitan Museum of Art, the city's largest museum, staunchly resisted all forms of modern art.[2]

The Museum of Modern Art in New York, founded in 1929, would advocate for the cause of modernism, though it also perpetuated the notion that the forefront of avant-garde art was predominantly Europe. As World War II approached, American art continued to grapple with the challenge of gaining international recognition and asserting its independent voice. The domestic art market remained fragile, with American collectors focused on acquiring European artworks, often sourced directly from Paris. As Titia Hulst observes, despite the United States achieving economic dominance in the Western world before the war, its local primary art market was slow to develop. Wealthy Americans preferred purchasing art from Paris, just as they did their wines and gowns. This preference hindered the formation of a critical mass of artists and collectors necessary for an American cultural flourishing. However, the war brought dramatic changes.[3]

THE GREAT DEPRESSION AND THE FEDERAL ART PROJECT

The artists who would be called Abstract Expressionists shortly after World War II began their careers in the 1930s, primarily in New York City. Among them were European immigrants such as Arshile Gorky (1904–1948), Mark Rothko (1903–1970), and Willem de Kooning (1904–1997), as well as second-generation immigrants like Lee Krasner (1908–1984). Others hailed from various parts of the United States, including Jackson Pollock (1912–1956) from Wyoming and Clyfford Still (1904–1980) from North Dakota.

It was the time of the Great Depression, triggered by the Wall Street Crash of October 1929. The economic downturn left 25 percent of the American workforce unemployed[4] and caused the collapse of one-quarter of the nation's banks.

In 1935, the Democratic administration of President Franklin D. Roosevelt (1882–1945) established the Federal Art Project (FAP), part of the New Deal's Works Progress Administration (WPA), in order to provide employment to thousands of artists during the Great Depression. The initiative funded public murals, sculptures, and all kinds of other art, aiming to make it accessible to the public while supporting struggling artists across the United States.

More than one hundred community art centers were set up throughout the country, and around ten thousand artists were involved. Mary Gabriel highlights that the FAP not only kept painters, sculptors, and other artists alive, but also fostered a sense of community where none had existed before, enabling isolated artists to connect and interact. Moreover, it instilled a sense of self-worth, as the government recognized artists as individuals with valuable talents that could benefit society. Significantly, women also took part in the FAP, constituting one-fifth of the artists employed and receiving the same pay as men.[5]

Regional Realism was the predominant artistic movement during the Great Depression, evolving in response to the political isolation and also as a counterpoint to European modernism and abstraction. Artists

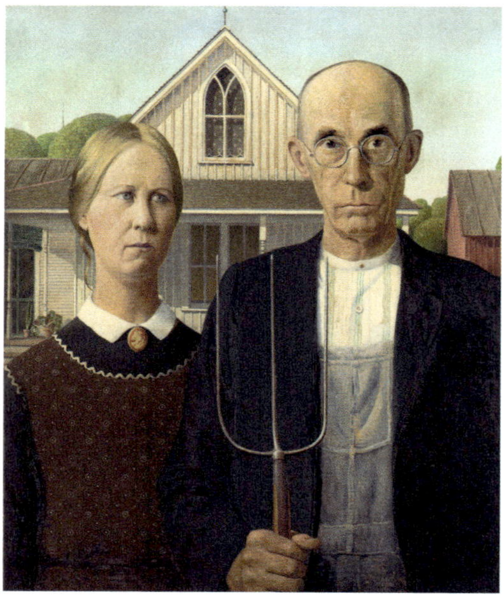

Grant Wood, *American Gothic*, 1930, Art Institute of Chicago

believed in their moral duty to society, expressed through a figurative and narrative style that celebrated American themes and values, often focusing on rural subjects. Thomas Hart Benton (1889–1975), who would teach Jackson Pollock at the Art Students League in New York, championed a return to an agrarian past perceived as authentically American; Grant Wood (1891–1942) portrayed the stern image of an Iowa farm couple in his iconic *American Gothic* (1930); Charles E. Burchfield (1893–1967) depicted both Midwestern landscapes and urban scenes.

Edward Hopper (1882–1967) captured the sense of alienation of the Great Depression, giving city and country scenes a haunting, introspective quality, in which light and shadow emphasize the emotional depth and solitude of his subjects. Georgia O'Keeffe explored natural forms, featuring large-scale, abstracted flowers, desert landscapes, and bones. She thus celebrated the beauty of the American Southwest, concentrating on organic shapes and vibrant colors, blending realism with abstraction, and expressing a deep connection to nature.

ABSTRACT EXPRESSIONISM TAKES SHAPE

Drawing inspiration from Mexican Muralism, Native American art, and European avant-garde movements, a new generation of American artists achieved maturity by the early 1940s, shaping their own distinctive and original artistic language.

Initially called "abstract Expressionism" by the writer and critic Robert Coates in a 1946 review of an exhibition by the German-born painter Hans Hofmann (1880–1966)[6]—and by others simply the "New York School," referring mainly to artists of the following decades—the style was elaborated by artists in the United States such as Pollock, Rothko, de Kooning, Gorky, Franz Kline (1910–1962), and Barnett Newman (1905–1970). There were talented women among the Abstract Expressionists—as part of the original group, Krasner and Elaine de Kooning (1918–1989); in the so-called second generation, Helen Frankenthaler (1928–2011), Joan Mitchell (1925–1992), and Grace Hartigan (1922–2008)—but they did not receive the recognition they deserved at the time. Similarly, Norman Lewis (1909–1979), the only African American in the first generation of the movement, saw his work overlooked by dealers and curators for decades.

The influence of Mexican Muralists on the abovementioned artists was highlighted by the Whitney Museum of American Art's 2020–21 exhibition *Vida Americana: Mexican Muralists Remake American Art, 1925–1945*. In Mexico, following the 1910–11 revolution that toppled the dictatorship of Porfirio Díaz and established a popular democracy (though armed conflict among different factions was continual until 1920), art assumed a vital role in educating the masses about the ideals of social justice. Starting in the early 1920s, the government commissioned José Clemente Orozco (1883–1949), Diego Rivera (1886–1957), and David Alfaro Siqueiros (1896–1974), among others, to create large murals. Named "Los Tres Grandes"

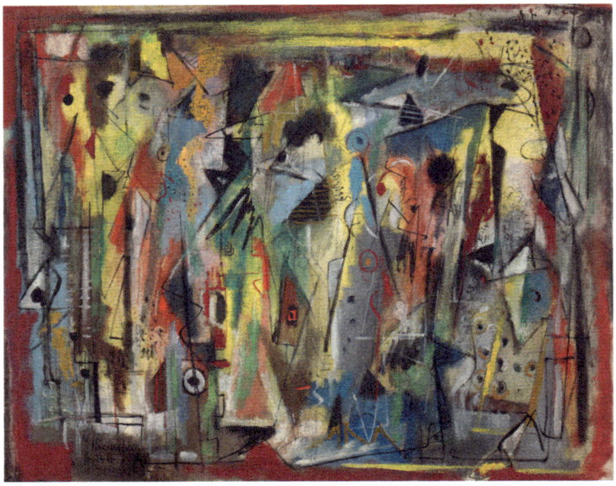

Norman Lewis, *Phantasy II*, 1946,
Museum of Modern Art, New York

(the Three Greats), the three painters were invited to the United States in the 1930s by various institutions, and the works they produced had a profound impact. For example, the young Pollock traveled with his brother to Pomona College in Claremont, California, to look at Orozco's *Prometheus* (1930). He also attended the Experimental Workshop near Union Square in New York, which Siqueiros founded in 1936. Believing that art should be revolutionary not only in its subjects but also in its materials and techniques, Siqueiros explored unconventional practices such as spraying, splattering, and pouring paint onto canvases placed on the floor.

The influx of intellectuals fleeing war-torn Europe, particularly Surrealists such as André Breton (1896–1966), Roberto Matta (1911–2002), Max Ernst (1891–1976), and Salvador Dalí (1904–1989), is often cited as a catalyst for the development of Abstract Expressionism. However, some scholars argue that their influence might have been overstated. Surrealist practices and theories—such as automatic writing and reliance on the unconscious mind in creation—were already familiar in New York during the 1930s. Solo exhibitions of Surrealists had been hosted by galleries like the eponymous Julien Levy and Pierre Matisse, and the Museum of Modern Art had presented the groundbreaking exhibition *Fantastic Art, Dada, Surrealism* in 1936–37. Additionally, the émigrés were not particularly friendly, according to Steven Naifeh and Gregory White Smith, and few American artists actually interacted with them.[7] Nevertheless, the European artists' arrival, as Deborah Solomon points out, coincided with a critical moment in American painting, when the political art of the 1930s had been abandoned, but a new style had not yet been found and defined.[8] The presence of the Surrealists in New York represented the final push for young artists toward liberation from existing rules and styles, including Surrealism itself.

Also profound in its influence on the younger generation of American artists was the Museum of Modern Art's 1941 exhibition *Indian Art of*

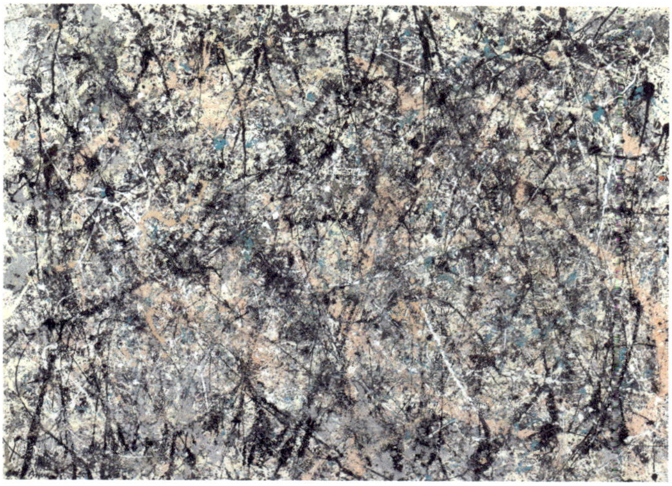

Jackson Pollock, *Number 1, 1950 (Lavender Mist)*, 1950, National Gallery of Art, Washington, DC

the United States. Presented for the first time to a broader audience, the bold, abstract forms and symbolic content of Native American art, with its rhythmic patterns, raw energy, and spiritual elements, encouraged the exploration of non-Western traditions, embracing emotion and ritual over traditional European influences.

Picasso's *Guernica* (1937)—on display at MoMA from 1939 to 1981, except when it traveled to other locations at various times until 1956—had a significant impact on the budding Abstract Expressionists. The painting's monumental scale, emotional power, and use of abstraction to convey political suffering deeply resonated with younger artists, inspiring the emergence of new forms of expression that emphasized spontaneity and intensity.

The horrors of World War II reinforced the belief among these artists that art needed to start from zero, demanding a revolutionary and uncharted approach to the canvas, unburdened by preconceived ideas. Painting evolved into a direct expression of the artist's emotions, with meaning emerging through the act of creation, engaging the entire body. Scale and gesture became central, leading to the development of the "allover composition" principle. Introduced by Clement Greenberg (1909–1994),[9] the definition indicated that the entire canvas—often of monumental dimensions—should be treated with equal importance, without one single focal point, and the paint applied uniformly across the surface to create a sense of continuous movement and space. Exemplified by Pollock's drip paintings, the allover composition rejected the traditional distinction between a clear foreground and background, instead emphasizing the process of painting itself, making every part of the canvas equally significant.

Having matured during the Great Depression and endured poverty and material hardships, the Abstract Expressionists saw themselves as

Collector, art lover, rebel, model of the liberated woman, black sheep of the Guggenheim family, savior of Abstract Expressionism, sexually outrageous: Peggy Guggenheim has triggered controversial reactions, and she still does. Several biographies have been dedicated to her, and she wrote her own story in 1946: *Out of This Century: Confessions of an Art Addict,* to scandalized reviews at the time.

Born in 1898 in New York into the wealthy Jewish Guggenheim family, she was the daughter of Benjamin Guggenheim, who died in the sinking of the *Titanic* in 1912 (his mistress, on board with him, survived), and his wife, Florette, from the even richer Seligman clan. Eccentricity and tragedy marked Peggy Guggenheim's life: besides the death of her father when she was a teenager, her beloved sister Benita and later her daughter Pegeen died prematurely. Guggenheim spent her youth in Europe and took part in the exuberant cultural life of Paris of the 1920s. She met intellectuals and artists, and she had affairs with many—the most famous of whom was the Irish-born playwright Samuel Beckett. She married twice: in 1922 to the artist Lawrence Vail (1891–1968), with whom she had a son and a daughter; and in 1941 to Max Ernst, who abandoned her for the painter Dorothea Tanning.

After opening the Guggenheim Jeune gallery in January 1938 on Cork Street in London's Mayfair district, where she exhibited works by many of her Surrealist friends, Guggenheim was planning to set up her own museum, but the war abruptly put an end to her project. The first winter of war was spent in Paris, where she compulsively added to her collection: "My motto was 'buy a picture a day,' and I lived up to it," she declared.[10] In 1941, being Jewish, she had to escape Europe; she went back to New York, shipping her collection along after the Musée du Louvre infamously refused to shelter it. Her New York gallery, Art of This Century, was fundamental in promoting the young American avant-garde. Guggenheim left New York in 1947 and settled in Venice, buying the Palazzo Venier dei Leoni on the Grand Canal, where she lived until her death in 1979 and is buried in the garden with her dogs. Her palazzo is now a museum, the Peggy Guggenheim Collection—the most visited one in Venice.

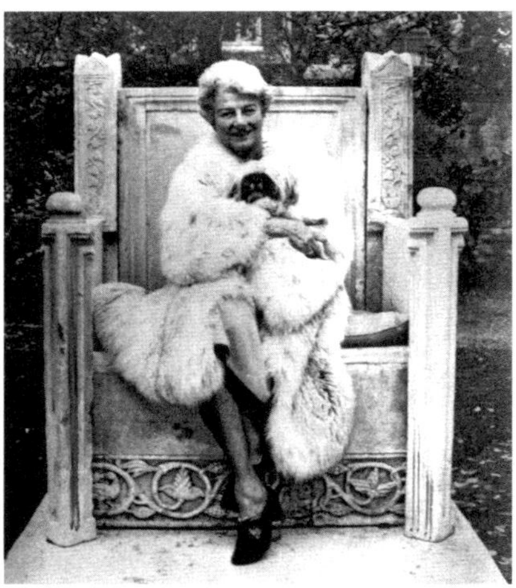

Peggy Guggenheim in her garden at the Palazzo Venier dei Leoni, Venice, 1978

outcasts and heroes in a perpetual struggle against society. They nurtured a sense of community, though, visiting one another's studios and gathering regularly in venues like the Waldorf Cafeteria and the Cedar Tavern in Greenwich Village. They endlessly discussed art, got drunk, and occasionally fought. "The fate of American art is being decided," wrote Greenberg, "by young people, few of them over forty, who live in cold-water flats and exist from hand to mouth. Now they all paint in the abstract vein, show rarely on 57th Street, and have no reputations that extend beyond a small circle of fanatics."[11]

PROMOTING THE NEW ART

The new language of the Abstract Expressionists was supported and promoted by a few bold dealers, with Peggy Guggenheim (1898–1979) and her gallery, Art of This Century, being the most influential among them. Opening at 30 East Fifty-Seventh Street in 1942, Art of This Century was the first venue to mount solo shows of William Baziotes (1912–1963), Robert Motherwell (1915–1991), Pollock, Rothko, and Still. Between the winter of 1942 and the summer of 1947, when it closed, the gallery organized fifty-five exhibitions showing 150 contemporary artists.

Initially, Guggenheim's plan was to exhibit well-established European modernist masters, whom she had personally known and collected during her extensive time in Europe. In 1938, she had launched the short-lived Guggenheim Jeune gallery in London, featuring artists such as Jean Arp (1886–1966), Constantin Brâncuşi (1876–1957), Jean Cocteau (1889–1963), Wassily Kandinsky (1866–1844), and Yves Tanguy (1900–1955).

The opening of Art of This Century on October 20, 1942, was attended by a huge crowd, curious to see Guggenheim's collection. An admission

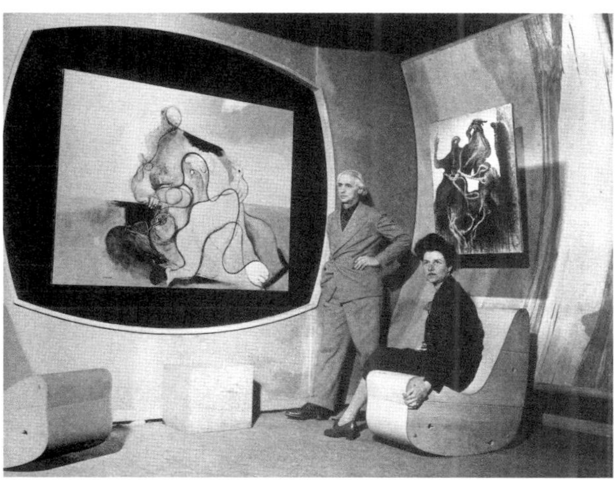

Max Ernst and Peggy Guggenheim at Art of This Century, New York, c. 1942

of $1 was charged, of which part of the proceeds went to the American Red Cross. Guggenheim notoriously wore two unmatched earrings, one by Alexander Calder (1898–1976) and one by Tanguy, to express her impartiality toward abstract and Surrealist art. Designed by the Austrian American architect Frederick John Kiesler (1890–1965), the spaces of Art of This Century were the antithesis of the neutral "white cube." The gallery displayed concave walls, paintings protruding or freely hanging in space, a lighting system that alternated between light and dark, and the recorded sound of a train. These eccentric features defined the three rooms devoted to Guggenheim's permanent collection, known as the "Kinetic," "Surrealist," and "Abstract" galleries. Only one room, the "Daylight Gallery," with white walls and natural light, was dedicated to commercial temporary exhibitions.

In the beginning, Art of This Century, like Guggenheim's town house on East Fifty-First Street, served as a hub for European émigré artists. Over time, however, its mission evolved toward championing the American avant-garde. This shift was catalyzed by Guggenheim's growing detachment from the Surrealists, following her separation from her second husband, the artist Max Ernst. Howard Putzel (1898–1945), an influential American critic, supplanted the French artist Marcel Duchamp (1887–1968) as her principal adviser.

"Pollock immediately became the central point of Art of This Century. From then on, 1943, until I left America in 1947, I dedicated myself to Pollock," she later declared.[12] And indeed, she was crucial in the initial promotion of the artist, whose gradual acceptance, rejection, and eventual success epitomize the path to triumph of Abstract Expressionism itself. It was a battle that involved pioneer gallerists, visionary art critics such as Greenberg and Harold Rosenberg (1906–1978), and the support of Alfred H. Barr Jr. (1902–1981) in the form of early acquisitions for the Museum of Modern Art.

Pollock's debut at Art of This Century was in a group show in 1943, which was part of the just-inaugurated "Spring Salons for Young Artists." Pollock exhibited *Stenographic Figure* (1943), which did not sell, but the press noticed him, and Coates in the *New Yorker* called the work (originally titled *Painting*) "a real discovery."[13] At Putzel's urging, Guggenheim agreed to visit Pollock's studio to consider offering him a solo show. Her first visit to his apartment at 46 East Eighth Street—where he lived with Lee Krasner—was not short of drama. Pollock had gotten drunk at a wedding and missed Guggenheim's arrival. Frustrated after climbing all the stairs to the apartment only to find Pollock absent, she had to be persuaded to go back. The effort proved worthwhile: she offered Pollock a solo exhibition in November 1943 and, more significantly, a one-year contract at $150 a month, to be deducted against the year's total sales. Pollock biographers Steven Naifeh and Gregory White Smith highlight that this was an unprecedented deal for an American artist. Even among Europeans, it was rare for an artist to receive more than informal and irregular support from dealers and collectors—unlike the long-term patronage arrangements in earlier centuries. As the two authors observe, "In one grand gesture, Peggy Guggenheim had shown her aesthetic faith in Jackson's future and

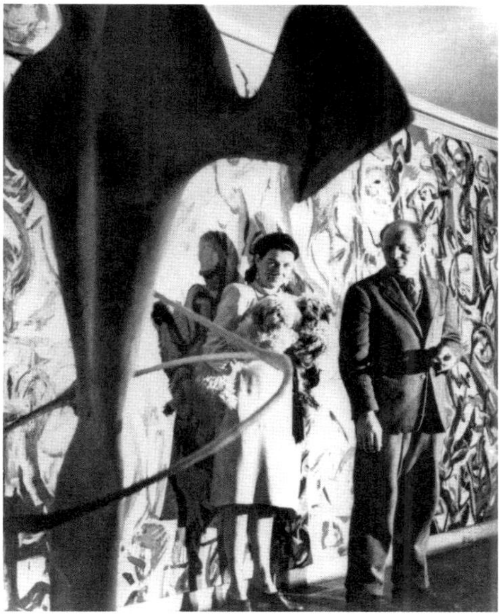

Peggy Guggenheim and Jackson Pollock in front of *Mural* (1943), c. 1946, New York

her financial faith in the future of the art market. It was, in its own way, a bolder statement than the gallery itself."[14]

The introduction to the catalogue for Pollock's solo exhibition was written by James Johnson Sweeney (1900–1986), then a curator at the Museum of Modern Art. The reviews by Coates and Greenberg were positive. This time, Coates mentioned several of Pollock's works and called him "an authentic discovery," referring to the "basic force and vigor" of Pollock's work and adding that "his color is always rich and daring, his approach mature, and his design remarkably fluent."[15] Greenberg reserved his praise for the smaller works, singling out two of them as being "among the strongest abstract paintings I have yet seen by an American."[16] Barr bought *The She Wolf* (1943) for $600 for MoMA. It was the first acquisition by a museum of any of Pollock's works. In 1944, Guggenheim renewed his contract and promised him three more solo shows. During this time, Greenberg identified the artist as the rising star of American art, capable of liberating it from its subordination to Europe. The critic devoted himself to promoting Pollock, aided by the unwavering support of the artist's future wife, Krasner. Pollock's final exhibition with Guggenheim, held in January 1947, featured works such as *Shimmering Substance* (1946), which marked his transition toward the dripping technique he is best known for. With one brief, anonymous exception, that show was reviewed solely by Greenberg, in *The Nation*.[17]

Another of the artists to have a solo exhibition at Art of This Century was Mark Rothko in February 1945, with fifteen paintings and some gouaches. Rothko was also instrumental in organizing the first solo show there of Clyfford Still—whom he had met in Berkeley in 1943—and Rothko wrote the essay for that catalogue.

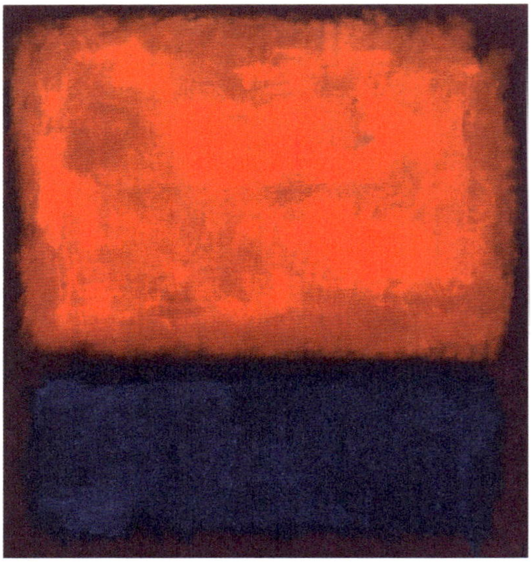

Mark Rothko, *No. 14, 1960*, 1960,
San Francisco Museum of Modern Art

It is also noteworthy that Art of This Century mounted the first exhibition solely dedicated to female artists, titled *31 Women*, in 1943. Guggenheim juried the exhibition with Duchamp, Breton, Ernst, Sweeney, and Putzel. The selected artists, hailing from sixteen different countries, were almost all younger than thirty years old, with Djuna Barnes (1892–1982) the sole exception.

In 1947, Guggenheim decided to close her gallery and move back to Europe. Betty Parsons (1900–1982), a New Yorker from a wealthy family and an artist herself, after studying in Paris and teaching in California, had opened her own space at 15 East Fifty-Seventh Street. Parsons would inherit all of Art of This Century's most important artists: Pollock, Newman, Rothko, and Still—whom she nicknamed the "Four Horsemen of the Apocalypse."[18] She declared, "I realized that they were saying something that no European could say."[19] From 1947 to 1951, it was Parsons who ran the vanguard gallery, which, as James E. B. Breslin points out, also became a place for painters to meet, discuss matters, and hang each other's shows.[20]

Pollock's drip paintings made their debut at the Betty Parsons Gallery in January 1948. The artist poured and dripped liquid paint directly onto canvases laid flat on the ground, to emphasize spontaneity, movement, and the physicality of painting. This first show featured seventeen paintings, most in his new style; they were priced as low as $150, but reportedly only one sold—to a friend of Guggenheim's. The exhibition was dismissed by all the critics except Greenberg. In an extensive review, he praised Pollock, then mentioned the artist John Marin, "with whom," he added, "Pollock will in time be able to compete for recognition as the greatest American painter of the twentieth century."[21]

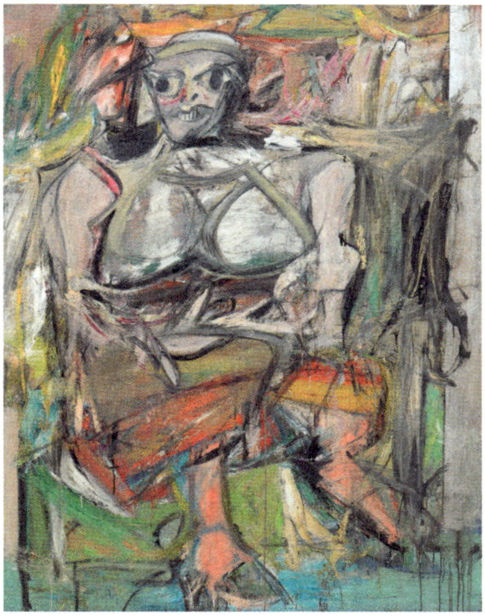

Willem de Kooning, *Woman I*, 1950–52, Museum of Modern Art, New York

Much more positive was the outcome of Pollock's second exhibition at Parsons's gallery, in January 1949. It led to the purchase by the Museum of Modern Art, one year later, of Pollock's *Number 1A, 1948* (1948) for $2,350. Pollock was also beginning to be known internationally: in 1948, six of his works had been exhibited at the Venice Biennale as part of Peggy Guggenheim's collection. In November 1949, Pollock's third Parsons show was a triumph; sales were impressive. And Abby Aldrich Rockefeller (1874–1948), whom the architect Philip Johnson (1906–2005) had brought to the artist's studio, bought *Number 1, 1949* (1949) for $1,000.

Willem de Kooning was never affiliated with Guggenheim's or Parsons's stable of artists. Although Guggenheim visited his studio, she did not offer him representation. The artist's first solo exhibition therefore did not occur until April 1948, hosted at the Charles Egan Gallery. Originally from Philadelphia and lacking formal art training or financial backing, Charles Egan (1911–1993) was well-connected with avant-garde artists. Inspired by their support, he opened his gallery in February 1946, occupying a modest space on the top floor of a residential building on East Fifty-Seventh Street.

De Kooning was almost forty-four years old at the time of his debut and had struggled for affirmation in New York for twenty-two years. He showed ten black-and-white abstract paintings, executed in oil and enamel, with a thick impastoed surface. They were priced between $300 and $2,000, and there were no sales. "By even the modest commercial standards of the time, the show was a failure," write biographers Mark Stevens and Annalyn Swan.[22] Egan could not afford any promotion or an opening party, and the mainstream press ignored the exhibition, with the exception of a short, quite negative review in the *New York Times* by Sam Hunter.[23] The exhibition's impact on the downtown community of artists was profound, though,

In 1958, the architect Philip Johnson approached Mark Rothko to create a series of paintings for the Four Seasons, a luxurious restaurant in the newly constructed Seagram Building in New York, designed by Johnson himself and by the modernist master Ludwig Mies van der Rohe (1886–1969). The contract allowed Rothko total freedom, just specifying that he had to cover five to six hundred square feet of walls. The payment was conspicuous: $35,000, of which $7,000 was paid to the artist upon his signing the contract. Rothko's market at the end of the 1950s was solid, and, as his biographer James E. B. Breslin notes, he was affluent, with an income that would rise from $21,000 in 1958 to about $61,000 in 1959.[24] The Seagram commission was enticing, though, as it would allow Rothko to engage in the creation of a whole, embracing pictorial space.

The artist enthusiastically plunged into the new endeavor, renting a larger studio on the Bowery and hiring a new assistant, Dan Rice. Adopting for the first time a dark palette of wine red and maroon, Rothko produced a first series of seven canvases, which did not satisfy him; two other series followed. After a trip in June 1959 to Italy, where he was deeply impressed by Michelangelo's Medici library and by frescoes in Pompeii, Rothko went to have dinner with his wife at the Four Seasons. Then he abruptly decided to give up the commission. During the transatlantic crossing to Italy, he had already declared his feelings toward the expensive restaurant in a conversation that happened by chance with John Fischer, then the editor in chief of *Harper's Magazine*: "I hope to paint something that will ruin the appetite of every son of a bitch who ever eats in that room. If the restaurant would refuse to put up my murals, that would be the ultimate compliment. But they won't. People can stand anything these days."[25]

None of the forty or so Seagram canvases Rothko created were ever installed in the Four Seasons, and they sat in storage until 1969 when, after years of negotiations, the artist donated nine of them to the Tate in London, where they remain, in a dedicated room. Thirteen are part of the collections of the National Gallery of Art in Washington, DC, and seven are in the Kawamura Memorial DIC Museum of Art in Sakura, Japan. Rothko's heirs have sold a few over the years.

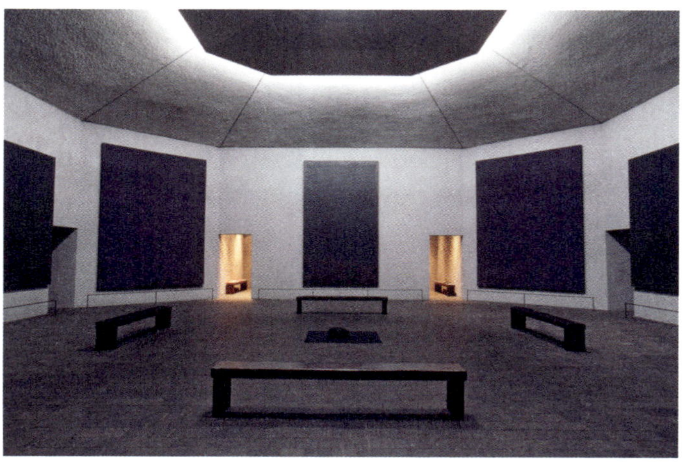

Rothko Chapel, Houston

Rothko's dream to create an embracing pictorial space, like a contemporary fresco, had to wait. In 1963, John and Dominique de Menil, a wealthy and cultivated French philanthropist couple living in Houston, proposed that the artist create murals for a nondenominational, meditative chapel. They offered him $250,000 and total freedom of execution. By that time, Rothko's success was consolidated. MoMA had dedicated a solo exhibition to him in 1961, and the artist had joined the Marlborough Galleries in 1963, a move that resulted in a dramatic rise in his prices.

Philip Johnson was in charge of designing the Houston chapel. Rothko immediately clashed with him, eventually leading to the architect's resignation in favor of two architects from Texas, Howard Barnstone (1923–1987) and Eugene Aubry (1935–1923).

In the octagonal brick building, fourteen huge, dark-toned monochromatic canvases—nine of them arranged in triptychs—create an environment for spiritual reflection that transcends religious boundaries and offers a profound, introspective experience to visitors of all backgrounds. However, Rothko himself was absent from the inauguration of his masterpiece, called the Rothko Chapel, in 1971. On February 25, 1970, at the age of sixty-six, he tragically took his own life.

CLEMENT GREENBERG AND HAROLD ROSENBERG: THE MILITANT CRITICS

Norman Kleeblatt describes two key figures in mid-twentieth-century American art in this way: "Clement Greenberg and Harold Rosenberg remain the two most influential critics of American art in the years after World War II. . . . They began as colleagues. . . . Both were Jewish intellectuals. Both were drawn to the new expressive abstraction in postwar New York. Yet each ultimately developed a singular, firmly entrenched interpretation."[26] Moving from different theoretical premises, Greenberg and Rosenberg not only supported the nascent Abstract Expressionism but, more importantly, provided the movement with a conceptual ground, of which they offered different theoretical interpretations.

Clement Greenberg, whose legendary career spanned fifty years—including as an

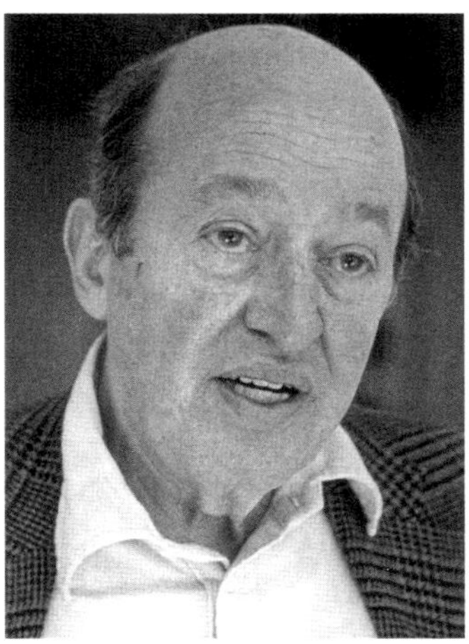

Clement Greenberg, 1977

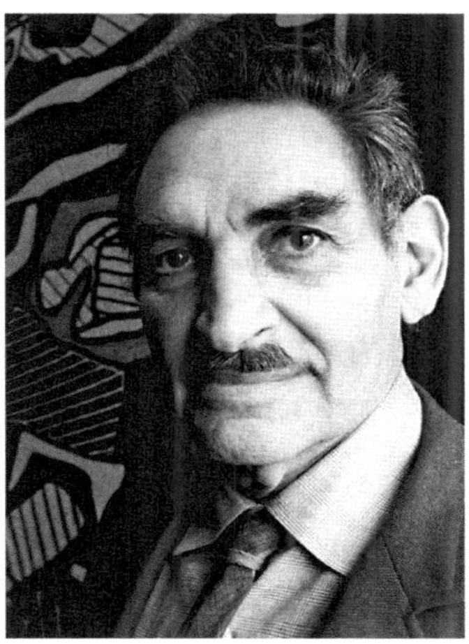

Harold Rosenberg

editor at *Partisan Review* from 1940 to 1942, as the art critic for *The Nation* from 1942 to 1949, and as an editor at *Commentary* from 1945 to 1957—emphasized a formal reading of Abstract Expressionism. He viewed it as an evolution of modernism that prioritized the purity of the medium (predominantly paint) and the flatness of the canvas, and he prophesied the death of the easel picture.[27] Artists such as Jackson Pollock abandoned the constraints of traditional easel paintings to pour and drip color directly onto canvases laid on the floor.

Harold Rosenberg, focusing on the existential and performative aspects of Abstract Expressionism, considered the movement a radical break from any historical artistic practice that had preceded it. He coined the term "action painting" to indicate that the act of painting itself, not just the final artwork, was a form of intense, spontaneous creation: "at a certain moment the canvas began to appear to one American painter after another as an arena in which to act. . . . What was to go on the canvas was not a picture but an event."[28]

and each of them went to see it.[29] Greenberg did cover it very positively in a long review in *The Nation*, calling it "this magnificent first show" and praising de Kooning as "one of the four or five most important painters in the country.[30] Hoping for sales, Egan extended de Kooning's show by a month, and eventually the Museum of Modern Art stepped forward to buy *Painting* (1948) for $700. If the exhibition did not improve de Kooning's financial situation, it succeeded in putting him on the map as one of the most interesting and talented artists of the New York School, and he was there to stay.

However, following another exhibition with Egan that failed to generate commercial success, de Kooning decided in 1953 to part ways with him and join the Sidney Janis Gallery, a move that numerous other artists were also making at the time. A wealthy Jewish clothing manufacturer from Buffalo, New York, Sidney Janis (1896–1989) had opened a gallery in 1948 at 15 East Fifty-Seventh Street, next door to Betty Parsons's gallery in the same building. His strategy was to alternate exhibitions of established European masters, like his inaugural exhibition of works by Fernand Léger (1881–1955) in 1948, with shows of young American artists. With the help of Leo Castelli (1907–1999), who would later become the most prominent promoter of the generation following the Abstract Expressionists, Janis organized the 1950 exhibition *Young Painters in U.S. and France*, in which Rothko was juxtaposed with Nicolas de Stäel (1914–1955), Franz Kline with Pierre Soulages (1919–2022), Pollock with André Lanskoy (1903–1976), and de Kooning with Jean Dubuffet (1901–1985).

INSTITUTIONAL RECOGNITION

During the 1950s, de Kooning, Pollock, Rothko, Kline, Krasner, Still, Newman, Frankenthaler, and Mitchell were honing their mature styles and gradually gaining recognition in museums and the press. Diana Crane observes that before 1948, the Abstract Expressionists were largely ignored by New York art magazines, the mass media, and museums in general. Only a few critics such as Greenberg and Sweeney wrote enthusiastically about them. By the end of the 1940s, however, they had gained a core group of influential supporters in the art world, including curators at the Museum of Modern Art, critics, dealers, and collectors.[31]

In 1950, Pollock was selected with de Kooning and Gorky, among a few others, to represent the United States at the Venice Biennale. Two years later, the Museum of Modern Art launched its International Program, to promote exhibitions of American art around the world. A highlight of the program occurred with the exhibition *The New American Painting* in 1958–59, which toured eight European cities. Curated by Dorothy C. Miller (1904–2003), the first female curator at the museum, the show marked a significant milestone in the recognition and acceptance abroad of the artists of the New York School.

Moreover, the mainstream press started to take notice of the emerging artists. In August 1949, *Life* magazine published a groundbreaking article about Pollock, posing the question "Is he the greatest living painter in the United States?" In the words of Mary Gabriel, "the artist as a celebrity was born."[32]

The debut exhibition of the New York School as a group, though, did not take place in a traditional gallery or museum setting, but rather in a vacant, dilapidated furniture store on East Ninth Street. Organized by the artists themselves and running from May 21 to June 10, 1951, it offered many of the participants their first opportunity to publicly show their work. Each artist was limited to presenting just one piece, for a total of eleven women and sixty-one men. Leo Castelli was tasked with hanging the artworks, while Kline was responsible for designing the poster. The opening was a landmark event, with Barr, Miller, and numerous critics in attendance. In the words of Gabriel: "The show . . . had a tremendous impact. . . . Not that every work in it was a masterpiece, far from it. Its strength lay in the realization that the seventy-two artists in the exhibition weren't *moving* in a new direction; they had already arrived there. It was an unequivocal artistic statement written in a new abstract language."[33]

Five years later, one of the leading figures of Abstract Expressionism, Jackson Pollock, died tragically in a car accident on August 11, 1956. Barr's planned solo exhibition for him at the Museum of Modern Art—originally intended to kick off a series featuring mid-career artists—turned into a memorial tribute.

Lee Krasner was appointed executor of Pollock's estate. After 1958, she chose to manage it independently of galleries. By carefully restricting the availability of his works and selecting the buyers, she was able to substantially increase the prices for Pollock's works. In 1957, the Metropolitan Museum of Art bought *Autumn Rhythm (Number 30)* (1950) for $30,000; before Pollock's death, Janis had asked Barr for $8,000 for it, but the MoMA director had failed to raise that amount.[34] The significance of this acquisition and its price cannot be overstated, as it marked the first time a major museum purchased an American painting for the same price as a European one. "That single sale reset the entire market for modern American work," Gabriel stresses.[35]

On January 15, 1951, *Life* magazine published a photo of fifteen of the eighteen painters who, along with ten sculptors, had protested against the Metropolitan Museum of Art's jury chosen to select the artists for the upcoming exhibition *American Painting Today, 1950*. The article was the last in an extended, heated debate triggered by an open letter addressed to Roland L. Redmond, president of the museum, and described in an article published on the front page of the *New York Times* on May 22, 1950. Drafted by the artist Adolph Gottlieb (1903–1974), the letter criticized the museum's selection process for the exhibition, arguing that it was biased against modern art. It was signed by many of the leading figures of the New York School—and by only three women: Louise Bourgeois (1911–2010), Mary Callery (1903–1977), and Hedda Sterne (1910–2011). Lee Krasner lamented not even being asked to sign. The publication in the *New York Times* was followed by critical coverage in the *New York Herald Tribune* on May 23, which labeled the group as "the Irascible Eighteen"; that name and "the Irascibles" became widely associated with the artists' movement against the established art world. Articles followed in *The Nation*, *Art Digest*, and *ARTnews*.

This would be the last battle that the New York School fought as a group. Despite the conservative attitude of the Metropolitan Museum, whose director, Francis Henry Taylor, famously referred more than once to the Museum of Modern Art as "that whorehouse on Fifty-third Street,"[36] the new art was gaining in public approval, and the large resonance of the protest in the press was proof of it.

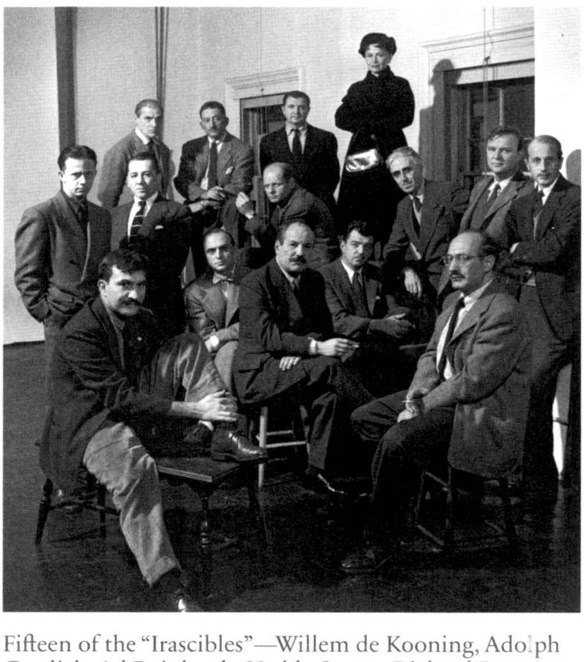

Fifteen of the "Irascibles"—Willem de Kooning, Adolph Gottlieb, Ad Reinhardt, Hedda Sterne, Richard Pousette-Dart, William Baziotes, Jackson Pollock, Clyfford Still, Robert Motherwell, Bradley Walker Tomlin, Theodoros Stamos, Jimmy Ernst, Barnett Newman, James Brooks, and Mark Rothko—posed for *Life* magazine, 1950

The ascent of Abstract Expressionism paralleled New York's emergence as the predominant art market. This status, as noted by A. Deirdre Robson, was achieved because American buyers began embracing their own compatriots' work, rather than solely focusing on European masters: "The key to the transformation of status of New York as art market centre was not just the greater willingness of Americans to buy art, but the changing prestige of American art in the 1950s. It was the greater openness of American collectors (particularly those crucial on-guard ones) to engage with the art of their own country." [37]

In his influential book *How New York Stole the Idea of Modern Art: Abstract Expressionism, Freedom, and the Cold War*, Serge Guilbaut argues that the rise of Abstract Expressionism was not solely due to its artistic innovation. Examining New York's ascendancy as the center of the art world after World War II through the lens of the political dynamics of the Cold War, the author suggests that the success of Abstract Expressionism was intertwined with a political agenda linked to the Marshall Plan and possibly the CIA. The American establishment favored this style for its political neutrality and the absence of the socially engaged, realistic subjects typical of 1930s art, making it ideal for international promotion as a fresh, noncontroversial, distinctly American movement.[38]

WOMEN OF THE ABSTRACT EXPRESSIONIST ERA

Women artists' major contributions to the emergence and evolution of Abstract Expressionism have only recently gained critical and market recognition.

Seminal publications and exhibitions are finally revisiting a narrative that had traditionally identified Abstract Expressionism as a white, male, or even macho movement.[39] The art historian Joan Marter stresses that to this day, the typical roll call of Abstract Expressionists, and associated events, usually includes only white urban males, occasionally a few women, and virtually no African American artists, although Norman Lewis was part of the original group.[40]

Women artists of the Abstract Expressionist period are currently experiencing a meteoric rise in the market, driven by a reassessment of their historical importance as well as practical considerations. Their work remains significantly more affordable than that of their male counterparts, making it an attractive investment. Additionally, pieces of exceptional quality are still available, which is rarer for their male peers. The Artnet Analytics Team examined the results at auction of five key women artists of that time: Helen Frankenthaler, Grace Hartigan, Agnes Martin (1912–2004), Louise Nevelson (1899–1988), and Vivian Springford (1913–2003). Since 1999, the total sales value for their work has increased astonishingly from just over \$1 million in 1999 to \$56.5 million in 2021. And the demand grows each year, with total sales value growing by more than \$10 million between 2020 and 2021. Nevertheless, their prices remain dramatically lower compared to the male Abstract Expressionist artists.[41]

Yet, during their lifetimes, women Abstract Expressionists confronted many obstacles in terms of both critical perception and the market.

The patriarchal society of 1940s and 1950s America made it difficult for women to gain recognition and credibility as artists. Few commercial galleries were willing to show female artists' work; collectors, who were predominantly men, were more inclined to buy and put their trust in what was considered a more solid and durable investment: works by men. Therefore, although many women artists were indeed actively part of the debate and of the birth of the Abstract Expressionist language, when the new art started to acquire financial value, they were left out. Gabriel's brilliant book *Ninth Street Women* follows the artistic development, careers, and lives of the five women included in the legendary 1951 *Ninth Street Show*. Of these, Krasner, Frankenthaler, and Mitchell are the ones who over the years, and particularly recently, have achieved the highest critical and market appreciation.

For Lee Krasner, the path to recognition was particularly hard. Gabriel notes that, despite significant advances for women in fields like medicine, law, and literature, professional art remained largely inaccessible. In early twentieth-century America, few men could survive as artists unless they were part of cultured circles with ties to Europe. For women, and especially for a working-class Jewish woman like Krasner, the daughter of Russian immigrants in Brooklyn, realizing such an ambition was nearly impossible.[42] Furthermore, Krasner's marriage to Jackson Pollock, to whom she devoted herself, supporting his success and battling his alcoholism at the expense of her own career, led to her being largely overlooked or dismissed during Pollock's lifetime. As John Yau notes, even after Pollock's death, Krasner remained mostly marginalized for nearly a decade, her contributions overshadowed by her husband's legacy.[43]

By the late 1930s, after studying at Cooper Union and Hans Hofmann's school, Krasner had become fully immersed in the American art scene, joining the American Abstract Artists group. "Lee was a formidable figure

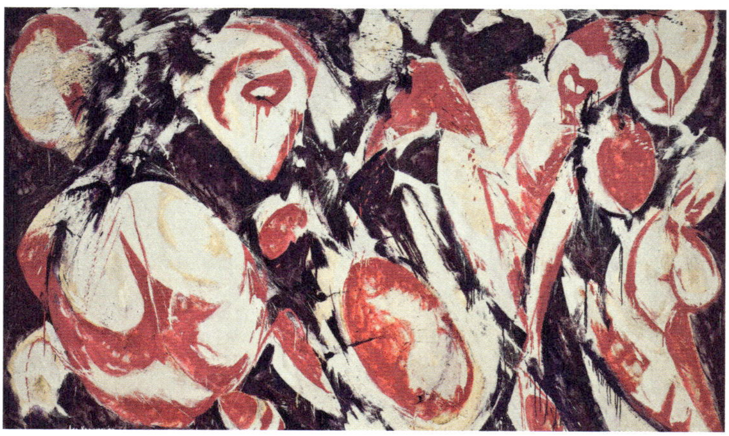

Lee Krasner, *Gaea*, 1966, Museum of Modern Art, New York

in the art world as a habitué of the scene, as a respected leader in the fight for artists' rights, and as a talented artist," Gabriel writes.[44] Still, success gradually came to Krasner only after Pollock's death. Previously, although her first solo exhibition at the Betty Parsons Gallery, in 1951—arranged by Pollock—received positive critical reviews, none of the fourteen paintings sold. Disappointed, Krasner destroyed the unsold works, later repurposing the fragments to create her renowned "collage paintings." These works were exhibited at the Stable Gallery in New York in 1955 and praised by critics as a very important contribution to the American art scene. Despite numerous setbacks, Krasner's presence in exhibitions grew steadily. Her 1958 show at the Martha Jackson Gallery in New York, featuring seventeen new paintings, received considerable attention. However, a planned exhibition at French & Company was abruptly canceled when Clement Greenberg, dissatisfied with her 1960 *Night Journeys* series, withdrew support. Krasner gained her first major international recognition in 1965 with *Lee Krasner: Paintings, Drawings and Collages* at the Whitechapel Gallery in London. A long-awaited traveling exhibition, *Lee Krasner: A Retrospective*, opened at the Museum of Fine Arts, Houston, in 1983 on the artist's seventy-fifth birthday, and it completed its American tour at the Museum of Modern Art, New York, in 1984–85. In between, on June 19, 1984, Krasner died.

Helen Frankenthaler and Joan Mitchell were part of the so-called second generation of Abstract Expressionists. Unlike their predecessors, they benefited from privileged backgrounds and formal fine arts training, which afforded them more consistent gallery representation and museum presence throughout their careers. The daughter of a New York State Supreme Court judge, Frankenthaler participated in the *Ninth Street Show* at only twenty-two years old, and that same year she had her solo debut at Tibor de Nagy, the New York gallery known for promoting the later Abstract Expressionists. In 1960, the Jewish Museum in New York hosted her first institutional exhibition, and six years later, she was one of just four artists who represented the United States at the Venice Biennale.

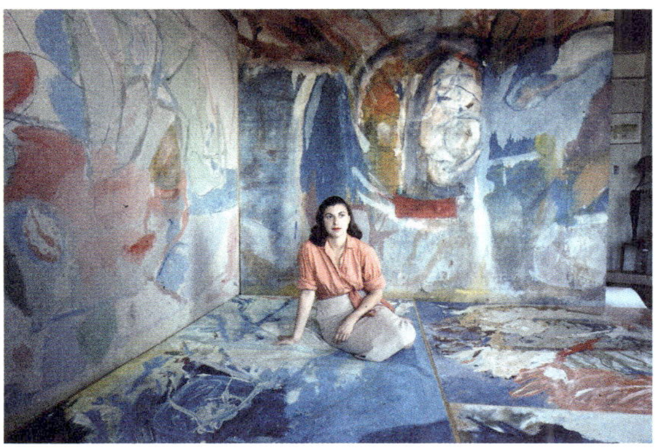

Gordon Parks, *Untitled*, New York, 1956. Parks photographed Helen Frankenthaler for the May 13, 1957, *Life* magazine article "Women Artists in Ascendance."

Mitchell, born into a prominent Chicago family, was one of the few women admitted to the artists' group called "the Club," and she socialized and drank with her peers at the Cedar Tavern. She, too, participated in the *Ninth Street Show* in 1951. Her first solo exhibition was at the New Gallery in 1952, with the Stable Gallery representing her through the 1950s. Marcia Tucker organized her first museum retrospective at the Whitney Museum in 1974.

On May 13, 1957, *Life* magazine featured an article titled "Women Artists in Ascendance," spotlighting young painters, including Frankenthaler and Mitchell. While this coverage showed that women had gained some visibility, Marter poignantly notes that although these two artists faced fewer barriers than the first generation of women Abstract Expressionists, they were still marginalized. As the movement gained wider recognition, women were systematically excluded and erased from its history.[45] A telling example is that Frankenthaler was never fully credited for inspiring the Color Field painting movement—a style defined by large, solid expanses of color designed to evoke emotion through that alone. Her groundbreaking 1952 work *Mountains and Sea*, where she poured diluted paint onto unprimed canvas placed on the floor in what came to be celebrated as her "soak-stain" technique, was foundational to the movement, yet her influence was overlooked at the time.

While the feminist movement of the 1960s was crucial in advancing the recognition of women artists, Krasner, Mitchell, and Frankenthaler had an ambivalent relationship with it. They resisted being labeled as "women painters" and showed little interest in the social causes championed by the movement, preferring to be recognized solely for the artistic merit of their work.

By the early 1960s, Mitchell's work had been acquired by the Museum of Modern Art in New York. In a comparison of prices, though, her paintings were selling in the 1980s for between $50,000 and $250,000, rising to $500,000 at the end of the decade; at the same time, de Kooning's works ranged from $500,000 to $1.5 million, with a record for *Interchange* (1955), sold privately for the record price of $20.7 million in November 1989.[46]

Even today, the market gap between Abstract Expressionist women and men remains enormous. The record price at auction for a work by Krasner, *The Eye Is the First Circle* (1960), sold at Christie's New York in May 2019, is $11,654,000; for Frankenthaler, it is $7,895,300, for *Royal Fireworks* (1975), sold at Sotheby's New York in 2020. De Kooning's *Woman as Landscape* (1954–55) sold at Christie's New York in 2018 for $68,937,504, and *Interchange* was privately sold again in 2015 for around $250 million; Pollock's *Number 17, 1951* (1951) sold in 2021 at Sotheby's New York for $61 million; and Rothko's record, set at Christie's New York in 2012, is $86.8 million, for *Orange, Red, Yellow* (1961).

While the art world's epicenter shifted after World War II to New York, where Abstract Expressionism, Pop art, and Minimalism arose, Paris did not lose its appeal as a leading art destination.

A significant number of artists indeed flocked to the French capital in the immediate postwar years, attracted by the still-alluring city's rich artistic heritage and the relatively low cost of living. The toll of the world conflict had been heavy on France, which suffered bombardment, Nazi occupation, and Jewish deportation. It was a physical and moral devastation that had left the country impoverished and shattered. Nevertheless, Paris, where Impressionism, Cubism, and Surrealism were born, still offered a free and fervent intellectual environment. Americans took advantage of the GI Bill (officially the Servicemen's Readjustment Act of 1944), which provided veterans with various benefits such as financial support for education, including the option of studying abroad.

Among the American artists who spent time in Paris, Sam Francis (1923–1994) was one of the most prominent. Initially studying medicine, Francis turned to painting while recovering from a war injury. In Paris, he absorbed European modernism, developing a distinctive style characterized by vibrant colors and dynamic compositions. In 1948, Ellsworth Kelly (1923–2015) moved to Paris, where the work of Matisse and Arp greatly influenced his focus on color, form, and spatial relationships. Joan Mitchell studied in France in 1948–49, visited Paris in 1955, and eventually made France her home. Norman Bluhm (1921–1999) also found his artistic direction in Paris after serving as a bomber pilot during the war. Al Held (1928–2005) moved to Paris in the early 1950s, studying at the Académie de la Grande Chaumière and drawing inspiration from European abstraction. Ed Clark (1926–2019), a pioneering African American abstract painter, found Paris to be a more inclusive environment, free from the racial discrimination he faced in the United States. This intellectual freedom allowed him to experiment with new techniques, including shaped canvases and the use of a broom instead of brushes for broader, dynamic strokes.

In 1950, a group of American GIs founded Galerie Huit at 8, rue Saint-Julien Le Pauvre on the Left Bank, a cooperative gallery that became the main hub for American artists, hosting exhibitions and serving as a gathering place for discussions.[47]

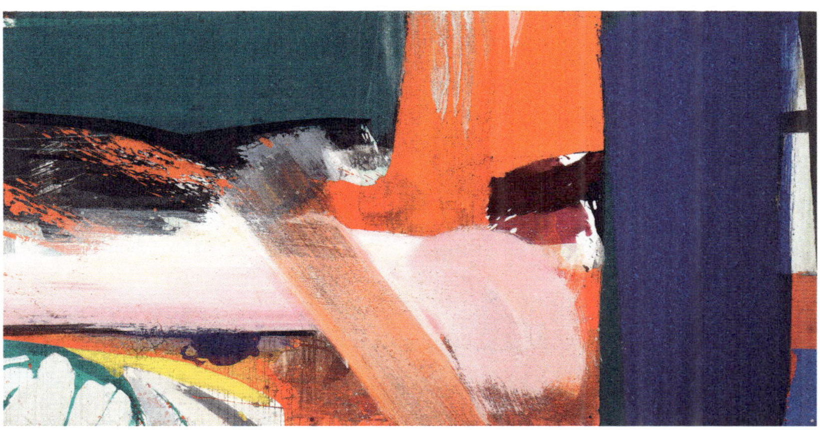

Ed Clark, *Locomotion*, 1963

NOTES

1 These institutions included the American Academy of Fine Arts (originally the New York Academy of Fine Arts), in New York, in 1802, and the Pennsylvania Academy of the Fine Arts, in Philadelphia, in 1805; by the late nineteenth century, there were other such schools, including the Art Students League in 1875 and the Architectural League in 1881, both in New York.

2 A. Deirdre Robson, "The Girl with the Gallery: Edith Halpert in the Mid-Twentieth-Century New York Art Market," in *Women Art Dealers: Creating Markets for Modern Art, 1940–1990*, ed. Véronique Chagnon-Burke and Caterina Toschi (London: Bloomsbury Visual Arts, 2024), 31–32.

3 Titia Hulst, "New York," in *A History of the Western Art Market: A Sourcebook of Writings on Artists, Dealers, and Markets*, ed. Titia Hulst (Oakland: University of California Press, 2017), 316.

4 The US population was about 125 million and the workforce about 50 million (in addition to children and older people, most married women were unemployed); at its peak, unemployment was about 12,830,000, or 24.9 percent.

5 Mary Gabriel, *Ninth Street Women: Lee Krasner, Elaine de Kooning, Grace Hartigan, Joan Mitchell, and Helen Frankenthaler; Five Painters and the Movement That Changed Modern Art* (New York: Little, Brown, 2018), 31.

6 Robert M. Coates, "The Art Galleries: Abroad and at Home," *New Yorker*, March 30, 1946, 83.

7 Steven Naifeh and Gregory White Smith, *Jackson Pollock: An American Saga* (Aiken, SC: Woodward/White, 1989), 418.

8 Deborah Solomon, *Jackson Pollock: A Biography* (New York: Cooper Square Press, 2001), 121.

9 Clement Greenberg, "'American-Type' Painting," *Partisan Review* 22, no. 2 (Spring 1955).

10 Peggy Guggenheim, *Out of This Century: Confessions of an Art Addict* (New York: Universe Books, 1979), 209.

11 Clement Greenberg, "The Present Prospects of American Painting and Sculpture," *Horizon*, October 1947, 29.

12 Guggenheim, *Out of This Century*, 315.

13 Robert M. Coates, review of "Spring Salon for Young Artists" at Art of This Century, with brief mention of Pollock, *New Yorker*, May 29, 1943, 49.

14 Naifeh and Smith, *Jackson Pollock*, 451.

15 Robert M. Coates, review of Pollock's solo exhibition at Art of This Century, *New Yorker*, November 20, 1943, 97.

16 Clement Greenberg, review of exhibitions, *The Nation*, November 27, 1943, 621.

17 Clement Greenberg, review of Pollock's fourth solo show at Art of This Century, *The Nation*, February 1, 1947, 137, 139.

18 Solomon, *Jackson Pollock*, 175.

19 James E. B. Breslin, *Mark Rothko: A Biography* (Chicago: University of Chicago Press, 1993), 250.

20 Breslin, *Mark Rothko*, 251.

21 Clement Greenberg, review of Pollock's first solo show at Betty Parsons Gallery, *The Nation*, January 24, 1948, 108.

22 Mark Stevens and Annalyn Swan, *De Kooning: An American Master* (New York: Alfred A. Knopf, 2004), 251.

23 Sam Hunter, review of de Kooning's first solo show, at Egan Gallery, *New York Times*, April 25, 1948.

24 Breslin, *Mark Rothko*, 397.

25 John Fischer, "Mark Rothko: Portrait of the Artist as an Angry Man," The Easy Chair, *Harper's Magazine*, July 1970, 131.

26 Norman L. Kleeblatt, "Introduction: Action, Abstraction, Reaction," in *Action/Abstraction: Pollock, de Kooning, and American Art. 1940–1976*, ed. Norman L. Kleeblatt, exh. cat. (New York: Jewish Museum, under the auspices of the Jewish Theological Seminary of America; New Haven, CT: Yale University Press, 2008), 1.

27 Clement Greenberg, "The Crisis of the Easel Picture," *Partisan Review* 15, no. 4 (April 1948).

28 Harold Rosenberg, "The American Action Painters," *ARTnews* 51, no. 8 (December 1952).

29 Stevens and Swan, *De Kooning*, 251.

30 Clement Greenberg, review of de Kooning's first solo show, at Egan Gallery, *The Nation*, April 24, 1948, 448.

31 Diana Crane, *The Transformation of the Avant-Garde: The New York Art World, 1940–1985* (Chicago: University of Chicago Press, 1989), 36.

32 Gabriel, *Ninth Street Women*, 270.

33 Mary Gabriel, "Dorothy Miller," in *Inventing the Modern: Untold Stories of the Women Who Shaped the Museum of Modern Art*, ed. Ann Temkin and Romy Silver-Kohn (New York: Museum of Modern Art, 2024), 222.

34 Solomon, *Jackson Pollock*, 253.

35 Gabriel, *Ninth Street Women*, 621.

36 Calvin Tomkins, *Merchants and Masterpieces: The Story of the Metropolitan Museum of Art* (New York: E. P. Dutton, 1970), 309.

37 A. Deirdre Robson, "The New York Art Market ca. 1960," in Hulst, *History of the Western Art Market*, 327.

38 Serge Guilbaut, *How New York Stole the Idea of Modern Art: Abstract Expressionism, Freedom, and the Cold War*, trans. Arthur Goldhammer (Chicago: University of Chicago Press, 1983).

39 These exhibitions include *Women of Abstract Expressionism*, Denver Art Museum, 2016; *Lee Krasner: Living Colour*, Barbican Art Gallery, London, 2019; *Pittura/Panorama: Paintings by Helen Frankenthaler, 1952–1992*, Museo di Palazzo Grimani, Venice, 2019; and Joan Mitchell retrospective, San Francisco Museum of Modern Art, Baltimore Museum of Art, and Fondation Louis Vuitton, Paris, 2021–23.

40 Joan Marter, "Missing in Action: Abstract Expressionist Women," in *Women of Abstract Expressionism*, ed. Joan Marter, exh. cat. (Denver: Denver Art Museum, in association with Yale University Press, New Haven, CT, 2017), 25.

41 Artnet Analytics Team, "Artnet Analytics Deep Dive: We Explore the Rising Market for Female Abstract Expressionist Artists," Artnet News, February 4, 2022, Artnet.com, https://news.artnet.com/buyers-guide/artnet-buyers-guide-ab-ex-women-2068206.

42 Gabriel, *Ninth Street Women*, 23.

43 John Yau, "Writing Rimbaud on the Wall," in *Lee Krasner: Living Colour*, ed. Eleanor Nairne, exh. cat. (London: Thames & Hudson, 2019), 34–35.

44 Gabriel, *Ninth Street Women*, 93.

45 Marter, "Missing in Action," 21.

46 This sale set a record at the time for the highest price paid for a work by a living artist. The transaction occurred during the Japanese asset price bubble, and the buyer was Shigeki Kameyama, a Japanese art dealer.

47 Debra Bricker Balken, "Americans in Paris: Artists Working in Postwar France, 1946–1962," in *Americans in Paris: Artists Working in Postwar France, 1946–1962*, ed. Lynn Gumpert and Debra Bricker Balken, exh. cat. (New York: Grey Art Gallery, New York University; Munich: Hirmer Publishers, 2022), 54–58.

8. New York Stories II: From the Harlem Renaissance and the Civil Rights Movement to Just Above Midtown

p. 169
The Harlem Renaissance

p. 170
The Role of Educators and the Works Progress Administration

p. 175
The Civil Rights Era

p. 179
The First Commercial Galleries for African American Artists

p. 181
Sam Gilliam and African American Abstraction

> You have propagated the notion that Blacks are not a part of the system. So until such time as you free your thinking enough to see that they've always been a part of it, and should rightly be included in the history books and what have you, we'll have to keep having black shows.
>
> —David C. Driskell quoted in C. Gerald Fraser, "'Black Art' Label Disputed by Curator," *New York Times*, June 29, 1977

Starting shortly after the dawn of the twentieth century, more than six million African Americans migrated from the segregated rural South to the industrial cities of the North, seeking better employment opportunities and more humane living conditions. In cities such as Chicago and New York, a Black middle class emerged and thrived, sparking a newfound racial consciousness that fueled the quest for a new form of art.

In particular, the neighborhood of Harlem in New York witnessed an artistic explosion that encompassed all creative fields. In the visual arts, a highly original vocabulary was created, yet racism and segregation hindered African American artists from receiving the exposure and market opportunities they deserved. Excluded from the mainstream system, these artists had to devise alternative models to promote, exhibit, and sell their art, with educators, community centers, and the support of the Federal Art Project taking on essential roles.

Racism and discrimination persistently continued to marginalize African American artists for decades. During the Civil Rights Movement, which peaked from the mid-1950s to the mid-1960s, they congregated into various groups and associations to advocate for acceptance within the mainstream art system. However, it took a considerable amount of time for African American artists to gain representation in major art institutions and museums, and for their market to develop. Courageous and pioneering African American dealers, such as the Davis brothers (Brockman Gallery) in Los Angeles and Linda Goode Bryant (Just Above Midtown) in New York in the late 1960s and 1970s, established the first, and for a long time almost the only, venues that gave African American artists such as David Hammons, Betye Saar, Senga Nengudi, and Howardena Pindell, to name just a few, the opportunity to exhibit and sell their work. Moreover, these galleries offered a model that went beyond serving as mere exhibition and sales spaces: they provided a venue for artists to convene, engage in discussions, and foster a sense of community with shared goals.

THE HARLEM RENAISSANCE

Music, literature, and visual arts thrived in Harlem, the international capital of Black culture in the early twentieth century. Driven by the writings and ideas of cultural leaders such as Alain Locke (1885–1954), a philosopher and editor of the very influential anthology *The New Negro*, published in 1925; and W. E. B. Du Bois (1868–1963), a prominent civil rights activist, sociologist, and cofounder in 1909 of the National Association for the Advancement of Colored People (NAACP), a new awareness arose for Black people. It was, as remarked by Howard Dodson, a period of an explosion of African American artistic and cultural creativity, marking a new stage of Black consciousness and development.[1]

The visual arts embraced a new vocabulary rooted in African heritage, the traditions of Black folklore, and every aspect of African American life. Furthermore, a new Black American identity was forged by the Harlem Renaissance artists, who for the first time took control of their own image. However, despite their hopes of finding a respectable place in American society, the participation of Black artists in American culture of the 1920s was virtually nonexistent, beyond music and dance—as the artist, scholar, and curator David C. Driskell (1931–2020) points out in the catalogue of the landmark 1976–77 exhibition he curated, *Two Centuries of Black American Art*, at the Los Angeles County Museum of Art and then museums in Atlanta, Dallas, and Brooklyn, New York. Harlem Renaissance artists were victims of a deeply segregated society, one that isolated its artists just as rigorously as it segregated its public schools, as Mary Schmidt Campbell emphasizes.[2] Their works were displayed in separate venues, such as "colored" branches of the YMCA, local public library branches, and private events hosted in wealthy African American homes. As a result, as Campbell laments, the visual artists of the Harlem Renaissance remained largely unknown to the wider public and were absent from the broader narrative of American art. Their artworks often stayed within family or close circles. It was not until the late 1960s, catalyzed by the Civil Rights Movement, that these artists and their contributions began to be rediscovered and appreciated.[3]

THE ROLE OF EDUCATORS AND THE WORKS PROGRESS ADMINISTRATION

In a context that prevented work by African American artists from being exhibited and traded within the main cultural system and market, the role of schools, community centers, and other organizations was crucial. These included the Savage Studio of Arts and Crafts, a school that the sculptor Augusta Savage (1892–1962) established in 1932; the Harlem Artists Guild (1935–41), which nurtured young talent and provided a platform for discussing visual arts within the community; and the Harlem Community Art Center, founded in 1937 with the aid of the federal Works Progress Administration. Even earlier, the wealthy white real estate developer and philanthropist William E. Harmon (1862–1928) founded the Harmon Foundation in 1922; through its exhibition program called "American Negro Artists," the Harmon Foundation was at the forefront of promoting and supporting the work of Black artists, particularly from 1928 to 1933.[4]

The significance of Augusta Savage, highlighted in a 2018 traveling exhibition,[5] lies in her brilliance not only as an artist but also as a teacher and educator. As Jeffreen M. Hayes notes, Savage dedicated her life to shaping Black America through her art and mentorship.[6] Despite her precocious talent, she faced major obstacles, not only in a society where it was nearly inconceivable for a woman of color to pursue an artistic career, but also in her family: her father, a fundamentalist Methodist minister, beat her often for sculpting clay into small objects that he regarded as biblically prohibited "graven images." Encouraged by the principal of her school in Florida, Savage moved to New York and earned a scholarship to the Cooper Union for the Advancement of Science and Art. After graduating, she was denied one organization's scholarship because of her race. In 1929, however, she was granted a Rosenwald Fellowship to study in Paris for a year, and then she received a second one. Meanwhile, she received her first public commission: a bust of W. E. B. Du Bois for the New York Public Library's 135th Street Branch (now the Schomburg Center for Research in Black Culture). After her return to New York, she created one of her masterpieces, *Lift Every Voice and Sing*[7] (which the fair's organizers renamed *The Harp*, a name she reportedly hated), a monumental sculpture commissioned for the 1939 New York World's Fair. Sadly, the original was destroyed when the fair closed in 1940, and it survives only in photographs and very small reproductions sold at the fair.

When Savage founded the Savage Studio of Arts and Crafts, it quickly became a vital hub for the Black community, providing a space for people to connect, share experiences, and receive artistic training. Through its activity, Savage emerged as Harlem's leading art educator and advocate, shaping the careers of many prominent young Black artists, including Jacob Lawrence (1917–2000) and Norman Lewis (1909–1979). She further expanded her influence as a cofounder of the Harlem Artists Guild and as

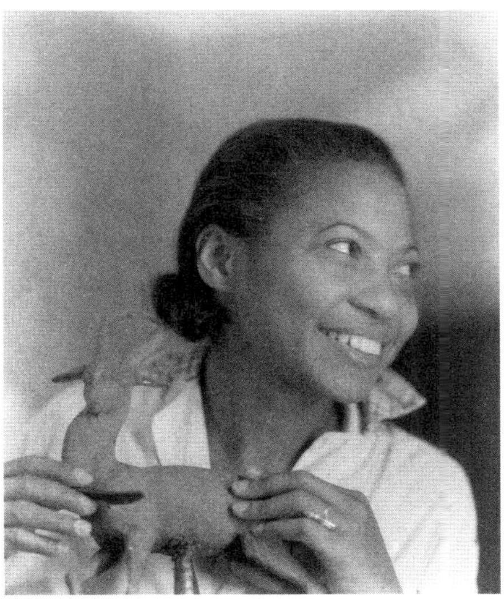

Augusta Savage, c. 1935

the inaugural director of the Harlem Community Art Center. In 1939, seeing the limited commercial opportunities for artists of color, Savage boldly opened New York's first gallery dedicated exclusively to exhibiting and selling works by African American artists, known as the Salon of Contemporary Negro Art. As Bridget R. Cooks remarks, Savage's establishment of the Salon was a groundbreaking event that directly challenged the art world's racially exclusive norms. Her initiative represented not just a platform for Black artists but a powerful statement that exposed the deep-seated racism and undemocratic practices within the art establishment.[8] The inauguration of Savage's gallery drew more than five hundred guests. Despite its ambitious program featuring artists from previous generations, such as the renowned sculptor Meta Vaux Warrick Fuller (1877–1968)—whose *Ethiopia Awakening* (c. 1914–21) is a powerful depiction of an African woman emerging from a mummy-like shroud, symbolizing the awakening of African consciousness and heritage—as well as the younger generation, like Norman Lewis, the venture lasted only three months due to insufficient sales. Nevertheless, its significance was profound, anticipating by three decades the activities of galleries such as Just Above Midtown in New York and the Brockman Gallery in Los Angeles.

Among the other educators who built and nurtured a community around them, Miriam Matthews (1905–2003), who operated in Los Angeles during the Great Depression, was the first credentialed African American librarian in California, in 1927, when she was hired to work for the Los Angeles Public Library. At a time when racial segregation was still the norm, Matthews not only developed and curated collections that celebrated African American literature, history, and culture, but created a welcoming space for all members of the community, regardless of race.

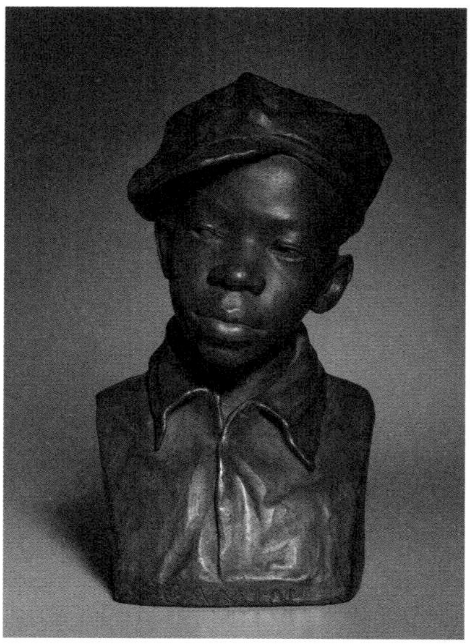

Augusta Savage, *Gamin*, c. 1929, Cleveland Museum of Art

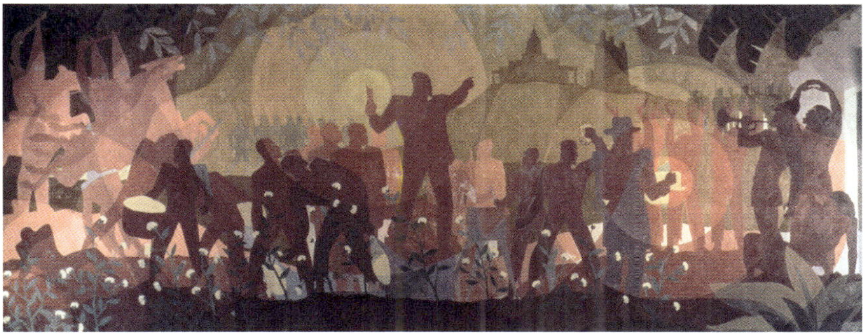

Aaron Douglas, *Aspects of Negro Life: From Slavery to Reconstruction*, 1934, Schomburg Center for Research in Black Culture, New York Public Library

Moving beyond the scope of the library, she also actively took part in the organization of exhibitions of African American artists. The sculptor and painter Beulah Woodard (1895–1955) exhibited in the Vernon Branch Library, thanks to Matthews; in 1937, Woodard would become the first African American to exhibit at the Los Angeles Museum of History, Science, and Art (forerunner of the Los Angeles County Museum of Art). In the same year, Woodard and Matthews cofounded the Los Angeles Negro Art Association to help promote African American artists.[9]

The New Deal's Federal Art Project (FAP) (see "New York Stories I," p. 142) was particularly crucial for African American artists during the Great Depression, as it provided them with essential opportunities to create, exhibit, and gain recognition as well as integrate their contributions into the broader American art scene, fostering greater equity and representation. In 1934, a New Deal predecessor to the FAP, the Public Works of Art Project, commissioned Aaron Douglas (1899–1979)—among thousands of artists who benefited from the short-lived program (1933–34)—to paint a series of murals, *Aspects of Negro Life*, for the 135th Street Branch of the New York Public Library. Douglas was thirty-five at the time and had been part of the Harlem Renaissance scene since 1925. He successfully worked as an illustrator for books and for magazines such as *Opportunity* and *The Crisis* (published by the National Urban League and the NAACP, respectively), but also for the mainstream magazines *Harper's* and *Vanity Fair*.

Aspects of Negro Life comprises four panels: *Song of the Towers*, *From Slavery through Reconstruction*, *An Idyll of the Deep South*, and *The Negro in an African Setting*. The murals address issues of discrimination and African American history, depicted in a highly original style, with flat figures turned into semi-transparent silhouettes, influenced by ancient Egyptian art and Art Deco.

One of a great many works supported by the later federal Works Progress Administration (1935–43), with help from Savage in obtaining funding, was Jacob Lawrence's *The Migration Series*, produced in 1940 and 1941. Comprising sixty tempera panels, the series depicts various episodes of the Great Migration, during which African Americans fled the racism of the

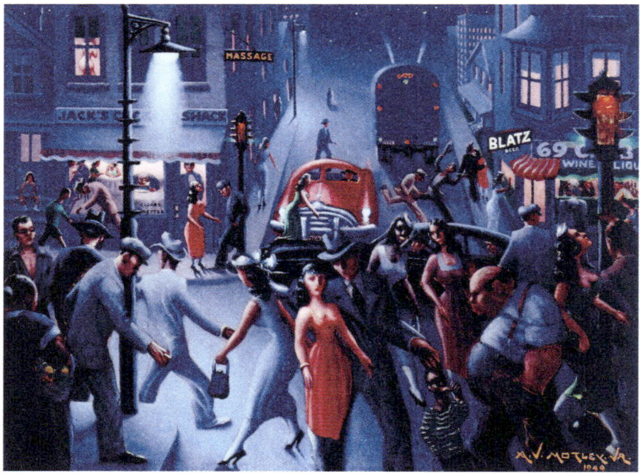

Archibald John Motley Jr., *Bronzeville at Night*, 1949, Art Bridges, Bentonville, Arkansas

South for opportunities in the North. Lawrence's distinctive style employed simplified geometric forms that reflect a sophisticated interpretation of Cubist techniques. The panels are accompanied by descriptive titles that contribute to the integrated narrative of the series.

After studying with Savage at the Harlem Community Art Center, Lawrence created *The Migration Series* when he was just twenty-four years old. The tempera paintings on hardboard were exhibited by Edith Halpert (1900–1970) at her Downtown Gallery in New York at the end of 1941, making Lawrence the first African American artist to have a solo show in a commercial gallery. Prior to this, twenty-six panels had been published in the November 1941 issue of *Fortune* magazine. Today, the series is jointly owned by the Phillips Collection in Washington, DC, and the Museum of Modern Art in New York. Lawrence's artworks are very rare on the market and coveted by collectors. His record price was set at $6,169,000 for *The Businessmen* (1947), which was sold at Sotheby's New York in 2018.

The South Side of Chicago, in a narrower area called the Black Belt, rose as another thriving center of African American culture, frequented by writers such as Arna Bontemps, Gwendolyn Brooks, Lorraine Hansberry, Margaret Walker, and Richard Wright; musicians such as Louis Armstrong, Thomas A. Dorsey, and Earl Hines; and visual artists such as Margaret Burroughs, Elizabeth Catlett, Eldzier Cortor, William Edouard Scott, and Charles White. The effervescence of "Bronzeville," the epicenter of the Chicago Renaissance, was captured by Archibald John Motley Jr. (1891–1981) in his paintings of jazz and cabaret nightclubs, depicted with an explosion of bright yellows, pinks, and reds against dark backgrounds.

Motley's iconic works, most of which are in the collections of universities and museums, have not come up at auction yet, so at the time of writing, the artist's record remains very low: $30,500 for *Guanajuato, Mexico* (1957), established at Treadway Toomey Auctions, Oak Park, Illinois, in 2015.

During the 1960s, African American artists began to organize both formally and informally into groups, aligning their agendas with those of political activists such as Dr. Martin Luther King Jr., who advocated for integration into mainstream American society. As Sharon F. Patton has observed, for visual artists, this meant moving away from segregation within Black colleges and cultural societies in predominantly Black neighborhoods, and instead striving to exhibit their work in mainstream museums and galleries.[10] The fight proved to be long and strenuous.

Spiral, founded in 1963 in New York by Charles Alston (1907–1977), Romare Bearden (1911–1988), Norman Lewis, and Hale Woodruff (1900–1980), emerged as an influential collective in the discourse of African American art during the Civil Rights Movement. While the group, which grew to more than a dozen members, did not adhere to a single aesthetic, it was instrumental in sparking crucial debates about how African American artists should portray the Black experience, exploring whether abstraction could be as impactful as figuration in expressing social realities and aspirations. The group's only exhibition, titled *First Group Showing (Works in Black & White)*, took place in 1965 in a rented space at 147 Christopher Street, showcasing the diverse approaches of its members.

Emma Amos (1937–2020), the sole woman in the group, exemplified the unique challenges faced by Black female artists of the era. For many, establishing an artistic identity involved a dual struggle: addressing misogyny from their male counterparts within the Black Power movement, while also confronting systemic racism within the predominantly white feminist movement of the time. For example, Faith Ringgold (1930–2024)—who worked in a variety of mediums but is perhaps best known for her artistic quilts, which blend storytelling, history, and activism, using fabric and paint to highlight African American experiences—was not accepted in the Spiral group.

Meanwhile, in Chicago, AfriCOBRA (African Commune of Bad Relevant Artists), founded in 1968, represented a parallel but distinct effort to shape

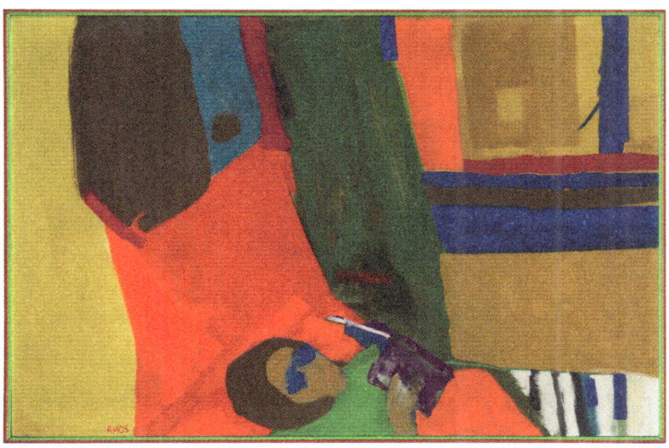

Emma Amos, *The Reader*, 1967, Crystal Bridges Museum of American Art, Bentonville, Arkansas

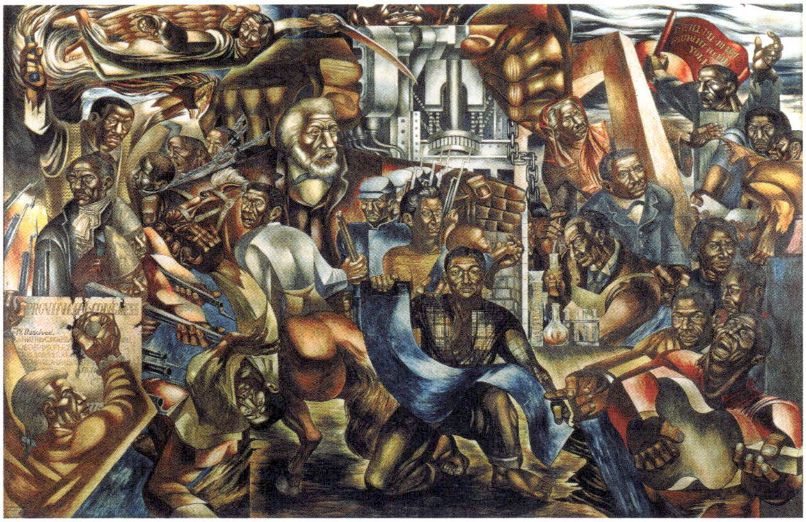

Charles White, *The Contribution of the Negro to Democracy in America*, 1943, Hampton University Museum, Virginia

a Black cultural aesthetic in art. Focused on creating works that were both accessible and deeply rooted in the Black experience, AfriCOBRA's art drew inspiration from African heritage, music, and everyday life. The collective developed a bold, recognizable style characterized by vibrant colors, dynamic compositions, and the integration of text, all aimed at affirming and celebrating Black identity and empowerment.

In Los Angeles during the 1960s, the towering figure of Charles White (1918–1979), previously part of the Chicago Renaissance and posthumously celebrated by a long-overdue retrospective at MoMA in New York in 2018–19, was the aggregator and mentor of the African American art community. Through his role as a teacher at the Otis Art Institute, White not only inspired and shaped young talents who would become influential in their own right, such as David Hammons (b. 1943) and Kerry James Marshall (b. 1955), but instilled in them a sense of social responsibility and the importance of using art as a tool for social change. At the heart of White's artistic practice was a commitment to portraying the dignity, resilience, and humanity of African Americans. For example, in the mural *The Contribution of the Negro to Democracy in America*, commissioned in 1943 by Hampton Institute in Hampton, Virginia, White depicted the achievements and struggles of African Americans throughout the nation's history, from slavery to emancipation to the present day.

Hammons, who by 1963 had settled in Los Angeles from his native Illinois to study with White, soon moved away from the flat surface of the canvas to examine and challenge common notions of Black identity. Before and after moving to New York in 1974, he created a series called *Body Prints*—the subject of an acclaimed exhibition at the Drawing Center in New York in 2021—not with naked models covered in blue paint, as the French postwar artist Yves Klein (1928–1962) used in his *Anthropométries* around 1960, but by using his own body, or other people's, greased with substances such as margarine and baby oil and then sprinkling the prints with charcoal or powdered pigment. He also sold snowballs on the Bowery in New York and made sculptures out of chicken bones, as well as hair from the floors of hairdressers' salons in Harlem. Hammons's sculptures exploring the theme of basketball address its significance as a symbol of aspiration and a potential pathway out of urban poverty for many African American youth. Critiquing the commodification of sports while highlighting its role as a form of cultural expression and resilience within Black communities, these works were initially perceived as bold social commentary, but they have since become highly sought-after by collectors and art institutions for their conceptual depth and cultural relevance. An untitled work showing a basketball hoop and backboard decorated with chandeliers was sold in 2013 at Phillips New York for $8,005,000. In 2016, always defying the art system, Hammons organized his first retrospective, *David Hammons: Five Decades*, not in a museum but in the blue-chip Mnuchin Gallery on New York's Upper East Side. That praised show was anticipated by two previous ones: one in which Hammons exhibited expensive fur coats stained with paint (2007), a statement about the insular wealth of the New York neighborhood where the gallery is located; and the other featuring paintings with rugs glued to the painted canvas (2011).

In Los Angeles, Betye Saar (b. 1926) investigated themes of female experience, sexuality, and Black identity through a variety of mediums. Her evocative assemblages, infused with elements of spirituality and African American folklore, challenge conventional notions of femininity and domesticity. *Black Girl's Window*, created in 1969, presents a scene of innocence: a young girl peering out of a window, her gaze fixed on something

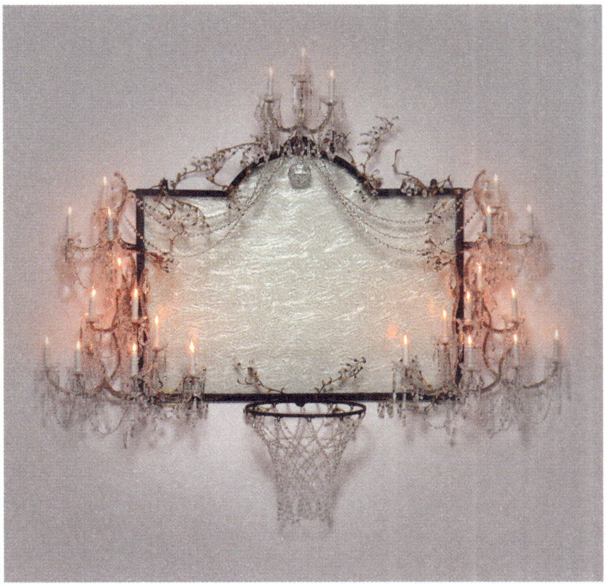

David Hammons, *Untitled*, 2000

beyond the frame. Through the window, which symbolizes both physical and psychological boundaries, Saar invites viewers to contemplate notions of confinement and liberation, questioning the limitations imposed upon marginalized communities. Saar's iconic *The Liberation of Aunt Jemima* (1972) addresses the racist fictional character of the Black "mammy" on boxes of Aunt Jemima pancake mix, and more broadly the stereotyped portrayal of Black American women. The "new" Aunt Jemima holds a rifle in one hand and a broom in the other, next to a grenade, thus becoming a symbol of empowerment and liberation. The market has only recently shown interest in Saar's work, following the surge in museum exhibitions dedicated to her.[11] The record auction for a work by Saar was established in November 2022 at Sotheby's New York, where *Rainbow Mojo* (1972) sold for $378,000.

Despite the formal and conceptual originality of their creations, institutional recognition did not come easily for African American artists in the 1960s and 1970s, and it was often accompanied by controversy and struggle. The few museum exhibitions dedicated to them were disappointing and met by harsh debates. In 1969, the Metropolitan Museum of Art's exhibition *Harlem on My Mind: Cultural Capital of Black America, 1900–1968* was conceived as a documentary display—but it did not include any actual works by African American artists. It was an outrageously reductive approach that sparked intense protest in the African American artistic community.[12]

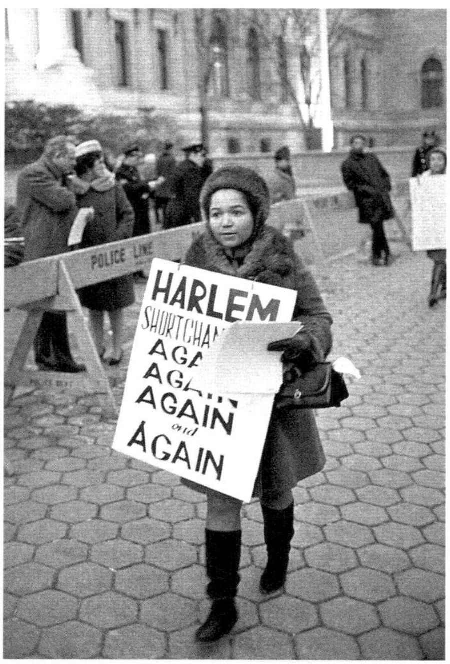

Demonstrators protesting the exhibition *Harlem on My Mind* at the Metropolitan Museum of Art, New York, January 16, 1969

The matter was broader than just presenting the art: how it was presented was fundamental. The lack of African American curators in museums was at the core of the problem, and the Black Emergency Cultural Coalition (BECC) was formed in 1969 to address such essential issues. Among its actions, the BECC promoted picketing the Metropolitan Museum's exhibition as well as the Whitney Museum of American Art's 1971 exhibition *Contemporary Black Artists in America*, for which a Black curator was not hired.

In this context, the importance of the establishment in 1968 of the Studio Museum in Harlem cannot be overemphasized. Located in the heart of the neighborhood, it was created by a group of local artists and supporters with the mission of providing a platform for African American artists, and it proved to be vital in fostering their careers and in advancing their visibility and wider appreciation of their work. The museum remains a cornerstone of cultural and artistic discourse in the contemporary world.

In Los Angeles, the Black Arts Council—active between 1968 and 1974—pursued an agenda similar to the BECC in New York: more inclusion for African American artists in museums and other institutions.

The Los Angeles County Museum of Art (LACMA), founded in 1961 as a spin-off from the Los Angeles Museum of History, Science, and Art and opened to the public in a complex of new buildings in 1965, stood out in this regard compared to its East Coast counterparts. As Kellie Jones points out, it was the first institution to hire external scholars and curators with recognized expertise in African American art—an approach that the Whitney Museum and the Metropolitan Museum in New York were not following at the time.[13] The groundbreaking exhibition *Sculpture of Black Africa: The Paul Tishman Collection* was organized at LACMA in 1968, followed by *Los Angeles, 1972: A Panorama of Black Artists*, among other shows.

THE FIRST COMMERCIAL GALLERIES FOR AFRICAN AMERICAN ARTISTS

The dearth of critical recognition and presence in public institutions also meant for African American artists a dramatic lack of representation in the leading commercial galleries. Because of this, the establishment in New York of Just Above Midtown (JAM) was crucial, offering Black artists a venue to exhibit and sell their work in the heart of the city's traditional art district on Fifty-Seventh Street. Founded in 1974 by Linda Goode Bryant (b. 1949), a young African American single mother who had begun her career as a fellow at the Metropolitan Museum and then worked in the education department of the Studio Museum in Harlem, Just Above Midtown marked a significant breakthrough. More than an exhibition space, it served as a self-described laboratory and cultural hub that fostered community and belonging for artists. Goode Bryant initiated various programs, including "Brunch with JAM," a series offering $5 meals alongside lectures by artists and museum curators.

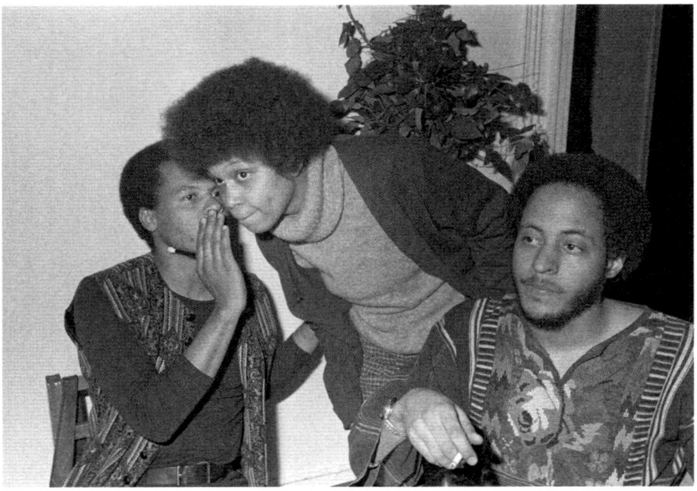

Linda Goode Bryant (center) and Houston Conwill (left) at Just Above Midtown, New York, March 18, 1978

In 2022, a revelatory exhibition at the Museum of Modern Art in New York finally acknowledged the pioneering role of Just Above Midtown and its visionary founder in providing vital support and visibility for African American artists during a time of systemic exclusion from mainstream art institutions and galleries. Among these artists was Hammons, who had famously told Goode Bryant, "I don't show in white galleries." For more than a decade, Goode Bryant and JAM provided a response to that.

Other artists whose varied works appeared at JAM included Senga Nengudi (b. 1943) and Howardena Pindell (b. 1943). Nengudi challenged traditional notions of sculpture with her innovative use of materials, particularly pantyhose, which she stretched, twisted, and otherwise manipulated to create dynamic installations and performances. Her work often explored themes of gender identity and the body, integrating elements of dance and ritual. Pindell's artistic practice encompassed painting, collage, video, and performance to examine themes of race, identity, and memory.

Due to constant financial struggles, including increasing rent, Just Above Midtown relocated in 1980 from Midtown to Franklin Street in Tribeca, which had not yet become an art destination as it is today. Eventually, after further moves, the gallery closed its doors in 1986, prompting Goode Bryant to redirect her efforts to documentary filmmaking and an urban farming initiative.

In Los Angeles, African American artists made significant contributions to the burgeoning art scene, yet, like their peers across the country, they had to create alternative institutional structures to exhibit and sell their work. Sadly, as Jones observes, the two major LA galleries at the time—Ferus and Dwan—largely ignored African American artists, offering them little to no support or visibility.[14] As a response to this discrimination, in January 1967 the artist brothers Alonzo Davis (1942–2025) and Dale Brockman Davis

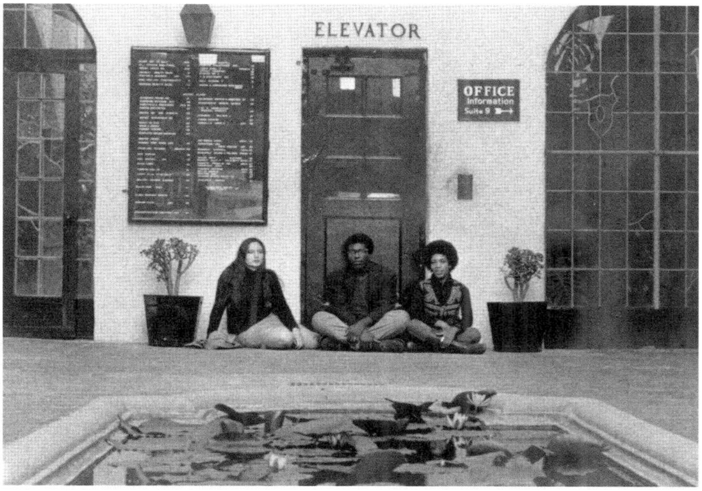

Annie Bianucci, George Evans, and Suzanne Jackson in front of Gallery 32, Los Angeles, 1969

(b. 1945) established the Brockman Gallery in a former frame store in the affluent neighborhood of Leimert Park in West Los Angeles. Its exhibition program showcased both emerging talents and established artists such as Jacob Lawrence, embodying, in Jones's words, an inclusive vision, which embraced a diverse array of artists and perspectives that mirrored the realities of Los Angeles and the nation. The Brockman Gallery also presented works by Chicano, Asian, and white artists. As early as 1969, for instance, a group exhibition titled *Oriental America* was mounted, highlighting Asian and Asian American artists.

In a similar vein, Gallery 32 was founded in 1968 by Suzanne Jackson (b. 1944), an artist and dancer. Her objective extended beyond merely offering exhibition opportunities in Los Angeles to underrepresented artists. She aimed at fostering community support for emerging artists, particularly among communities of color, thereby cultivating something truly remarkable.[15]

SAM GILLIAM AND AFRICAN AMERICAN ABSTRACTION

The *Drape* paintings by Sam Gilliam (1933–2022) represent one of the most groundbreaking artistic innovations of the 1960s. These free-hanging, lyrical abstractions, suspended from ceilings and walls without stretchers, defied the conventions of Abstract Expressionism and Color Field painting by engaging with the physical space around them. Born in Tupelo, Mississippi, Gilliam moved to Washington, DC, in 1962. He joined fellow African American artists such as Richard Hunt (1935–2023), Alvin Loving (1935–2005), and William T. Williams (b. 1942) in embracing abstraction—a bold choice that was unconventional and even criticized at the height of the Civil Rights Movement. As Sharon F. Patton notes, abstraction was often seen as "white" or "art for art's sake," contrasting with the figurative style favored by many Black artists seeking to confront social issues directly.[16]

In 1972, Gilliam became the first African American artist to represent the United States at the Venice Biennale, a landmark achievement. However, broader critical acclaim and market recognition were slow to follow. Over the years, his work appeared in important exhibitions, including at the Studio Museum in Harlem in 1982, Kunstmuseum Basel in Switzerland in 2018, and the Hirshhorn Museum and Sculpture Garden in Washington, DC, in 2022. In 2021, his monumental *Double Merge* (1968) was jointly acquired by the Dia Art Foundation and the Museum of Fine Arts, Houston, marking a significant acknowledgment of Gilliam's enduring impact on modern art.

A record-breaking price of $2,172,500 was achieved at Christie's New York in 2018 for Gilliam's *Lady Day II* (1971).

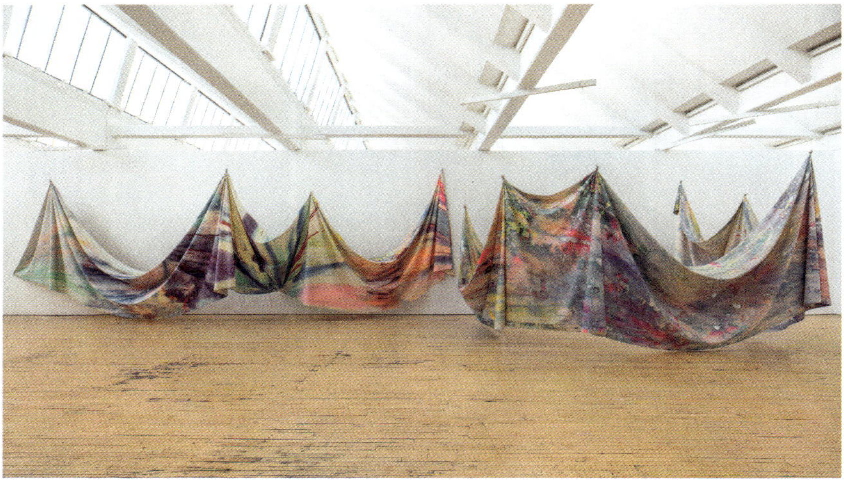

Sam Gilliam, *Double Merge*, 1968

NOTES

1 Howard Dodson, introduction to *Augusta Savage: Renaissance Woman*, by Jeffreen M. Hayes, with contributions by Bridget R. Cooks and Kirsten Pai Buick, exh. cat. (London: Giles, in association with the Cummer Museum of Art & Gardens, Jacksonville, FL, 2018), 12.

2 Mary Schmidt Campbell, introduction to *Harlem Renaissance: Art of Black America*, by David Driskell, David Levering Lewis, and Deborah Willis Ryan, exh. cat. (New York: Studio Museum in Harlem and Harry N. Abrams, 1987), 13.

3 Campbell, introduction to *Harlem Renaissance*, 11–14.

4 Bridget R. Cooks, "The Harlem Renaissance in Exhibition," in *The Harlem Renaissance and Transatlantic Modernism*, ed. Denise Murrell, exh. cat. (New York: Metropolitan Museum of Art, 2024), 123.

5 Hayes et al., *Augusta Savage*.

6 Jeffreen M. Hayes, "Labor, Love, Legacy: Augusta Savage's Art," in Hayes et al., *Augusta Savage*, 16.

7 This was the title of a spiritual hymn, originally written as a poem by James Weldon Johnson, then set to music by his brother, John Rosamond Johnson, and widely considered the Black "national anthem" then.

8 Bridget R. Cooks, "Augusta Savage: A Gallery of Their Own," in Hayes et al., *Augusta Savage*, 32–33.

9 Kellie Jones, *South of Pico: African American Artists in Los Angeles in the 1960s and 1970s* (Durham, NC: Duke University Press, 2017), 141.

10 Sharon F. Patton, *African-American Art* (Oxford, UK: Oxford University Press, 1998), 210.

11 These exhibitions include *Betye Saar: Call and Response*, Los Angeles County Museum of Art (2019–20); and *Betye Saar: The Legends of "Black Girl's Window,"* Museum of Modern Art, New York (2019–20).

12 Patton, *African-American Art*, 211. In February–July 2024, the exhibition *The Harlem Renaissance and Transatlantic Modernism* at the Metropolitan Museum of Art, curated by Denise Murrell, finally offered a thorough exploration into the rich creations of the movement.

13 Jones, *South of Pico*, 170.

14 Jones, *South of Pico*, 160.

15 Jones, *South of Pico*, 154.

16 Patton, *African-American Art*, 218.

9. New York Stories III: The Castelli-Sonnabend Model

p. 185
New Horizons

p. 188
Cy Twombly

p. 189
The Leo Castelli Gallery

p. 191
Leo Castelli

p. 193
Ileana Sonnabend Gallery in Paris

p. 194
Ileana Sonnabend

p. 196
Virginia Dwan

p. 197
The Castelli-Sonnabend Model

p. 199
Andy Warhol

p. 200
Warhol's Factory

p. 202
A Changing Scenario

p. 204
Women Artists of the Pop Era and Beyond

We should discover a genius! It's been two weeks since we last discovered a genius!

—Ivan Karp quoted in Peter Schjeldahl, "Leo the Lion," *New Yorker*, May 31, 2010

Toward the close of the 1950s, when Abstract Expressionism was gaining international recognition, a new artistic movement known as Pop art emerged. Anticipated by the pioneering achievements of Jasper Johns and Robert Rauschenberg, Pop artists broke away from the extreme subjectivity of their predecessors to focus their attention on the material world around them. As New York solidified its status as the epicenter of the contemporary art market, artists such as Andy Warhol and Roy Lichtenstein embraced the depiction of the real world and consumerism.

At the forefront championing this new generation of artists were the dealers Leo Castelli (1907–1999) and Ileana Sonnabend (1914–2007), who employed a series of exemplary practices that are still revered today as the gold standard for art galleries. Discovering new talent, showing total devotion to the artist, nurturing relationships with institutions, building an international network of collaborations to expand the reach of their artists' market—these were the cornerstones of this successful model. Its efficacy was demonstrated when Rauschenberg won the Grand Prize for Painting at the 1964 Venice Biennale (a precursor to today's Golden Lions), marking the first time an American—in fact, any non-European artist—received this prestigious award. The enthusiastic support of Castelli and Sonnabend was instrumental in securing early critical and commercial success for both Rauschenberg and Johns.

NEW HORIZONS

In 1953, two young artists from the American South, Robert Rauschenberg (1925–2008) and Jasper Johns (b. 1930), met in New York and embarked on a profound artistic and personal collaboration. Their creative exchange, which Calvin Tomkins likens to the transformative dialogue between Pablo Picasso and Georges Braque that birthed Cubism in the early twentieth century, was instrumental in establishing a new art form called Neo-Dada.[1] The term underscores its connection to the original Dada movement of the early 1900s, maintaining Dada's irreverent spirit and the use of found objects, mundane materials, and elements of chance to challenge established notions of art.

Born in Port Arthur, Texas, Rauschenberg had experienced a sporadic and largely unsuccessful exhibition history in New York prior to meeting

Johns. His solo debut, at the Betty Parsons Gallery in May 1951, with large monochrome paintings incorporating fragments of the "real" world such as fabric, hair, and broken mirrors, was ignored by the critics, and nothing was sold. That same spring, Rauschenberg was invited to participate in the legendary *Ninth Street Show*, financially supported and installed by Castelli. Rauschenberg's inclusion of the outside world into his artworks continued with the *White Paintings* of 1951, canvases coated with white paint that reflected the changing light of their surroundings. The *Black Paintings* (1951–53) followed, characterized by thick impasto interwoven with torn newspaper fragments. In 1953, in a bold move to distance himself from the previous generation, Rauschenberg obtained from Willem de Kooning (1904–1997) a drawing by the master—and erased it (leaving only traces of the original marks), defiantly signaling a break with past artistic conventions; the result was *Erased de Kooning Drawing*, now part of the collection of the San Francisco Museum of Modern Art.

Despite the lack of critical and commercial recognition, Rauschenberg persisted with his artistic experimentation, creating the *Red Paintings* (1953–54), which incorporated fabrics and newspaper into the texture of the works. They were exhibited in December 1954 in the solo exhibition *Joyeux Noël* at the Charles Egan Gallery, the same venue where de Kooning had made his New York debut in 1948. The immediate effect of the show, as remarked by Tomkins, was to reinforce the artist's reputation as an "enfant terrible." The only positive review came from Frank O'Hara (1926–1966), a young poet and critic, and later a curator at the Museum of Modern Art, New York, who in *ARTnews* described the collages as "ecstatic works" made by a "serious lyrical talent."[2]

Johns, born in Augusta, Georgia, enrolled briefly at the Parsons School of Design in New York in 1949, before being drafted into the US Army and stationed in Sendai, Japan, in 1952–53, during the Korean War. His early works pictured universally known and recognizable images such as flags, maps, targets, letters, and numbers, which he defined as "things the mind

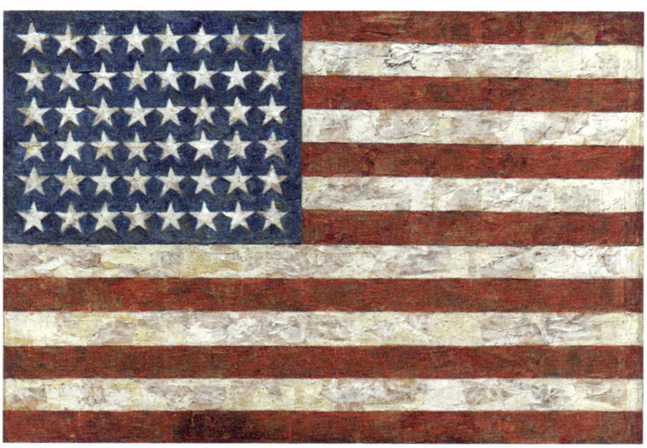

Jasper Johns, *Flag*, 1954–55, Museum of Modern Art, New York

already knows."[3] The first *Flag*, begun in 1954 after the artist dreamed of an American flag, used the ancient Egyptian encaustic technique (mixing wax with pigments) to create a thick surface incorporating torn newspapers. A small *Flag* was incorporated into a Rauschenberg work, *Short Circuit*, in the 1955 *Fourth Annual Exhibition of Painting and Sculpture* at the Stable Gallery, founded by Eleanor Ward in 1953, which quickly became a launchpad for major artists. *White Flag* (1955–58) was displayed in a window of the Bonwit Teller luxury department store in 1956, followed by *Flag on Orange Field* in 1957. To fully grasp the revolutionary impact of Johns's *Flags* and his subsequent series *Targets*, it is crucial to consider the context of American painting during that era. As Morgan Meis points out, Barnett Newman was still creating his iconic "zips" (vertical lines on fields of color), de Kooning was producing his signature canvases filled with dynamic shapes and colors, and Jackson Pollock, though deceased by 1956, had set the standard for "serious painting" with his allover drip technique. In stark contrast, Johns's flag paintings appeared to risk utter banality.[4]

The expansion of art beyond its traditional boundaries and into the "real," catalyzed by Rauschenberg and Johns, culminated in the triumph of Pop art. This movement, which emerged simultaneously in the United Kingdom and the United States in the mid- to late 1950s and thrived in the 1960s, was defined by its incorporation of imagery from popular and mass culture, as well as its embrace of the mechanical reproduction techniques typical of advertising. Generally considered the first recognized work of Pop art is a collage by Richard Hamilton (1922–2011), *Just What Is It That Makes Today's Homes So Different, So Appealing?* (1956), created for the seminal 1956 exhibition *This Is Tomorrow* at London's Whitechapel Gallery. At the same time in the United States, artists such as Roy Lichtenstein (1923–1997), Andy Warhol (1928–1987), Claes Oldenburg (1929–2022), Tom Wesselmann (1931–2004), and James Rosenquist (1933–2017) "chose to depict everything previously considered unworthy of notice, let alone of art," as Lucy Lippard explains. They embraced "every level of advertising, magazine and newspaper illustration, Times Square jokes, tasteless bric-à-brac and gaudy furnishings, ordinary clothes and foods, film stars, pin-ups, cartoons. Nothing was sacred, and the cheaper and more despicable the better."[5]

The emergence of Pop art in the United States coincided with a period of exceptional economic expansion and prosperity. The US measurement then used, the gross national product, had increased by 250 percent since the end of World War II, and the median family income, adjusted to inflation, had almost doubled, as David Farber reports.[6] For the middle class, the economic boom meant increased purchasing power, leading to widespread ownership of numerous consumer products such as cars, telephones, and kitchen appliances. However, this era was also marked by profound contradictions, including heightened tensions of the Cold War, racial discrimination, the civil rights struggles, the rise of the feminist movement, the Vietnam War, and student protests.

Nine Discourses on Commodus (1963) by Cy Twombly (1928–2011) embodies the artist's extraordinarily layered and conceptually sophisticated language. It also epitomizes the complex journey to his critical acclaim and commercial recognition.

Inspired by the assassination of the Roman emperor (161–192 CE), *Nine Discourses on Commodus* eschews easy interpretation. In nine separate canvases, it majestically combines potent gestural brushstrokes with calligraphic and cryptic symbolism. When *Nine Discourses on Commodus* was first exhibited at Leo Castelli's gallery in April 1963, the New York art scene was excited by, and embracing, Pop and Minimal art. *Discourses* belonged to neither style. As such, it triggered controversial reactions and Donald Judd's famous scathing criticism, calling it a "fiasco."[7] The work did not find a buyer in New York and ended up in an Italian collection, from which it was eventually sold, in 2007, via Gagosian, to the Guggenheim Museum Bilbao in Spain, where it is now on permanent display.

Born in Lexington, Virginia, Twombly shared his initial artistic and personal path with the two other artists from the South who were about to shake up the New York art scene, Johns and Rauschenberg. With the latter, Twombly traveled to Italy and North Africa, and shared his first presentation in 1953 at the Stable Gallery in New York. After serving in the US Army as a cryptographer, Twombly returned to Rome in 1957, where he met his wife-to-be, the aristocrat Tatiana Franchetti. A local gallery, La Tartaruga, showed his work in 1958.

From the beginning and throughout his career, Twombly's art defied easy categorization, and it is indeed his singularity that made it difficult for his contemporaries to grasp and appreciate its value. "Any attempt to bundle him into the ism of the day is generally confounded by the restive fecundity of his reinventions," writes Simon Schama.[8] Twombly's artistic path developed between Italy—first in Rome and then also in the small coastal town of Gaeta—and his native Lexington. In an increasingly refined but emotionally immediate style, imbued with mythological, literal, and personal narratives, Twombly produced series of masterpieces, such as the *Ferragosto* paintings (1961) and the iconic *Blackboards* (1966–71), characterized by repetitive, looping white chalk lines on dark gray backgrounds. Institutional appreciation grew slowly. In 1968, the Milwaukee Art Center mounted the artist's first American museum exhibition, curated by Robert Pincus-Witten; in 1979 came the long-awaited retrospective in New York, which took place at the Whitney Museum of American Art.

A "grand late phase" characterized Twombly's later years, with monumental and majestic series of paintings such as *Bacchus* (2005), *The Rose* (2008), and his last one, *Camino Real* (2010–11). In terms of market appreciation, although the auction record at $70.5 million belongs to *Untitled (New York City)* (1968), sold at Sotheby's New York in November 2015, from the *Blackboard* series, the late works seem to be in demand. Displaying a joyful use of color and vigorous gestural brushstrokes, these late paintings appear to resonate with a global younger generation of collectors. One example from the *Bacchus* series sold at Christie's New York in 2017 for $46,437,500, and a gigantic and colorful *Untitled* (2007) made $58,863,000 at Sotheby's New York in November 2021.

In January 1958, an exhibition dedicated to Jasper Johns's *Flags*, *Targets*, and *Numbers* opened at the Leo Castelli Gallery, and his first solo show, in the words of Calvin Tomkins, "hit the art world like a meteor."[9] Alfred H. Barr Jr., then director of collections at the Museum of Modern Art, obtained three works for MoMA: *Target with Four Faces* (1955), *Green Target* (1955), and *White Numbers* (1957). And during the same month of the show, *ARTnews* put *Target with Four Faces* on its cover. The attention was virtually unprecedented for a modern artist only twenty-seven years old, and it marked a fundamental shift in the New York art scene: a new language was replacing Abstract Expressionism as the avant-garde movement, and Leo Castelli was its champion.

The Castelli Gallery was a newcomer in New York: it had opened less than a year earlier, in February 1957, in two rooms of Castelli's apartment at 4 East Seventy-Seventh Street. The first exhibitions presented established European artists such as Wassily Kandinsky, Fernand Léger, Piet Mondrian, and Pablo Picasso, along with various Abstract Expressionists like Willem de Kooning, Jackson Pollock, and David Smith.

By then, Castelli, an Italian Jewish émigré who had arrived in 1941 in New York with his wife Ileana (later Ileana Sonnabend), after escaping Europe at war, was a known fixture of the New York art world. The couple were friends with many of the Abstract Expressionists—Willem and Elaine de Kooning used to vacation at the Castellis' home in the Hamptons—and were among the only three nonartists (along with the dealer Charles Egan) to have been admitted to "the Club," the legendary discussion group founded in 1948. Castelli also financially supported and hung the *Ninth Street Show* in 1951. However, when at almost fifty years old Castelli finally opened his own gallery, he decided not to focus on the Abstract Expressionists but to promote the next emerging generation of artists. "I was looking for new people that had something new to say," he said in a television interview by Barbaralee Diamonstein in 1976.[10]

Castelli first encountered the work of Johns in March 1957 while visiting *Artists of the New York School: Second Generation* at the Jewish Museum in New York, in which *Green Target* was included. Castelli reported to Sonnabend: "I am not sure about the show, . . . but I did see a green canvas. I can't say I understood it, but I liked it immensely. It intrigued me so much that I can't think of anything else."[11] The first meeting between Johns and the Castellis is almost legendary. As Annie Cohen-Solal puts it, "Few discoveries in the history of art have risen to the status of revelation as did Castelli's first sighting of Johns's work." [12] The couple were visiting Rauschenberg's studio on Pearl Street. The artist offered them a drink but, not having ice, said he would go down to his friend Johns to get it. Castelli followed him, "and there I was confronted with an astonishing sight: paintings of flags, red, white and blue . . . all white one . . . targets . . . alphabets; numbers; and all in a material I hardly knew—encaustic."[13] It was an epiphany, and Castelli immediately offered Johns a solo show for January 1958. Rauschenberg's was to follow suit in March of the same year.

Cohen-Solal points out: "Castelli put at Johns's service a cultural and commercial network, the means of national and international exposure and, within a few months, the work had circulated throughout the world. . . . He also found the artist his earliest collectors in New York, in the persons of Ben Heller, Robert Scull, Mrs. Donald Peters, Robert Rosenblum, Leo Steinberg, Mrs. H. W. Glaswall, and Michael Sonnabend."[14] After the debut at Castelli, Johns's success was meteoric: *Two Flags* (1958) was included in the *Annual Exhibition: Contemporary Painting* at the Whitney in December 1959–January 1960; at about the same time, ten of Johns's paintings were exhibited in *Sixteen Americans* at MoMA; and in September 1960, *Jasper Johns and Kurt Schwitters* at the Ferus Gallery in Los Angeles brought his work to the West Coast. In 1964, the Jewish Museum in New York mounted a ten-year retrospective, which then traveled to the Whitechapel Gallery in London; the Pasadena Museum of Art in California had a retrospective in 1965.

As for Rauschenberg, his Combines (begun in 1954) triggered a very different reaction than Johns's *Flags* when they were first exhibited at Castelli's in March 1958. It was a "succès de scandale," and there were very few sales. The works, now considered groundbreaking, incorporated found objects of various kinds—not just photographs and newspaper clippings but also such items as a tire, a stuffed Angora goat, a stuffed eagle—onto the canvas. This abrupt and playful intrusion of the "real" into the realm

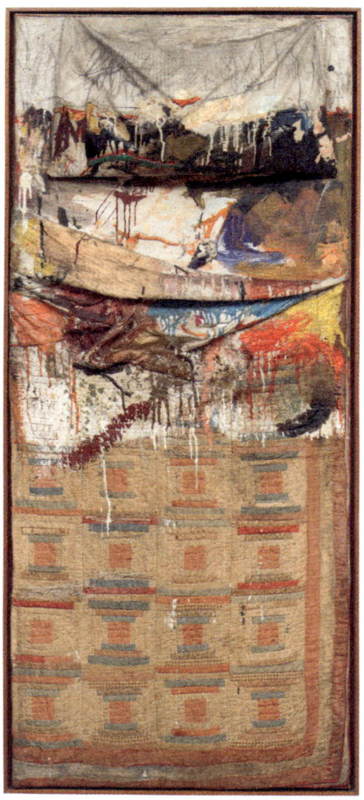

Robert Rauschenberg, *Bed*, 1955, Museum of Modern Art, New York

of art was unprecedented and provoked outraged reactions. *Bed* (1955), one of the most prominent and iconic works in the show, was bought by Castelli—who would eventually donate it to MoMA—but Barr did not acquire anything for the museum.

In 1959, however, Rauschenberg was included in the important exhibition *Sixteen Americans* at MoMA, and he started working on thirty-four illustrations for Dante's *Inferno.* They would be shown at Castelli in December 1960 and eventually acquired by MoMA, in 1963, as an anonymous gift from a donor who purchased them from Castelli for $30,000. Slowly, the art world consideration of Rauschenberg was changing positively, and he was no longer considered an "enfant terrible."

In 1962–64, he made dozens of silkscreen paintings, moving away from the three-dimensionality of the Combines. They were canvases on which gestural brushstrokes were combined with silkscreened images taken from diverse sources—*National Geographic*, *Life*, *Esquire*, and various newspapers, as well as Rauschenberg's own photographs. The outside world was still included in the paintings but in a two-dimensional way.

In 1963, the Jewish Museum finally mounted the first retrospective dedicated to Rauschenberg, curated by its new director, Alan Solomon.

Lee Bontecou, Christo, Marisol Escobar, Donald Judd, Roy Lichtenstein, James Rosenquist, Frank Stella, and Andy Warhol, to name just a few: the Castelli Gallery launched and nurtured the careers of many artists of the new generation—in the words of Cohen-Solal, "the major figures who broke with Abstract Expressionism."[15] "The art of the 1960s would have not looked the way it did if Leo Castelli had not assembled his group of artists and promoted them into international prominence," affirms Diamonstein.[16] Castelli's reach embraced not only Pop art but also the nascent Minimalism. Emerging as a reaction against the emotional intensity and expressiveness of Abstract Expressionism, Minimalism sought to distill art to its essential elements, emphasizing simplicity, formal rigor, and objectivity. In sculpture, this vision translated into the pure geometric forms of Donald Judd (1928–1994), Dan Flavin (1933–1996), and Carl Andre (1935–2024); in painting, it produced the large-scale monochromatic canvases of Frank Stella (1936–2024), devoid of external references and personal emotions; the abstract compositions of Ellsworth Kelly (1923–2015), celebrating pure form, color, and the interplay of shape; and the subtle and meticulous grid compositions of Agnes Martin (1912–2004), rendered with delicate brushstroke and a muted palette.

LEO CASTELLI

"Few were truly immune to Leo's charm," states Annie Cohen-Solal in her comprehensive biography dedicated to the gallerist.[17] "Small of stature, impeccably dressed," is how Calvin Tomkins describes him in a 1980 *New Yorker* profile, also quoting Ivan Karp (1926–2012), former director of the gallery, in referring to Castelli's "mixture of European charm and American ease."[18]

Born in the international city of Trieste in 1907 into an affluent Jewish family named Krauss, Leo adopted his mother's name, Castelli, in 1932, after the Italian Fascist regime forced its citizens to abandon foreign names. He studied law in Milan, but his passion was literature, which he read in four languages, and he was an excellent athlete. Castelli's first job was with an insurance company that in 1932 sent him to Bucharest, where he met and married Ileana Schapira, the daughter of one of the richest Romanian industrialists. With Castelli having secured a position in a bank in Paris, in 1935 the couple arrived in the capital on the Orient Express and settled in the elegant Parisian suburb of Neuilly-sur-Seine, with a cook, a laundress, a chauffeur, and chambermaids. Their daughter, Nina, was born in 1936. Backed by Ileana's father, in 1939 Castelli opened a gallery with René Drouin at place Vendôme, showing Art Deco furniture and Surrealist paintings. The enterprise was short-lived, though: World War II broke out in September, and the Castellis, being Jewish, were forced to flee from Europe. In 1941, they arrived in New York, following an adventurous journey via Tangier and Cuba. Castelli volunteered for the US Army and served in an intelligence unit; at the war's conclusion, he was granted American citizenship.

The couple soon immersed themselves in New York's burgeoning avant-garde scene, forging friendships with curators and artists. In 1957, Castelli inaugurated his gallery, which would support and shape the new course of American art. After his divorce from Ileana, with whom he remained on amicable terms and continued a fruitful collaboration, Leo married Antoinette Fraissex du Bost (1928–1987), twenty years younger, in 1963. The couple had a son, Jean-Christophe, born the same year. A temporary location on the Upper West Side of Manhattan, the Castelli Warehouse, was opened in December 1968 with an exhibition organized by Robert Morris (1931–2018) and featuring environmental sculptures by Bruce Nauman (b. 1941) and Richard Serra (1938–2024), along with works by Eva Hesse (1936–1970) and several other artists. In 1971, Castelli was one of the first dealers to establish a gallery in the then-degraded SoHo neighborhood in Lower Manhattan, at 420 West Broadway—he took the second floor and Sonnabend the third in the same building. In 1995, Leo married the young Italian historian Barbara Bertozzi. In older age, Castelli inspired, and sometimes partnered with, a younger generation of dealers, such as Jeffrey Deitch and Larry Gagosian. He died in New York on August 21, 1999.

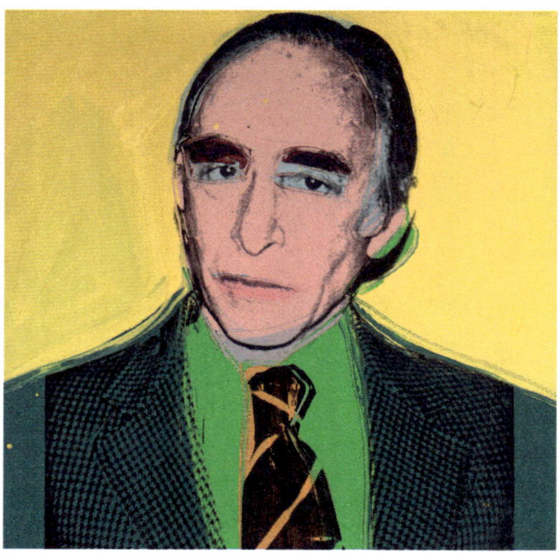

Andy Warhol, *Leo Castelli*, 1975

Equally crucial for promoting the new American art was Ileana Sonnabend's Parisian gallery.

After divorcing Castelli in 1959 and marrying Michael Sonnabend, she moved to Europe with the intention of opening her own venue. Rome was the city the couple first considered, but instead they preferred to settle in the more international Paris. In November 1962, Sonnabend's gallery was inaugurated at 37, quai des Grands-Augustins, on the Left Bank of the Seine, with a solo exhibition dedicated to Johns. The artist had previously been included in the Venice Biennale of 1958 and presented in Paris at the Galerie Rive Droite in January 1959, to the indifference of local critics. Some of them were decidedly hostile, like the influential Pierre Restany (1930–2003), promoter of Nouveau Réalisme—a movement that emerged in France in the early 1960s, characterized like Pop art in Britain and the United States by the incorporation of everyday objects and urban life into art, along with the use of assemblage, collage, and performance. Sonnabend was advised not to show Johns's *Flags*, as they could have been taken as a political provocation, but she ignored the recommendation. As Manuela Gandini remarks, "The inauguration of this little unknown gallery caused a great sensation," a mixture of praise and outrage.[19]

Rauschenberg's Combines followed in 1963, presented in two consecutive shows. Tomkins describes the initial exhibitions of Johns, Rauschenberg, Stella, Lichtenstein, and other Castelli artists at the Sonnabend Gallery in Paris as revolutionary events.[20] In January 1964, Andy Warhol's solo show *Death in America* was mounted there. Its images of car crashes and electric chairs serigraphed on canvas shocked Paris and put the artist on the international map with authority. As Gandini notes, the Sonnabends brought a new energy to Europe that contrasted sharply with the prevailing stillness. They revolutionized the promotion and dissemination of contemporary art, circulating irreverent and provocative images from another world.[21]

During the early 1960s, while the Castelli Gallery was rapidly gaining a following among American collectors, Sonnabend faced the challenges of a cultural landscape often hostile to women and generally wary of American art. Despite these obstacles, she successfully cultivated a network of influential supporters. Among them were the German chocolate manufacturer Peter Ludwig and his wife, Irene, who donated their collection to the newly created Ludwig Museum in Cologne in 1976 and to more than two dozen others; and Count Giuseppe Panza di Biumo, a significant part of whose collection in Italy was sold to the new Museum of Contemporary Art (MOCA) in Los Angeles in 1984. She also earned the backing of prominent museum directors such as Pontus Hultén (1924–2006) of the Moderna Museet in Stockholm, who in 1964 organized the groundbreaking exhibition *American Pop Art: 106 Forms of Love and Despair*, which subsequently traveled to the Stedelijk Museum in Amsterdam and the Louisiana Museum of Modern Art in Humlebaek, Denmark.

Catherine Dossin notes that by the time Abstract Expressionism made its European debut in the late 1950s, highlighted by prestigious exhibitions such as *The New American Painting* (see "New York Stories I," p. 142), it was already well established and commanded high prices. In contrast, Pop art arrived in Europe from its very inception, offering works at prices that were still accessible to many collectors. It also resonated more deeply with European audiences, who were already familiar with, and intrigued by, American popular culture through Hollywood films, comic books, and the vibrant pages of *Life* magazine. Likewise facilitating its rapid acceptance, Pop art was perceived as more relatable and easier to understand than the often abstract and enigmatic Abstract Expressionism. Ultimately, the triumph of American art in Europe was the success of Pop art, not Abstract Expressionism, as the later style arrived at the right moment to fulfill European expectations of what American art should represent.[22]

ILEANA SONNABEND

"She epitomizes an essential figure within the history of modern art: the woman art dealer." That's how Ann Temkin describes the subject of the exhibition *Ileana Sonnabend: Ambassador for the New*, which was mounted in 2013 at the Museum of Modern Art in New York to celebrate the donation of important works by Sonnabend's heirs. Temkin notes that Sonnabend was one of several such women—Peggy Guggenheim, Betty Parsons, and others had preceded her in New York, Denise René and Iris Clert in Paris—and observes that whereas "the decision makers at art institutions were primarily men, the role of the dealer offered a rare opportunity for a woman who wanted to use her creative intelligence to make a mark."[23]

Born Ileana Schapira in 1914 in Bucharest, a member of one of the richest industrial families in Romania, she grew up in a cultural and international environment. Annie Cohen-Solal describes her as "beautiful, sophisticated, elegant, and rich. She

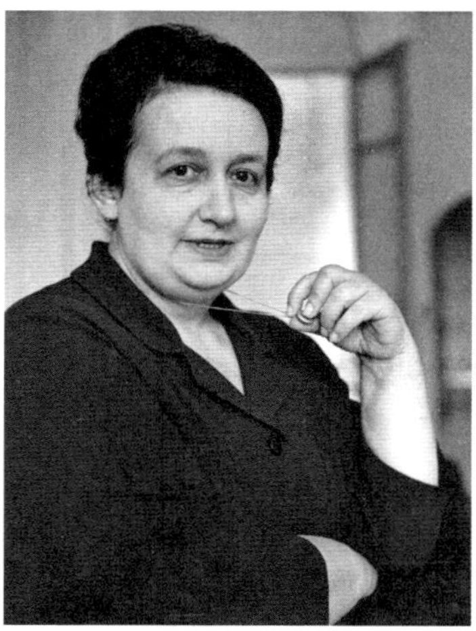

János Kender and Harry Shunk, *Ileana Sonnabend*, c. 1960s

was also, as Leo would discover, provocative, willful, whimsical, and curious."[24] In 1933, at only eighteen, she married Leo Castelli and moved with him to Paris in 1935 and then to New York not long after the outbreak of World War II. After the Castellis divorced, she married Michael Sonnabend, a literary scholar whom she had met at Columbia University, and the couple moved to Europe, eventually settling in Paris, where she opened her own gallery. Animated by an unconventionally courageous and adventurous spirit, Sonnabend championed artists whose work at the time was considered impossible to sell.

In 1968, amid student protests and broader social unrest, Sonnabend decided to close her Paris gallery. She returned to New York, initially opening a space uptown at 924 Madison Avenue before establishing a full-fledged gallery in 1971 at 420 West Broadway in SoHo, sharing the building with Castelli. In Paris, Sonnabend had introduced American artists to European audiences, and upon returning to New York, she reversed the approach by presenting European artists to the American public. Her legendary opening show, in September 1971, was a performance by Gilbert (b. 1943) and George (b. 1942): the two self-described "living sculptures," painted in gold and wearing tweed suits, sang an old British popular song, "Underneath the Arches," repeatedly for hours. Many pioneering exhibitions—often considered outrageous—followed. In January 1972, Vito Acconci (1940–2017) masturbated underneath a wooden ramp eight hours a day for the duration of his three-week show, called *Seedbed*. In 1991, Jeff Koons (b. 1955) presented *Made in Heaven*, a series of paintings and sculptures that depicted him engaged in sexual acts with his then wife, the porn star La Cicciolina (Ilona Staller). In 2000, Sonnabend's gallery moved to the Chelsea neighborhood of Manhattan, its last location. Sonnabend died in 2007, leaving her daughter, Nina, and adopted son, Antonio Homem, as her heirs. The gallery closed in 2014.

The coronation of Castelli's and Sonnabend's combined efforts in promoting American art came in 1964, when Rauschenberg was awarded the Grand Prize for Painting at the Venice Biennale, the first time ever for an American artist. Until then, from 1948 to 1962, of twenty-four

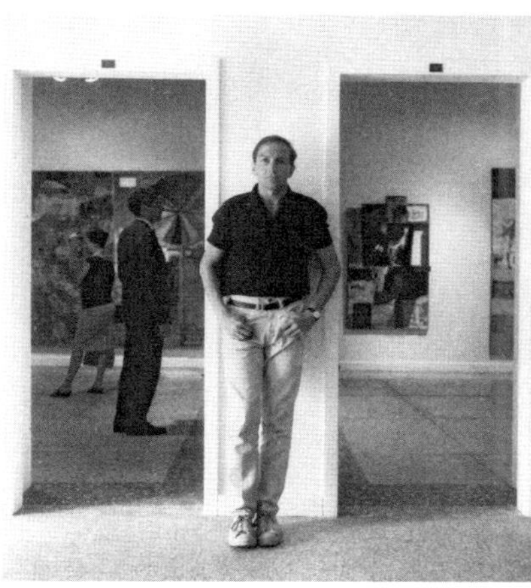

János Kender and Harry Shunk, *Robert Rauschenberg exhibition, Venice Biennale, 1964 June 21*, 1964

international prizes awarded, ten had gone to the French Pavilion and fourteen to artists associated with the School of Paris.[25]

Rauschenberg's recognition marked an epochal passage: American art was no longer considered derivative of a European model, but the real harbinger of novelty. Rauschenberg's Venice Biennale success triggered endless polemics, though, talk of conspiracy, and sometimes outrage. Cohen-Solal reports that the Church forbade its clergy to visit the Biennale and that the Vatican paper *Osservatore Romano* called it "the complete and utter downfall of culture!"[26]

VIRGINIA DWAN

Virginia Dwan (1931–2022) founded her eponymous gallery in a Los Angeles storefront in 1959. The city's interest in modern art at the time was limited, and much like the Hollywood film industry—as remarked by art historian Germano Celant (1940–2020)—Los Angeles society rejected any endeavor not centered on amusement and entertainment. Art was often deemed either unnecessary or a conduit for immorality and political dissent.[27] A contemporary art museum did not yet exist; the Los Angeles Museum of History, Science and Art had turned down the offer of the extraordinary Louise and Walter Arensberg collection of modern art—particularly remarkable for its extensive holdings of works by Marcel Duchamp—and it was eventually donated to the Philadelphia Museum of Art. Collectors' support in general was lacking, and the few existing galleries, such as Frank Perls, Felix Landau, and Paul Kantor, were promoting Californian artists like Richard Diebenkorn (1922–1993) or established European masters. The opening of the Ferus Gallery in 1957 with a group exhibition including art by Edward Kienholz (1927–1994), around whom an experimental scene was emerging, marked a first fundamental step toward a structural change in the Los Angeles scene. Kienholz's provocative and immersive works employed found objects to address social and political issues, by challenging viewers to confront uncomfortable truths within everyday settings.

Dwan's program had a significant impact, as she operated on two fronts: promoting American artists such as Rauschenberg, Franz Kline (1910–1962), Philip Guston (1913–1980), and Joan Mitchell (1925–1992); and introducing European artists including Arman (1928–2005)—with whom Dwan's new spaces on Lindbrook Drive were inaugurated in 1962—as well as Yves Klein (1928–1962), Niki de Saint Phalle (1930–2002), and Martial Raysse (b. 1936).

Expanding its presence to New York in 1965, Dwan Gallery became the hub for artists exploring Minimalism, Conceptual art, and Land art. The latter, also known as Earth art or Environmental art, emerged in the late 1960s and early 1970s, driven by a desire to overcome the limitations of the physical space of galleries and museums. Embracing the vastness and temporality of the earth itself, Land artists produced works in the natural landscape that were designed to change over time and were subject to the forces of erosion, weathering, and growth. This impermanence challenged the commodification of art, as these pieces are not easily bought, sold, or collected. However, such complex interventions in the natural landscape required considerable funding. Land art turned into a guiding principle for Dwan's gallery, informing its selection of artists, exhibitions, and programming. The groundbreaking *Earthworks* exhibition in 1968 showed a diverse group of artists whose large-scale installations, ephemeral sculptures, and immersive experiences invited viewers to contemplate their place in the natural world, as well as to consider the impact of human activity on the environment.

Dwan's unwavering commitment to Land art, bolstered by her considerable personal fortune, enabled her to finance iconic projects such as *Double Negative* (1969) by Michael Heizer (b. 1944), *Spiral Jetty* (1970) by Robert Smithson (1938–1973), *35-Pole Lightning Field* (1973) by Walter De Maria (1935–2013), and *Star Axis* (1976–) by Charles Ross (b. 1937). The creation of the Dwan Light Sanctuary at the United World College–USA in Montezuma, New Mexico—completed in 1996—embodied Dwan's holistic vision of art as a transformative and contemplative force. Her dedication to philanthropy was central to Dwan's decision to close her gallery in 1971, and it materialized in generous gifts to various US institutions, most notably more than 250 works to the National Gallery of Art in Washington, DC. The exhibition *Los Angeles to New York: Dwan Gallery, 1959–1971*, organized in 2017 by the National Gallery of Art and the Los Angeles County Museum of Art, paid Dwan a too-long-expected tribute.

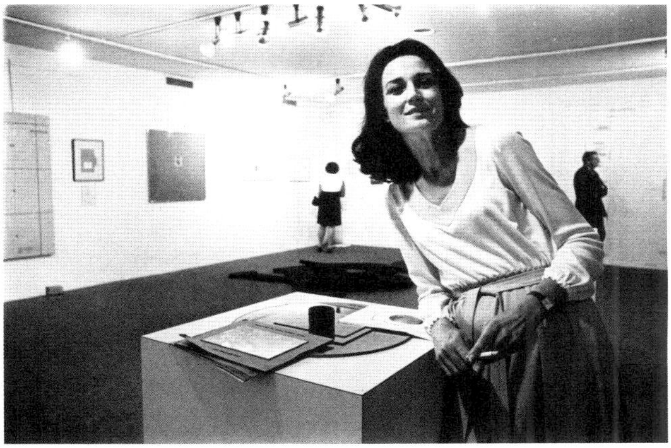

Virginia Dwan at the exhibition *Language III*, Dwan Gallery, New York, 1969

THE CASTELLI-SONNABEND MODEL

Castelli and Sonnabend harnessed a model of artist representation—which Paul Durand-Ruel inaugurated in the nineteenth century with his Impressionist stable (see "Paul Durand-Ruel and the Birth of the Impressionist Market," p. 94)—that has long been considered the gold standard of promotion and dedication.

I prefer to call it "Castelli-Sonnabend"—not only "Castelli," as it usually is referred to—because Sonnabend's role cannot be overemphasized. When working in New York, her approach complemented her husband's. In the words of Rauschenberg, "Ileana was more sensual and imaginative, while Leo was more analytical and art-history-aware, and it was the tension between their two approaches that made the gallery."[28] The decision to take on new artists was always a joint one between the Castellis. When she moved to Europe and opened her Parisian venue in 1962, Sonnabend became a trailblazer in promoting in Europe the artists whom Castelli was promoting in America.

Castelli had total dedication to his artists; to him, as Tomkins says an unnamed museum director put it, "The artist always comes before the money." This translated into awarding regular stipends to artists, Tomkins adds, regardless of whether they were productive or not—another cornerstone of the Castelli-Sonnabend model.[29] William Rubin (1927–2006), director of the Department of Painting and Sculpture at MoMA from 1973 to 1988, declared, "Leo is always ready to sacrifice his own interests to those of his artists. . . . I think he is in the tradition of men like Ambroise Vollard, who have been devoted and committed to the artists they handled, to helping their art find its rightful place. To me, he is a model art dealer."[30] At one point, Ivan Karp, then director of the Castelli Gallery, suggested cutting John Chamberlain's stipend in half because he was too slow at making work and happened to be $40,000 in debt to the gallery. "How could I?" Castelli replied. "He couldn't get along on that."[31]

The primary function of the art dealer, as Castelli stated, was to discover new artists and make them known to the public before museums would. This involved finding opportunities for the artists at museums and other public institutions, meaning exhibitions or acquisitions for their permanent collections.[32] Castelli therefore nurtured relationships with all the major museum directors and curators—Alfred Barr of MoMA, Alan Solomon of the Jewish Museum, Henry Geldzahler (1935–1994) of the Metropolitan Museum of Art—as did Sonnabend in Europe, although museums there were slower to open their doors to contemporary art. International promotion was also central to the Castelli-Sonnabend strategy, and was based on setting up a network of satellite galleries that were provided with works to show and sell. Virginia Dwan in Los Angeles, John Berggruen in San Francisco, David Mirvish in Toronto, Konrad Fischer in Düsseldorf, and Gian Enzo Sperone in Turin were some of their most active collaborators. Although Castelli repeatedly declared that selling art was not his goal, but only the means necessary to finance his enterprise, he successfully built a solid clientele including Robert and Ethel Scull, Emily and Burton Tremaine, Philip Johnson, and Harry N. Abrams, among others, while Sonnabend was pursuing the same goal in Europe. Art dealer Jeffrey Deitch calls Castelli's strategy "counter-commercial," but he notes that—ironically—galleries with a commercial orientation usually do not succeed as well as galleries that are primarily motivated by an artistic mission.[33]

The late collector Donald Marron said in an interview by Cohen-Solal: "Leo identified a time that was coming, he identified a number of the great players, and then he created an atmosphere in which they would flourish. I have no idea how he did financially, but he created this atmosphere of discovery and success."[34]

And indeed there was additional value in a work bought at Castelli's, still considered today the most prestigious provenance for that period.

Between Leo Castelli and Andy Warhol, who would become the most celebrated artist of his generation and the icon of Pop art, it was not love at first sight.

Warhol had visited the Castelli Gallery in May 1961 as a collector, buying a drawing by Johns for $350. According to Ivan Karp, the gallery's director, Warhol then noticed a Lichtenstein painting leaning against the wall and exclaimed, "I am doing something like this myself!" Warhol was shocked. "I actually am doing cartoon things and commercial subjects. But they're different, of course; they're very different. Would you come and look?"[35] Karp went, but Castelli declined to represent Warhol at that time, as he feared it would be detrimental to exhibit works so similar to Lichtenstein's. However, Cohen-Solal writes, Sonnabend perceived Warhol's potential right away, and she empathized with his nature.[36] After Karp's visit, Warhol abandoned the use of comic strips as sources for his pictures and focused on simple consumer objects such as Campbell's Soup cans and Coca-Cola bottles. These were initially executed by hand, but later, starting in 1962, around the time that Rauschenberg was making his silkscreen paintings, Warhol discovered the same technique, which he would embrace until his death, as it allowed him to be as impersonal as a machine.

In April 1961, Warhol had displayed some early Pop art works in the window of the Bonwit Teller department store in New York, as Johns and Rauschenberg had done a few years earlier. However, it was on the West Coast, at the Ferus Gallery in Los Angeles, that Warhol had his debut solo exhibition of Pop art, in July–August 1962. The now iconic thirty-two *Campbell's Soup Cans*, one for each different flavor of soup, were displayed on a ledge around the gallery as if sitting on grocery shelves. Ferus Gallery partner Irving Blum had encountered Warhol's work during a trip to New York the summer before, and although he admitted to still being drawn to Abstract Expressionism, he was intrigued

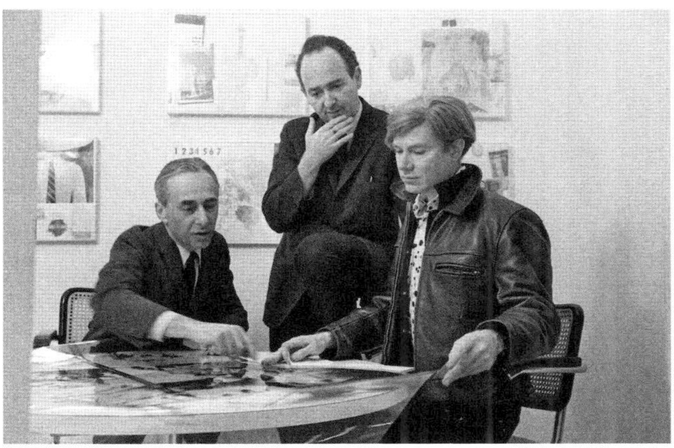

Leo Castelli, Ivan Karp, and Andy Warhol, 1966

The Factory was not only Andy Warhol's studio, but the epicenter of both his artistic output and his public persona, which were deeply intertwined and mutually dependent. Gerard Malanga (b. 1943), one of Warhol's closest collaborators during those years, reminisces: "In contrast to other artists who were very private in their studios, Andy just opened the doors. The Factory became a very open environment, not intentionally, but Andy enjoyed being around people. He was a people person, a collector of people."[37]

The first Factory opened on the fifth floor at 231 East Forty-Seventh Street, near the newly constructed United Nations building, in a neighborhood devoid of artistic activity at the time. Its walls were adorned with silver foil, earning it the nickname "Silver Factory," and it quickly became a gathering place for celebrities—and aspiring ones—and vibrant parties often accompanied by amphetamine use.

In early 1968, Warhol relocated the Factory downtown to the Decker Building at 33 Union Square West, where he was later shot, almost fatally, by the radical feminist writer and activist Valerie Solanas on June 3, 1968. In 1974, the Factory moved again, to 860 Broadway, on the northwest side of Union Square. Reflecting on this era, Henry Geldzahler, then a curator at the Metropolitan Museum of Art, remembers: "There was always this feeling that something incredible was going to happen, something really exciting or fun or new. . . . You didn't know what corner it was going to come from. And you could sit just languidly and wait for it to happen. . . . Andy brought a new sense of strategy and possibility into American art that's still reverberating."[38]

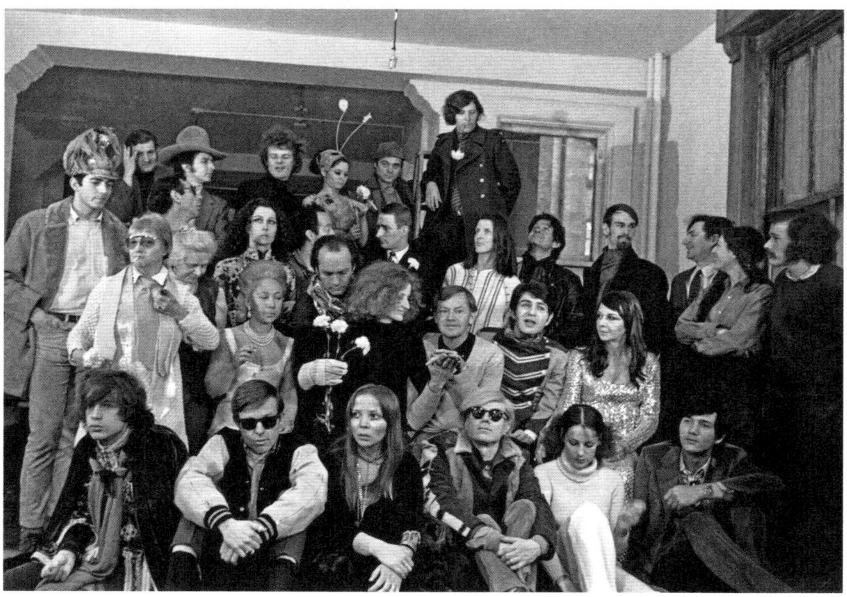

Group portrait taken at Andy Warhol's Factory, New York, March 6, 1968

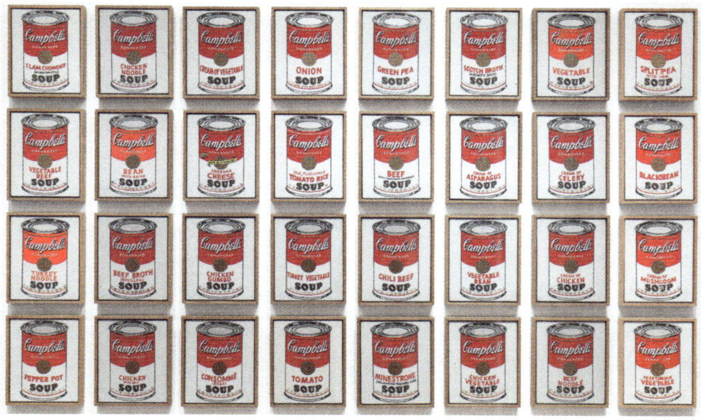

Andy Warhol, *Campbell's Soup Cans*, 1962, Museum of Modern Art, New York

by what Warhol did: "I remember not being able to make head or tails of these paintings. They were radical, and I wasn't at all prepared for them. . . . However art evolved, I didn't think that would be the way."[39] In the Ferus Gallery's 1962 show, there were a few sales, but Blum and Warhol decided to keep the *Campbell's Soup* series together and bought back the paintings that had been purchased. The thirty-two canvases are now part of the collection of the Museum of Modern Art in New York.

In November of the same year, the Stable Gallery in New York mounted an exhibition of *Marilyn* and *Elvis* paintings, among others. In that show, the architect Philip Johnson bought *Gold Marilyn Monroe* (1962), to donate to MoMA. The *Elvis* series was also shown in September 1963 at the Ferus Gallery. As mentioned above, an exhibition of Warhol's *Death and Disaster* paintings at Sonnabend's gallery in Paris in January 1964 was a breakthrough for the artist on the European scene and market. That April, after a last show at the Stable Gallery, of hundreds of *Campbell's*, *Brillo*, *Heinz*, and other wood boxes representing various grocery products, Philip Johnson commissioned Warhol to produce a mural for the façade of the New York State Pavilion, which Johnson designed, at the 1964–65 New York World's Fair. As the subject, Warhol chose mug shots of the thirteen men described as most wanted in a New York Police Department booklet. The mural triggered controversy and was removed a few days before the opening—by being covered with silver paint.

Finally, in November 1964, Warhol had his much-awaited debut with Castelli. The somber mood of the disaster paintings was abandoned in favor of just one subject: flowers. Based on a photograph of four hibiscus blossoms by Patricia Caulfield—who in 1966 would successfully sue Warhol for appropriating her images without authorization—the series depicted the flowers in different colors, combinations, and sizes, representing a new artistic departure for the artist. Blake Gopnik writes that Castelli displayed thirty-six of the canvases in the exhibition, while keeping dozens more in his inventory, and that within two months more than thirty had sold, priced from $150 to $1,200. Castelli and Karp were able to sell another fifty over the course of the following year, grossing around $50,000, nearly quadrupling the total amount that Warhol's first show at the Stable Gallery had generated.[40] Warhol's reputation was growing, along with his status as a celebrity; his studio, known as the Factory at its different locations over the years, was the site of not only the creation of art but also filmmaking, a variety of performances, and seemingly nonstop parties. In October 1965, the first museum survey dedicated to the artist was organized by the Institute of Contemporary Art in Philadelphia, and the opening was, in Gopnik's words, "a madhouse."[41] By his second show at Castelli, in 1966, security guards had to be stationed to manage the overwhelming crowd. In an unusual move, no paintings were displayed; instead, the exhibition featured silver "pillows" and wallpaper adorned with silkscreened cows.

A CHANGING SCENARIO

A. Deirdre Robson writes that by the end of the 1950s, the support system for modern art in New York was undergoing significant changes:

> The status of modern art museums had increased and was accompanied by much higher annual attendances.... At the same time, the number of galleries in New York had increased from some 70 establishments in 1940 to more than 115 in 1954, and about 275 in early 1960, with a concurrent expansion in the number of artists and variety of shows staged. The total volume of auction sales had also trebled, and those in private galleries had increased by a similarly substantial proportion, with a concomitant rise in general price levels. Finally, the number of collectors seemed to be burgeoning nationwide.[42]

In this evolving environment, characterized by general growing economic prosperity and wider social and cultural openness, success and acceptance came faster and more easily to the Pop artists compared to the previous generation.

The Abstract Expressionists came of age during the Great Depression, experienced material and financial deprivation, and had to struggle for their art to be accepted. For years, they felt rejected by the cultural establishment, heroes against a society that did not understand or appreciate them. When, at the end of the 1950s, recognition finally arrived, the Abstract Expressionists had to face the emergence of a younger group of artists, immediately acclaimed as the new avant-garde, and they reacted with profound hostility. After Sidney Janis mounted the *International Exhibition of the New Realists*, which put together European and American Pop, in 1962, Adolph Gottlieb (1903–1974), Philip Guston, Robert Motherwell (1915–1991), and Mark Rothko (1903–1970) decided to protest by abandoning Janis's gallery, which at the time represented them. "The Abstract Expressionists' anger was not really so hard to understand," explains Tomkins. "They had struggled for many years in total obscurity, their achievements recognized only by one another. . . . The recognition that they had so recently and so arduously won was now being usurped, or so they believed, by a new generation of brash youngsters who had become 'artists overnight,' who had not earned anything the hard way, and whose most apparent common bond seemed to be mockery and rejection of all serious art."[43]

It was not only that recognition and success were easier to achieve for the new artists; the same approval mechanism was undergoing a profound transformation. In an interview, Castelli affirmed that Pop art was primarily a collector's movement, that collectors were the principal champions of the group.[44] As Diana Crane points out, Pop art incorporated images of banal consumer objects and used the language of advertising and comics, thus creating a new type of relationship between the artist, the spectator, and the art object. The spectator could immediately relate to what the artists represented, the highly familiar world of popular culture; Pop art was easy to like, and it coincided with a mood of openness and excitement in the larger society. The role of art critic as a mediator and interpreter was therefore no longer needed, or at least was much diminished.[45]

Furthermore, buying contemporary American art was beginning to be perceived as a profitable investment. Confirmation arrived on October 18, 1973, with the Scull auction at Sotheby Parke Bernet. Robert Scull, a New York taxicab entrepreneur and, with his wife Ethel, an early collector of postwar American art, put up for sale fifty of the best paintings from the collection, in an auction that became one of the first media events of its kind—it was reported on by CBS—and was accompanied by marketing and publicity. All the artists included were American; apart from Franz Kline and Barnett Newman, still alive; and an average of around forty years old. The results of the auction were extraordinary, establishing several records. A painting by Twombly sold for $40,000, more than fifty times the $750 Scull had paid; Johns's *Double White Map* (1965), bought by Scull for $10,200, went for $240,000; Rauschenberg's Combine painting *Thaw*, acquired by Scull for $900, made $85,000. This triggered Rauschenberg's famous confrontation with Scull after the auction, captured by a documentary film crew: the artist accused the collector of profiteering off his own hard work; Scull responded that these auction results would raise primary-market prices for Rauschenberg and his fellow artists when selling their future works. The auction marked a turning point: it put postwar and contemporary American art on the map and established the idea that it could be a moneymaking tool.

Pop art marked a radical departure from the introspective, individualistic nature of Abstract Expressionism, yet despite its innovations, the movement fell short in addressing or advancing gender equality. The attitude of the consumer society of the 1960s toward women was contradictory. In Linda Nochlin's words: "On the one hand, they were considered the primary agents of consumerism; ads for hard goods, innovative products, new cleansers, clothes, and cosmetics as well as food and drink were aimed directly at them; on the other hand, women themselves were made into a product in popular culture, or at least productlike: passive, sexual creatures, miniskirted big-breasted 'dollies' made to be consumed—or thrown away—by hungry male admirers."[46]

In the aftermath of World War II, women were largely pushed back into traditional domestic roles. Betty Friedan's landmark 1963 book, *The Feminine Mystique*, provided a profound analysis of the postwar shift, quickly becoming a cornerstone of feminist literature. As men returned from military service, many women left their wartime jobs, leading to the reassertion of a "mystique" that reinforced traditional roles, emphasizing women's place within the family and the home. The societal transformation not only affected married women but also influenced a younger generation. By the end of the 1950s, for example, the percentage of women attending college significantly declined, from 47 percent in 1920 to 35 percent in 1958, as many young women opted to leave college in pursuit of marriage.

In this context, fully appreciating the contributions of female artists to Pop art requires a reevaluation of the movement itself. Moreover, the conventional understanding of Pop art as an exclusively American and London-based phenomenon must be reconsidered, as highlighted by such exhibitions as the eye-opening *The World Goes Pop* at Tate Modern in London in 2015–16. Pop art was, in fact, a complex, global, and multifaceted movement, far broader than a simple embrace of consumerism. Women artists of the time often challenged the reduction of the genre to stereotypes—such as comic-strip heroines

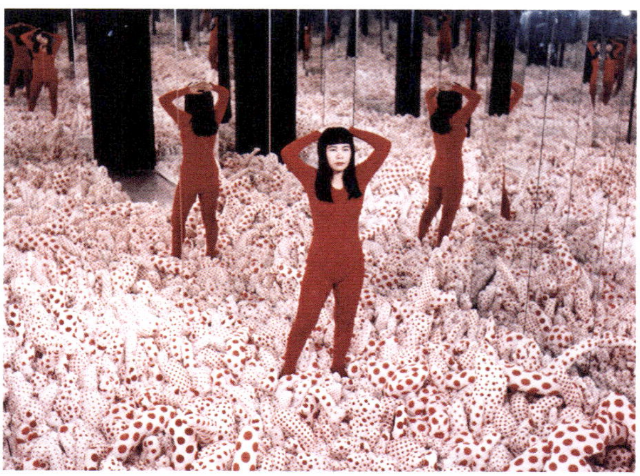

Yayoi Kusama with *Infinity Mirror Room–Phalli's Field* (1965), Castellane Gallery, New York, 1965

and flattened, faceless nudes—by offering a different, more caustic and critical gaze on consumerist society, or by experimenting with new, unorthodox materials traditionally associated with female crafts.

The now widely celebrated Yayoi Kusama (b. 1929), whose immersive *Infinity Mirror Rooms* and other large-scale installations captivate audiences and quickly become Instagram sensations, holds an auction record of $10,496,000 for her work. However, she initially faced significant struggles to gain visibility and approval in the art world. Born into a wealthy and traditional family from rural Japan, since childhood Kusama suffered from anxiety and hallucinations, seeing the dots that would become her artistic signature. In the United States, where she moved in 1957 and remained until 1973, mostly in New York, the young artist developed her own distinctive interpretation of Pop art through an uncompromising and bold artistic practice. In 1962, at the same time as Claes Oldenburg, she produced the first soft sculptures, in the form of phalluses accumulated to cover various objects—but only Oldenburg was credited for the invention at the time. And as early as 1965, Kusama pioneered immersive ambient experiences with her first *Infinity Mirror Room*.

With her series *Nanas*, starting in 1964, Niki de Saint Phalle celebrated femininity by reimagining primitive female goddesses with a bold, contemporary, and grotesque twist. For one of them, *Ana Lena en Grèce* (1965–67), the auction record was established at Sotheby's New York in November 2005 at $1,136,000.

Marisol Escobar (1930–2016), commonly referred to simply as Marisol, was known for her carved wood sculptures characterized by their boxy, totemic forms. By the mid-1960s, Warhol described her as "the first girl artist with *glamour*."[47] Shown regularly at Castelli, Marisol received prices that were in line with those of her male peers at the time: in 1965, for example, her sculptures were selling for up to $7,500, compared to Lichtenstein's and Warhol's up to $8,000.[48] After a gradual eclipse from collective memory, in recent years there has been a resurgence of interest in and a reevaluation of her work. But Marisol's market is still soft, with an auction record of $912,000—very far from the multimillion-dollar prices achieved now by Lichtenstein and Warhol—for *The Cocktail Party* (1965–66), an assemblage of fifteen freestanding figures that sold at Sotheby's New York in May 2005.

Lee Bontecou (1931–2022) gained recognition with her celebrated expansive, wall-mounted sculptures. Bearing the influence of World War II, these innovative works were crafted using industrial materials such as conveyor belts, mailbags, and dryer components. Bontecou always rejected the attempt by some to read them as vaginal images expressing an aggressive sexuality. She was one of the very few women to have consistent representation by Leo Castelli. Bontecou's market is finally rising, with an auction record of $9,176,500 for one of her wall sculptures, *Untitled* (1959–60), which sold at Christie's New York in November 2021.

Mirroring the retreat of Bontecou from the public eye, Lee Lozano (1930–1999) earned acclaim in the 1960s before similarly disappearing for forty years. Recent exhibitions (such as *Strike*, at Pinacoteca Agnelli, Turin, in 2023, and Bourse de Commerce, Paris, in 2023–24) have presented her work to a broader public. Developing a very personal aesthetic, Lozano interpreted the Pop spirit of her time in her *Tool Paintings* series. Enlarged hammers, screws, clamps, bolts—all are monochromatically rendered with obvious phallic allusions. The market for Lozano reached $602,500 in an auction at Phillips in 2010 for an untitled canvas from 1970.

Among the artists who transformed traditional feminine crafts into fine art, Faith Ringgold (1930–2024) stands out. Her quilts are vibrant, narrative-rich tapestries that weave together African American heritage, feminism, and the struggles of the Civil Rights Movement. These works, imbued with cultural depth and social critique, have gradually gained recognition in the art world. Her record price was established at Sotheby's New York in May 2024 for *Dinner at Gertrude Stein's: The French Collection Part II, #10* (1991), which sold for $1,572,500, more than twice the low estimate.

Rosalyn Drexler (b. 1926) created paintings inspired by atmospheric film noir. Her work is still ignored by a larger public and by the market, with a record price of only $37,800 for *Zoo Bandit Killed* (1963), sold at Christie's New York in May 2022.

Marjorie Strider (1931–2014) dabbled with the theme of eroticized women in her three-dimensional canvases depicting bikini-clad beauties. *Girl with Pink Rose* (2014) sold for $180,000 at Sotheby's New York in July 2024.

Pauline Boty (1938–1966) produced paintings and collages in which she used appropriated images from various sources. *Epitaph to Something's Gotta Give* (1962) sold for $1,665,607 at Christie's London in March 2024.

Martha Rosler (b. 1943) created photomontages juxtaposing disparate elements to reveal hidden truths and criticize cultural norms, for example by condemning "the suburban home as complicit with US imperialism and the atrocities of the Vietnam War."[49] Her auction record for such a work, *Bringing the War Home: House Beautiful* (1990), which sold at Christie's New York in May 2006, is $156,000.

Judy Chicago (b. 1939), whose career spanned five decades, is considered an undisputed feminist icon. Her groundbreaking installation piece *The Dinner Party* (1974–79), on permanent display at the Brooklyn Museum in New York, features a triangular table with elaborate place settings such as ceramic plates adorned with vulva-like forms, representing thirty-nine historically significant women. It is a celebration of women's achievements throughout history, but also a critique of the patriarchal structures that have marginalized them. Recent exhibitions, such as *Judy Chicago: Herstory* at the New Museum in New York in 2023–24, celebrate Chicago's relevance and the versatility of her practice, which encompasses painting, sculpture, installation, drawing, textiles, photography, stained glass, needlework, and printmaking. In terms of the market, though, her record price dates back to 2007, when *Car Hood* (1964) sold for $288,000 at Los Angeles Modern Auctions.

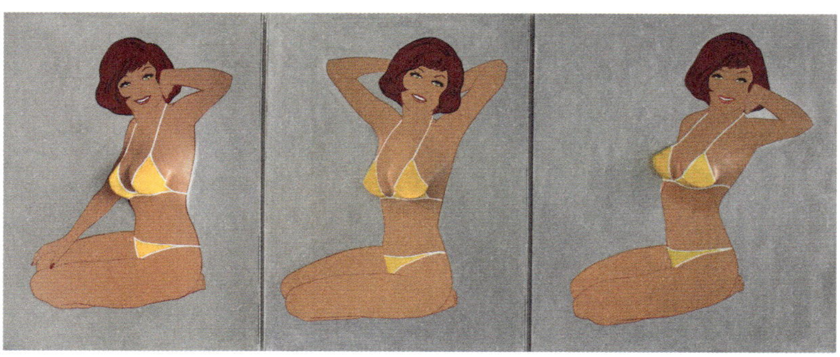

Marjorie Strider, *Triptych II (Beach Girl)*, 1963

NOTES

1 Calvin Tomkins, *Off the Wall: A Portrait of Robert Rauschenberg* (New York: Picador, 2005), 107.

2 Frank O'Hara quoted in Tomkins, *Off the Wall*, 98.

3 *Jasper Johns: Writings, Sketchbook Notes, Interviews*, ed. Kirk Varnedoe, comp. Christel Hollevoet (New York: Museum of Modern Art, 1996), 149.

4 Morgan Meis, "Is the Painting Counting?," in *Jasper Johns*, ed. Roberta Bernstein, exh. cat. (London: Royal Academy of Arts in collaboration with the Broad, 2017), 38.

5 Lucy R. Lippard, *Pop Art*, with contributions by Lawrence Alloway, Nancy Marmer, and Nicolas Calas (New York: Frederick A. Praeger, 1966), 82.

6 David Farber, *The Age of Great Dreams: America in the 1960s* (New York: Hill and Wang, 1994), 8.

7 Judd's full quote reads: "Twombly has not shown for some time, and this adds to the fiasco. In these paintings there are a couple of swirls of red paint mixed with a little yellow and white and placed high on a medium-gray surface. There are a few drips and splatters and an occasional pencil line: There isn't anything to the paintings. The poster for the show is an example of Twombly's earlier work and is easily the best thing present. Twombly usually scribbles on a white ground, using color infrequently." Donald Judd, "Cy Twombly," *Arts Magazine* 58, nos. 8–9 (May–June 1964): 38.

8 Simon Schama, "Cy Twombly," in *The Essential Cy Twombly*, ed. Nicola Del Roscio (London: Thames & Hudson, 2014), 11.

9 Tomkins, *Off the Wall*, 131.

10 Leo Castelli, interview by Barbaralee Diamonstein, *About the Arts*, WNYC, November 17, 1976.

11 Annie Cohen-Solal, *Leo and His Circle: The Life of Leo Castelli*, trans. Mark Polizzotti with the author (New York: Alfred A. Knopf, 2010), 243.

12 Cohen-Solal, *Leo and His Circle*, 248.

13 Cohen-Solal, *Leo and His Circle*, 243.

14 Cohen-Solal, *Leo and His Circle*, 249.

15 Cohen-Solal, *Leo and His Circle*, 257.

16 Castelli, interview by Diamonstein.

17 Introduction to Cohen-Solal, *Leo and His Circle*, xii.

18 Calvin Tomkins, "A Good Eye and a Good Ear," *New Yorker*, May 26, 1980, 40.

19 Manuela Gandini, *Ileana Sonnabend: "The Queen of Art"* (Rome: Castelvecchi, 2008), 153.

20 Tomkins, "A Good Eye and a Good Ear," 71.

21 Gandini, *Ileana Sonnabend*, 155.

22 Catherine Dossin, *The Rise and Fall of American Art, 1940s–1980s: A Geopolitics of Western Art Worlds* (Farnham, UK: Ashgate, 2015), 180–81.

23 Ann Temkin and Claire Lehmann, *Ileana Sonnabend: Ambassador for the New*, exh. cat. (New York: Museum of Modern Art, 2014), 10–11.

24 Cohen-Solal, *Leo and His Circle*, 122.

25 Dossin, *Rise and Fall of American Art*, 86.

26 Cohen-Solal, *Leo and His Circle*, 287–88.

27 Germano Celant, *Virginia Dwan and Dwan Gallery* (Milan: Skira, 2016), 17.

28 Tomkins, "A Good Eye and a Good Ear," 62.

29 Tomkins, "A Good Eye and a Good Ear," 40.

30 Tomkins, "A Good Eye and a Good Ear," 41.

31 Tomkins, "A Good Eye and a Good Ear," 62.

32 Castelli, interview by Diamonstein.

33 Magnus Resch, *Management of Art Galleries* (London: Phaidon, 2015), 6.

34 Cohen-Solal, *Leo and His Circle*, 258.

35 Cohen-Solal, *Leo and His Circle*, 263–64.

36 Cohen-Solal, *Leo and His Circle*, 338.

37 Stephen Shore, *Factory: Andy Warhol*, with text by Lynne Tillman (London: Phaidon, 2016), 36.

38 Shore, *Factory*, 137.

39 Blake Gopnik, *Warhol* (New York: Ecco, 2020), 249.

40 Gopnik, *Warhol*, 395.

41 Gopnik, *Warhol*, 511.

42 A. Deirdre Robson, "The New York Art Market ca. 1960," in *A History of the Western Art Market: A Sourcebook of Writings on Artists, Dealers, and Markets*, ed. Titia Hulst (Oakland: University of California Press, 2017), 324.

43 Tomkins, *Off the Wall*, 169.

44 Castelli, interview by Diamonstein.

45 Diana Crane, *The Transformation of the Avant-Garde: The New York Art World, 1940–1985* (Chicago: University of Chicago Press, 1989), 37.

46 Linda Nochlin, "Running on Empty: Women, Pop and the Society of Consumption," in *Seductive Subversion: Women Pop Artists, 1958–1968*, ed. Sid Sachs and Kalliopi Minioudaki, exh. cat. (Philadelphia: University of the Arts; New York: Abbeville Press, 2010), 15.

47 Grace Glueck, "It's Not Pop, It's Not Op—It's Marisol," *New York Times Magazine*, March 7, 1965, 34.

48 Sid Sachs, "Beyond the Surface: Women and Pop Art, 1958–1968," in *Seductive Subversion*, 33.

49 Kalliopi Minioudaki, "Feminist Eruptions in Pop, Beyond Borders," in *The World Goes Pop*, ed. Jessica Morgan and Flavia Frigeri, exh. cat. (London: Tate Publishing, 2015), 79.

9 New York Stories III

10. Breaking the Rules: Damien Hirst's Auction *Beautiful Inside My Head Forever*

p. 211	p. 212	p. 217
Beautiful Inside My Head Forever	Damien Hirst	Hirst's Market after the Auction

In a move that some say has the potential to change the face of art dealing, Mr. Hirst has cut out his dealers . . . and taken his work straight to auction.

—Carol Vogel, "Damien Hirst's Next Sensation: Thinking outside the Dealer," *New York Times*, September 14, 2008

The unprecedented case of Damien Hirst's *Beautiful Inside My Head Forever*, a two-day auction held at Sotheby's London in September 2008, challenged the conventional notion of the gallery as the exclusive venue for showing an artist's primary production. Hirst directly consigned a significant group of works from his studio to the auction house, thus excluding his dealers and gallerists from the proceeds of the sale. The auction itself was enormously successful—but afterward, the secondary market for works by Hirst declined. Why?

BEAUTIFUL INSIDE MY HEAD FOREVER

In an unheard-of move for a living artist that has never been repeated since, Hirst consigned 244 works fresh from his studio to market directly through auction in 223 lots. Proceeding in this way limited any control over the clients or pricing and increased the visibility of potential failure. It also forced those already with significant holdings of Hirst's work to bid to protect the artist's market. The presentation offered examples, all made within the previous two years, across the artist's oeuvre—animals in formaldehyde, spin and butterfly paintings, medicine cabinets, and so on. The move was bold, as artists typically prefer more controlled market conditions. Only an artist with confidence in his market—and a conceptual interest in the art world—would attempt it. With *Beautiful Inside My Head Forever*, Hirst transformed the art market itself into his artistic medium, blurring the lines between creation and commerce, turning market dynamics themselves into a performative and provocative extension of his conceptual practice. The art world awaited the results with curiosity and apprehension. Would the market, though robust at the time, be able to absorb such a huge output by a single artist in just two days of auction? If so, was the gallery's role no longer fundamental, and could other artists start selling their new work directly through auction houses?

Sotheby's heavily marketed the sale: traveling exhibitions, a luxurious limited-edition catalogue, videos on YouTube. Hirst was personally involved in the promotion, opening his studio to the most important collectors for private previews. Twenty-one thousand people visited the

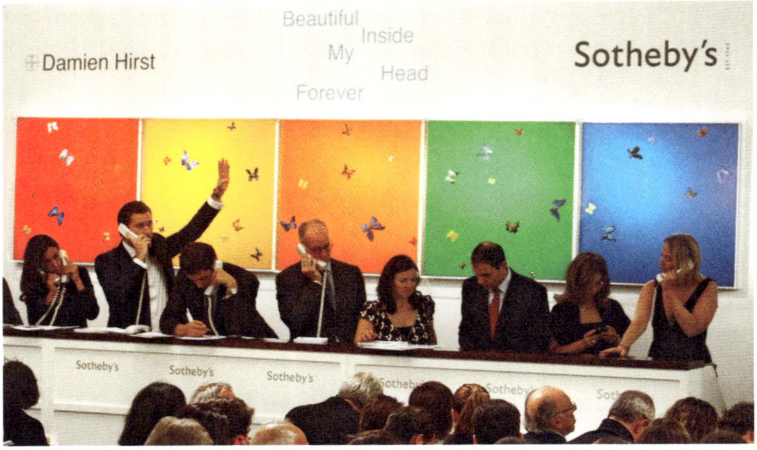

Telephone bidders vie for Damien Hirst's work at the *Beautiful Inside My Head Forever* evening sale, Sotheby's, London, September 15, 2008.

New Bond Street galleries where the works to be sold were displayed in advance of the sale.

The auction took place on September 15 and 16, 2008, in a packed and vibrant salesroom. On the opening day of the auction, Lehman Brothers, an illustrious investment bank that had been operating since the 1850s and was heavily committed to mortgage-backed investments, collapsed and filed for bankruptcy across the ocean in New York. Its failure erupted into a global financial crisis that had shown troubling warning signs since early 2007, and that by late 2008 quickly became one of the worst in recent history. However, as reported by Carol Vogel in London, "It was as if Sotheby's here was a little oasis far removed from the grim news of the financial world."[1] Her first-day article describes the setting: "The headlines had little effect on the scene outside the salesroom.... The street was filled with television camera crews; fans hoping to spot celebrities like Bianca Jagger; and a crowd of collectors, dealers and curiosity seekers waiting for the doors to open."[2]

The auction was indeed an astounding success: it totaled $200.7 million, more than the high estimate of $177.6 million—breaking the record for a single-artist auction, set at Sotheby's New York in 1993 when the sale of eighty-eight Picassos brought in $32 million. One-third of the purchasers at the Hirst auction were new buyers.

DAMIEN HIRST

Born in Bristol, England, in 1965 and raised in Leeds in a working-class environment, Hirst is one of the most significant living creators, and the most prominent of the so-called Young British Artists (YBAs). Used for

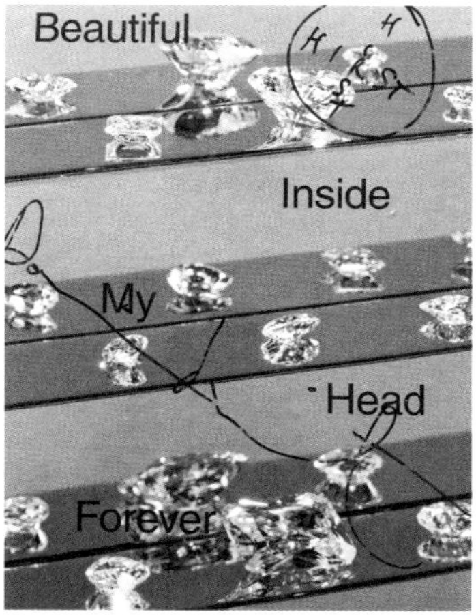

Signed cover of the *Damien Hirst: Beautiful Inside My Head Forever* auction catalogue

the first time by Michael Corris, the term loosely referred to the generation of artists who emerged at the end of the 1980s in London.[3] Confronting viewers with the most grim and startling facets of reality, they were united by the use of highly unorthodox and found materials, such as Hirst preserving animals in formaldehyde; Marc Quinn (b. 1964) using ten pints of his own frozen blood in the sculpture *Self* (1991); Sarah Lucas (b. 1962) working with cigarettes and women's nylon tights—as in the series *Bunny* (1997)—to challenge traditional representations of femininity by transforming everyday objects into provocative sculptures that explore themes of sexuality, gender, and power; and Tracey Emin (b. 1963) turning her own unmade bed, surrounded by personal items, into the sculpture *My Bed* (1998), a raw and intimate portrayal of vulnerability, emotion, and the chaos of everyday life. While Hirst's works may be unsettling, they engage with timeless themes deeply embedded in centuries of artistic tradition. Through a unique vocabulary, he explores life and death, the transience of human existence, and the tension between beauty and decay. Besides animals in formaldehyde, his oeuvre includes butterfly wings, flies on decomposing flesh, pill-filled cabinets, and both abstract and figurative paintings.

In addition, Hirst's disruptive creativity has consistently challenged established market and production models, demonstrating entrepreneurial innovation throughout his career. His debut on the London art scene came with the legendary 1988 exhibition *Freeze*, which he organized while still a student at Goldsmiths College, where the Young British Artists were nurtured by the progressive teaching of Michael Craig-Martin. Hirst curated a three-part group show in an abandoned Port of London Authority warehouse, marking the beginning of a new era in contemporary British art. In the words of Richard Stone: "*Freeze* occupies a mythical place in the written and verbal history of recent British art and announced a new

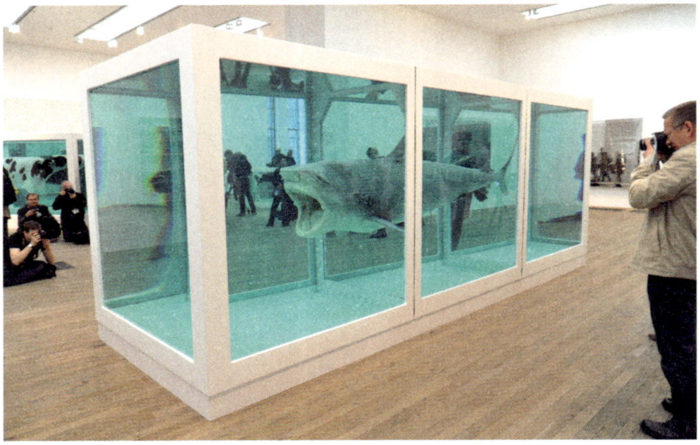

Installation view, *Damien Hirst: A Retrospective*, Tate Modern, London, April 4–September 9, 2012. Featuring *The Physical Impossibility of Death in the Mind of Someone Living* (1991)

direction."[4] The show attracted the attention of Jay Jopling, who in 1993 would open his gallery called White Cube, on London's Duke Street, and would play a key role in launching the careers of many leading YBAs; and of the collector Charles Saatchi, who had founded his own exhibition space in North West London in 1985. Saatchi helped finance one of Hirst's most iconic works, the vitrine containing a shark preserved in formaldehyde titled *The Physical Impossibility of Death in the Mind of Someone Living* (1991), which he would sell years later to Steven A. Cohen for an undisclosed amount said to be as high as $12 million.

The exhibition *Sensation*, at London's Royal Academy of Arts in 1997, introduced to a larger public the new art of the YBAs, showing some of their most controversial works from the Saatchi Collection. When the show traveled to the Brooklyn Museum in New York in October 1999 (after a stop in Berlin the previous year), it sparked a significant controversy, including the furious disapproval of then Mayor Rudolph Giuliani, who temporarily cut off city funding to the museum. "So what is new about the art in *Sensation*?" asks Norman Rosenthal in his essay in the exhibition catalogue. "The answer lies surely in this generation's totally new and radical attitude to realism, or rather to reality and art itself."[5] Amid scandals and controversies, the YBAs quickly achieved fame and success, while Hirst continued to explore new market possibilities.

The 2008 example was not the first time Hirst had gone direct to auction, although the previous instance did not involve consigning works directly from his studio. In October 2004, the dedicated auction *Pharmacy* at Sotheby's London successfully sold all the contents of the restaurant of the same name that Hirst had opened in 1998 in the city's Notting Hill district.

Hirst had a knack for creating boundary-pushing and headline-grabbing works as part of his art practice. In June 2007, *For the Love of God*, a sculpture consisting of a platinum cast of an eighteenth-century human

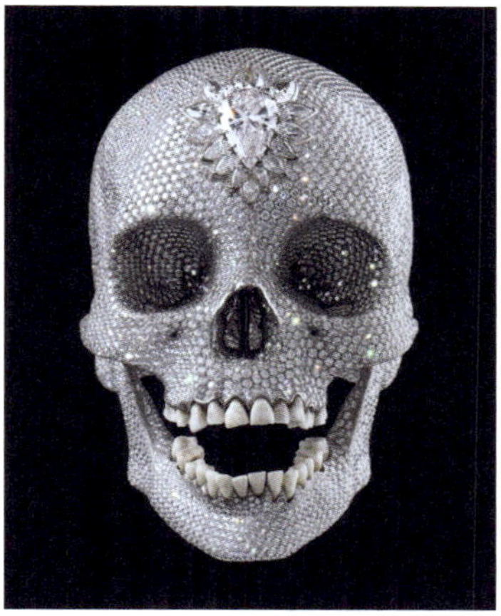

Damien Hirst, *For the Love of God*, 2007

skull encrusted with 8,601 real diamonds, was displayed at the White Cube gallery in London. The significant security challenge required the construction of a darkened room similar to a bank vault, which protected the multimillion-dollar artwork while enhancing its aura of exclusivity and intrigue. The subject of *For the Love of God*, inspired by an Aztec crystal skull, aligns with the tradition of a *memento mori*, or reminder of mortality. However, the astronomical reported cost of $23.6 million[6] to create it challenged conventional notions of art—engaging with, and perhaps satirizing, the excesses of the art market.

Hirst began showing his work at Gagosian galleries in 1996. At the beginning of 2012, all of Gagosian's then eleven locations in eight

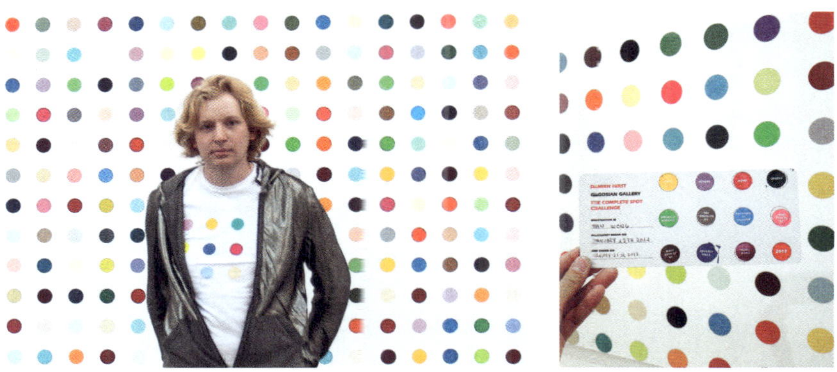

Left: Valentine Uhovski, the first person to visit every location of *Damien Hirst: The Complete Spot Paintings, 1986–2011*, stands before a Spot painting at Gagosian, Britannia Street, London. Right: Third-place winner Tanley Wong holds up a completed Spot Challenge card.

cities—New York, London, Paris, Los Angeles, Rome, Athens, Geneva, and Hong Kong—were simultaneously occupied with *Damien Hirst: The Complete Spot Paintings, 1986–2011*. This was a global exhibition that showed the artist's series of meticulously arranged, colorful Spot paintings, varying in size, patterns, and color combinations and spanning twenty-five years. No artist had ever attempted—nor has any ever since—to exhibit in all Gagosian venues at the same time. Globe-trotting gallerygoers also had the opportunity to participate in The Complete Spot Challenge, which awarded a signed Spot print to anyone who visited all eleven exhibitions.

In 2015, Hirst opened Newport Street Gallery in South London to display his personal collection and organize exhibitions. Two years later, for collector and Christie's owner François Pinault's dual venues in Venice, Palazzo Grassi and Punta della Dogana, Hirst conceived a visionary exhibition titled *Treasures from the Wreck of the Unbelievable*. The artist staged a narrative to contextualize the works—purportedly the salvaged contents of a sun temple–bound shipwreck, belonging to a freed slave and collector named Cif Amotan II. Accompanied by a faux documentary detailing the recovery process, the statues and artifacts—crafted from materials including bronze, marble, and semiprecious stones—were unveiled to the public, eliciting a range of reactions from enthusiastic approval to profound outrage. These pieces were subsequently made available for sale through Hirst's galleries.

Hirst has never shied away from his interest in the market or sensationalism. In response to the rising market in non-fungible tokens (NFTs), he embarked on a provocative project called *The Currency* in 2016. Hirst produced ten thousand unique Spot paintings on paper, each corresponding to a digital-only certificate of ownership. Each owner was given one year to decide whether to keep the NFT or the physical painting—and

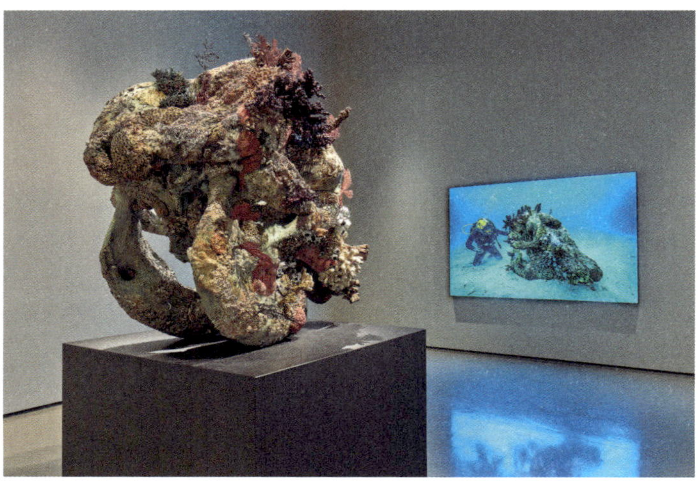

Installation view, *Damien Hirst: Treasures from the Wreck of the Unbelievable*, Palazzo Grassi and Punta della Dogana, Venice, April 9–December 3, 2017

whichever version was not kept would be destroyed. The result, announced in mid-2022, was an almost equal split: 5,149 collectors chose the physical artwork, while 4,851 kept the NFT.

HIRST'S MARKET AFTER THE AUCTION

It is difficult to evaluate the consequences of *Beautiful Inside My Head Forever* on Hirst's market, which retreated after the auction, as the entire art market was deeply struck by the erupting 2008 financial crisis, shrinking by 40 percent between the end of 2008 and the end of 2009. The recovery for the art market in general was relatively fast, though; in 2011, sales were again robust and at the level they had been in 2007. New auction records were established even before that, such as $103 million for Alberto Giacometti's *Walking Man I* (1960) in February 2010 at Sotheby's London, and $106 million for Pablo Picasso's *Nude, Green Leaves and Bust* (1932) at Christie's New York in May 2010.

Hirst's annual auction sales shrank from $270 million in 2008 to $19 million in 2009—an unsurprising contraction, given the volume of work offered at the 2008 Sotheby's two-day mega-sale. The average price paid at auction for one of his works in 2008 was $831,000, and in September 2010 just $136,000; through 2017, around a third of the works by Hirst available at auction since 2009 did not sell.[7] Why? Many explanations have been given, but the most compelling is that by circumventing galleries, Hirst undermined the traditional processes of market validation and curation that galleries provide. This direct-to-auction approach at such a large scale signaled that his production was potentially unlimited, leading to fears of

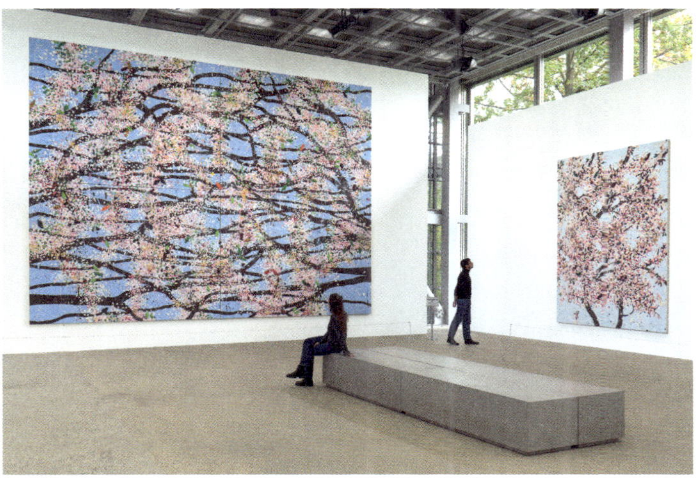

Installation view, *Damien Hirst: Cherry Blossoms*, Fondation Cartier pour l'art contemporain, Paris, July 5, 2021–January 1, 2022

market saturation. Collectors and investors, who rely on scarcity to drive long-term value, began to question the sustainability of Hirst's market. The perception of his work as less exclusive, combined with the general global economic recession, led to a decline in demand and prices for his artworks in the years following the auction. If one looks at the fate of the lots included in *Beautiful Inside My Head Forever*, as Tim Schneider did, it is undeniable that when they resurface at auction, they perform poorly.[8]

This has marked a significant divergence since 2008 between Hirst's secondary market, considerably weakened after his solo auction, and his primary market, which has continued to perform strongly. Already in 2012, Jay Jopling reported $110 million in sales of Hirst's new works. The sculptures in the 2017 Venice exhibition *Treasures from the Wreck of the Unbelievable* were said to have sold for more than $330 million.[9] In addition, unlike these highly conceptual works, Hirst returned to a traditional painterly process with his later *Veil Paintings* and *Cherry Blossoms*, inspired by Pierre Bonnard's chromatic palettes. Both these series were received with critical and commercial acclaim. The *Veil Paintings* were exhibited at Gagosian, Beverly Hills, in 2018 and immediately sold out; the *Cherry Blossoms* series, combining gestural brushstrokes with Pointillism, was shown in 2021–22 at the Fondation Cartier in Paris to a very positive reception.

NOTES

1 Carol Vogel, "Bull Market for Hirst in Sotheby's 2-Day Sale," *New York Times*, September 16, 2008.

2 Carol Vogel, "Hirst's Art Auction Attracts Plenty of Bidders, Despite Financial Turmoil," *New York Times*, September 15, 2008.

3 Michael Corris, "British? Young? Invisible? w/Attitude?," *Artforum* 30, no. 9 (May 1992).

4 Richard Shone, "From 'Freeze' to *House*: 1988–94," in *Sensation: Young British Artists from the Saatchi Collection*, exh. cat. (London: Thames & Hudson, in association with the Royal Academy of Arts, 1998), 17.

5 Norman Rosenthal, "The Blood Must Continue to Flow," in *Sensation*, 10.

6 Alan Riding, "Alas, Poor Art Market: A Multimillion-Dollar Head Case," *New York Times*, June 12, 2007.

7 Anny Shaw, "Art Market: Damien Hirst's Market Looks Poised for a Comeback," Artsy.net, January 17, 2017, https://www.artsy.net/article/artsy-editorial-damien-hirsts-market-poised-comeback.

8 Tim Schneider, "A Decade after Damien Hirst's Historic 'Beautiful Inside My Head Forever' Auction, Resale Prices Are Looking Ugly," Artnet News, September 12, 2018, Artnet.com, https://news.artnet.com/market/damien-hirst-beautiful-resales-1346528.

9 Felix Salmon, "The False Narrative of Damien Hirst's Rise and Fall," *New Yorker*, December 6, 2017.

11. Blurring the Boundaries: The Rise of Blockbuster Museum Exhibitions in Commercial Galleries

p. 221

Case Study No. 1: *Picasso: Mosqueteros*, Gagosian, New York, March 26–June 6, 2009

p. 225

How Gagosian's *Picasso: Mosqueteros* Was Put Together

p. 226

The Public's and Critics' Reactions and the Impact on Picasso's Market

p. 227

Case Study No. 2: *Piero Manzoni: A Retrospective*, Gagosian, New York, January 24–March 21, 2009

p. 228

Why Is Piero Manzoni Still Relevant?

p. 230

Manzoni Retrospective at Gagosian

p. 231

Reaction to the Exhibition and Market Results

The staggering exhibition of Picasso's late paintings and prints at the Gagosian Gallery [is] one of the best shows to be seen in New York since the turn of the century. . . . Like the retrospective of Piero Manzoni . . . "Picasso: Mosqueteros" should make any museum glow green with envy. . . . This show should relieve doubts about the essential role of commercial galleries in a vital art scene.

—Roberta Smith, "Going All Out, Right to the End," *New York Times*, April 16, 2009

In the past fifteen years, major contemporary art galleries in New York, Los Angeles, and London—which traditionally present new works by living artists—have begun to focus on organizing retrospectives dedicated to historical as well as modern masters. These presentations, marked by scholarly curation, meticulous exhibition design, and high-quality academic catalogues, used to be exclusively the domain of museums. An early example was Larry Gagosian's 1995 show dedicated to the Baroque master Peter Paul Rubens (1577–1640), an unprecedented move for a contemporary gallery. Exhibitions at this scale and level of quality are phenomenally expensive to produce—so why are galleries investing in them? And what are the results for the galleries that organize them? What is their cultural and market impact?

During my eleven years (2005–16) as a director at Gagosian in New York, I organized several groundbreaking exhibitions of historical artists, two of which I will examine as case studies: *Picasso: Mosqueteros* at Gagosian's 522 West Twenty-First Street gallery and *Piero Manzoni: A Retrospective* at its gallery at 555 West Twenty-Fourth Street, both presented in New York in 2009.

CASE STUDY NO. 1: *PICASSO: MOSQUETEROS*, GAGOSIAN, NEW YORK, MARCH 26–JUNE 6, 2009

The title *Mosqueteros* (*Musketeers*) references a body of work that Pablo Picasso (1881–1973) created between 1962 and 1972, in the last decade of his life. These paintings feature imagined figures such as musketeers, matadors, cavaliers, and prostitutes, influenced by old master painters including El Greco (1541–1614), Diego Velázquez (1599–1660), Rembrandt van Rijn (1606–1669), and Francisco de Goya (1746–1828), as well as Édouard Manet (1832–1883). Picasso's musketeers were presented alongside his late large nudes and self-portraits. One goal of the show was to reaffirm Picasso's late work, which had not been shown in New York since the pivotal 1984 exhibition *Picasso: The Last Years, 1963–1973* at the Solomon R. Guggenheim Museum, and which was still largely overlooked by critics, the public, and

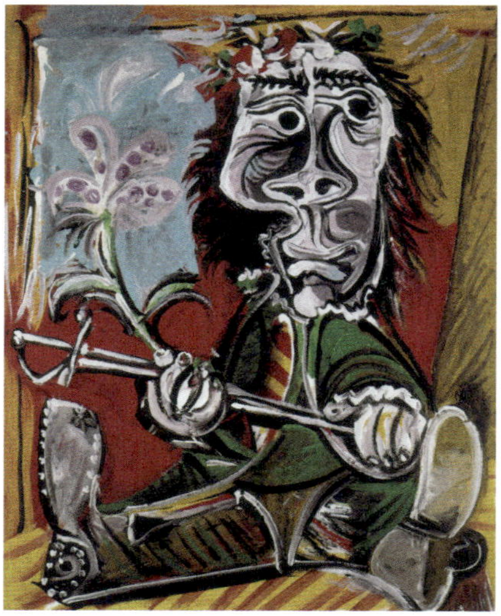

Pablo Picasso, *Portrait de l'Homme à l'epée et à la fleur*, 1969

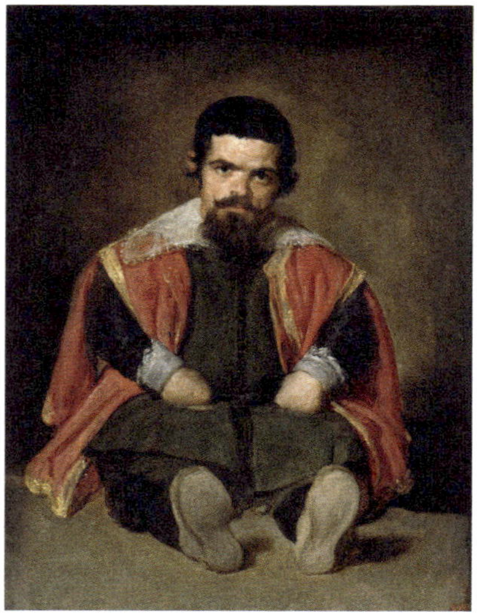

Diego Velázquez, *El bufón el Primo*, 1644, Museo Nacional del Prado, Madrid

the market. By highlighting the artist's continued innovation and exploration even in his later stages of life, the 2009 thematic show aimed to reexamine this period of the artist's production and reintroduce it to a new audience of collectors, thus expanding its market.

When Picasso painted his *Mosqueteros*, he was in his early eighties and residing in the South of France with his second wife, Jacqueline Roque. Despite his wealth and fame, he was facing a changing perception in the artistic community. As Picasso's biographer John Richardson (1924–2019), a British art historian celebrated for his authoritative multivolume biography titled *A Life of Picasso*,[1] notes in the exhibition catalogue for the show, "By the mid-1960s his fans were melting away. Artists and intellectuals no longer perceived Picasso as the leader of the avant-garde."[2] Gone were the days of Picasso's revolutionary Cubism, the sensual Surrealist depictions of Marie-Thérèse in the 1930s, and his inventive interpretations of *Women of Algiers*, by Eugène Delacroix (1798–1863), from 1954–55 or *Las Meninas*, by Velázquez, in 1957. After World War II, however, the epicenter of the Western art world shifted from Paris to New York, where Abstract Expressionism, and later movements such as Pop art, Minimalism, and Conceptual art, dominated the scene. Picasso, Richardson writes, loathed abstraction and American art.[3]

The Spanish-born Picasso remained revered in his adopted homeland of France. A major retrospective at the Grand Palais, Petit Palais, and Bibliothèque Nationale in Paris in 1966 (*Hommage à Pablo Picasso*) and a smaller celebration of his ninetieth birthday in the Grande Galerie at the Musée du Louvre in 1971—where he was the first living painter to receive such an honor—cemented his status as a master, but Picasso was no longer seen as being at the forefront of the avant-garde.

In 1964, Françoise Gilot's memoir *Life with Picasso* was published, revealing infidelities and other private aspects of the artists' personal life that were not flattering and which had previously been kept shielded from the public. Picasso was outraged and viewed Gilot's book as a betrayal. He attempted—but failed—to stop its publication by suing Gilot for defamation and severing ties with their two children, Claude and Paloma, in retaliation for the memoir's release.

The following year, Picasso underwent surgery for a duodenal ulcer, an event that forced him to temporarily halt his painting. During his long recovery, he delved deeply into Spanish and other European literary traditions, immersing himself in the Spanish poems of Luis de Góngora y Argote (1561–1627) and Lope de Vega (1562–1635). These figures, emblematic of Spain's Golden Age, likely stirred memories of his homeland and its rich cultural legacy. Alongside these, Picasso explored the writings of the French novelist Honoré de Balzac (1799–1850), the timeless dramas of William Shakespeare (1564–1616), and illustrated books featuring the art of Rembrandt, the Dutch master he greatly admired.

This period of reflection and intellectual engagement reinvigorated Picasso's imagination and profoundly influenced his later work. Among

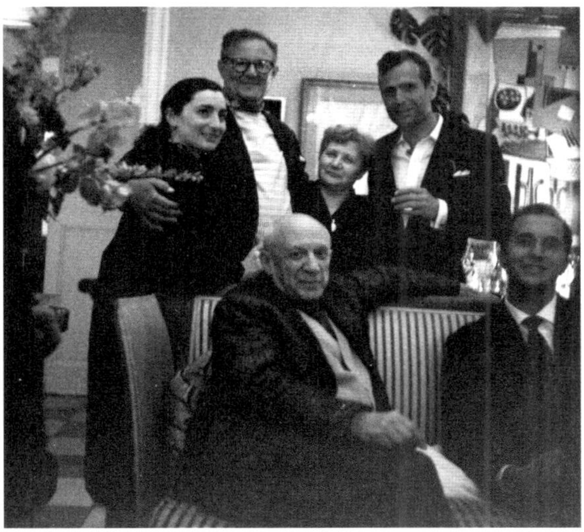

Clockwise, from upper left: Jacqueline Roque, Douglas Cooper, Henriette Gomès, John Richardson, Luis Miguel Dominguín, and Pablo Picasso at the Château de Castille, Argilliers, France, n.d.

the most significant outcomes of this introspection was his *Mosqueteros* series. These flamboyant, swashbuckling figures provided Picasso with a creative avenue to engage in a symbolic "dialogue" with masters of the past, blending historical inspiration with his innovative modern style. The *Mosqueteros* also served as a deeply personal gesture, reconnecting Picasso

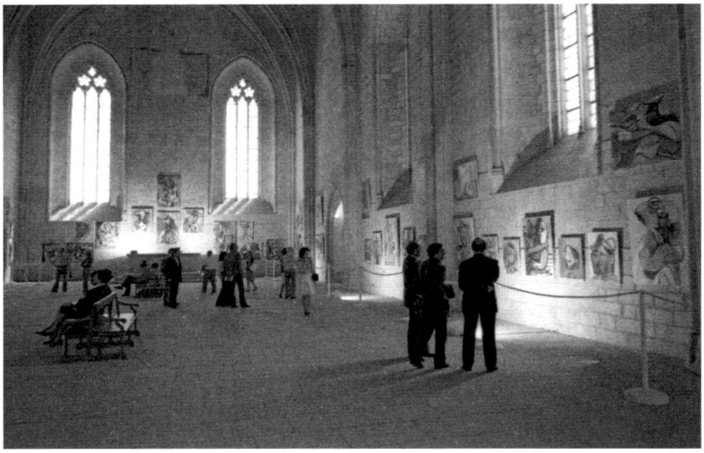

Installation view, *Picasso: Peintures et dessins: 1969–1970*, Palais des Papes, Avignon, France, May 1–September 30, 1970

with his Spanish roots—a poignant act of cultural reclamation given his self-imposed exile following the Spanish Civil War (1936–39) and throughout the oppressive regime of Francisco Franco (1939–75). For Picasso, these works were not only artistic explorations but also a symbolic homecoming, reestablishing ties with the Spain he had left behind, both physically and emotionally, decades earlier.

In May 1970, when Picasso's *Mosqueteros*—along with his new self-portraits and large nudes—were first unveiled at the Palais des Papes in Avignon, audiences were not impressed. Critics found the works raw, incoherent, and "ugly," dismissing them as poorly executed. Douglas Cooper, a Cubist collector and friend of the artist, famously described them as "incoherent doodles done by a frenetic dotard in the anteroom of death."[4]

Picasso was deliberately pushing the boundaries of painting by integrating the rapid, expressive techniques of Abstract Expressionism while retaining a strong focus on the figure. This daring, innovative approach was largely misunderstood at the time. As Richardson notes, these works marked Picasso's final "Great Late Phase," created "in a race against death."[5] The author highlights that the lack of appreciation for Picasso's late works when they were first unveiled stemmed from a fear of the new and unexpected. These boldly outrageous paintings, with their farcical irony, caricatural exuberance, abundance of genitalia, science-fiction elements, and subversive dark humor, did not fit into his accepted image. The master, once again, "had broken all the rules."[6]

HOW GAGOSIAN'S *PICASSO: MOSQUETEROS* WAS PUT TOGETHER

The core of the Gagosian exhibition featured significant and seldom displayed paintings and prints from the collection of Bernard Ruiz-Picasso, the artist's grandson, whose invaluable collaboration enriched every aspect of the project. Surrounding his works, we secured loans from museums, other members of the Picasso family, and private collectors. In total, the exhibition comprised fifty paintings and forty-nine prints that Picasso created between 1962 and 1972. John Richardson was invited to curate the exhibition.

I first contacted Richardson in 2008 while organizing an exhibition for the Gagosian gallery at 980 Madison Avenue titled *Isabel and Other Intimate Strangers: Portraits by Alberto Giacometti and Francis Bacon*, which focused on Isabel Rawsthorne (1912–1992), model and muse to both Giacometti (1901–1966) and Bacon (1909–1992). In her unpublished diary, held in the Tate Modern archives, Rawsthorne mentioned being portrayed during her years in Paris not only by Giacometti but also by Picasso. I reached out to Richardson seeking his assistance in identifying these paintings so that they could potentially be included in the exhibition. Although our attempts to locate these specific works were unsuccessful, this initial contact led to a beautiful friendship and collaboration. Together, we organized five exhibitions at Gagosian dedicated to Picasso. In addition to *Mosqueteros*, they were *Picasso: The Mediterranean Years (1945–1962)*, Britannia Street, London (2010); *Picasso and Marie-Thérèse: L'amour fou*, West Twenty-First Street, New York (2011); *Picasso and Françoise Gilot: Paris–Vallauris, 1943–1953*, 980 Madison Avenue, New York (2012); and *Picasso & the Camera*, West Twenty-First Street, New York (2014–15).

The decision to mount *Picasso: Mosqueteros* in the West Twenty-First Street gallery in Chelsea, designed by Richard Gluckman as a spacious

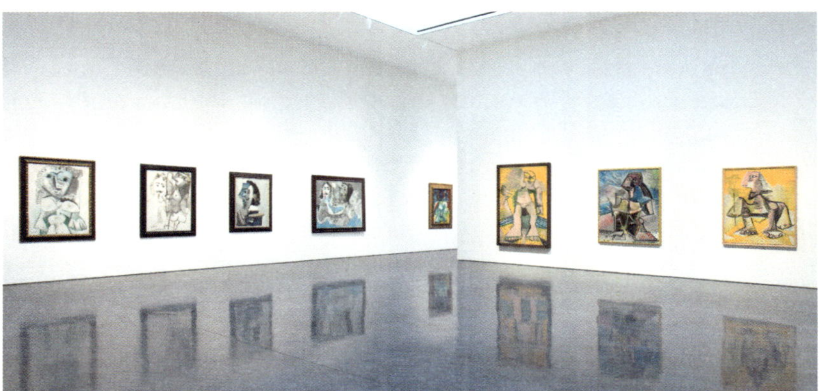

Installation view, *Picasso: Mosqueteros*, Gagosian, West 21st Street, New York, March 26–June 6, 2009

and luminous "white cube," proved crucial to its success. In the New York neighborhood where commercial galleries usually show the work of living contemporary artists, the exhibition of Picasso's works was a bold and unexpected move. The environment breathed new life into Picasso's historically significant pieces, typically exhibited in museums, enhancing their contemporary freshness and vigor. Annabelle Selldorf was tasked with designing the exhibition space. Her approach involved a minimalist layout that gently guided visitors through the gallery, allowing the artworks to speak for themselves. The hanging of the paintings was deliberately unconventional, at times adopting a salon style reminiscent of their original presentation in the Palais des Papes in Avignon, an arrangement overseen by Picasso himself.

On a personal note, working with Annabelle Selldorf, as well as John Richardson and Bernard Ruiz-Picasso, was an immensely intellectually rewarding experience, which turned into friendship and extended to subsequent exhibitions. My dear Gagosian colleague Michael Cary would also become a crucial collaborator in the subsequent shows dedicated to Picasso.

THE PUBLIC'S AND CRITICS' REACTIONS AND THE IMPACT ON PICASSO'S MARKET

The exhibition was a resounding success. Roberta Smith of the *New York Times* praised it as "one of the best shows to be seen in New York since the turn of the century," adding that it could make any museum "glow green with envy."[7] She also emphasized that the show underscored the crucial role of commercial galleries in sustaining a vibrant art scene. More than one hundred thousand visitors attended the exhibition during its ten-week run. Importantly, free admission attracted a diverse audience, including those less likely to visit traditional museums. When the International Association of Art Critics handed out its annual awards, honors for "Best Show in a Commercial Gallery in New York City" went to *Picasso: Mosqueteros*.

The timing of the exhibition, however, coincided with one of the most challenging periods for the global economy and the art market. Conceived in 2007, when the art market was thriving, *Picasso: Mosqueteros* opened in January 2009, amid the financial crisis triggered by the collapse of the housing market and of the subprime mortgage business. Following the bankruptcy of Lehman Brothers in September 2008, the art market also suffered a significant downturn. Collectors and investors, facing financial uncertainty, adopted a more circumspect approach, prioritizing liquidity over acquisitions. The gallery managed to hit its sales targets, despite collectors' caution at this difficult moment. However, the impact of *Picasso: Mosqueteros* extended far beyond sales. It solidified Gagosian's authority in the Picasso market, sending a strong message to both current owners and prospective buyers of Picasso's work. It resonated deeply with collectors and artists alike, enhancing the gallery's reputation as a premier venue of unparalleled quality and cultural significance in a global art market. Furthermore, the exhibition provided a fresh lens through which to view Picasso's late works, emphasizing their profound originality and challenging the conventional understanding of this period of his oeuvre. Notably, this significant cultural reappraisal originated not from a traditional public institution but from a commercial gallery, a sign of how roles have blurred.

Picasso: Mosqueteros also had a significant impact on Picasso's market in general. Prices for late paintings, previously undervalued, experienced a notable surge. This shift was underscored by the decision by Christie's to feature *Mousquetaire à la pipe* (1968) on the cover of its prestigious Impressionist and Modern evening auction catalogue in May 2009, which sold for $14,642,500. Before the Gagosian exhibition, the highest price for a painting from the *Mosqueteros* series was $16,841,000 for *Homme à la pipe* (1968), sold by Christie's New York in November 2007; after the exhibition, it rose to $30,965,000 for *Mousquetaire à la pipe* (1969), sold by Sotheby's New York in November 2013.

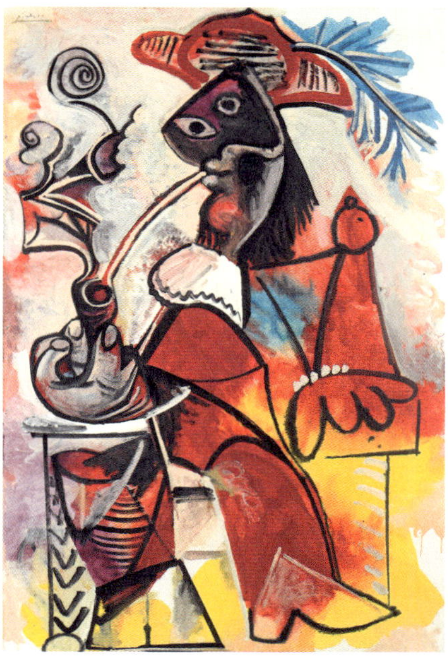

Pablo Picasso, *Mousquetaire à la pipe*, 1969

CASE STUDY NO. 2: *PIERO MANZONI: A RETROSPECTIVE*, GAGOSIAN, NEW YORK, JANUARY 24–MARCH 21, 2009

In 2007, I proposed organizing a retrospective for the Italian artist Piero Manzoni (1933–1963), driven by two simple and compelling considerations. First, although Manzoni was a major European postwar figure alongside Yves Klein (1928–1962), Alberto Burri (1915–1995), and Lucio

Fontana (1899–1968), he had never been the subject of a retrospective in the United States. Second, Gagosian had yet to engage with Manzoni's market or the broader Italian postwar market, which was experiencing substantial growth at the time.

WHY IS PIERO MANZONI STILL RELEVANT?

Despite his tragically short life—he died at only twenty-nine years old—Manzoni reshaped and challenged the very notion of art, anticipating Conceptual practices leading toward the complex era of postmodernism. Manzoni was active in an Italy undergoing rapid transformation. Within a few years after the devastation of World War II, which had brought German occupation of part of the country in late 1943 and a brutal civil conflict leaving deep physical and moral scars, the country began experiencing an economic boom known as the *miracolo italiano* (Italian miracle). This period was marked by a cultural rebirth that spanned all creative fields—art, architecture, design, literature, and cinema. Milan, where Manzoni would make his mark, stood as the pulsing epicenter of the cultural resurgence.

Born in Soncino, near Milan, into an aristocratic family, Manzoni initially embraced the Art Informel style, dominant in postwar Europe and characterized by spontaneous, abstract, and gestural brushstrokes conveying raw emotion. His artistic direction shifted dramatically after encountering Klein's eleven identical canvases covered in a vibrant blue—which the artist later patented as International Klein Blue (IKB)—in the exhibition *Proposte monocrome, epoca blu* (*Monochrome Proposition, Blue Epoch*) at Galleria Apollinaire in Milan in January 1957. Influenced also by Burri's use of unconventional materials such as burlap and burnt plastic, and by Fontana's radical puncturing (1949) and slashing (1958) of the canvas, Manzoni created his groundbreaking *Achromes*. The term—coined by the artist and used to name all his paintings from that moment until his death—indicates

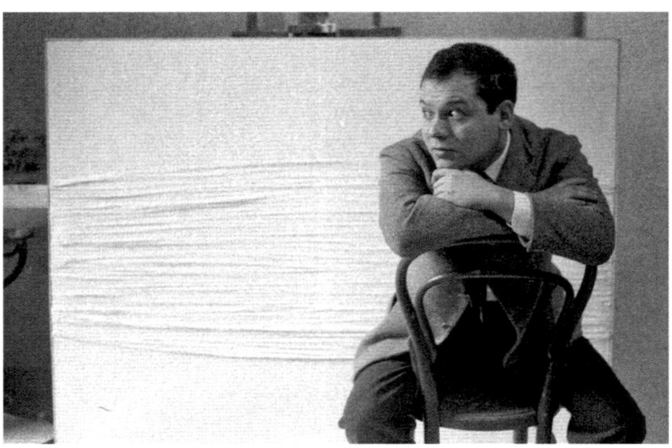

Piero Manzoni with one of his *Achromes*, Milan, 1959

a surface devoid of color. The first *Achromes* were canvases imbued with kaolin, a porcelain clay. The drying process naturally created wrinkles and folds, transforming the painting into a neutral, self-forming surface devoid of narrative or symbolism. In Manzoni's words, "We absolutely cannot consider the picture as a space on to which to project our mental scenography. It is the area of freedom in which we search for the discovery of our first images. Images which are as absolute as possible, which cannot be valued for that which they record, explain and express, but only for that which they are: to be."[8] Later *Achromes* would utilize materials such as straw, cotton balls, gravel, fiberglass, polystyrene, felt, bread rolls dipped in kaolin, and cobalt chloride (which changed color over time).

Manzoni's artistic exploration soon shifted toward more conceptual and uncharted territories. His infamous *Merda d'artista* (*Artist's Shit*) (1961)—consisting of ninety sealed tin cans, each allegedly containing thirty grams of the artist's feces and sold at the equivalent of the daily price of gold—shocked the art world of his time, and it still does. With the *Sculture viventi* (*Living Sculptures*) (1961), in which models became "sculptures" upon being signed by the artist, and the *Base magica* (*Magic Base*) (1961), a pedestal that transformed anyone standing on it into a sculpture, Manzoni asserted the agency of the artist and pushed the limits of creativity. These works questioned the essence of art itself, intertwining the roles of artist and viewer, and blurring the boundaries between art and life.

In 1959, Manzoni cofounded *Azimuth*, a magazine, and Azimut, an exhibition space, with Enrico Castellani (1930–2017), who was exploring the innovative use of nails to create monochromatic surfaces with three-dimensional effects of light and shadow. Opened in the basement of a furniture store in Milan, Azimut became a hub to foster dialogue between Italian and international artists.

During his lifetime, Manzoni's work triggered contrasting reactions. Some contemporaries hailed him as a radical innovator, while others dismissed his works as provocative stunts. Manzoni's market began to develop significantly after his untimely death in 1963. The 1970s and 1980s saw a growing appreciation among collectors and institutions, fostered by key retrospectives and exhibitions that further solidified his status. In the decade prior to the Gagosian exhibition, Manzoni's market firmly established itself, with his works being sought after by major international collectors and commanding substantial prices at auction, in particular for his creased *Achromes*, which were recognized as his most iconic creations. The auction record for one of them at the time of the Gagosian exhibition stood at $10,121,000, established at Sotheby's New York in May 2008.

Crucial for the expansion and consolidation of Manzoni's market and for the postwar and contemporary Italian art market in general, on an international level, have been the thematic auctions titled 20th Century Italian Art. The first auction was organized by Sotheby's London in October 1997, followed by another at Christie's in 1998. As a junior specialist in the Sotheby's Contemporary Art Department in London, I was tasked with cataloguing the works included in that inaugural sale. The auction was led by Sotheby's specialists Elena Geuna and Claudia

Dwek, whose dedication and expertise fueled my passion for postwar and contemporary Italian art. Prestigious Italian galleries—which I do not name here for fear of overlooking any—have also consistently presented Manzoni's work at international fairs such as Art Basel, making invaluable contributions to the development of his global market. Their dedication cannot be overstated.

MANZONI RETROSPECTIVE AT GAGOSIAN

The Gagosian exhibition was envisioned as a comprehensive survey of the artist's entire body of work. No other retrospective had been dedicated to Manzoni in the United States before, a fact that remains unchanged since then, at the time of writing. It was organized in collaboration with the Archivio Opera Piero Manzoni in Milan, which is overseen by the artist's family and with which I had a long-standing relationship since my Sotheby's days. I asked Germano Celant (1940–2020), renowned for authoring both the 1975 and 2004 catalogues raisonnés of Manzoni's oeuvre, to curate it. (With Celant, who soon became a dear friend, I would organize another exhibition in 2012 for Gagosian, New York, dedicated to Lucio Fontana: *Ambienti spaziali*. It was the first presentation of the artist's pioneering spatial environments in the United States. Annabelle Selldorf designed the complex and sometimes challenging installation of the show.)

The loans for the exhibition were sourced from the Manzoni archive, private collections, and museums worldwide, including the Herning Kunstmuseum in Denmark, which graciously provided key works never previously exhibited in the United States, such as the *Base magica* and the

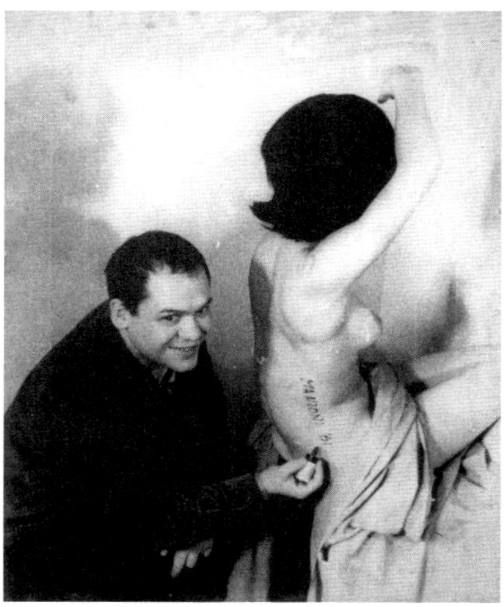

Piero Manzoni signing a model to create a *Scultura vivente* (*Living Sculpture*), Milan, January 13, 1961

Socle du monde (*Base of the World*) (1961)—an inverted plinth positioned upside down on the ground, conceptually transforming the entire planet into a work of art.

Installed in the elegant and airy large spaces of the 555 West Twenty-Fourth Street gallery in Chelsea, the exhibition also featured works by contemporary American and European artists who were active during Manzoni's era, such as Robert Rauschenberg (1925–2008), Yayoi Kusama (b. 1929), and Frank Stella (1936–2024), as well as Klein, Fontana, and Burri. This inclusion aimed to contextualize Manzoni's art within an international framework, highlighting connections and influences across borders.

REACTION TO THE EXHIBITION AND MARKET RESULTS

Opening on January 24, 2009, *Piero Manzoni: A Retrospective* was a public and critical triumph. Holland Cotter wrote in the *New York Times*: "Manzoni's art has, in general, been a mystery in the United States. . . . Sonnabend Gallery organized a survey in 1972. Then there was pretty much nothing until 'Manzoni: A Retrospective,' now at the Gagosian Gallery in Chelsea. Maybe that's why the show feels like such an amazement."[9] *Piero Manzoni: A Retrospective* would be chosen best solo show of the year in a gallery by the artist Rob Pruitt for his first annual Art Awards (*Picasso: Mosqueteros* was also nominated in the same category), announced at a ceremony at the Guggenheim Museum, and Benjamin H. D. Buchloh contributed a feature on the exhibition to *Artforum*'s "Best of 2009" year-end issue.[10]

Thousands of visitors—among them, many artists—flocked to see the retrospective, taking advantage of this first opportunity to admire a

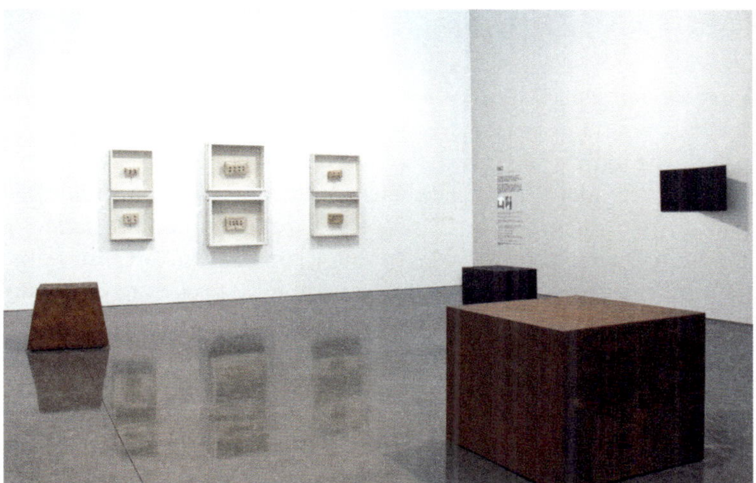

Installation view, *Manzoni: A Retrospective*, Gagosian, 555 West 24th Street, New York, January 24–March 21, 2009

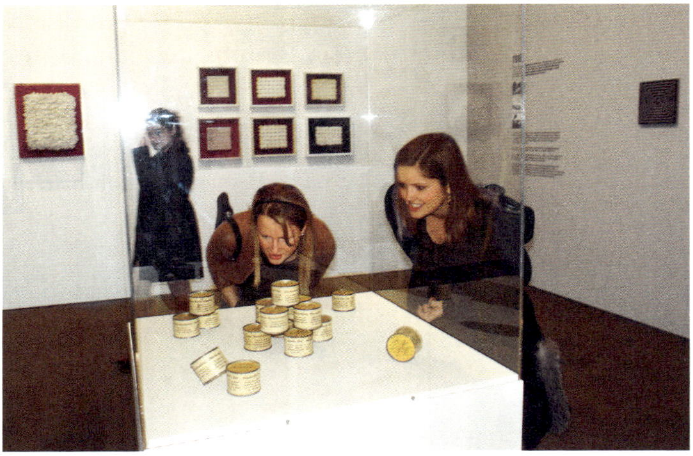

Gallerygoers viewing *Merda d'artista* (*Artist's Shit*) (1961) at *Manzoni: A Retrospective*, Gagosian, 555 West 24th Street, New York, 2009

full survey of the complexity of Manzoni's pioneering vision. The show, originally conceived at the peak of the market in 2007, opened amid the financial crisis in January 2009. In those cold and gloomy days, though, Manzoni's works were able to convey—or so I felt—the artist's playful confidence that art has the power to make our life better, and somehow change the world. In the long term, the show also proved instrumental in establishing Gagosian's presence in a market where the gallery had not previously been active. Additionally, it sparked broader collector interest in Manzoni's work. Because of its reputation, Gagosian's involvement served as a form of validation that further solidified Manzoni's position in the market. A record price, still unmatched, of about $20 million for an *Achrome*—double the auction record before the Gagosian exhibition—was achieved at Sotheby's London in October 2014.

As demonstrated by the cases explored, the decision to mount historical or monographic retrospectives by commercial galleries, despite their high costs, is driven by several factors. First, these exhibitions enhance the prestige and stature of the gallery within the art world, through increased press coverage, public attendance, and international recognition. They demonstrate a commitment to art historical scholarship and deepen the gallery's relationship with estates, institutions, academics, curators, and art historians.

From a market perspective, these exhibitions have proven to be financially rewarding, particularly in the long run. They attract serious collectors who may be interested in both historical and contemporary works. Finally, they provide an opportunity for the public to engage deeply with significant works from the past in a context that is different from, and sometimes less intimidating than, a museum.

NOTES

1 Richardson's biography, *A Life of Picasso*, ends in 1943, thirty years before the artist's death. Random House in New York published the first two volumes: *1881–1906* (1991) and *1907–1917: The Painter of Modern Life* (1996); Alfred A. Knopf in New York, the final two volumes: *The Triumphant Years, 1917–1932* (2007) and, posthumously, *The Minotaur Years, 1933–1943* (2021).

2 John Richardson, "Great Late Picasso," in *Picasso: Mosqueteros*, by Richardson et al., exh. cat. (New York: Gagosian Gallery, 2009), 15.

3 Richardson, "Great Late Picasso," 15.

4 John Richardson, *The Sorcerer's Apprentice: Picasso, Provence, and Douglas Cooper* (New York: Alfred A. Knopf, 1999), 300. Widely quoted, Cooper's harsh criticism originally appeared in a letter to the editor in the French magazine *Connaissance des arts* in July 1973, not long after Picasso's death.

5 Richardson, "Great Late Picasso," 15, 21.

6 Richardson, "Great Late Picasso," 34.

7 Roberta Smith, "Going All Out, Right to the End," *New York Times*, April 16, 2009.

8 Germano Celant, *Piero Manzoni*, exh. cat. (Milan: Skira, 2009), 28.

9 Holland Cotter, "To Bump Off Art as He Knew It," *New York Times*, February 12, 2009.

10 Benjamin H. D. Buchloh, "Manzoni: A Retrospective," *Artforum*, December 2009, 160–63.

12. The Rebirth of China's Art Market and Its Rising International Clout

p. 236
From State-Controlled to Free Market: The Origin of the Chinese Art Market

p. 238
The Development of an Art Ecosystem

p. 242
Chinese Artists' Journey from Instruments of the Party to Global Recognition

p. 247
The Rise and Evolution of Chinese Collectors

p. 248
What Now?

Today, China is the only major art market in the world where an immense state-endorsed-and-censored art system and a significant market-oriented art system coexist in parallel.

—Kejia Wu, *A Modern History of China's Art Market*

China's art market accounts for one-third of all global art transactions; in 2011, it even passed the United States and United Kingdom to become the country with the largest value of sales. Growth since the turn of this century has been particularly rapid in contemporary art. In Beijing before 1990, for example, no commercial outlets specialized in that; by 2000, there were 5 contemporary art galleries; by 2008, the number had jumped to 300, and almost every major New York gallery had signed at least one Chinese artist. Four years later, the 798 Art District in Beijing alone counted 207 galleries.[1]

By 2013, China had more than 350 auction houses, and in less than a decade since then, auction revenues soared by 900 percent.[2] Since the 2010s, all the major Western auction houses—Christie's, Sotheby's, and Phillips—have opened outposts in mainland China or Hong Kong (which retained significant independence until 2020, when enactment of the National Security Law saw its autonomy and freedoms significantly diminished), as have the major galleries. This expansion has been complemented by the emergence of art fairs across the country, with Art Basel thriving in Hong Kong for more than a decade.

The remarkable market expansion highlighted by the aforementioned data has occurred in a country governed by the Communist Party, which traditionally upholds centralized control, state ownership, and Marxist-Leninist principles. However, ever since the economic reforms of Chinese leader Deng Xiaoping (1904–1997) starting in 1978, China has progressively embraced market-oriented mechanisms, private enterprise, and global trade, evolving into what is termed a "socialist market economy." It is through the paradoxical lens of an aggressively free market operating within a still-authoritarian regime that the birth and development of the art market and system in China need to be considered. Initially during this period, the government triggered and supported the development in the country of an ecosystem encompassing museums, art districts, galleries, and fairs, where public and private initiative met.

Chinese artists, who were denied freedom of expression and isolated from the rest of the world for decades, have been catapulted to international attention in this century, with their works achieving prices in six figures. While an integral part of the art scene beyond China, however, they are still under the scrutiny of government censorship.

China's art market is now a key element in the worldwide art system, and a financially crucial one. Furthermore, counting the most active group of young collectors, trends and tastes that unite millennials (born in the 1980s and 1990s) and Generation Z (born in the late 1990s and early 2000s) globally are often anticipated there.

FROM STATE-CONTROLLED TO FREE MARKET: THE ORIGIN OF THE CHINESE ART MARKET

In the People's Republic of China (PRC), instituted in 1949, the economy was state planned and private property not allowed. Art education was centralized, and all artistic endeavors had to serve as political instruments under the auspices of the Department of Propaganda. Widespread destruction of cultural heritage, stringent artistic censorship, isolation of Chinese artists from the international scene, and the extensive looting of art and antiquities collections tragically marked this time. Any form of art trade was officially prohibited.

As Li Ma explains: "Art markets in the West have long benefited from established infrastructure. Participants, from artists to curators, from dealers to critics, have together nurtured social norms of evaluation. In comparison, China's art market had a truncated history until postreform cultural entrepreneurs reinvented its formal and informal institutions. From the late 1950s to the 1980s, China had been deprived of the economic infrastructure to manage interactions between artists, traders, and consumers."[3]

The embryo for a resurgence of an art market in China is identified by Kejia Wu in the 1984 government's decision to return works of art and antiquities confiscated during the Cultural Revolution (1966–76) to their original owners or their heirs.[4] Short for "Great Proletarian Cultural Revolution," the Cultural Revolution, encouraged by Chinese leader Mao Zedong himself and his wife Jiang Qing, was aimed at destroying the "Four Olds"—old ideas, old cultures, old customs, and old habits. In August 1966, three hundred thousand Red Guards looted and ravaged numerous homes in Beijing, requisitioning and destroying artworks and books. China's long history of sophisticated collecting, rooted in the imperial court and the aristocracy, thus ended drastically. State-owned antiquities shops were set up to sell the confiscated goods at low prices, either to state-owned museums, like the Palace Museum in Beijing and the Shanghai Museum, or to international buyers, in order to generate foreign currency for the government. The state-owned antiques stores remained for a long time the only places where individuals could sell their artworks. As a consequence, they accumulated a high-quality inventory and dominated the supply of artworks.[5]

In the early 1990s, the bold economic reforms that Deng had instituted in 1978–89, aimed at transforming China's centrally planned economy into a free market, had a decisive impact on the development of the art market. Chinese entrepreneurs were allowed to take part in the trading for cultural relics, and as a consequence, the first private auction houses were founded. On August 21, 1992, Duo Yun Xuan Auctions Co. Ltd. was registered to sell Chinese antiquities; in January 1993, the Shanghai Cultural Relics Management Commission granted the company permission to expand from selling antiquities to holding auctions, too, of cultural relics from other periods. In May of that year, China Guardian Auctions Co. Ltd. was established by the entrepreneur Chen Dongsheng, making it China's first comprehensive auction house specializing in Chinese art and artifacts, including international sales of them. Today, it is the second-largest auction house in China and the fourth largest in the world, having expanded its categories to include not only traditional Chinese paintings and calligraphy but also ceramics, furniture, and contemporary art.

Commenting on the success of Duo Yun Xuan's and China Guardian Auctions' first sales, Wu writes:

> On the supply side, the sourcing of artworks mostly came from state-owned antiquities shops, and this enabled the auction houses' specialists to include some of the highest quality artworks in their sales. On the demand side, in addition to renowned international collectors who came to China to participate in the auctions, around 50 percent of the buyers were newly wealthy Chinese entrepreneurs who benefited from the country's fast economic growth and began collecting art.
>
> These two auctions were a turning point for the art market in the PRC. Before this occurred, the art trade was controlled by state-owned antiquities shops under a planned economy; afterwards, art commerce started to operate similarly to a market-based economy.[6]

The mid-2000s witnessed a surge in demand for Chinese art and antiques globally, while the interest of Chinese collectors began to shift toward Western art, mainly modern and contemporary.

International auction houses such as Sotheby's and Christie's, recognizing the enormous potential of the Chinese market, started establishing a presence in the country. In 2012, Sotheby's signed a joint agreement with state-owned Beijing Gehua Cultural Development Group, as foreign auction houses were not yet allowed to conduct business independently in China. It was Christie's, though, that in 2013 became the first to be granted a license to operate independently in mainland China, and it held an auction in Shanghai in September of that year. Phillips entered the Asian market in November 2015, with an auction in Hong Kong featuring a curated selection of contemporary art and design. The three auction houses now regularly hold successful sales in Hong Kong and Shanghai.

Galleries, the backbone of the Western contemporary market, did not exist in China until 1991, when the Australian-born Brian Wallace founded the Red Gate Gallery in Beijing. It took another fifteen years, though, for Western galleries to start establishing outposts in the country. The Italian Galleria Continua paved the way, by presenting an international program in China in 2004. Its new venue in Beijing's 798 Art District was inaugurated in 2005 with an exhibition featuring sixteen artists representing five continents. In the following years, Almine Rech, Axel Vervoordt, Ben Brown Fine Arts, Blum & Poe, David Zwirner, Gagosian, Hauser & Wirth,

Lehmann Maupin, Massimo De Carlo, Pace (shut down in 2018), Perrotin, Simon Lee, and White Cube each opened one venue in Hong Kong, Beijing, or Shanghai. These galleries' programs in China have been presenting Western artists from their rosters as well as local ones. Significantly, all the most important Chinese artists are now represented by major Western galleries.

The entry of Western galleries into the Chinese art market has been supported by the establishment of international fairs: in Shanghai, ART021 and West Bund Art & Design were founded in 2013 and 2014, respectively. The most important is Art Basel Hong Kong, which has been successfully operating since 2013. Held annually in March at the Hong Kong Convention and Exhibition Centre, it is the Asian edition of the prestigious Art Basel fair, which takes place every year in Basel, Miami Beach, Paris, and Doha.

THE DEVELOPMENT OF AN ART ECOSYSTEM

The expansion of the art market in China has been accompanied by the development in record time of a comprehensive art system, encompassing the establishment of new museums and art districts. No country has ever witnessed a surge in the number of new museums as has China in the past twenty years. In 2002, the State Administration of Cultural Heritage (a governmental agency in China responsible for the preservation, protection, and management of the country's cultural heritage) set the ambitious goal of building one thousand museums by 2015. Every large and medium-sized city within the country would have at least one. China not only achieved this goal but surpassed it. By 2013, almost fifteen hundred museums had already been added. And the program has continued apace. By way of comparison, in the United States, between twenty and forty museums were being built annually in the decade preceding the 2008 financial crash. As Georgina Adam points out, the push to build museums in China stems from various factors, including government policy that emphasizes culture as a key element of "soft power" and a desire to catch up with the West in terms of the number of museums per capita. Beyond major cities like Shanghai and Beijing, second- and third-tier cities have also established their own cultural institutions.[7]

The history of museums in China reflects the nation's evolving relationship with its cultural heritage and the influence of global trends. The concept of the museum, as understood in the West, was introduced to China in the late nineteenth and early twentieth centuries, a period of internal upheaval and external pressures. Before this, the idea of publicly accessible spaces dedicated to the preservation and exhibition of artifacts was virtually unknown. Instead, the Chinese tradition of collecting was dominated by private collections held by emperors, scholars, and aristocrats; objects of art, archaeology, and natural history were kept within palatial walls or private estates.

The first museum in China, the Nantong Museum, was established in 1905 by Zhang Jian (1853–1926), an industrialist and intellectual. Located in Jiangsu Province, it was the first institution to adopt a Western-style approach to curating and displaying cultural relics—a significant departure from the elite collections of the past. This was followed by several other early museums that emerged during the Republican era (1912–49). The Palace Museum in Beijing, founded in 1925, turned the Imperial Palace, or "Forbidden City," into a public museum. Opening the emperor's residence and personal collection to the public marked a significant shift in societal values, reflecting the demystification of the emperor's divine status and a newfound embrace of national heritage by the Chinese people.

After the founding of the People's Republic of China in 1949, museums became powerful tools for the new government to propagate socialist ideology and foster a unified national identity. During the Maoist period, the focus was primarily on revolutionary history, emphasizing the achievements of the Communist Party and the proletariat. However, the decade-long Cultural Revolution saw widespread destruction of cultural heritage, and many museum collections were damaged or lost.

The post-Mao era, following his death in 1976, brought a resurgence in cultural preservation, coupled with a rapid expansion of the museum sector. The late twentieth and early twenty-first centuries have seen a remarkable growth in the number and variety of museums in China. Major cities such as Beijing, Shanghai, Xi'an, and Nanjing have developed world-class institutions. Today, China boasts thousands of museums, ranging from those dedicated to ancient history or archaeology to others with a focus on modern art or science, reflecting a renewed commitment to cultural preservation, education, and tourism. Notably, nearly a third of the country's fine art museums are small enterprises. Over the past few decades, private museums have proliferated, with a common trend being the involvement of property developers, who often incorporate public museums into their projects to take advantage of tax benefits.[8]

Museums have also appeared within shopping centers, such as Chi K11 art space, part of the K11 Art Mall in Shanghai, which opened in 2013. Built to museum standards, Chi K11 hosts exhibitions featuring both emerging and established contemporary artists. This blend of art and commerce is common in China, where cultural appreciation intersects with economic pragmatism. Private museums often follow a self-sustaining model, treating art as both a cultural asset and an economic driver, with commercial elements woven into the visitor experience. K11's founder, Adrian Cheng (b. 1979), acknowledged that art malls may seem unconventional to international visitors, as they appear to demystify the traditional museum experience; at the same time, though, they make art more accessible and less intimidating by embedding it in familiar retail settings. However, the post-pandemic contraction of China's luxury market has posed significant challenges to the innovative K11 model, as decreased consumer spending has impacted the viability of such experiential retail concepts, resulting in severe financial losses. In September 2024, Cheng resigned as CEO of New World Development Company, the family's company businesses encompassing property development and investment, infrastructure and services, department stores and hotels.

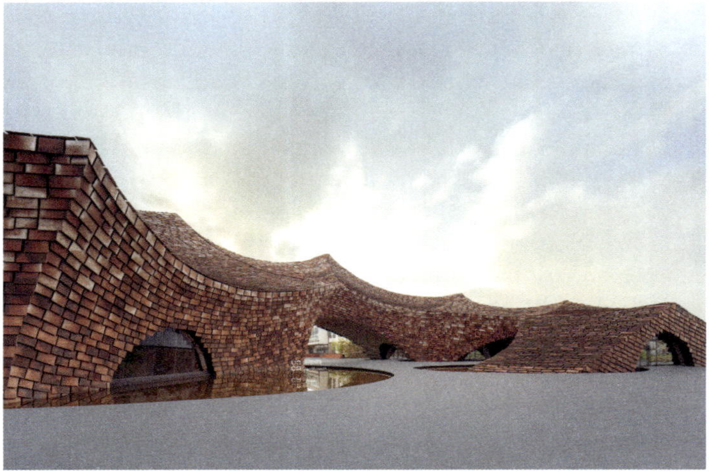

Exterior of UCCA Clay, Yixing, China

The Ullens Center for Contemporary Art (UCCA), founded in 2007 by Belgian collectors Guy Ullens (b. 1935) and his wife Myriam (1952–2023) in Beijing's 798 Art District, was the first museum dedicated to contemporary Chinese artists. It displayed the extensive collection of its founders, among the earliest Western entrepreneurs to engage with China's art scene. In 2017, the museum evolved into the UCCA Group, backed by new investors, and in 2018, it opened UCCA Dune, an architectural marvel beneath the sands of Aranya's coastal community in Beidaihe. The company opened a third location, UCCA Edge, in Shanghai in May 2021, and a fourth, UCCA Clay, in Yixing, Jiangsu Province, in October 2024.

Husband-and-wife collectors Liu Yiqian and Wang Wei established the Long Museum in Shanghai in 2012 to house their wide-ranging collection, from traditional Chinese art to Western modern masterpieces. Liu was catapulted to international attention in 2014 after a photo showed him sipping tea from a Ming dynasty (1348–1644) porcelain cup he had purchased for $36.3 million. The following year, the couple acquired Amedeo Modigliani's *Nu couché* (*Reclining Nude*) (1917) for a record $170.4 million. Liu's rise from taxi driver to billionaire collector intrigued the art world, leading to a 2016 profile in the *New Yorker.*[9] Since its founding, the museum has expanded to three more venues: Long Museum Pudong, Long Museum West Bund, and Long Museum Chongqing.

In 2007, Indonesian Chinese entrepreneur and art collector Budi Tek (1957–2022) created the Yuz Foundation, a nonprofit organization dedicated to promoting contemporary art and artists. In May 2014, Tek opened the Yuz Museum in Shanghai's West Bund, transforming a former aircraft hangar into a contemporary art museum. The museum has hosted numerous significant exhibitions, including the world's largest Alberto Giacometti retrospective, in 2016, in collaboration with the Fondation Giacometti, and the Asian premiere of Andy Warhol's *Shadows* (an installation of 102 silkscreened canvases from his longtime series) in 2016, as well as the first institutional exhibition in mainland China of the American artist known as KAWS, in 2017. The museum also focuses on supporting local talent by frequently showcasing emerging Chinese artists.

The HOW Art Museum was founded by Chinese collector Zheng Hao, with Yun Cheagab serving as its director since 2012. The museum operates two locations: one in Shanghai, which opened in 2017, and another in Wenzhou, established in 2013. It is known for public engagement and educational outreach, such as the "Night Art Museum" initiative, which extends its hours to make art more accessible.

By Art Matters, a contemporary art museum designed by Renzo Piano Building Workshop and supported by fashion brand JNBY, was established in Hangzhou in 2021. Cofounded by Li Lin and Wu Jian and led by Italian curator Francesco Bonami, it also features an innovative residency program for contemporary artists and researchers worldwide.

Notable also is the Guangda Art Museum, established in 2015 as a private institution in Hangzhou's Shangcheng District. The museum's collection has a rich trove of works by Balthus, Pierre Bonnard, Paul Cézanne, Giacometti, and Giorgio Morandi, as well as by contemporary Chinese artists.

The M+ Museum, located in Hong Kong's West Kowloon Cultural District, opened to the public in November 2021. Designed by Herzog & de Meuron in collaboration with TFP Farrells and Arup, the museum represents a blend of government and private support. Its collection focuses on Asian art across diverse mediums, including design, painting, sculpture, video, and installations. Adjacent to M+ is the Hong Kong Palace Museum, a government-established institution that opened in July 2022. This museum displays Chinese art and cultural artifacts, offering visitors a comprehensive view of China's rich heritage.

Prestigious international collaborations have been flourishing in China as well. In 2019, the Centre Pompidou in Paris opened a branch within the West Bund Museum called the Centre Pompidou × West Bund Museum Project to showcase Chinese culture globally while introducing international art to Chinese audiences. Similarly, the National Gallery in London launched a promotional event in June 2018 by transforming a Shanghai Metro station to display reproductions of key artworks, with QR codes linking to related merchandise; the London museum also exhibited fifty-two of its masterpieces, by Raphael, Titian, Caravaggio, Rembrandt, Claude Monet, Vincent van Gogh, and many more, in Shanghai and Hong Kong (with a stop in South Korea in between) in 2023–24.

Developing art hubs has also been an essential aspect of government cultural policy, blending public and private efforts. A prime example is the 798 Art District in Beijing's Chaoyang District. Originally the 798 Electronics Factory, a state-owned complex, it was transformed from a declining industrial site into an art landmark, reflecting a nationwide trend of revitalizing industrial spaces to support artistic innovation and cultural engagement. Its spacious, Bauhaus-inspired architecture was repurposed into affordable studios, galleries, exhibition halls, and cafés. Now, the 798 Art District is one of Beijing's top cultural destinations, drawing artists, collectors, tourists, and art lovers worldwide. Similar districts have since emerged across China. In Shanghai, the M50 Art District on Moganshan Road has become a major attraction, housing a diverse range of galleries and artists' studios. In Kunming, a former rubber factory has been repurposed into an art hub, art galleries, dozens of artists' workshops, and more. The 22 Art District in Shenzhen, located in Bao'an District, once an industrial zone, now hosts galleries, studios, and cultural spaces.

CHINESE ARTISTS' JOURNEY FROM INSTRUMENTS OF THE PARTY TO GLOBAL RECOGNITION

Contemporary Chinese artists are now featured in both local and international collections, with some commanding prices in the millions. Yet, just a few decades ago, creative freedom for artists was nonexistent, as their work was expected to serve the Communist Party and the state. Ma explains that in the 1950s, shortly after the revolution, the Communist Party adopted a Soviet-style model to control artistic and cultural production, mandating that art promote the socialist agenda. Artists were required to join the China Artists Association, a state-sanctioned organization that oversaw all artistic output. Under these restrictions, art was state-funded and had to adhere to prescribed themes, images, and styles. With no independent exhibition spaces, alternative markets, or room for experimentation, artists were forced to conform to these strict regulations.[10]

In 1966, the Cultural Revolution established an even more tightly controlled artistic regime impacting the entire art system, including schools, exhibitions, and publications. As a result, Chinese art lost its individuality, and artists were expected to remain anonymous and create works solely for the collective good of the revolutionary masses, rather than for personal expression.

Censorship and state control of all creative activities remained stringent until the late 1970s, when the first timid attempts of rebellion against the system appeared. The most striking case was the exhibition illegally organized in Beijing by a group of twenty-three independent artists called Xing Xing (the Stars). Largely self-taught and from elite families, the Stars boldly displayed on September 27, 1979, approximately 150 artworks on the fences of the National Museum of China. Authorities shut down the exhibition after just two days, but as Philip Tinari observes, it conveyed a unified expression of new creativity that challenged the stagnant confines of Socialist Realist aesthetics.[11] Despite the repression of the Stars exhibition, the emancipation of the Chinese art scene and its opening to the outside world continued to gain momentum after decades of isolation.

Beginning in the 1980s, Western art began to permeate China more widely through reproductions, exhibitions, and the translation and publication of art books, as described by Ma.[12] In 1983, more than two dozen works by Pablo Picasso were shown for the first time in China, during the visit of French president François Mitterrand. And the impact in Beijing

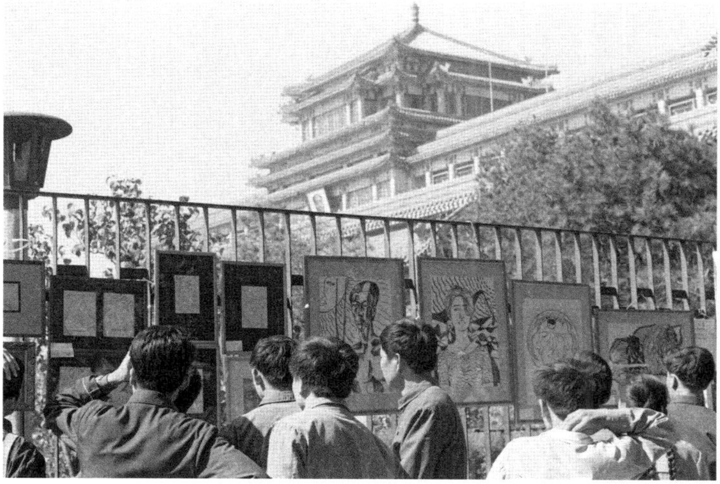

The first Stars exhibition, installed without permission on railings adjoining the National Art Museum of China, Beijing, c. September 27, 1979

of the 1985 exhibition presented by the Rauschenberg Overseas Culture Interchange (ROCI) was strong, particularly for Robert Rauschenberg's use of collage.[13] Funded by the artist, the project, for which Rauschenberg traveled to countries with restricted artistic expression to foster dialogue through creativity, embodied his dedication to human rights and artistic freedom. From 1985 to 1990, ROCI reached ten nations—Mexico, Chile, Venezuela, China, Tibet, Japan, Cuba, the USSR, Germany, and Malaysia—culminating in a 1991 exhibition at the National Gallery of Art, Washington, DC.

Ma notes that the 1980s were a period of cultural awakening for a younger, educated generation of Chinese who eagerly absorbed Western influences. Improved relations between China and the United States enabled cultural exchanges, allowing Chinese artists to connect with the global art scene. By the mid-1980s, around two hundred young Chinese artists were studying in the United States.[14] Meanwhile, foreign curators began to show interest in Chinese art. In 1980 and 1982, China was invited to make its debut in the general group show at the Venice Biennale, with the hope that contemporary art would be exhibited; however, to preserve the ideal of a national art form, the Chinese government chose instead to exclusively submit traditional crafts, embroidery and paper-cutting.[15] It was only in the following decade that the situation began to change at the Biennale, but solely at an individual level.

Marie Leduc highlights two exhibitions that were significant in the effort to both regulate the art scene in China and gain international recognition for Chinese artists. *China/Avant-Garde*, which opened on February 5, 1989, at the National Art Museum of China, in Beijing, was the first large-scale exhibition to provide a comprehensive overview of Chinese avant-garde art. *Magiciens de la terre* (*Magicians of the Earth*) at the Centre Pompidou

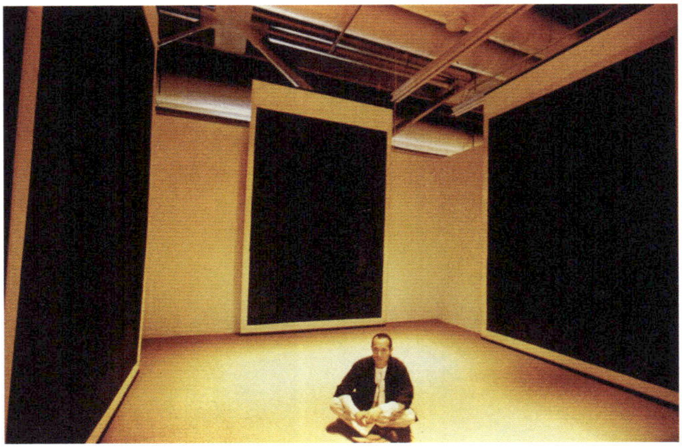

Yang Jiechang with works from his *One Hundred Layers of Ink* series at *Magiciens de la terre*, Centre Pompidou, Paris, May 18–August 14, 1989

and the Grande Halle de la Villette in Paris, in mid-1989, included three Chinese artists: Gu Dexin (b. 1962), Huang Yong Ping (1954–2019), and Yang Jiechang (b. 1956).[16] (Almost thirty years later, in 2016, Huang would be invited to conceive an installation as part of the prestigious *Monumenta* commissions at the Grand Palais in Paris.)

Curated by Jean-Hubert Martin, the legendary *Magiciens de la terre* exhibition challenged the Eurocentric dominance in the art world and the conventional notions of cultural hierarchy by presenting fifty works from Western artists alongside fifty from non-Western artists on an equal footing. Martin's innovative approach demonstrated the richness and diversity of artistic practices globally, emphasizing the need for cultural exchange and dialogue in an interconnected world.

Before and during the exhibition, which ran from May 18 to August 14, 1989, the Tiananmen Square demonstrations and crackdown occurred in Beijing. On June 4, 1989, the Chinese government brutally suppressed pro-democracy protests led primarily by students demanding political reform and an end to corruption; the government has never confirmed the death toll, but estimates range up to two thousand or more. Renewed censorship and other severe restrictions on freedom of expression followed, leading many young artists to adopt sarcasm as a form of resistance and expression of their despair. This gave rise to movements like Political Pop and Cynical Realism, which captured their disillusionment with political repression. Political Pop blended Chinese propaganda imagery with elements of Western consumer culture to offer a subversive critique of the political landscape. Cynical Realism used satirical and often dark humor to depict the alienation and absurdities of life under authoritarian rule. Wang Guangyi (b. 1957) juxtaposed images of Communist propaganda with Western consumer logos in his *Great Criticism* series (1990–2007). The *Bloodline* paintings by Zhang Xiaogang (b. 1958), a series he began in 1993, use haunting portraits reminiscent of family photographs from the Cultural Revolution era to explore themes of identity, memory, and collective trauma. The "laughing man" self-portraits by Yue Minjun (b. 1962), also started in 1993, convey the absurdities of modern life.

The witty, bold, and provocative works that Political Pop and Cynical Realist artists created would gain international acclaim and achieve record market prices. Zhang's *Bloodline: Big Family No. 2* (1995) sold at Christie's Hong Kong in December 2020 for $12,646,903; Yue's *Gweong-Gweong* (1993) made $6,932,517 at Christie's Hong Kong in May 2008.

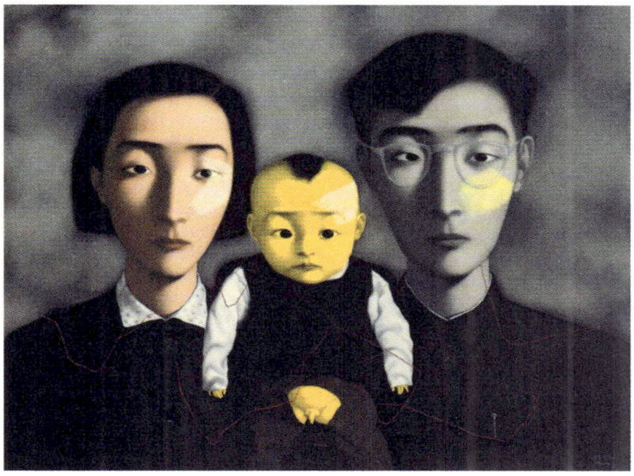

Zhang Xiaogang, *Bloodline: Big Family No. 2*, 1995

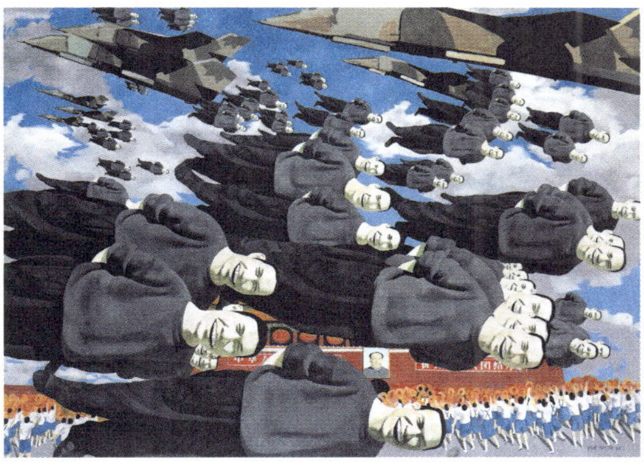

Yue Minjun, *Gweong-Gweong*, 1993

The work of Chinese artists continued to be presented abroad, in exhibitions such as *Chine demain pour hier* (*China Tomorrow for Yesterday*) in July 1990 in the village of Pourrières, near Aix-en-Provence in the South of France; and *China Avant-Garde* (1993–94) in Berlin; Rotterdam, the Netherlands; Oxford, England; Odense, Denmark; and Hildesheim, Germany. During the same decade, China's market economy began to form its now-supportive ecosystem for artists.[17]

The presence of Chinese artists on the international stage expanded significantly throughout the 1990s and 2000s. Starting in 1993, Chinese artists began to participate unofficially in the Venice Biennale. Fourteen were featured in *Nuova pittura cinese* (*New Chinese Painting*), part of *Passaggio a Oriente* (*Passage to the Orient*) in the Aperto (Open) section. By 1997, the number of Chinese artists invited grew to nineteen under the curatorship of Harald Szeemann. The same year, however, the Chinese government exhibited academic oil paintings at the Biennale. In 2003, the Centre Pompidou hosted the first large-scale exhibition of contemporary Chinese artists, signaling growing international interest. Two years after that, China established its own permanent national pavilion at the Venice Biennale, managed by the Chinese Ministry of Culture, solidifying the country's presence in the global art scene. Domestically, the Chinese government began to actively support and organize international art events within its borders. The Shanghai Biennale, launched in 1996, began accepting foreign artists from 2000 on. According to Wu Hung, the opening of the Shanghai Biennale to international participation marked a turning point for contemporary art in China. It symbolized official acceptance of global exhibitions within the country and the inclusion of experimental artists in state-run museums, highlighting China's evolving cultural openness.[18]

Now fully integrated into the global system, China's contemporary art scene remains complex, characterized by the unlikely coexistence of a thriving and liberal market with a still-challenging state censorship of artists. A major thorn in China's side is the internationally renowned Ai Weiwei (b. 1957), who has continually challenged the Chinese government's policies and practices, particularly regarding corruption, environmental degradation, and human rights abuses. *Remembering* (2009), for example, consisting of nine thousand children's backpacks arranged on the façade of the Haus der Kunst in Munich to spell out "She lived happily for seven years in this world" in Mandarin, commemorated the thousands of schoolchildren who perished in the 2008 Sichuan earthquake due to shoddy construction and government negligence. Ai himself was detained in 2011 by Chinese authorities for eighty-one days without charge, to an international outcry and condemnation. Since 2015, the artist—a symbol of Chinese dissidence and one of the most popular artists worldwide—has

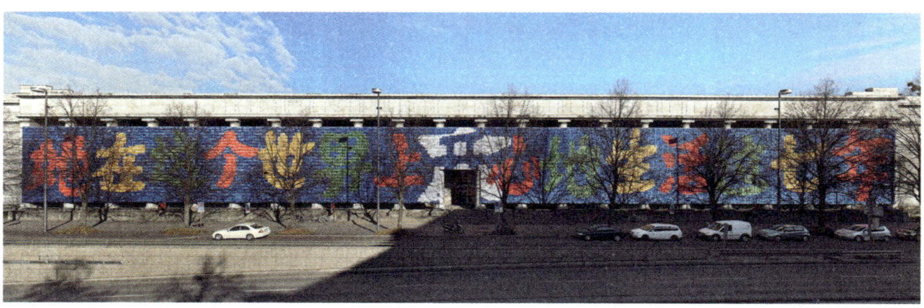

Installation view, *Ai Weiwei: So Sorry*, Haus der Kunst, Munich, October 12, 2009–January 17, 2010. Featuring *Remembering*, 2009

been living in exile, but he continues to advocate for freedom of expression and respect for human rights in China, both through his work and through social media platforms such as Twitter (now X) and Instagram.

THE RISE AND EVOLUTION OF CHINESE COLLECTORS

As previously discussed, China has experienced a remarkable transformation in the early twenty-first century, driven by Deng's economic reforms. This era of rapid growth saw the middle-income segment of China's population rise dramatically from 3.1 percent in 2000 to more than 50 percent by 2018. Even more significant for the art market is the surge in the number of millionaires, which has skyrocketed to 6.2 million—second only to the United States. According to the Hurun Rich List, China had 753 "dollar billionaires" in mid-2024. Notably, the average age of these billionaires is sixty-one, years younger than their Western peers, signaling a potentially more dynamic group of art collectors and investors.

The escalating surge in personal wealth most years has translated into an appetite for luxury goods.[19] And Western auction houses, as Adam points out, have cleverly cultivated demand by associating art with luxury goods and an upscale lifestyle. China, in particular, has shown a strong fascination with luxury brands, accounting for an impressive 30 percent of the global $285 billion luxury goods market in 2016.[20]

Record-breaking acquisitions—$17.4 million by Joseph Lau for Andy Warhol's *Mao* (1972) in 2006, $28.2 million by Wang Jianlin for Picasso's *Claude and Paloma* (1950) in 2013, and the previously mentioned $170.4 million by Liu Yiqian for a Modigliani—have catapulted to the world's attention the financial power of the Chinese billionaires, as well as their determination to put together world-class collections. Ma explains that while economic growth and wealth accumulation typically translate into a thriving art market, China's boom follows a unique logic. Decades of egalitarian Communist campaigns from the 1950s to the 1980s prevented transfer of assets across generations. As a result, Chinese collectors who experienced that era of egalitarianism and poverty have now embraced lavish spending habits. Billionaires such as Liu, Wang, and Lau have swiftly assembled impressive art collections, often focusing on iconic and trophy paintings acquired at auctions.

China also boasts the largest cohort of young collectors in the world. Born after China's economic reform began, they enjoy opportunities unavailable to previous generations, have a strong interest in Western contemporary artists, see themselves as global citizens, and frequently spend time and money abroad.[21]

This is reflected in information summarized by Quek Jie Ann from major auction houses and the online art brokerage Artsy. According to a 2023 report by Christie's, millennials account for nearly 40 percent of its buyers in the Asia Pacific region, a stark contrast to the 20 percent in the Americas, Europe, and the Middle East. The report also highlights a remarkable 65 percent surge in new Gen Z buyers. Sotheby's has observed a similar significant increase, noting that younger collectors expanded to 30 percent of its bidders, up from just 6 percent in 2018. In terms of art preferences, only 11 percent of the younger collectors consider it a priority to collect blue-chip art, compared with 23 percent of the older buyers, as Artsy's *Art Collector Insights 2023* reports.[22]

A multitude of factors—including international education and experiences, and a keen interest in technology and online platforms—have shaped the preferences of millennial and Gen Z collectors worldwide. While the impact of social media on the art market is a global phenomenon, it is particularly pronounced in China. Since 2008, China has led the world in the number of people with Internet access.[23] Particularly popular is WeChat, which serves multiple functions beyond messaging. Since its launch in 2011, WeChat has grown to become the world's largest stand-alone mobile app by 2018, boasting more than one billion monthly active users. Its use as a primary search engine in China has extended into the art world, and its capability to disseminate information in Mandarin makes it an invaluable tool for reaching Chinese collectors, especially those residing outside major urban centers. Chinese social media influencers, known there as "key opinion leaders," or KOLs, initially employed by luxury brands to target millennials, are now increasingly engaged with the art scene.

WHAT NOW?

The evolution of China's art scene and market has been closely intertwined with, and shaped by, political and past events, each leaving a lasting impact. As pointed out by Ma: "Unlike the West, whose small and insular art world is hardly affected by politics, China's art market has been in a delicate dance with geopolitical forces that sometimes take a firm lead. Historical transitions of decolonization, nationalism, liberalism, and developmentalism provide the backdrop of the art story."[24] Shifts in governance, economic policies, and cultural movements have affected the definition of artistic production and consumption, as well as the relationships among artists, collectors, and institutions.

The thriving market and its dynamic art ecosystem have developed within the paradox of a liberal, market-oriented economy coexisting with an authoritarian regime. Government support has been crucial in establishing art districts, museums, and an environment conducive to private investment. However, the tension between freedom and state control persists, influencing every aspect of the art system and daily life for Chinese citizens.

For artists in China, who have long navigated a precarious landscape where creativity contends with restriction, the tightening grip of censorship has intensified since the COVID-19 pandemic began, including an increase in digital surveillance. This shift reflects the government's growing control over cultural and social expression, further constraining artistic freedom and pushing boundaries on what can be publicly created and shared.

More artists are being detained or having their works banned in China. Tighter controls on digital platforms have also been enforced, with algorithms now more aggressively filtering out politically sensitive material. Ai Weiwei's documentary *Coronation* (2020), about severe government restrictions during the pandemic on the city of Wuhan, where COVID-19 was first reported, was blocked from being shown in China.

Nevertheless, Chinese artists' visibility abroad remains strong. On May 22, 2024, for example, *ARTnews* reported that Ai would have his first US retrospective in ten years at the Seattle Art Museum (SAM).[25] *Ai, Rebel: The Art and Activism of Ai Weiwei*, opened on March 12, 2025, showing more than 130 works spanning four decades. And for the first time in its ninety-year history, SAM presented works by a single artist at all three of its locations: at the Seattle Asian Art Museum, *Ai Weiwei: Water Lilies*, his interpretation in LEGO blocks of Monet's iconic late-career series; and at the Olympic Sculpture Park, *Ai Weiwei: Circle of Animals/Zodiac Heads (Bronze)*, comprising twelve monumental sculptures.

Meanwhile, the role of Hong Kong, which has been the epicenter of the international art market in Asia, is also vacillating, threatened both by the increasing restrictions that the Chinese government has imposed and by the rise of other Asian cities such as Seoul and Tokyo as art hubs. Under British rule from 1842 to 1997, the strategically located Hong Kong flourished as a free port, where minimal restrictions and low tariffs and duties facilitated international trade. The 1997 handover of Hong Kong to China, while marking the end of its colonial era, transitioned the city into a Special Administrative Region, maintaining some autonomy under the "one country, two systems" principle. Initially, Hong Kong enjoyed significant freedoms not found in mainland China, and it was allowed a separate legal system and democratic elections for some local positions. However, the introduction on June 30, 2020, of the National Security Law, which aims to prevent, stop, and punish acts of secession, subversion, terrorism, and collusion with foreign forces, grants Beijing significant control over Hong Kong's legal and political systems, increasing police powers as well.

These challenges prompt critical questions about the future trajectory of China's art market and its evolving role on the international stage. The interplay between censorship, economic shifts, and a growing base of affluent collectors will shape how the market develops and how Chinese art is positioned globally.

Will the forces of censorship stifle or significantly restrict artistic expression? How might this scenario impact the strength of the country's art market? If censorship is deeply ingrained in the lives and practices of Chinese artists, can it be seen as a driving creative force and a reflection of their time and society?

NOTES

1 Wu Hung, *Contemporary Chinese Art: A History, 1970s–2000* (London: Thames and Hudson, 2014), 432.

2 Li Ma, *China's Art Market since 1978: Regional Entrepreneurship and Global Impact* (London: Palgrave Macmillan, 2023), 5.

3 Ma, *China's Art Market since 1978*, 215.

4 Kejia Wu, *A Modern History of China's Art Market* (Abingdon, UK: Routledge, 2023), 5–9.

5 K. Wu, *Modern History of China's Art Market*, 32.

6 K. Wu, *Modern History of China's Art Market*, 32. The two auctions took place on June 20, 1993, and March 27, 1994.

7 Georgina Adam, *Dark Side of the Boom: The Excesses of the Art Market in the 21st Century* (London: Lund Humphries, 2017), 56–57.

8 Adam, *Dark Side of the Boom*, 56–57.

9 Jiayang Fan, "Letter from Shanghai: The Emperor's New Museum," *New Yorker*, November 7, 2016, 28–33.

10 Ma, *China's Art Market since 1978*, 35–36.

11 Philip Tinari, "Between Palimpsest and Teleology: The Problem of 'Chinese Contemporary Art,'" in *Art and China after 1989: Theater of the World*, by Alexandra Munroe, Hou Hanru, and Philip Tinari, exh. cat. (New York: Guggenheim Museum Publications, 2017), 53. Associated with the Stars were Ai Weiwei (b. 1957), cofounders Huang Rui (b. 1952) and Ma Desheng (b. 1952), and members including Wang Keping (b. 1949) and Li Shuang (b. 1957).

12 Ma, *China's Art Market since 1978*, 61.

13 Marie Leduc, *Dissidence: The Rise of Chinese Contemporary Art in the West* (Cambridge, MA: MIT Press, 2018), 28.

14 Ma, *China's Art Market since 1978*, 10.

15 Leduc, *Dissidence*, 129.

16 Leduc, *Dissidence*, 44–49.

17 Ma, *China's Art Market since 1978*, 69.

18 Wu H., *Contemporary Chinese Art*, 352.

19 Ma, *China's Art Market since 1978*, 174.

20 Adam, *Dark Side of the Boom*, 62.

21 Ma, *China's Art Market since 1978*, 137–41.

22 Quek Jie Ann, "Asia's Young and Wealthy Are Fueling Demand for Art—What Are They Collecting?," CNBC.com, January 7, 2024, https://www.cnbc.com/2024/01/08/asias-young-and-rich-are-fueling-art-demand-what-are-they-collecting.html.

23 Ma, *China's Art Market since 1978*, 130.

24 Ma, *China's Art Market since 1978*, 9.

25 Alex Greenberger, "Ai Weiwei to Get His First US Retrospective in a Decade at Seattle Art Museum," *ARTnews*, May 22, 2024, https://www.artnews.com/art-news/news/ai-weiwei-us-retrospective-2025-seattle-art-museum-1234707464/.

12 The Rebirth of China's Art Market and Its Rising International Clout

13. The Art Market in a Global, Post-Pandemic, Turbulent Time

p. 253 COVID Strikes

p. 254 Instagram, NFTs, AI: How Digital Transformations Are Affecting the Art World

p. 260 Passing the Torch: From Baby Boomers to Millennials and Gen Z

p. 262 The Rise of the Art Market for African American Artists

p. 265 Jean-Michel Basquiat

p. 266 The Renaissance of Women Artists

p. 268 The Market for Female Surrealists

p. 272 Concerns about the Environment

p. 273 Shortening the Distance between Primary and Secondary Markets

p. 273 The Patronage Model in Qatar, Saudi Arabia, and the United Arab Emirates

p. 276 What Model Now?

> What sort of beauty will save the world?
>
> —Fyodor Dostoyevsky, *The Idiot*

In 2020, the COVID-19 pandemic shook the world to its core, and the art community was no exception. Lives were tragically lost, people laid off, galleries shut down. The upheaval necessitated a swift transition to online platforms for all business operations. However, this crisis also catalyzed a crucial and transformative restructuring, with digitization becoming a driving force for change.

The art market that has recovered from the pandemic is in many aspects a transformed one. Cultural and social changes, along with a generational shift in the demographics of collectors, are deeply affecting tastes, prices, and modes of conducting business. Marginalized and otherwise overlooked groups of artists, most notably women and African Americans, are finally receiving long-overdue critical and market attention.

No other artist has followed Damien Hirst in consigning a significant batch of freshly created works to an auction house, but the gap between primary and secondary markets has markedly diminished.

The gallery model remains central to the art world, with major galleries expanding geographically and embracing digital strategies. Nevertheless, it faces substantial challenges. As information becomes decentralized and widely accessible online, and opinions are increasingly shared through social media, the dynamics of artists' validation are becoming more complex.

New models are also emerging, such as artists' agencies, which offer comprehensive promotion and management of all aspects of their careers.

Lastly, artificial intelligence (AI) is impacting the art system by offering tools that enhance creativity as well as algorithms that aid in authentication and valuation, while simultaneously raising critical and contentious issues.

COVID STRIKES

At the beginning of 2020, COVID-19, a complex and often life-threatening respiratory illness caused by a virus, spread so rapidly that within a couple of months, it had brought much of the world to an unprecedented and unimaginable halt.[1] Lockdowns—mandatory closings of schools and businesses and prohibition on most other gatherings—were declared and enforced in many countries, even as deaths escalated and health systems and economies were severely strained. Vaccines were developed after several months—in record time—and began to be administered near the end of 2020; life slowly started to get back to normal.

Still, the long-term effects were profound, and the art world was not spared. Among those who tragically lost their lives due to COVID were art historians and curators Maurice Berger, Germano Celant, and David C. Driskell. Art businesses, too, experienced countless layoffs, and some of those that had closed their doors never reopened. The forced paralysis that had blocked the mobility of individuals and goods had deep repercussions on every aspect of the art system. All activity had to be moved online—it was a matter of survival. Auction houses, along with major galleries, were better positioned, due to their structured operations and readiness to sell digitally. However, like all businesses in 2020, they were still drastically affected. According to the annual Art Basel and UBS report on the art market published in early 2021, aggregate sales for dealers declined from 2019 to 2020 by 20 percent and public auction sales by 30 percent. Of the 365 planned global art fairs, 61 percent were canceled, though 37 percent did hold live events and the remaining 2 percent held hybrid, alternative events. One sector doubled in value: unsurprisingly, that of aggregate online sales. As pointed out by cultural economist Clare McAndrew, author of the report and founder of the research and consulting firm Arts Economics, the crisis provided the impetus for change in a market that, in terms of digitization, had lagged behind compared to other industries.[2] And as the following year's report noted, recovery in 2021 was robust and fast, with combined sales of art and antiques by dealers and auction houses reaching an estimated $65.1 billion, up 29 percent from 2020, and "with values also surpassing pre-pandemic levels in 2019."[3]

During the 2020 pandemic, the strong stock market performance fueled pent-up demand among wealthy collectors, leading them to lavishly invest in the art sector starting later that year.

INSTAGRAM, NFTS, AI: HOW DIGITAL TRANSFORMATIONS ARE AFFECTING THE ART WORLD

With upwards of 2 billion users, 95 million daily posts, and a valuation exceeding $100 billion, Instagram has become a dominant force in social media since the app was released in 2010. Its focus on visuals has fueled its rapid growth, and its significance in the art world became clear during the pandemic, when the platform served as an effective alternative exhibition space and source of information. Today, Instagram goes beyond just marketing and outreach for artists, galleries, and institutions; it functions as a virtual exhibition space where artists share behind-the-scenes glimpses of their process and the ongoing lives of their artworks. Moreover, it has evolved into a direct communication channel between artists and a global audience, unrestricted by time or geography.

Unlike physical galleries, Instagram is accessible to anyone with a smartphone, tablet, or desktop computer—which means several billion people, a large majority of the world's population. This global virtual gallery is breaking down traditional barriers and democratizing access to art. By amplifying voices that might struggle for recognition in traditional art circles, Instagram fosters greater inclusivity and diversity within the art world.

Established artists use Instagram to engage dynamically with their followers, while for many emerging artists, the platform has been crucial in launching their careers. By sharing images, stories, and videos, artists can connect directly with followers and potential buyers, sometimes leading to direct sales that bypass traditional galleries and dealers. The use of hashtags and geotags allows artists to align themselves with specific topics or communities, while metrics like follower counts and "likes" might enable them to gauge their work's impact and audience preferences.

As one example among many, Instagram was instrumental in exponentially expanding the career of Salman Toor (b. 1983), providing a means for sharing his art with a global audience. Born in Lahore, Pakistan, Toor creates intimate, small-scale oil paintings that merge old master influences with vignette-style narratives, reflecting his experiences as a queer brown man living between New York and South Asia. His visually striking style—highly "Instagrammable"—and resonant content have strongly connected with a young audience worldwide, making Instagram the ideal platform for his work. Interest surged among collectors, galleries, and institutions, culminating in Toor's solo exhibition, *How Will I Know*, at the Whitney Museum of American Art in 2020–21, which catapulted him into the global spotlight. This attention was further amplified by the remarkable auction results that followed. In December 2020, Toor became the first Pakistani artist to be featured in a major auction at Christie's New York, where his painting *Rooftop Party with Ghosts 1* (2015) sold for $822,000—eight times its low estimate. The auction frenzy continued with *Liberty Porcelain* (2012), which sold at Phillips London in the same month for $505,688—nine times its low estimate. As of the summer of 2024, Toor's auction record stands at $1,562,500, set at Sotheby's New York in November 2022 for *Four Friends* (2019). This meteoric rise in prices has been driven by the limited availability of his work on the primary market, combined with a global demand fueled by his strong resonance on social platforms.

Many African artists, historically operating outside traditional international art market channels, have also found Instagram to be a remarkably effective tool for gaining international exposure. This is the case with the Ghanaian painter Amoako Boafo (b. 1984), who has exhibited with Gagosian since 2023; his auction record of $3,420,438 was established at Christie's Hong Kong in December 2021 for *Hands Up* (2018). Boafo's breakthrough came when African American artist Kehinde Wiley (b. 1977) discovered his work on Instagram, leading to connections with galleries such as the prestigious Mariane Ibrahim, with venues in Paris, Chicago, and Mexico City, and exposure to collectors. The market for Boafo's distinctive portraits celebrating Black identity skyrocketed due to a combination of strategic gallery representation, critical acclaim, and social media influence. Fashion collaborations, such as with Dior, further pushed his renown.

Boafo stands as just one example among the many ultra-contemporary African artists—born after 1974—who experienced a jump in the art market. In an article for Artnet in 2022, Katya Kazakina reported that auction

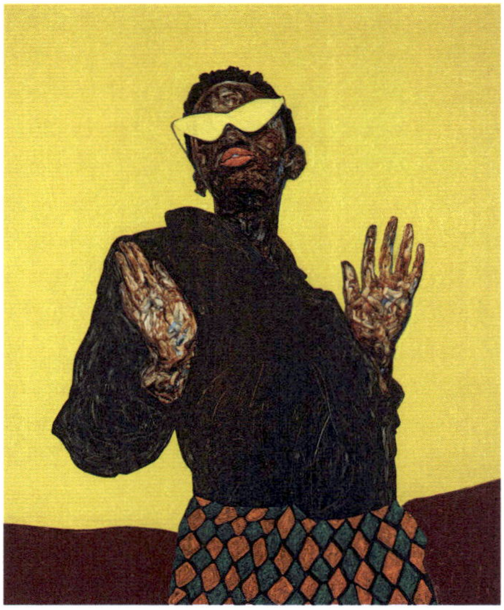

Amoako Boafo, *Hands Up*, 2018

sales for this particular group of artists witnessed a staggering increase over just two years, soaring from a cumulative $7.5 million in 2019 to almost $40 million in 2021. Kazakina identifies several factors as drivers of the explosion in the market for emerging African artists: the digital revolution in the art world during the pandemic, which facilitated unprecedented access to the abundant talent across the continent; the growing desire among buyers to diversify their collections, moving away from a predominantly white and Western focus; and the influx during the lockdown of new collectors who tend to favor figuration, a style embraced by numerous young African painters.[4]

In this context, the traditional separation between primary and secondary markets is almost nonexistent. Acquired by the consignor directly from the artist, *Sisters in Pink* (2021), by the Ghanaian Emmanuel Taku (b. 1986), sold at Phillips for $189,000—seven times its low estimate—in November of the same year it was painted. The artist's large-scale portraits that blend traditional African elements with contemporary themes attracted significant attention from international collectors, driven by Taku's strong social media presence and positive critical reception. However, the speculative nature and overexposure of his market led soon to a saturation point. When Taku's auction results began to soften, collectors started to resell his works at lower prices. The abovementioned *Sisters in Pink* reappeared at Phillips New York in March 2024, and it sold for only $10,160. The decline highlights the volatility of a market that rose too fast and hazardously, without consistent and sound gallery and institutional support. Rachel Corbett points out that the market for young African figurative artists dramatically shrank in 2024, warning that "anti-woke sentiment had infected the mainstream and interest in showy egalitarianism and visible diversity was noticeably lower."[5]

While Instagram has democratized the art world and market, it also risks homogenizing artistic tastes and content. The platform favors art that is easily consumable online, leading to the rise of "Instagrammable art." This term refers to photogenic works, from immersive installations to figurative art, that translate well digitally. Although Instagram has expanded access to the art market, artists can also feel pressured to prioritize trends and commercial success over their true vision, potentially marginalizing more challenging or unconventional art forms.

On March 11, 2021, the art world was abuzz with the news that *Everydays: The First 5000 Days* (2021) had sold at Christie's New York for an astounding $69,346,250, making its creator, Beeple (b. 1981), the third-most-expensive living artist and marking the first time a major auction house sold a purely digital work. A collection of images that Beeple—born Mike Winkelmann—had been posting online since 2007, *Everydays: The First 5000 Days* is an NFT, or non-fungible token, meaning that it exists solely in digital form. The buyer was Vignesh Sundaresan, who purchased the work on behalf of his fund Metapurse with the purpose of dividing it into fractional shares to sell. Amy Whitaker and Nora Burnett Abrams observe that the single-lot sale of this work "brought both a record price . . . and a collision of seemingly unrelated fields that destabilized the pillars of the contemporary art world."[6]

Zachary Small describes the event as "a bidding war constructed from overlapping economic and technological interests."[7] Small's investigation into the rise and fall of the NFT market highlights the fact that younger generations have embraced NFTs as a symbol of their own rising economic power in society, representing a break with older models of cultural production.[8] The arrival of crypto in the art world coincided with the pandemic, the industry's migration to online sales, and the moment when, as Small puts it, "millennials had become leading spenders in the art market."[9]

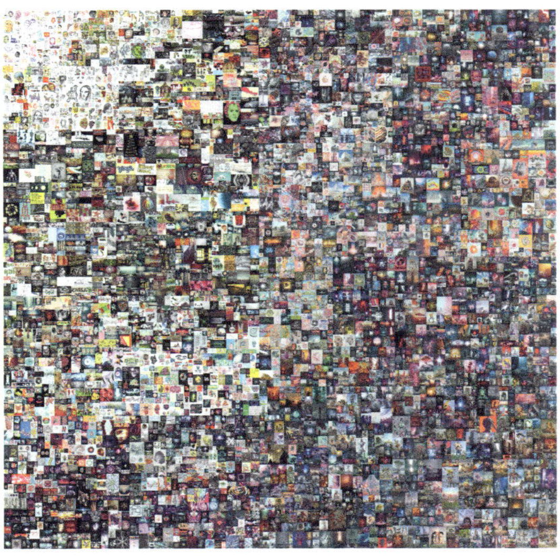

Beeple, *Everydays: The First 5000 Days*, 2021

What is an NFT? It is a unique encoded token that represents ownership or proof of authenticity for a specific digital-only asset—which could be an artwork, a video clip, a PFP (profile picture), or a tweet, to name but a few examples—not occupying physical space like a traditional artwork but, instead, typically stored on a blockchain. That refers to a secure database, an online ledger of sorts, in which information is linked together using cryptographic techniques that make any alterations easily detectable. This technology allows the creation of unique identifiers—like a certificate of authenticity—for digital files, which would otherwise be infinitely replicable. NFTs enable consumers to verify authenticity and origin, significantly reducing the risk of counterfeiting. The process of converting something into a digital token on a blockchain is known as "tokenization." NFTs are now used across various industries, including gaming, music, sneakers, and even real estate, where they may or may not represent ownership of physical properties.

In the digital art space, NFTs enable artists to tokenize their work, establish verifiable ownership and transparent provenances, and monetize directly. Furthermore, NFTs can be sold via "smart" or self-executing contracts that grant the artists resale royalties, allowing them to receive percentages of secondary-market sales, unlike at a standard auction house. Whitaker and Abrams wonder: "Contemplating the span of art history from the Renaissance to the present, and the changes in patronage, artistic working style, and power, is blockchain the biggest artistic intervention since the Renaissance? What seismic shifts will it bring in the power structure of the arts?"[10]

After Beeple's record price, it indeed seemed that blockchain technology had the potential to reshape the traditional power dynamics that have long defined the art world.

Interestingly, in March 2022, Beeple mounted a personal exhibition, at the now-shuttered Jack Hanley Gallery in New York, called *Uncertain Future*—which featured thirteen paintings and prints, and which sold out. The initial excitement surrounding NFTs has now waned. The 2024 Art Basel and UBS report notes that spending on digital art accounted for only 3 percent of collectors' total expenditures, with digital artworks constituting just 8 percent of their collections, down from 15 percent in 2022.[11] In 2024–25, per the same source, spending on digital art rebounded to 14 percent. Paintings remained both the most popular medium to collect and the largest category within collections across generations and wealth levels, and regardless of the length of time collecting.[12]

For nearly a year beginning in the fall of 2022, the installation *Unsupervised* (2021–22), part of the ongoing series *Machine Hallucinations* (2016–) by the Turkish-born artist Refik Anadol (b. 1985), captivated audiences at the Museum of Modern Art in New York. According to the museum's website, Anadol utilized a sophisticated machine-learning model trained on publicly available data from MoMA's collection. As the model navigated through its interpretation of this extensive array of artworks, it reimagined the history of modern art and speculated on future possibilities. Moreover, site-specific inputs from the museum lobby's environment, including

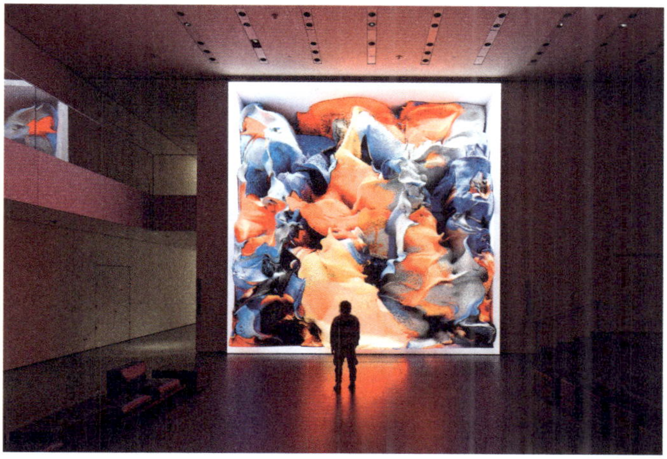

Installation view, *Refik Anadol: Unsupervised*, Museum of Modern Art, New York, November 19, 2022–October 29, 2023

changes in light, sound, motion, and external weather conditions, dynamically influenced the algorithm and the continuously evolving imagery and soundscapes it generated.

Unsupervised represents a remarkable application of AI to the realm of art, showing how technology can reshape artistic expression and viewers' engagement. Shortly before the end of the exhibition, MoMA acquired Anadol's artwork for its permanent collection.

On a broader scale, the ethical implications and concerns surrounding the use of AI across various domains have ignited intense debate and left many critical questions unresolved. In response, on October 30, 2023, President Joseph Biden issued an executive order to ensure the responsible development and deployment of AI technologies. This included the creation of a White House Artificial Intelligence Council across federal agencies, designed to address the ethical and societal implications of AI and to establish governance frameworks, with a focus on transparency, accountability, cybersecurity, and data privacy protection.

The intersection of AI and the art world has sparked a mix of excitement and caution. AI-generated art often draws from algorithms trained on extensive datasets of human-created works (without the authors' or artists' permission). Yet AI lacks inherent creative intuition; it mimics styles and patterns observed in existing art rather than generating ideas organically. As such, can AI-produced artworks truly be considered original creations?

Artnet News launched a series of discussions on how artists are engaging with AI, as well as its impact on their work and our perception of art. Laurie Simmons (b. 1949), known for her staged photographs exploring themes of domesticity, identity, and femininity, has integrated machine-learning algorithms into her images. She views AI as just another tool, akin to a camera, that adds to her creative process without defining her as an "AI artist." Mario Klingemann (b. 1970) trains AI on vast image datasets to produce new, often surreal compositions, emphasizing the creative process as much as the final work. His piece *Memories of Passersby I* (2018) continuously generates unique portraits in real time, inviting viewers to see AI as a relatable and collaborative force in art.[13] Meanwhile, in Australia, at the National Gallery of Victoria Triennial in 2023–24, Agnieszka Pilat (b. 1973) trained robotic dogs to paint in real time. Pilat advocates for artists not to resist this technological development but, rather, to embrace AI as a tool, like any other, that can shape culture.

As artificial intelligence rapidly transforms industries around the globe, the art world finds itself on the cusp of unprecedented change. From authentication and curation to creation and market prediction, AI is poised to reshape long-standing practices. Jo Lawson-Tancred captures the gravity of this moment, declaring, "The implications of artificial intelligence are hard to predict, but one thing experts do agree on is that they are almost impossible to overstate. . . . It would be absurd to imagine that the art world could be exempt from such seismic shifts."[14]

Copyright and intellectual property are prime areas impacted by AI advancements. AI systems can generate pieces that closely resemble or replicate existing artworks, thus challenging traditional notions of attribution and ownership.

The application of AI to art authentication and valuation was catapulted to the world's attention with the case of the *de Brécy Tondo*, a sixteenth-century circular painting depicting the Madonna and Child and usually attributed to a follower of Raphael (1483–1520) or his workshop. A UK research team, using AI-based facial recognition, suggested that the painting was created by Raphael himself. The claim was later challenged by the Swiss AI firm Art Recognition, which used its own model to determine, with 85 percent certainty, that the work was not by Raphael.

Lawson-Tancred points out that the *de Brécy* debacle exposes the fact that AI can be objective only if it uses the same model and is trained on the same data—which did not happen in that case.[15] Nevertheless, the scathing question—whether AI can one day surpass, and replace, human expertise—hovers over us.

As for art valuation, which traditionally relies on secondary-market data and experts' interpretation of them, this is another area where AI could be effective, with the possibility of predicting the trajectory of an artist's success.

PASSING THE TORCH: FROM BABY BOOMERS TO MILLENNIALS AND GEN Z

It is estimated that by 2045, the baby boomers' generation will pass down $84.4 trillion in assets, with $72.6 trillion going directly to their heirs, in particular, millennials.[16]

Born between 1946 and 1964, baby boomers accumulated their wealth during the favorable climate of the prosperous post–World War II years in various sectors, from industry to real estate and financial markets. In terms of art collecting, their choices have been routed to the major art movements and creators to which they were exposed: Abstract Expressionism, Pop art, and Minimalism, and European masters such as Francis Bacon, followed by artists such as Damien Hirst, Jeff Koons, Richard Prince, Gerhard Richter, Cindy Sherman, and Christopher Wool. Like the majority of museum collections from the baby boomers' time period, this has also meant choosing the work of mainly white and male artists.

As a new generation of collectors—the children of the baby boomers—enters the art market, a reevaluation is taking place. Artists long regarded as stable cornerstones of art history and market consensus are being reassessed. The work of Jasper Johns (b. 1930) is a case in point. His canonical status remains firmly anchored, as demonstrated by the major dual-venue retrospective at the Whitney Museum of American Art and the Philadelphia Museum of Art in 2021–22, as well as the sale of *Small False Start* (1960) for $55,350,000 at Christie's in November 2022. At the same time, results from the May 2023 contemporary auctions at Christie's—where three paintings by Johns from the S. I. Newhouse collection sold slightly below their low estimates—point to a more selective market response, which reflects a broader generational reorientation in taste and values.

Another significant example is *White Disaster (White Car Crash 19 Times)* (1963) by Andy Warhol (1928–1987), which sold at Sotheby's New York in November 2022 for $85,350,496. This was indeed a remarkable price in absolute terms, but it fell below expectations; furthermore, the painting did not produce much bidding and was bought by a collector in his seventies. By comparison, a decade earlier, Warhol's *Silver Car Crash (Double Disaster)* (1963) had prompted a fierce bidding competition at Sotheby's New York in November 2013 and established a record price for the artist of $105,445,000. It was a time when baby boomers were still leading the market—indeed, they were responsible for the exceptional price spike in the first fifteen years of the twenty-first century.

Each generation naturally gravitates toward artistic expressions that resonate with its sensibilities. However, the entry of millennials (born in the 1980s and 1990s) and Generation Z (born in the late 1990s and early 2000s) into the art market has brought structural changes, including widespread use of digital technology and heightened focus on social and environmental issues. As digital natives, they are drawn not only to acquiring digital art such as NFTs but also to accessing art and information through nontraditional channels. While millennials and Gen Z art collectors still visit galleries and fairs, online platforms and virtual galleries—which often aim to be more transparent, accessible, and equitable—are increasingly their go-to sources. Their collecting choices are also influenced by both a desire to prioritize authentic narratives and a strong emphasis on social and political issues. This shift has been crucial in driving the rise of the market for women and African American artists; however, the exponential growth of these markets has attracted buyers from all generations, as traditional collectors seek to diversify their holdings and ensure that their collections remain relevant.

The enduring interest in works rich with personal and narrative content may explain why postwar masters like David Hockney (b. 1937) and Francis Bacon (1909–1992)—gay artists known for their powerful figurative paintings—continue to resonate with changing tastes. Hockney's *Portrait of an Artist (Pool with Two Figures)* (1972) sold for $90.3 million at Christie's New York in November 2018, at the time the most expensive work by a living artist ever sold at auction. Bacon's *Study for Portrait of Lucian Freud* (1964) fetched $52.7 million at Sotheby's New York in June 2022, and *Figure in Movement* (1976) brought in $52.2 million at Christie's New York in November 2023.

The anticipated $84.4 trillion wealth transfer from baby boomers is expected to bring high-quality collections to the market in the coming years, whether through single-owner estate sales or inherited works, as seen with sales of Paul Allen's and S. I. Newhouse's estates at Christie's.

Another epochal shift with transformative potential is the massive wealth transfer set to impact American women by 2030. According to a McKinsey & Company report by Pooneh Baghai, Olivia Howard, Lakshmi Prakash, and Jill Zucker in July 2020, women are expected to administer around $30 trillion in financial assets, a figure that is about the same as the annual GDP of the United States. The authors write:

> Today, women control a third of total US household financial assets—more than $10 trillion. But over the next decade, large sums of money are expected to change hands. The biggest driver of this shift is demographics. Today, roughly 70 percent of US affluent-household investable assets are controlled by baby boomers. Furthermore, two-thirds of baby-boomer assets are currently held by joint households (where a female is present but not actively involved in financial decisions), meaning that roughly $11 trillion in assets are likely to be put into play. As men pass, many will cede control of these assets to their female spouses, who tend to be both younger and longer lived. . . . After years of playing second fiddle to men, women are poised to take center stage.[17]

This significant wealth transfer will inevitably influence art market dynamics, challenging a field traditionally dominated by men. For 2022, the Art Basel and UBS report notes the overall gender breakdown of buyers as 39 percent female and 61 percent male, with 0.5 percent identifying as nonbinary.[18] In 2025, the same source indicates that Gen Z and millennial women spent more than men, while for Gen X and boomers, the opposite was true.[19]

THE RISE OF THE ART MARKET FOR AFRICAN AMERICAN ARTISTS

Sociocultural, economic, and institutional changes have propelled the exponential rise of the market for African American artists. The COVID-19 lockdown in 2020 marked a pivotal moment, coinciding with the resurgence of the Black Lives Matter movement and widespread protests following the brutal murder of George Floyd by police in Minneapolis on May 25, 2020. Black Lives Matter originated in 2013 after the acquittal of George Zimmerman, a member of the neighborhood watch program in his Florida gated community, who had killed teenager Trayvon Martin the year before. The decentralized movement organized protests of police brutality after the deaths of unarmed Black men in 2014 and after. Such events were part of a broader effort to increase diversification in society and redress historical injustices—and it profoundly impacted the art world too, amplifying the voices of both current and earlier African American artists, including an increased presence in museums and galleries.

The 2018 unveiling of the official portraits of Barack and Michelle Obama at the National Portrait Gallery in Washington, DC, was historic. These portraits, by Kehinde Wiley and Amy Sherald (b. 1973), respectively, marked the first commissions for African American artists to paint portraits of a former president and first lady, symbolizing a shift toward inclusivity in the art establishment.

A critical reassessment of African American artists' contributions to art history, driven by scholarly research and prominent exhibitions, has fueled market growth. (Swann Galleries, a family-run New York business established in 1941 and known for its specialization in rare books, became the first and, so far, only auction house to establish a department dedicated to African American art, in 2006.) Between 2008 and 2021, the market for African American artists soared by nearly 400 percent, according to Artnet, though it still accounted for only 4 percent of global auction sales in 2021,

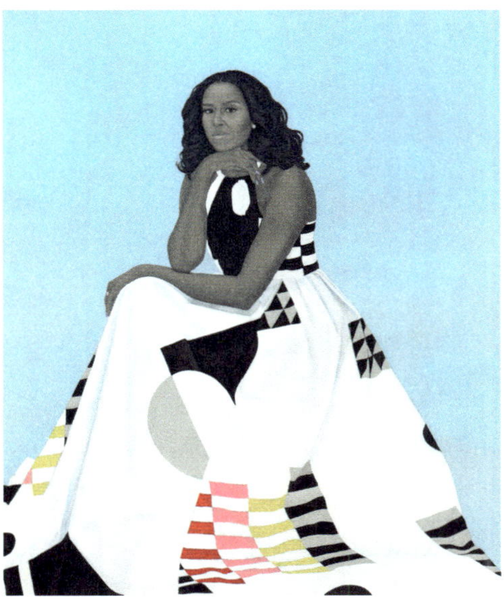

Amy Sherald, *Michelle LaVaughn Robinson Obama*, 2018, National Portrait Gallery, Washington, DC

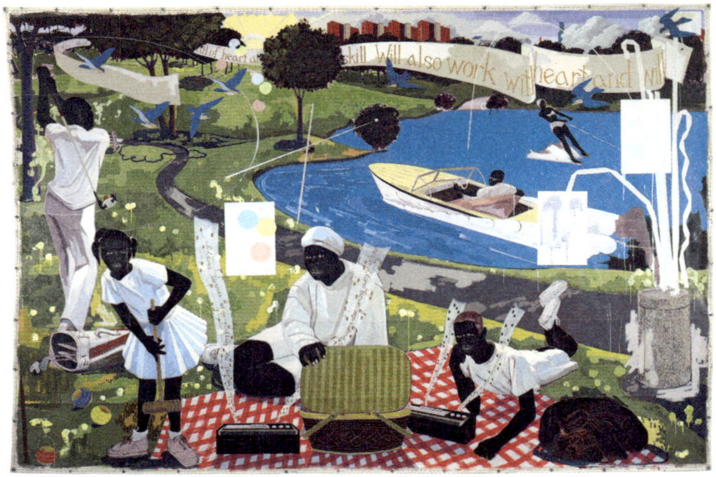

Kerry James Marshall, *Past Times*, 1997

and less in 2022.[20] Leading galleries such as Hauser & Wirth, Gagosian, and David Zwirner have increasingly featured Black artists, both historical and contemporary. Initially, the market surge focused on younger African American artists, with limited availability in the primary market driving significant auction prices. Notable examples include Mark Bradford (b. 1961), whose *Helter Skelter I* (2007) sold for $11,987,144 at Phillips London in March 2018; the Ethiopian-born American artist Julie Mehretu (b. 1970), whose *Walkers With the Dawn and Morning* (2008) sold for $10,737,500 at Sotheby's New York in November 2023; the Nigerian-born American artist Njideka Akunyili Crosby (b. 1983), whose work *The Beautyful Ones* (2012) sold for $4,740,000 at Christie's New York in November 2022; and Amy Sherald, whose painting *The Bathers* (2015) sold for $4,265,000 at Phillips New York in December 2020.

A landmark moment came when *Past Times* (1997) by Kerry James Marshall (b. 1955) sold for $21.1 million at Sotheby's New York in May 2018. This set a new benchmark for a living African American artist and underscored the recognition of older artists who had long struggled for mainstream acceptance. Born in Birmingham, Alabama, Marshall creates works that highlight the marginalization of African Americans in art. His large-scale paintings, inspired by Western art traditions, depict African American lives in a dark, almost black color palette to address their historical invisibility. Despite earlier achievements, such as participation in the 50th Venice Biennale (2003) and museum acquisitions, it was his retrospective *Mastry* (which opened at the Museum of Contemporary Art Chicago in 2016 and traveled to the Metropolitan Museum of Art in New York and the Museum of Contemporary Art, Los Angeles, through 2017) and the record-breaking auction result a year later that cemented his global prominence.

Recognition is also expanding to much earlier masters of the twentieth-century Harlem Renaissance, such as Jacob Lawrence (1917–2000) and Norman Lewis (1909–1979). As previously mentioned, Lawrence's *The*

Businessmen (1947) sold for $6.17 million at Sotheby's New York in November 2018, while Lewis's *Ritual* (1962) fetched $2.78 million at Sotheby's New York in 2019. These sales reflect a growing appreciation for underexplored niches and the investment potential of their works.

Jean-Michel Basquiat (1960–1988) holds the record for the most expensive painting by an African American artist. His *Untitled* (1982) sold for $110.5 million at Sotheby's New York in May 2017—which, in fact, was the highest price at the time for any American artist. Basquiat's market trajectory is unique. Despite his short life, he achieved early commercial success, becoming highly sought-after by collectors and partially embraced by the art establishment. Basquiat's rise coincided with the 1980s return to figuration as well as economic prosperity, and his work attracted young, wealthy collectors. Initially priced at $2,500 during his first solo show in the United States, at Annina Nosei Gallery in New York in 1982, Basquiat's works posthumously skyrocketed in value, with *In This Case* (1983) selling for $93.1 million at Christie's New York in May 2021, up from $999,500 in 2002.

JEAN-MICHEL BASQUIAT

Like a dazzling meteor, Jean-Michel Basquiat's genius crossed the firmament of the New York art world, leaving an indelible mark that would influence generations to come.

In less than a decade, the artist forged a distinctive and potent visual language, drawing inspiration from a diverse array of sources including Cy Twombly, Leonardo da Vinci, and his own Caribbean and African heritage, while crafting a personal pantheon that celebrated Black jazz musicians and athletes.

Reflecting on the widespread admiration for Basquiat during the 1980s, Marc Mayer notes that from the artist's very first exhibition, his work resonated across contemporary art communities in North America, Europe, and Japan. By the age of twenty-five, Basquiat had garnered international recognition. Yet it is only now, with the passage of time and our current perspective on the twentieth century, that we can truly grasp the enduring uniqueness of his work and understand why it was revered as exemplary even in 1983.[21]

Born into a middle-class family—his father Haitian and his mother Puerto Rican—Basquiat was a self-taught artist and a precocious child, fluent in three languages. His mother often took him to museums, particularly the Brooklyn Museum, where he became its youngest member. Leaving home as a teenager, Basquiat began covering the walls of downtown Manhattan with graffiti alongside his friend Al Diaz, signing their work "SAMO©." Having participated in the influential *Times Square Show* in 1980, Basquiat gained further recognition with a feature in the December 1981 issue of *Artforum* titled "The Radiant Child." His first solo exhibition took place in Modena, Italy, at Emilio Mazzoli's gallery, in May 1981.

Annina Nosei provided Basquiat with a studio in the basement of her SoHo gallery in New York, leading to a groundbreaking exhibition in March 1982, for which his painting *Arroz con Pollo* (1981) was prominently featured on the invitation card. (In 1989, the year after Basquiat's death, *Arroz con Pollo* appeared at auction at Christie's New York and sold for $440,000.)

Also in 1982, Basquiat became the youngest artist ever included in the prestigious Documenta exhibition in Kassel, Germany, and he was invited to take part in the Whitney Museum's Biennial in 1983. Larry Gagosian began representing Basquiat in

Los Angeles, along with Mary Boone in New York and Bruno Bischofberger in Zurich. The Swiss dealer encouraged a collaboration with Andy Warhol, resulting in about 160 paintings, which were the subject of a comprehensive and revelatory exhibition at the Fondation Louis Vuitton in Paris in 2023.

Basquiat's international presence expanded in 1987 with solo shows at Galerie Daniel Templon in Paris and Akira Ikeda Gallery in Tokyo. However, despite the growing recognition, New York museums hesitated to acquire his work. Meanwhile, as his success soared, Basquiat's heroin addiction worsened. He tragically passed away on August 12, 1988, at the age of twenty-seven, from an overdose.

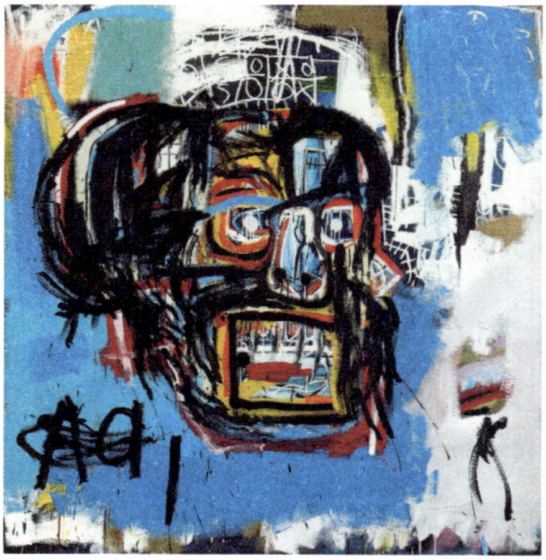

Jean-Michel Basquiat, *Untitled*, 1982

THE RENAISSANCE OF WOMEN ARTISTS

A remarkable resurgence in the market for female artists is reshaping narratives that have historically marginalized women, as discussed in earlier chapters. This shift is being propelled by art institutions and museums, alongside growing societal awareness of gender inequalities. In this context, the 2022 Venice Biennale, curated by Cecilia Alemani, marked a significant milestone: for the first time, about 90 percent of the artists featured were women or nonbinary.

A flurry of institutional exhibitions by women artists in New York soon followed. An eight-month-long survey of work by Cecily Brown (b. 1969) opened in the spring of 2023 at the Metropolitan Museum of Art; *Cecily Brown: Death and the Maid* featured some fifty paintings and other works by the British painter who moved to New York in the mid-1990s. For almost as many months, the museum's rooftop garden was home to an architectural installation by Lauren Halsey (b. 1987) that blended ancient Egyptian inspirations with contemporary contexts from South Central Los Angeles, where she lives and works. At the Whitney Museum that spring and summer, a retrospective of Jaune Quick-to-See Smith (1940–2025), of the Confederated Salish and Kootenai Nation, marked the first solo

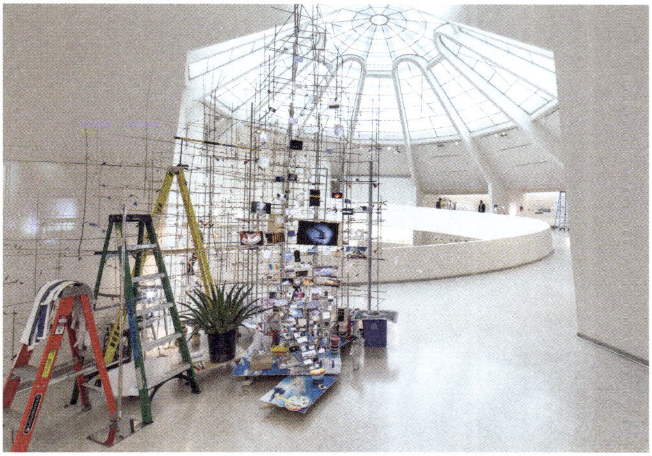

Installation view, *Sarah Sze: Timelapse*, Solomon R. Guggenheim Museum, New York, March 31–September 10, 2023

exhibition of a Native American female artist in a major American museum. Meanwhile, the Solomon R. Guggenheim Museum's rotunda showcased drawings and sculptures by Gego (Gertrud Goldschmidt) (1912–1994), a German-born Venezuelan artist who fled Nazi persecution in 1939, while Sarah Sze (b. 1969) had a solo exhibition, *Timelapse*, that comprised several site-specific multimedia installations placed throughout the museum's interior—and even outside.

Despite these advancements, substantial disparities between male and female artists persist across all fields. Women remain underrepresented in public collections—usually only 5 to 15 percent of the works are by women—partly because many artworks have entered museums through donations from collections that often prioritized male artists. Compounding this issue, many of the leading museums worldwide—including the British Museum in London and the Metropolitan Museum of Art and MoMA in New York—have never had a female director; in 2021, the Musée du Louvre in Paris named a woman, Laurence des Cars, to be its director for the first time since it was established—in 1793.

On the other hand, several women do occupy important positions. In November 2023, the Solomon R. Guggenheim Museum and Foundation selected Mariët Westermann as its new director and CEO. In London in 2017, Maria Balshaw became the first woman to be named director of the Tate. The late Pope Francis named Barbara Jatta director of the Vatican Museums starting on the first day of 2017; Anne Pasternak became director of the Brooklyn Museum in New York in 2015; Thelma Golden has been leading the Studio Museum in Harlem as director and chief curator since 2005; and Lisa Phillips was named director of the New Museum in New York in 1999. In New York, women are also at the helm of the Drawing Center, with Laura Hoptman as executive director since 2018, and the Dia Art Foundation, with Jessica Morgan becoming director in 2015.

Commercial galleries are increasing the number of women in their rosters, greatly enhancing their visibility. Simultaneously, auction houses have been crucial in setting record prices for female artists. The global turnover in this market surged from $419 million in 2012 to $975 million in 2021, marking a remarkable 132 percent increase over a decade. Initially impacting ultra-contemporary women artists, this trend has extended to older generations as well. Abstract Expressionists, Surrealists, and even female old masters such as Artemisia Gentileschi are experiencing meteoric rises in their prices.

Significant differences exist between the ultra-contemporary category—coined in a 2019 Artnet News report and defined as artists born anytime between 1975 and the present—and older artists. In one section of the *Women Artists Market Report 2023* for Artsy, Casey Lesser highlights that the market for ultra-contemporary women artists has expanded dramatically, from $5.28 million in 2012 to $220.24 million in 2022. Lesser points out that in the younger age category, works by women artists often lead in market performance. The data she presents are illuminating: in 2022, for artists born in or after 1975, women had 43.6 percent of the auction market share, compared to 56.1 percent for male artists; the rest were categorized as nonbinary (0.28%) or N/A (0.02%). If we consider an even younger category, artists born in or after 1985, the results are dramatic: female artists accounted for 63.6 percent of the market share in 2022, compared to just over 36 percent for men, the rest being nonbinary (0.33%) or N/A (0.04%).[22]

Despite this good news for women, Arun Kakar and Lesser observe in another section of the Artsy report that the overall data from 2022 still reveal the persistence of stark gender disparities in the total auction market for artists of all ages. Out of the total $11 billion worth of artworks sold at auction, those by male artists accounted for $9.7 billion, while those by female artists totaled just over $1 billion, or only 9.3 percent of the total market share. Furthermore, among the one hundred best-selling artworks, only two were by women: Georgia O'Keeffe (1887–1986) and Louise Bourgeois (1911–2010).[23] While collectors and investors are increasingly recognizing the artistic merit and financial potential of works by female artists, their presence in the market remains substantially inferior compared to male artists.

THE MARKET FOR FEMALE SURREALISTS

The unique perspectives and themes explored by Surrealist women artists resonate strongly with contemporary audiences. Delving into issues of identity, gender, and subconscious experience, their dreamlike compositions challenge traditional narratives and offer a rich, unconventional view of the human experience. As a result, Surrealist women are experiencing an explosion of both critical and commercial acclaim. Group exhibitions and solo retrospectives dedicated to them have proliferated in institutions and museums around the globe, accompanied by record prices at auction.[24]

The growing interest goes beyond a general reassessment of female artists' contributions to art history. Many Surrealist women led independent and unconventional lives, a trait now highly valued by the market when revisiting past creators. Moreover, women's participation in Surrealism was both extensive and influential, surpassing their involvement in any other twentieth-century artistic movement. This prominence was largely due to Surrealism's rejection of bourgeois conventions and traditional gender roles. Many women entered the movement through personal relationships with male Surrealists: Leonora Carrington and later Dorothea Tanning with Max Ernst, Kay Sage with Yves Tanguy, and Remedios Varo with the poet Benjamin Péret. However, the attitude of Surrealist artists toward women was complex and controversial. Although women were celebrated as muses and sources of inspiration, they were often marginalized in these roles, despite many having received formal artistic training prior to, or independent of, their involvement with the movement. Nevertheless, as Whitney Chadwick points out, Surrealist women successfully transcended the role of muse, forging their own identities by uniquely blending elements of artifice with natural or instinctual life.[25]

Hailing from a wealthy and conservative English family, Leonora Carrington (1917–2011) left everything behind, driven by a passionate "amour fou" with Max Ernst (1891–1976). She followed him to France, endured time in an asylum in Spain after a nervous breakdown, and eventually departed for Mexico in 1942, where she found stability and creative fulfillment. Mexico, with its revolutionary government that valued art for its educational role, held a profound allure for European expatriates escaping fascism and war. In Mexico City, Carrington joined a thriving circle of intellectuals, artists, writers, and poets, including the Spanish painter Remedios Varo (1908–1963), another refugee from Europe's Surrealist milieu. Carrington and Varo formed a profound and enduring friendship, anchored by a mutual fascination with mysticism, magic, and the esoteric. This bond significantly shaped their artistic evolutions, characterized by an imaginative blend of storytelling, oneiric visions, and rich symbolism. Drawing inspiration from the intricate and symbolic compositions of Hieronymus Bosch (c. 1450–1516) as well as the Renaissance's precise perspective-based spatial constructions, Carrington and Varo rendered highly detailed otherworldly landscapes filled with strange creatures and unexpected juxtapositions.

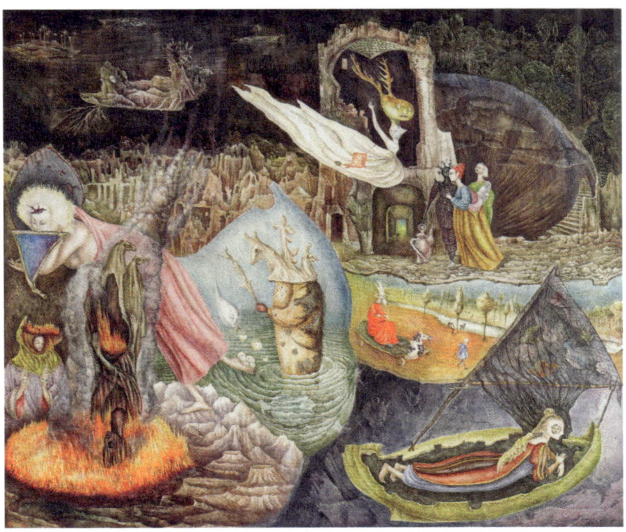

Leonora Carrington, *Les Distractions de Dagobert*, 1945

With their works coveted by collectors, the market for both artists has grown dramatically. Varo's *Armonía (Autorretrato Sugerente)* (*Harmony [Suggestive Self-Portrait]*) (1956) sold for $6,186,800 at Sotheby's New York in June 2020; Carrington's *Les Distractions de Dagobert* (1945) achieved $28,485,000 at Sotheby's New York in May 2024.

Merging personal symbolism with Surrealist elements, as well as Mexican and pre-Columbian traditions, Frida Kahlo (1907–1954) created her most renowned works in Mexico, the country of her birth, where she became an iconic figure in both art and popular culture. Her painting *Diego y yo* (1949), which sold for $34.9 million at Sotheby's in 2021, is one of the most expensive artworks ever made by a Surrealist or a woman artist. (The highest price for any woman artist still belongs to Georgia O'Keeffe's *Jimson Weed/White Flower No. 1* from 1932, which sold for $44,405,000 at Sotheby's New York in November 2014.) Kahlo's self-portrait features an image of Diego Rivera on her forehead, symbolizing her deep and often turbulent love for the famous political muralist and painter, whom she married twice. Her charismatic persona and dramatic life story have also amplified her appeal to collectors and the general public.

Kahlo faced profound health challenges that left a lasting impact on her work. At six, she contracted polio, which caused a lifelong limp. Then, at eighteen, she was in a devastating bus accident that resulted in multiple fractures, chronic pain, numerous surgeries, and prolonged periods of bed rest. This relentless suffering became a central theme in Kahlo's art, as seen in her raw portrayals of medical struggles, fractured bodies, and deep psychological distress. Her self-portraits—marked by vulnerability and resilience—depict both her physical fragility and her emotional turmoil. Through her work, Kahlo transformed personal agony into a powerful statement of strength and defiance, and ultimately she became a global icon revered by the public and highly sought-after by collectors.

Leonor Fini (1907–1996) and Dorothea Tanning (1910–2012) are also attracting growing interest from both institutions and collectors. Fini, born in Buenos Aires but raised in cosmopolitan Trieste, began her artistic journey in Italy. During her teenage years, she suffered from an eye disease that necessitated two months of being blindfolded. This period of forced darkness inspired her eerie, nocturnal landscapes, populated by birds, saints, and exotic women depicted with Gothic accents, as observed by Robert Zeller.[26] Rebellious and fiercely independent, Fini mingled with leading figures of the Surrealist movement in Paris, yet she never formally joined the group. Her art is distinguished by its portrayal of powerful, enigmatic, intimidating women who subvert traditional gender roles. These figures embody themes of independence, sexual liberation, and a direct challenge to patriarchal norms, blending allure with dominance to redefine feminine strength. An example of them, her *Autoportrait au Scorpion* (1938), sold for $2,319,000 at Sotheby's New York in 2021, more than doubling her previous auction record set the year before.

Tanning, an American artist, first encountered Surrealism in 1936 at MoMA's groundbreaking exhibition *Fantastic Art, Dada, Surrealism,* while she was living in New York and working as a commercial painter for Macy's department store. Her career began to flourish in 1941 with a solo show at the Julien Levy Gallery, followed by her participation in Peggy Guggenheim's influential 1943 exhibition *31 Women* at the Art of This Century gallery. It was there that Tanning met Ernst, Guggenheim's husband at the time, sparking a deep romantic and artistic partnership that would last for decades. The couple initially settled in Arizona before moving to France, where they continued to shape the Surrealist movement and each other's artistic evolution. Over her six-decade production, Tanning developed an original vocabulary that incorporated elements from the Gothic novels she had read in her youth, transforming them into dreamlike and surreal scenarios. Her auction record was set by *Le Mal oublié* (*The Ill Forgotten*) (1955), which sold for $1,440,000 at Christie's New York in May 2022.

Kay Sage (1898–1963) achieved her auction record in February 2014 when Sotheby's London sold *Le Passage* (1956) for $7,070,000. A poignant sense of loneliness pervades the unsettling and desolate landscape of the painting, characteristic of her distinctive style, which often incorporates architectural elements as remnants of a vanished civilization. Sage came from a wealthy industrial family in Albany, New York, and enjoyed a privileged upbringing that included extensive travel in Europe. Settling in Paris in 1937, she was introduced to Surrealism and deeply influenced by the metaphysical landscapes of Giorgio de Chirico. She returned to America with her future husband, Yves Tanguy (1900–1955), in 1939, just as World War II began. Following successful solo exhibitions in New York at the Pierre Matisse and Julien Levy galleries, Sage's career continued to flourish, thanks to the representation of gallerist Catherine Viviano.

The market is also experiencing a notable expansion for highly innovative photographers such as Claude Cahun (born Lucy Schwob [1894–1954]), Dora Maar (1907–1997), and Lee Miller (1907–1977). The first comprehensive exploration of Surrealist photography was a 1985 survey exhibition, *L'Amour fou: Photography and Surrealism*, cocurated by Rosalind Krauss and Jane Livingston at the Corcoran Gallery of Art in Washington, DC.[27]

A younger generation of female artists, including Giulia Andreani (b. 1985), Louise Bonnet (b. 1970), Inka Essenhigh (b. 1969), Ewa Juszkiewicz (b. 1984), Christina Quarles (b. 1985), Beatrice Scaccia (b. 1978), and Anna Weyant (b. 1995), has been actively incorporating Surrealist elements and themes into their artistic language. Drawing inspiration from the movement's symbolic imagery, distortions, and exploration of the subconscious, these artists have created works that resonate with both critics and collectors. This revival of Surrealist aesthetics has been met with considerable enthusiasm, leading to increasing demand and rising prices.

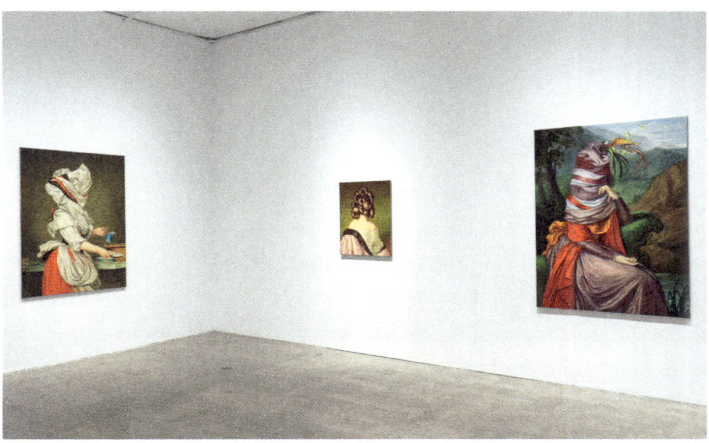

Installation view, *Ewa Juszkiewicz: In vain her feet in sparkling laces glow*, Gagosian, Park & 75, New York, November 17, 2020–January 4, 2021

As the world grapples with the urgent crises of climate change, deforestation, pollution, and biodiversity loss, artists, collectors, galleries, and cultural institutions are becoming increasingly aware of the environmental toll of their practices. Many traditional art supplies contain hazardous materials, including heavy metals, solvents, and nonrenewable pigments, which can harm the environment during both production and disposal. In response, a growing number of eco-conscious artists are embracing sustainable methods, choosing recycled or repurposed materials, natural pigments, and eco-friendly mediums. Beyond material choices, the carbon footprint of the global art market has become a pressing concern. Major art events—such as art fairs, biennials, and international exhibitions—demand extensive transportation of artworks and personnel, which dramatically contributes to greenhouse gas emissions. Digital technologies offer the potential to reduce this environmental impact by limiting the need for physical transport, but even digital assets can present challenges, as is the case with NFTs; their minting processes are notoriously energy-intensive.

To create a more sustainable and environmentally responsible art ecosystem, initiatives such as carbon offset programs for art events and eco-certifications for artworks are on the rise. For instance, the Gallery Climate Coalition (GCC), founded in 2020, has assembled a diverse group of more than 279 galleries, 140 art businesses, 180 nonprofit organizations, 190 professionals, and 230 artists and collectives to work toward cutting greenhouse gas emissions in the visual arts sector by at least 50 percent by 2030. This target aligns with the Paris Agreement's objective to limit global warming to below 1.5°C. The GCC also champions zero-waste policies, encouraging practices that can support a cleaner, greener art world.

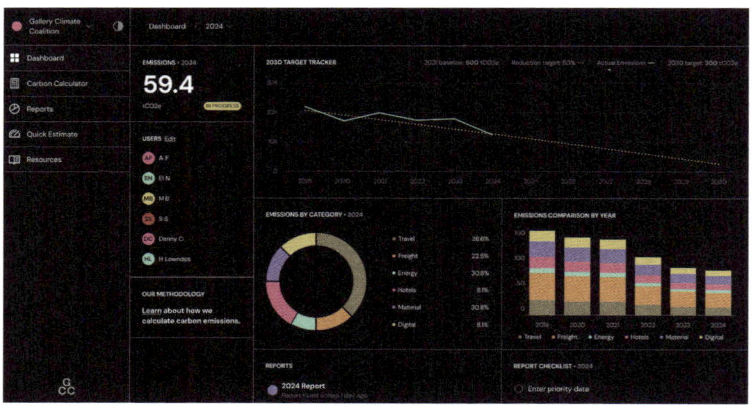

The free-to-use, sector-specific GCC Carbon Calculator at https://calculator.galleryclimatecoalition.org

SHORTENING THE DISTANCE BETWEEN PRIMARY AND SECONDARY MARKETS

While no artist has replicated Damien Hirst's bold 2008 decision to organize a dedicated auction of works fresh from the studio (see "Breaking the Rules," p. 210), the distance between the primary and secondary art markets has narrowed significantly. In the past, artworks by emerging artists typically had to gain recognition and value before entering the secondary market, but this is no longer the norm. An increasingly global audience covets the same trendsetting artists, making it particularly challenging, if not impossible, especially for new buyers, to access primary works by these artists through their representing galleries, which naturally have limited supply. Furthermore, galleries, acting as gatekeepers, often prioritize established collectors they have long-standing relationships with, who are less likely to flip works at auction as their value increases. In this scenario, auctions become for many collectors the only opportunity to buy works by contemporary artists they cannot access through galleries.

A comprehensive study published in Artnet News in the fall of 2022 examined the overall presence of artists and the average time between their debuts and their first appearances at auction—day and evening (the latter is significantly more important)—at major houses such as Sotheby's, Christie's, and Phillips, and shows how the distance has dramatically shortened. The study further underscores that from 2013 to mid-July 2022, the growth in auction sales of works by artists born after 1975 has far outpaced that of those born between 1900 and 1974. Auction sales of art by the younger cohort surged by more than 700 percent, from $91.4 million in 2013 to $739.3 million in 2021. In contrast, the peak sales value for the older group of artists was achieved in 2014 at $6.95 billion, reflecting an increase of roughly 16 percent over the 2013 total.[28]

Auction houses are indeed effectively reaching into the primary market itself, evolving their focus from older, more established artists to increasingly spotlight young ones and reshaping their strategies through curated sales and even direct collaborations with artists and galleries. Though this approach may open new doors for artists and collectors, the swift entry of young artists into the secondary market can encourage speculation and inflated prices, which could ultimately influence the direction of their careers. Artists who still may not have solid gallery support and an established reputation risk being very negatively affected by a sudden rise and fall in their auction results.

THE PATRONAGE MODEL IN QATAR, SAUDI ARABIA, AND THE UNITED ARAB EMIRATES

Qatar, Saudi Arabia, and the United Arab Emirates have risen as prominent forces on the international art scene, presenting art models that echo historical patronage, but on a state level.

"Being able to build the piece in the desert at this scale is like meeting the Medicis in the fifteenth century," declared Richard Serra (1938–2024) following the inauguration of his installation *East-West/*

West-East in the Brouq Nature Reserve in Qatar in 2014.[29]

Consisting of four steel plates, each thirteen feet wide and either fifty-five or forty-eight feet high, placed along half a mile in a line that traverses the desert, *East-West/West-East* creates an immersive experience that prompts contemplation of scale, materiality, and the relationship between human intervention and the natural world. It also required substantial financing. Serra's comparison to the Florentine family, the epitome of the Renaissance patronage model (see "Church, Royalty, Bankers," p. 12), alludes to the role of the ruling Al Thani family and in particular of Sheikha Al Mayassa in the flourishing of the arts in Qatar. Absolute sovereigns of the small Middle Eastern country on the northeastern coast of the Arabian Peninsula, the Al Thani family's financial support of the arts and its use in image building is certainly comparable to the great European patrons of centuries past. The investment in culture is driven by Qatar's desire to diversify its economy by positioning art as an asset class and investment opportunity, beyond natural resources. The Qatar Museums Authority is the entity that oversees and manages the country's museums and cultural initiatives. The first such institution to be built was the Museum of Islamic Art, designed by I. M. Pei and inaugurated in 2008, followed by remarkable buildings commissioned to the most famous architects in the world and completed in record time: the Mathaf, the Arab Museum of Modern Art, designed by Jean-François Bodin, opened in 2010; the Qatar National Library, designed by Rem Koolhaas, opened to the public in 2017; and the Qatar National Museum, by Jean Nouvel, was inaugurated in 2019. Strategically linked to the edifications of museums are commissions of permanent installations and artworks to major artists. Damien Hirst's *The Miraculous Journey* (2013) consists of fourteen bronze sculptures depicting different stages of fetal development during pregnancy. Placed outside Sidra Medicine, a medical and research center for women and children in Ar-Rayyan, it was said to have cost $20 million.

Qatar's cultural investment has gathered together a spectacular collection both of Islamic art and of Western modern and contemporary art—with record purchases such as Paul Cézanne's *The Card Players* (1892–93), allegedly for $250 million from the collection of Greek shipping magnate George Embiricos in 2011, and Paul Gauguin's *Nafea faa ipoipo?* (*When Will You Marry?*) (1892) for $210 million in 2015. These acquisitions, whether at auctions or through private transactions, made Qatar the biggest art buyer of the first decades of the twenty-first century. Its impact on the art market, despite the absence of widespread collecting in the country, has been profound, pushing prices for iconic artworks to unprecedented levels.

Saudi Arabia is regarded as one of the most conservative and restrictive governments worldwide, with extensive use of the death penalty, slavery not officially abolished until 1962, and strict gender-based regulations—women were granted the right to drive only in 2018—and yet the country has also been gaining visibility for its ambitious, large-scale arts project. Producer of more than 10 percent of all the world's oil and with about 40 percent of its population younger than twenty-five years old, Saudi Arabia registered growth that was one of the biggest of all the countries of the economic Group of 20 (G20) nations in 2023. As in Qatar, a series of transformative initiatives have been put in place by the de facto absolute ruler, the young Crown Prince Mohammed bin Salman, effectively in power since 2015. His Saudi Vision 2030, unveiled in 2016, is a multifaceted project aimed at diversifying Saudi Arabia's economy and reshaping its global image through cultural exchange and international partnerships. It seeks to position

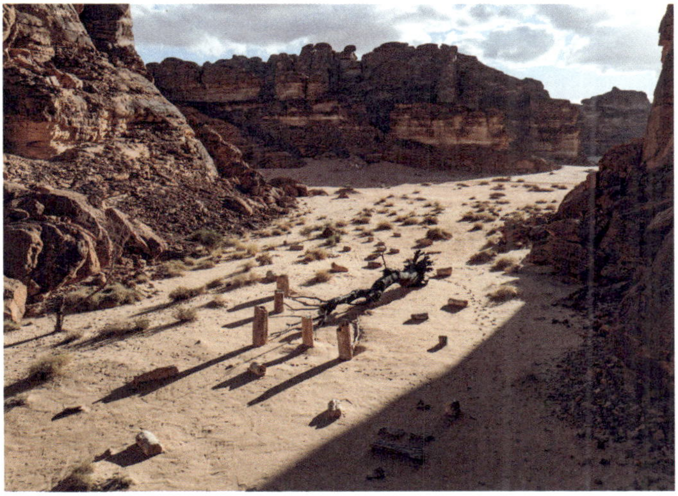

Installation view, *Desert X AlUla*, Saudi Arabia, February 9–March 23, 2024. Featuring Giuseppe Penone's *La logica del vegetale–Metamorfosi* (*Vegetal Logic–Metamorphosis*), 2024

the country as an art destination, including substantial investments toward the establishment of cultural institutions, promotion of creative industries, and empowerment of local talent.

Pillars of the broad project include the creation of the Saudi Arabia Museum of Contemporary Art (SAMoCA) in Riyadh, the nation's premier institution devoted to contemporary art, designed by Lina Ghotmeh; and of the Incense Road Museum, which pays homage to the ancient trade routes that have connected civilizations for millennia, and was designed by Asif Khan.

One of the most emblematic plans under Saudi Vision 2030 is the ambitious $15 billion "Journey through Time Masterplan," which seeks to revitalize the ancient city of AlUla. Settled by the Nabataeans, an Arab population that flourished between the fourth and the second centuries BCE, controlling commercial routes and founding Petra in Jordan, AlUla was located on the incense route that connected producers from Oman and Yemen to the Mediterranean. It includes several archaeological sites such as Hegra (Mada'in Saleh), Saudi Arabia's first UNESCO World Heritage Site. Managed by the Royal Commission for AlUla, the comprehensive three-part strategy is designed to transform AlUla into an important tourist destination, with the goal of attracting two million visitors each year. As reported by *Arab News*, the plan is expected to generate thirty-eight thousand new jobs, significantly contributing to the national economy with an estimated boost of $32 billion.[30]

Despite controversies in the West about the project due to alleged human rights abuses by the Saudi regime,[31] many countries have been supporting it. For example, France signed a ten-year agreement to help promote AlUla as a global tourism destination, and several major museum leaders from Europe and the United States have been on the project's advisory board. In 2020, the California public art biennial Desert X hosted the first exhibition in AlUla to present open-air installations in the desert.

Abu Dhabi, the capital and the largest of the seven emirates that constitute the United Arab Emirates (UAE), is home to the Arabian Peninsula's most extensive museum, the Louvre Abu Dhabi. Situated on Saadiyat Island, it officially opened in 2017 as a partnership with the Musée du Louvre in Paris. Central to this collaboration is the concept of cultural diplomacy, in which both institutions leverage their collections, resources, and expertise to foster mutual respect and appreciation among diverse audiences. Jean Nouvel's design drew inspiration from the traditional Arabian medina, unfolding as a micro-city composed of fifty-five distinct buildings. This intricate layout is further enhanced by waterways reminiscent of Abu Dhabi's ancient *falaj* irrigation systems, weaving through the museum complex. Above, a latticed dome delicately filters sunlight, casting shadows akin to those beneath palm groves. The museum's permanent collection features approximately seven hundred artworks, complemented by an additional three hundred on loan from prestigious institutional partners.

The Louvre Abu Dhabi is a key component of the ambitious $27 billion transformation of Saadiyat Island as an emblem of the UAE's cultural development. Among the other projects under construction are the Zayed National Museum, conceived by the architectural firm Foster and Partners, and the Guggenheim Abu Dhabi, designed by Frank Gehry, poised to become the largest Guggenheim museum globally.

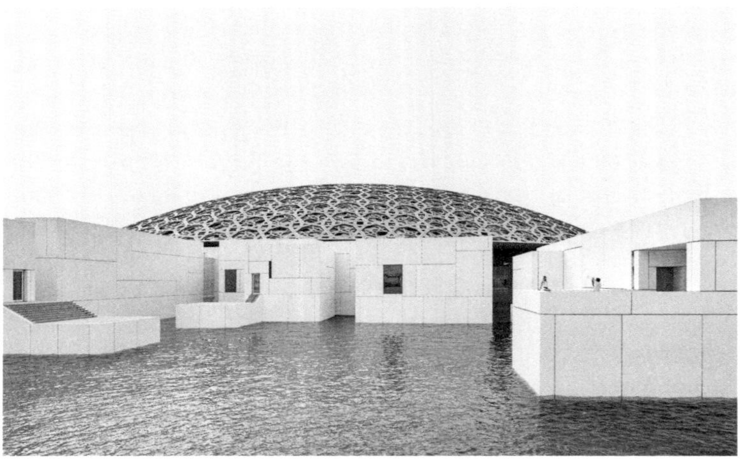

Exterior of Louvre Abu Dhabi

WHAT MODEL NOW?

The art market is a dynamic and ever-evolving system, mirroring the economic and social structures of its time. Over the centuries, various models have defined its shape: from the patronage system of the Renaissance, in which the Church and wealthy individuals or families dictated artistic production, to the rise of the free market during the Dutch Golden Age, and the influence of the French Académie Royale de Peinture et de Sculpture and its post-Revolution successor, the Académie des Beaux-Arts, which dominated from the seventeenth through the nineteenth centuries. In more recent history, the late nineteenth-century Parisian art scene marked the ascendancy of the gallery-centered market, epitomized by Paul Durand-Ruel's promotion of the Impressionists. This model gained further traction in the twentieth century, thanks to trailblazing dealers such as Ambroise Vollard and Paul Rosenberg, who played pivotal roles in shaping the market for innovators of modern art such as Cézanne and Pablo Picasso.

After World War II, as the revolutionary language of the New York School found an audience through the efforts of dealers such as Peggy Guggenheim and Betty Parsons, the art world's epicenter shifted from Paris to New York. By the late 1950s and 1960s, Leo Castelli and Ileana Sonnabend furthered the role of the gallerist, by unconditionally supporting pathbreaking artists like Jasper Johns and Andy Warhol. The Castelli-Sonnabend model set a standard for future generations of art dealers, inspiring towering figures such as Larry Gagosian and Jeffrey Deitch.

Today, galleries—ranging from intimate, independent spaces to vast multinational enterprises—are flourishing worldwide, reflecting the ever-growing scope of the art market. Regardless of their size, the fundamental mission of galleries remains unchanged: they show, promote, and facilitate the sale of artworks on behalf of the artists they represent.

While large galleries often symbolize the pinnacle of success, smaller galleries play a vital role in discovering and fostering emerging talent. Yet they face increasing challenges: escalating overhead costs, stiff competition from mega-galleries, and the financial burden of adapting to an increasingly digital world. These pressures, compounded by economic volatility and high fees for participating in art fairs, have left many smaller galleries struggling, with some even closing their doors. In response, a number of these galleries have embraced creative solutions through collaboration. Such efforts as Condo, a gallery-sharing initiative conceived by Vanessa Carlos of the London-based gallery Carlos/Ishikawa, and Vacation, which followed a time-sharing model in which ten international galleries subleased an exhibition space on New York's Lower East Side for a month at a time in 2018, enabled the pooling of resources, offering new opportunities and audiences to both artists and gallerists. Furthermore, organizations such as the New

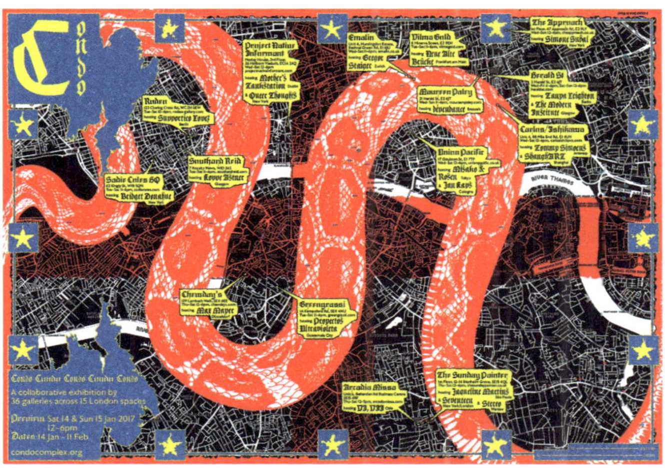

Map of exhibition locations for Condo London 2017, January 14–February 11, 2017

Art Dealers Alliance champion innovation by facilitating joint exhibitions and fairs, often showcasing underrepresented artists, thereby invigorating the art scene.

The traditional gallery model has faced increasing scrutiny as more artists opt to manage their careers independently. A notable example came in 2023, when Peter Doig parted ways with his longtime gallerist, Michael Werner, to take control of his own sales and promotion. As Anny Shaw highlights in the *Art Newspaper*, this trend of artists "ditching dealers" is gaining momentum.[32] This shift is further underscored by the fact that in 2023, the top ten positions on *ArtReview*'s "Power 100" list were occupied by artists rather than dealers—a marked departure from the past.[33]

Further transforming the landscape, agencies traditionally associated with entertainment, such as United Talent Agency (UTA), have ventured into the fine art market. UTA launched its fine art division in 2015, representing artists such as Judy Chicago and Isaac Julien, and opening exhibition spaces in Los Angeles and Atlanta—but the division and galleries lasted only until mid-2024, though the agency still represents the artists. Meanwhile, other major agencies, including Endeavor and Creative Artists Agency (CAA), also offered artists representation models akin to those used in the music, film, and sports industries. In this evolving system, galleries often serve as platforms for exhibitions and sales, while artists maintain greater control over their career paths, with agents overseeing and strategizing every aspect of their professional development. Having been involved for some time in the past with 291 Agency, founded in New York in 2021 by Max Teicher, soon joined by Andrea Crane, Jessy Arisohn, and Rysia Murphy as partners, I have witnessed firsthand the positive response that the model triggers in artists.

Despite the growing trend of artists managing their careers independently, galleries continue to play an indispensable role in validating an artist's career. Historically, dealers such as Paul Durand-Ruel and Leo Castelli were instrumental in securing the acceptance of movements like Impressionism and Pop art. Today, Gagosian, Zwirner, and Hauser & Wirth, among others, remain gatekeepers in the contemporary art world, bestowing legitimacy upon the artists they represent. In a 2008 book, Don Thompson argued that the value of contemporary art was largely determined by powerful dealers, followed by branded auction houses. Museum curators, while influential through special exhibitions, played a minor role, with critics holding little sway and buyers virtually none.[34] But is this still the case? The validation process has indeed become more complex. While the endorsement of prestigious galleries is still crucial in bolstering an artist's market value and reputation, the influence of social media, as previously discussed, has grown significantly. Artists can now cultivate their own followings and gain visibility through digital platforms, reshaping traditional hierarchies in the art world.

Nevertheless, galleries remain the primary channel for art sales. According to an Art Basel and UBS report in 2025, a substantial 83 percent of respondents made acquisitions through a gallery in person, online, or at an art fair in 2024 and the first half of 2025. Spending at auction, meanwhile, dropped to 49 percent (down from 74 percent in 2023), further emphasizing the continued dominance of galleries in the art market.[35]

Patronage still represents a crucial force in sustaining the arts, with private collectors, foundations, corporations, and even nation-states such as Qatar providing indispensable financial support for large-scale projects (see "The Patronage Model in Qatar, Saudi Arabia, and the United Arab Emirates," p. 273). In particular, corporate sponsorship has become a key pillar of contemporary art patronage, as companies leverage art to enhance their public image, contribute to civic initiatives, and mitigate perceptions of corporate greed. The motivations driving modern-day patrons are as varied as the patrons themselves—ranging from a deep, genuine passion for art and a belief in its transformative power, to a more pragmatic desire for visibility and prestige. As Daniel Haxall observes, corporations often engage in art sponsorship as a way to boost their public standing, align themselves with cultural and social causes, and address public concerns about corporate excess and greed.[36] This strategic intersection of business and art patronage continues to shape the landscape of contemporary cultural support. Reflecting on Julie Mehretu's *Mural* (2009)—a colossal twenty-three-by-eighty-foot wall painting commissioned for the lobby of the Goldman Sachs headquarters in Lower Manhattan, at a cost of $5 million, that traces the history of the capitalist system—Haxall points out: "Today, private companies are increasingly the only viable option for realizing large-scale art and architectural projects. . . . In the past few decades in particular corporations have increasingly been motivated by civic responsibility, tax incentives, or redefining their brand image, and now they not only collect and sponsor new art, but also subsidize exhibitions, museums, and projects that fuse fine art with advertising or product design."[37]

As cultural values evolve and the structural dynamics of the art world shift, the market is transitioning toward a hybrid model defined by greater flexibility and fluidity. While traditional galleries will remain integral, new forms of representation—artist-led initiatives, agencies, and collaborative ventures—are steadily gaining ground. This transformation holds the promise of a more decentralized and democratic art market, one that embraces greater diversity and fosters a wider array of opportunities for artists. In this unfolding landscape, the boundaries between creator, dealer, and audience may blur, reshaping the very foundations of how art is seen, shared, and valued.

To conclude on a personal note, my study of how artists have navigated the creative process over the centuries—surfacing limitations, societal constraints, and the barriers imposed by race and gender—has deepened my awe for the unstoppable force of human creativity. Whether constrained by the amount of ultramarine blue their patrons provided or the subject chosen by them, or by institutional obstacles restricting access to education, professional opportunities, or the simple right to express oneself, artists have always found a way to channel their unique visions. Through it all, art has remained and remains capable of provoking deep reflection on our condition as human beings, and uplifting our spirit.

NOTES

1 Chinese authorities notified the World Health Organization (WHO) on December 31, 2019, about a cluster of cases of pneumonia of unknown origin in the city of Wuhan. A type of virus known as a coronavirus and later named SARS-CoV-2 was identified as the cause of the disease now known as COVID-19.

2 Clare McAndrew, *The Art Market 2021: An Art Basel & UBS Report* (Basel: Art Basel; Zurich: UBS, 2021), https://theartmarket.artbasel.com/previous-reports.

3 Clare McAndrew, *The Art Market 2022: An Art Basel & UBS Report* (Basel: Art Basel; Zurich: UBS, 2022), 18, https://theartmarket.artbasel.com/previous-reports.

4 Katya Kazakina, "Emerging African Artists Have Amassed Nearly $65 Million at Auction since 2019. Some of Them Don't Even Have Galleries Yet," Art Detective, Artnet News, January 13, 2022, Artnet.com, https://news.artnet.com/market/ultra-contemporary-african-art-detective-2060089.

5 Rachel Corbett, "How the Black Portraiture Boom Went Bust," *New York*, May 5–18, 2025, 80.

6 Amy Whitaker and Nora Burnett Abrams, *The Story of NFTs: Artists, Technology, and Democracy* (New York: Rizzoli Electa, 2023), 9.

7 Zachary Small, *Token Supremacy: The Art of Finance, the Finance of Art, and the Great Crypto Crash of 2022* (New York: Alfred A. Knopf, 2024), 54.

8 Small, *Token Supremacy*, 12.

9 Small, *Token Supremacy*, 49.

10 Whitaker and Abrams, *Story of NFTs*, 49.

11 Clare McAndrew, *The Art Basel & UBS Art Market Report 2024 by Arts Economics* (Basel: Art Basel; Zurich: UBS, 2024), 72, https://theartmarket.artbasel.com/download/The-Art-Basel-and-UBS-Art-Market-Report-2024.pdf.

12 Clare McAndrew, *The Art Basel & UBS Survey of Global Collecting 2025 by Arts Economics* (Basel: Art Basel; Zurich: UBS, 2025), 15, 60, https://theartmarket.artbasel.com/download/The-Art-Basel-and-UBS-Survey-of-Global-Collecting-in-2025.pdf.

13 Min Chen, "'A Collaborator Who Understood My Vision': Laurie Simmons, Casey Reas, and Mario Klingemann on How A.I. Is Fueling Creativity," Artnet News, December 19, 2023, Artnet.com, https://news.artnet.com/art-world/artists-ai-creativity-2340982.

14 Jo Lawson-Tancred, *AI and the Art Market* (London: Lund Humphries, 2024), 10–11.

15 Lawson-Tancred, *AI and the Art Market*, 24, 28.

16 The estimates are the result of an analysis by the financial market intelligence firm Cerulli and Associates. See Jack Kelly, "The Great Wealth Transfer from Baby Boomers to Millennials Will Impact the Job Market and Economy," *Forbes*, August 9, 2023, https://www.forbes.com/sites/jackkelly/2023/08/09/the-great-wealth-transfer-from-baby-boomers-to-millennials-will-impact-the-job-market-and-economy/.

17 Pooneh Baghai, Olivia Howard, Lakshmi Prakash, and Jill Zucker, "Women as the Next Wave of Growth in US Wealth Management," McKinsey & Company, July 29, 2020, https://www.mckinsey.com/industries/financial-services/our-insights/women-as-the-next-wave-of-growth-in-us-wealth-management.

18 McAndrew, *Art Market 2022*, 209.

19 McAndrew, *Art Basel & UBS Survey of Global Collecting 2025*, 15.

20 Julia Halperin and Charlotte Burns, The Burns Halperin Report, "Perceptions of Progress in the Art World Are Largely a Myth. Here Are the Facts," Artnet, December 13, 2022, https://news.artnet.com/art-world/perceptions-of-progress-in-the-art-world-are-largely-a-myth-here-are-the-facts-2227941.

21 Marc Mayer, "Basquiat in History," in *Basquiat*, ed. Marc Mayer, exh. cat. (London: Merrell, in association with the Brooklyn Museum, New York, 2005), 42–43.

22 Casey Lesser, "The Ultra-Contemporary Women Artists at the Forefront of the Art Market," in *The Women Artists Market Report 2023*, Artsy, March 8, 2023, https://www.artsy.net/article/artsy-editorial-ultra-contemporary-women-artists-forefront-art-market.

23 Arun Kakar and Casey Lesser, "The State of the Market for Women Artists' Work," in *The Women Artists Market Report 2023*, Artsy, March 8, 2023, https://www.artsy.net/article/artsy-editorial-state-market-women-artists-work.

24 Among the many solo exhibitions are *Dorothea Tanning*, Tate Modern, London, 2019; *Dora Maar*, Centre Pompidou, Paris, 2019; *Toyen, l'écart absolu*, Musée d'Art Moderne de la Ville de Paris, 2022; and *Meret Oppenheim: My Exhibition*, Museum of Modern Art, New York, 2022–23. Among the group shows are *Angels of Anarchy: Women Artists and Surrealism*, Manchester Art Gallery, UK, 2009–10; *Fantastic Women: Surreal Worlds from Meret Oppenheim to Louise Bourgeois*, Schirn Kunsthalle Frankfurt, Germany, 2020; and *Surréalisme au féminin?*, Musée de Montmartre, Paris, 2023.

25 Whitney Chadwick, *Women, Art, and Society* (London: Thames and Hudson, 1990), 325–26.

26 Robert Zeller, *New Surrealism: The Uncanny in Contemporary Painting* (New York: Monacelli Studio, 2023), 90.

27 For the accompanying catalogue, see Rosalind Krauss and Jane Livingston, *L'Amour fou: Photography and Surrealism*, with an essay by Dawn Ades (Washington, DC: Corcoran Gallery of Art; New York: Abbeville Press, 1985).

28 "From the Studio to the Auction Block: How the Path between These Two Poles Shrank in the 21st Century—and What It Means for the Art Market," Artnet News and Morgan Stanley, November 3, 2022, https://news.artnet.com/market/from-the-studio-to-the-auction-block-morgan-stanley-2202991.

29 Nicolas Niarchos, "Richard Serra in the Qatari Desert," *New Yorker*, April 16, 2014.

30 Shane McGinley, "Royal Commission for AlUla Confirms $15 Billion Masterplan Opportunity for Public-Private Partnerships," Arab News, April 28, 2021, https://www.arabnews.com/node/1850136/bu.

31 Outrage and concern were triggered over labor conditions at Saadiyat Island, highlighted in a 2009 Human Rights Watch report, "'The Island of Happiness': Exploitation of Migrant Workers on Saadiyat Island, Abu Dhabi," https://www.hrw.org/report/2009/05/19/island-happiness/exploitation-migrant-workers-saadiyat-island-abu-dhabi. It revealed that laborers often pay exorbitant recruitment fees in their home countries, putting them in substantial debt before even arriving. When they reach the UAE, contractors frequently seize their passports and maintain full control over their welfare, leaving workers vulnerable, particularly when wages are unpaid.

32 Anny Shaw, "Why Are Ever More Artists Ditching Dealers?," *Art Newspaper*, December 12, 2023, https://www.theartnewspaper.com/2023/12/12/why-ever-more-artists-are-ditching-the-dealers.

33 *ArtReview*, "Power 100," https://artreview.com/power-100?year=2023.

34 Don Thompson, *The $12 Million Stuffed Shark: The Curious Economics of Contemporary Art* (New York: Palgrave Macmillan, 2008), 26.

35 McAndrew, *Art Basel & UBS Survey of Global Collecting 2025*, 16–17.

36 Daniel Haxall, "From Bank Lobbies to Sportswear: Julie Mehretu, Kehinde Wiley, and the Shift in Corporate Patronage in the Twenty-First Century," in *Corporate Patronage of Art and Architecture in the United States: Late 19th Century to the Present*, ed. Monica E. Jovanovich and Melissa Renn (London: Bloomsbury Visual Arts, 2019), 225.

37 Haxall, "From Bank Lobbies to Sportswear," 239–40.

Acknowledgments

The inspiration for writing this book originated from a course on the history of the western art market that I was invited to teach by Professor Sandra Lang in the Master's program in Visual Arts Administration at NYU Steinhardt. She is the first person to whom I wish to convey my gratitude. I am also deeply thankful to my colleagues Melissa Rachleff Burtt and Amy Whitaker for their encouragement and support.

I owe a special debt of gratitude to my students, whose intellectual curiosity and active engagement in my classes motivated me to explore new ideas and embrace diverse perspectives. The insights shared by my guest speakers—Cecilia Alemani, Giovanna Bertazzoni, Stefania Bortolami, Jinqing Cai, Amalia Dayan, Pepi Marchetti Franchi, Tobias Meyer, Marc Payot, Jenny Saville, Annabelle Selldorf, Nick Simunovic, Max Teicher, and Cheyenne Westphal—have significantly enriched my understanding and informed my work.

My heartfelt thanks go to Michael Cary and Adele Minari, who patiently read most of my chapters, offering invaluable support that strengthened my confidence throughout this project. I am also deeply appreciative of Stefano Albertini, Vera Alemani, Francesco Bonami, Lorenzo Cherubini, Domenico Filipponi, Mark Fletcher, Massimiliano Gioni, Manuele Gragnolati, Silvia Grilli, Harvey Molotch, Francesca Pistone, Beatrice Scaccia, Rebecca Sternthal, Francesca Valiani, and Ersilia Vaudo, whose thoughtful feedback on parts of the manuscript, or advice in general, proved both insightful and encouraging. Georgia Aliya Collyer and Ginevra De Blasio provided initial assistance during the first research phase of this work.

I am particularly grateful to Richard Slovak, whose meticulous copy-editing and fact-checking have been exemplary.

Andrea Crane was fundamental in helping me finding a publisher in Larry Gagosian, to whom I would like to express my most profound gratitude. Collaborating with his gallery's outstanding publication department, led by Alison McDonald—with whom I already had the pleasure of working on catalogues for the exhibitions I organized as a director at the gallery—felt like a homecoming. I am especially thankful to my editor, Priya Bhatnagar, whose thorough and thoughtful work transformed my manuscript into a finished book. At Gagosian I also would like to thank Andisheh Avini, Shiori Kawasaki, and Helen Redmond.

The collaboration with Giuseppina Leone and Silvia Fiocco from my Italian publisher Allemandi has also been precious. Eugenia Testa worked with Gagosian on image permissions, and Sofia Salvatori conceptualized an elegant and visually striking layout.

I am very grateful to Philipp Hubert for shepherding the graphic design of the book through to completion.

It is a true privilege to feature a cover artwork by Maurizio Cattelan—an artist I greatly admire and have had the pleasure of calling a friend for over two decades.

Finally, and most importantly, I want to thank my husband, Gianluca. Nothing would be possible without him.

INDEX

Page numbers in **bold** indicate pages with illustrations. Numbers followed by "n" indicate endnotes.

20th Century Italian Art auction (Christie's, 1998), 229
20th Century Italian Art auction (Sotheby's, 1997), 229–30
20 Years in the Evolution of Picasso, 1903–1923 (Jacques Seligmann & Co.), 125
22 Art District (Shenzhen), 241
31 Women (Art of This Century, 1943), 154, 270
35-Pole Lightning Field (De Maria), 197
291 Agency, 278
291 gallery, 130, **130**, 144–45
798 Art District (Beijing), 241–42
2008 financial crisis, 212, 217, 226, 231–32, 238
2008 Sichuan earthquake, 246

A

Abrams, Harry N., 198
Abrams, Nora Burnett, 257, 258
Abstract Expressionism, 143, 145–65, 167n39, 185, 189, 191, 194, 202–4, 222, 224, 261, 268
Abu Dhabi, 275–76, 281n31
Académie d'Architecture (Academy of Architecture), 95
Académie de France, 56
Académie de la Grande Chaumière, 165
Académie de Musique (Academy of Music), 95
Académie de Peinture et de Sculpture (Academy of Painting and Sculpture), 95
Académie de Poésie et de Musique (Academy of Poetry and Music), 56
Académie des Beaux-Arts (Academy of Fine Arts), 90, 95–96, 276
Académie Française (French Academy), 56
Académie Julian (Paris), 90, 144
Académie Royale d'Architecture (Royal Academy of Architecture), 56
Académie Royale de Danse (Royal Academy of Dance), 56
Academie Royale de Peinture et de Sculpture (Royal Academy of Painting and Sculpture), 55–56, 86, 276
academies, 29, 54, 55–56, 90
Académie Suisse, 101
Accademia del Disegno (Academy of Drawing), 29, 84
Accademia di San Luca, 83
Acconci, Vito, 195
Achromes series (Manzoni), **228**, 228–29, 232
Acrobat and Young Harlequin (Picasso), 137
The Acrobat's Family with a Monkey (Picasso), 123
action painting, 158
Adam, Georgina, 238
Adelson, Warren, 67
Advancing Women Artists, 81
Afghanistan, 19
African American artists, 144, 147, 170–82, 205–6, 261, 262–65
  Chicago Renaissance, 174, 176
  in France, 165, 171
  Harlem Renaissance, 169–70, 264–65
  Two Centuries of Black American Art (LACMA, 1976–77), 170
African art, 129–31, **130**, 137, 138
African artists, 255–56, **256**, 264
AfriCOBRA (African Commune of Bad Relevant Artists), 175–76
After Dinner at Ornans (Courbet), 96
The Agnew Clinic (Eakins), 143
Agnews, 70
AI (artificial intelligence), 253, 259–60
AI-generated art, 259
Ai Weiwei, **246,** 246–47, 249, 250n11
Alaric, 14
Alba Madonna (Raphael), 79
Alcuin of York, 16
Alemani, Cecilia, 266
Alexander the Great, 59
Alidosi, Francesco, 30
Allen, Paul, 262
Allom, Charles, 74
Allori, Alessandro, 82
allover composition principle, 149
Al Mayassa, Sheikha, 273
Alpers, Svetlana, 42, 45
Alston, Charles, 175
Al Thani family, 273
Altman, Benjamin, 70
AlUla, Saudi Arabia, 275, **275**
Ambienti spaziali (Gagosian, 2012), 230
Amelia, Piermatteo d', 30
American Abstract Expressionists, 105
American Academy of Fine Arts, 166n1
American art, 143, 152, 200, 203, 222
American Art Association, 108
American artists, 165
American Gothic (Wood), **146**, 147
American Negro Artists exhibition program (Harmon Foundation), 170
American Painting Today, 1950 (Metropolitan Museum of Art), 160
American Pop Art: 106 Forms of Love and Despair (Moderna Museet, 1964), 193
Amos, Emma, 175, **175**
L'Amour fou: Photography and Surrealism (Corcoran, 1985), 271
Amsterdam, Holland, 42, 50
Anadol, Refik, 258–59
Ana Lena en Grèce (Saint Phalle), 205
An Allegory of Peace and the Arts (Gentileschi and Gentileschi), 85
The Anatomy Lesson of Dr. Nicolaes Tulp (Rembrandt), 41–42, **42**
Andreani, Giulia, 271
Andre, Carl, 191
Angelica Kauffman (Royal Academy of Arts, 2024), 92n36
Angels of Anarchy: Women Artists and Surrealism (Manchester Art Gallery, 2009–10), 281n24
Anguissola, Sofonisba, 80–82, 92n36
Anne of Austria, 57
Anne of Brittany, 65
Annual Exhibition: Contemporary Painting (Whitney, 1959–60), 190
The Annunciation (van Eyck), 79
Anthropométries (Klein), 176–77

antipopes, 31
Antwerp, Belgium, 29, 44–45
Apollinaire, Guillaume, 124, 130, 131
Apollo, 59
Apparition of the Virgin and Child to Saint Hyacinth (El Greco), 137
Arab News, 275
Aragonese, 21
architects, 26
Architectural League (New York), 166n1
architecture
  Gothic, 17–18, 22
  Romanesque, 17
Archivio Opera Piero Manzoni (Milan), 230
Arensberg, Louise and Walter, 135, 196
Argyrol, 137
Ariosto, Ludovico, 25
Arisohn, Jessy, 278
Aristotle, 28
Aristotle with a Bust of Homer (Rembrandt), 72
Arman, 196
Armonía (Autorretrato Sugerente) (Harmony [Suggestive Self-Portrait]) (Varo), 270
Armory Show (New York, 1913), 119, 135, 145
Armstrong, Louis, 174
Arp, Jean, 151, 165
Arroz con Pollo (Basquiat), 265
ART021, 238
Art Awards, 231
Art Basel, 230, 238, 254, 258, 262, 278–79
Art Basel Hong Kong, 235, 238
Art Collector Insights 2023 (Artsy), 248
Art Deco, 173, 192
Art Digest, 160
Arte dei Medici e Speziali (Doctors and Apothecaries) guild, 27
Artemisia (National Gallery, 2020), 92n36
art fairs, 49, 254
Artforum, 231, 265
art hubs, 241–42
artificial intelligence (AI), 253, 259–60
Art Informel, 228
Art Institute of Chicago, 137
art investment funds, 113, 128–29
artists
  ditching dealers, 278
  representation, 278
  status of, 26–29, 48–49, 222
Artists of the New York School: Second Generation (Jewish Museum, 1957), 189
Artnet, 255–56, 263
Artnet Analytics Team, 161
Artnet News, 259–60, 268, 273
ARTnews, 78, 82–83, 160, 186, 189, 249
Art Newspaper, 278
Art of This Century gallery (New York), 150, **151**, 151–54, 270
Art Recognition, 260
Les Arts à Paris, 131
Arts Club of Chicago, 133
Arts Economics, 254
Art Students League (New York), 147, 166n1
Artsy, 247–48, 268
The Ascetic (Picasso), 137
Asian American artists, 181
Asian art, 241
Asian artists, 181
Asian market, 237
Aspects of Negro Life series (Douglas), 173, **173**
Assouline, Pierre, 96, 98, 103, 108, 127
ateliers de demoiselles (girls' studios), 87
Aubry, Eugene, 157
Aubusson, 54
Auclert, Hubertine, 90
auction houses, 236–37, 254, 268, 273, 278. *See also specific houses by name*
auctions, 108, 202, 203, 254, 273
  20th Century Italian Art (Christie's, 1998), 229
  20th Century Italian Art (Sotheby's, 1997), 229–30
  Damien Hirst: Beautiful Inside My Head Forever (Sotheby's, 2008), 211–12, **212**, **213**
  Goldschmidt (Sotheby's, 1958), 116
  Impressionist and Modern evening auction (Christie's, 2009), 227
  record prices, 53, 63, 68, 69, 71, 81, 91n10, 104, 107, 116, 167n46, 174, 182, 205–6, 217, 229, 232, 245, 255, 261, 262, 264, 265–66, 270–71
  Salvator Mundi (Christie's, 2017), 69
  Scull (Sotheby Parke Bernet, 1973), 203
  Skin of the Bear ("La Peau de l'Ours") (1914), 113, 128–29
auction sales, 273, 279
Augustulus, 14
authentication, 64–65, 73, 260
Autoportrait au Scorpion (Fini), 270
Autumn Rhythm (Number 30) (Pollock), 159
avant-garde art, 97, 113–14, 122–34, 143–45, 150, 152, 155, 189, 192, 202, 222
  China Avant-Garde (1993–94), 245
  China/Avant-Garde (National Art Museum of China, 1989), 243
Avercamp, Hendrick, **40**, 48
Axelrod, Alan, 71
Azimut (Milan), 229
Azimuth, 229

B

baby boomers, 260–62
Bacchus (Twombly), 188
Bacon, Francis, 225, 261, 262
Baghai, Pooneh, 262
Baldassari, Anne, 134
Bal du moulin de la Galette (Dance at the Moulin de la Galette) (Renoir), 107, **107**
Baldwin II, 18
Ballet Rehearsal (Degas), 77
Balshaw, Maria, 267
Balthus, 241
Baltimore Museum of Art, 123, 167n39
Balzac, Honoré de, 223
Bambach, Carmen, 67
Bamiyan, Afghanistan, 19
bankers, 12–35
A Bar at the Folies-Bergère (Manet), 108
Barbero, Alessandro, 16
Barber, Tabitha, 89
Barbican Art Gallery (London), 167n39
Barbizon school, 104
Barker, Sheila, 80, 84
Barnes, Albert C., 123, 131, 135, 137–38
Barnes Collection (Philadelphia), 137–39, **138**
Barnes, Djuna, 154

Barnes Foundation, 139
Barnstone, Howard, 157
Baroque style, 60
Barr, Alfred H., Jr., 119, 125, **132**, 135–37, 143, 152, 153, 159, 189, 191, 198
Barr, Margaret Scolari, **132**
Bartolomeo, Michelozzo di, 22
Base magica (Magic Base) (Manzoni), 229, 230–31
basilicas, 15, 18, 28, 29, 31, 37
Basket of Fruit (Caravaggio), 43
Basquiat, Jean-Michel, 53, 265–66, **266**
The Bathers (Courbet), 96
The Bathers (Sherald), 264
Baudelaire, Charles, 98
Bauhaus, 241
Baxandall, Michael, 10, 19
Bazille, Frédéric, 97–99
Baziotes, William, 151, **160**
Bearden, Romare, 175
The Beautyful Ones (Crosby), 264
Beckett, Samuel, 150
Bed (Rauschenberg), **190**, 191
Beeple, 257, **257**, 258
Behrman, S. N., 72, 73
Beijing Gehua Cultural Development Group, 237
Belgium, 38
Benedictine abbeys, 15
Benedictine Rule, 15
Benedict of Norcia, 15
Benhamou, Judith, 129
Benois Madonna (Leonardo), 64, 71
Benton, Thomas Hart, 147
Berenson, Bernard, 72–73, 76
Berger, Maurice, 254
Berggruen, John, 198
Bernheim, Gaston, 118
Bernini, Gian Lorenzo, 56
Bertozzi, Barbara, 192
Bianucci, Annie, **181**
Bibliothèque Nationale (Paris), 222
Biden, Joseph, 259
Bikker, Jonathan, 41–42
Biltmore House (Asheville, North Carolina), 71
Biro, Yaëlle, 130
Birth of Venus (Naissance de Vénus) (Cabanel), 100, **100**
Bischofberger, Bruno, 266
Black artists, 264
Black Arts Council (Los Angeles), 179
Black Belt, 174
Blackboards (Twombly), 188
Black Emergency Cultural Coalition (BECC), 179
Black Girl's Window (Saar), 177–78
Black Lives Matter movement, 263
Black Paintings (Rauschenberg), 186
Black Power movement, 175
Blacks, 169
Bliss, Lillie P., 135, 136
blockbuster exhibitions, 220–33
Bloodline: Big Family No. 2 (Zhang), 245, **245**
Bloodline paintings (Zhang), 244–45
blue-chip art, 248
Blue Nude: Memory of Biskra (Matisse), 123
Bluhm, Norman, 165
Blum, Irving, 199–201
Blum & Poe, 237–38
Boafo, Amoako, 255, **256**
Bodin, Jean-François, 273
Body Prints (Hammons), 176–77
Bohn, Babette, 82
Boiardo, Matteo Maria, 25
Boileau, 56
Bolnes, Catharina, 46
Bologna, Italy, 29, 82
Bologna University, 18
Bonami, Francesco, 241
Bondanella, Julia Conaway, 29
Bondanella, Peter, 29
Le Bonheur de vivre (The Joy of Life) (Matisse), 123, 138
Bonheur, Rosa, 88, **88**
Bonnard, Pierre, 134, 218, 241
Bonnet, Louise, 271
Bontecou, Lee, 191, 205
Bontemps, Arna, 174
Bonwit Teller, 187, 199
books, 16
Boone, Mary, 266
Borghese, Scipione, 31
Borgia, Cesare, 26
Borgia family, 25
Borgia, Lucrezia, 26
Boriaud, Jean-Yves, 21–22
Borromeo, Federico, 43
Bosch, Hieronymus, 269
Botticelli, Sandro, 23, 75, 76
Boty, Pauline, 206
Boudin, Eugène, 101, 108
Bourgeois, Louise, 160, 268, 281n24
Bourse de Commerce (Paris), 205
Bouvier, Yves, 67–69
Boy in a Red Waistcoat (Garçon au gilet rouge) (Cézanne), 116, **116**, 137
Bracquemond, Félix, 101
Bradford, Mark, 264
Brady, Aoife, 83
Bramante, Donato, 28, 31, 53
Branchi, Filippo, 54
Brâncuşi, Constantin, 151
Brandon, Édouard, 101
Brandt, Isabella, 45
Braque, Georges, 97, 124, 126, 127, 135, 140n29, 145, 185
Braun, Emily, 122
Brenner, Michael, 128
Breslin, James E. B., 154, 156
Breton, André, 125, 148, 154
Bringing the War Home: House Beautiful (Rosler), 206
Brisson, Adolphe, 120
British Museum (London), 267
British Royal Collection (Windsor Castle), 65
Brockman Gallery (Los Angeles), 169, 172, 180–81
Bronzeville, 174
Bronzeville at Night (Motley), 174, **174**
Bronzino, Agnolo, 82
Brooklyn Museum (New York), 77, 78, 206, 214, 265, 267
Brooks, Gwendolyn, 174
Brooks, James, **160**
Brouq Nature Reserve (Qatar), 274
Brown, Cecily, 266
Brown, David Alan, 67
Ben Brown Fine Arts, 237–38
Bruce, Ailsa Mellon, 79
Brueghel, Jan the Elder, 45
"Brunch with JAM" series (JAM), 179

Brunelleschi, Filippo, 21–22, 28
Buchloh, Benjamin H. D., 231
Buckingham Palace, 65
Buddha, 19
El bufón el Primo (Velázquez), **222**
Bunny series (Lucas), 213
Buonarroti, Michelangelo, 23
Burchfield, Charles E., 147
Burri, Alberto, 227, 228, 231
Burroughs, Margaret, 174
The Businessman (Lawrence), 174, 264–65
By Art Matters (Hangzhou), 241
By Her Hand: Artemisia Gentileschi and Women Artists in Italy, 1500–1800 (Detroit Institute of Arts, 2021–22), 92n36
Byzantine Empire, 14

C

Cabanel, Alexandre, 100, **100**
Cahiers d'art, 133
Cahn, Isabelle, 117
Cahun, Claude, 271
Caillebotte, Gustave, 106, **106**
Calder, Alexander, 79, 152
Callery, Mary, 160
The Calling of Saint Matthew (Caravaggio), 32
Calvin, John, 38
Cambridge University, 18
Campbell, Mary Schmidt, 170
Campbell's Soup Cans (Ferus Gallery, 1962), 199–201
Campbell's Soup Cans (Warhol), **201**
Campi, Bernardino, 81
Capet, Hugh, 17
Caravaggio, 32–33, **33**, 43, 44, 68, 241
carbon offset programs, 272
The Card Players (Cézanne), 273
Car Hood (Chicago), 206
Carlos, Vanessa, 277
Carnegie, Andrew, 74
Carnegie Steel Company, 74
Carolingian Renaissance, 16
Carolingian renovation (Renovatio Carolingia), 16
Carrère and Hastings, 74
Carrington, Leonora, 81, **269**, 269–70
Carter, Jimmy, 79
Carter, Morris, 76
Cary, Michael, 226
Cassatt, Mary, 77, 101, 103, 109, 144
Cassirer, Paul and Bruno, 109, 117, 118
Castellani, Enrico, 229
Leo Castelli Gallery (New York), 188–93, 199, 201–2, 205
Castelli, Jean-Christophe, 192
Castelli, Leo, 158, 159, 185, 186, 189, 191–92, 195, 198, 199, **199**, 201–3, 277, 278
  Castelli-Sonnabend model, 197–98, 277
  Leo Castelli (Warhol), **192**
Castelli, Nina, 192, 195
Castelli Warehouse (New York), 192
Castello Sforzesco (Milan), 26
Castel Sant'Angelo, 31
Castiglione, Baldassare, 25
cathedrals, 17, 18
Catholic Church. *See* Roman Catholic Church
Catlett, Elizabeth, 174
Caulfield, Patricia, 201
CBS, 203
Celant, Germano, 196, 230, 254
celebrity, 159
Cennini, Cennino, 19, 27
censorship, 235, 236, 242, 244–49
Central Pacific Railroad, 71
Centre Pompidou (Paris), 241, 243–45, **244**, 246, 281n24
Centre Pompidou × West Bund Museum Project, 241
Cézanne, Paul, 78, 96–97, 101, 122, 123, 133, 137, 145, 241
  The Card Players, 273
  Exposition rétrospective d'oeuvres de Cézanne (Salon d'Automne, 1907), 117
  Garçon au gilet rouge (Boy in a Red Waistcoat), 116, **116**, 137
  Goldschmidt auction (Sotheby's, 1958), 116
  market for, 113, 114–17
  Portrait of Ambroise Vollard, **115**
  Toward Mont Sainte-Victoire, 138
Chadwick, Whitney, 84–85, 88, 90, 269
Chamberlain, John, 198
Charlemagne, 16
Charles I of England, 33, 45, 65, 85
Charles II of England, 65
Charles II of Spain, 83
Charles V, Holy Roman emperor, 25, 29
Charles VIII of France, 23
Charles IX of France, 56
Château de Versailles, 56, **56**
Château du Cloux (Clos Lucé), 31
Chavannes, Pierre Puvis de, 123
Chen Dongsheng, 237
Cheng, Adrian, 239
Cherubini, Laerzio, 33
chiaroscuro, 39
Chicago, Illinois, 174
Chicago, Judy, 206, 278
Chicago Renaissance, 174, 176
Chicano artists, 181
Chigi, Agostino, 31
Chi K11 art space (Shanghai), 239
Chile, 243
China
  art hubs, 241–42
  art market, 235–38, 248–49
  art system, 235, 238–42
  auction houses, 236–37
  COVID-19 pandemic, 280n1
  Cultural Revolution, 236, 239, 242, 245
  galleries, 237–38
  museums, 238–41
  State Administration of Cultural Heritage, 238
  Tiananmen Square demonstrations (1989), 244
China Artists Association, 242
China Avant-Garde (1993–94), 245
China/Avant-Garde (National Art Museum of China, 1989), 243
China Guardian Auctions Co. Ltd., 237
Chine demain pour hier (China Tomorrow for Yesterday) (1990), 245
Chinese art and artifacts, 237, 241, 242
Chinese artists, 235, 241, 242–47, 249
Chinese collectors, 247–48
Christ as Salvator Mundi ("Savior of the World") (Leonardo), 67

Christianity, 16
Christie's, 63, 65, 107, 235, 237, 247–48, 261, 273
  20th Century Italian Art auction (1998), 229
  Impressionist and Modern evening auction (2009), 227
Christie's Hong Kong, 245, 255
Christie's London, 81, 206
Christie's New York, 81, 104, 123, 164, 182, 188, 206, 217, 227, 255, 257, 262, 264–65, 271
  Salvator Mundi auction (2017), 69
Christ in the House of Martha and Mary (Vermeer), 46
Christo, 191
Church. *See* Roman Catholic Church
Church of Our Lady (Antwerp), 49
CIA, 161
La Cicciolina (Ilona Staller), 195
Cif Amotan II, 216
Cimabue, 28, 68
Cirque Fernando, 109
Civil Rights Movement, 169, 170, 175–79, 181, 206
Claesz, Pieter, **43**, 46
Claridge's (London), 72
Clark, Ed, 165, **165**
Clark, Kenneth, 65
Claude and Paloma (Picasso), 247
Claudius, Appius Caecus ("the Blind"), 34n21
Clemenceau, Georges, 105
Clement VII, 24, 25
Clert, Iris, 194
Clos Lucé (Château du Cloux), 31
the Club, 164, 189
Coady, Robert J., 128
Coates, Robert, 147, 152, 153
The Cocktail Party (Marisol), 205
Cocteau, Jean, 151
Cohen-Solal, Annie, 189–91, 194–96, 198, 199
Cohen, Steven A., 214
Colbert, Jean-Baptiste, 54, 56, 59, 60, 95
Cold War, 187
Cole, Thomas, 143
collage paintings, 163
collectors, 113, 128, 131, 159, 199, 202, 203, 268
  Chinese, 247–48
  Gilded Age, 73–75
  women, 75–78
  young, 235–36, 247
Colman, Samuel, 78
Colnaghis, 70
Colonne Vendôme, 96
Color Field movement, 164
comacine (stonemason) masters, 26–27
Combines (Rauschenberg), 190–91, 193, 203
Commentary, 158
commercial galleries, 198, 268. *See also specific galleries by name*
  for African American artists, 179–81
  blockbuster museum exhibitions in, 220–33
commissions, 45, 156–57, 201. *See also* patronage
  contracts, 18
  never delivered, 32
  public, 171
  rejected, 32–33
Commonwealth Sale, 65
The Complete Spot Challenge (Hirst), **215**, 216
Composition: The Pheasants (Picasso), **138**
Conceptual art, 196, 222
The Concert (Vermeer), 76
Condo (London), 277, **277**
Cone, Claribel and Etta, 123, 135
Confraternity of the Immaculate Conception, 32
Connaissance des arts, 233n4
Constantine, 14, 15, 18, 31
Contarelli Chapel (Rome), 32–33
contemporary art market, 276–79
Contemporary Black Artists in America (Whitney, 1971), 179
contracts, 18
The Contribution of the Negro to Democracy in America (White), 176, **176**
Conwill, Houston, **180**
Cook, Francis, 65, 66
Cooks, Bridget R., 172
Cooper, Douglas, **223**, 224, 233n4
Cooper Union for the Advancement of Science and Art, 162, 171
Copernicus, Nicolaus, 22
Coquiot, Gustave, 122
Corbett, Rachel, 256
Corcoran Gallery of Art (Washington, DC), 271
Cornelia, Mother of the Gracchi (Kauffman), 81
Coronation (Ai), 249
Corot, Jean-Baptiste-Camille, 104, 132
corporate sponsorship, 279
Correggio, Niccolò da, 25, 44
Corris, Michael, 213
Cortor, Eldzier, 174
Costa, Lorenzo, 25
Cotter, Holland, 231
Counter-Reformation, 37–38
Courbet, Gustave, 95, 96, 103
Couture, Thomas, 98, 109
COVID-19 pandemic, 248, 249, 253–54, 262–63, 280n1
Cranach, Lucas the Elder, **38**
Crane, Andrea, 278
Crane, Diana, 143, 158–59, 203
Creative Artists Agency (CAA), 278
The Crisis, 173
critics, 157–59
Crosby, Njideka Akunyili, 264
crypto, 257
Cuba, 243
Cubism, 113, 114, 124, 126, 127–28, 131, 132, 135, 137, 165, 174, 185, 222
Cubism and Abstract Art (MoMA, 1936), 135
cultural diplomacy, 276
Cultural Revolution (China), 236, 239, 242, 245
The Currency (Hirst), 216–17
Cuyp, Aelbert, 41
Cynical Realism, 244–45

D

Dada, 135, 148, 185, 270
Dale, Chester, 79, 135
Dale, Maud, 135
Dalí, Salvador, 148
Dallas Museum of Art, 67
Damer, Anne Seymour, 89
Danaë (Gentileschi), 81
The Dance (Matisse), 134, 138, **138**
Dante Alighieri, 20, 191

Daranyi, Sylphide de, 130, 131
Dark Ages, 14
David (Donatello), 22
David (Michelangelo), 24, 29
Davis, Alonzo, 169, 180–81
Davis, Dale Brockman, 169, 180–81
dealers, 48–50, 113–22, 127–33, 151, 159, 192, 194–95, 254, 277–78
Death and Disaster series (Warhol), 201
Death in America (Sonnabend Gallery, 1964), 193
The Death of Lucretia (Botticelli), 76
Death of Sardanapalus (Delacroix), 104
The Death of the Virgin (Caravaggio), 32, 33, **33**, 44
de Brécy Tondo, 260
De Carlo, Massimo, 238
de Chirico, Giorgio, 130, 131, 137, 271
The Declaration of the Rights of Women (de Gouges), 86
Degas, Edgar, 76, 77, 101, 103, 108, 109, 125, 133
de Gouges, Olympe, 86
Deitch, Jeffrey, 192, 198, 277
Le Déjeuner sur l'herbe (Manet), 98, **98**, 109
Dekker, Erwin, 99
de Kooning, Elaine, 147, 189
de Kooning, Willem, 78, 145, 147, **155**, 155, 158–59, **160**, 164, 186, 187, 189
Delaborde, Henri, 88
Delacroix, Eugène, 78, 104, 132, 222
de la Fontaine, Jean, 128
Delft, Holland, 39, 46, 50
Delieuvin, Vincent, 64–65
The Deluge (Michelangelo), 30
De Maria, Walter, 197
de Menil, John and Dominique, 157
Les Demoiselles d'Avignon (Picasso), 124–25, **125**, 127, 133, 136, 137
de Monfreid, Georges-Daniel, 121
Deng Xiaoping, 235, 236, 247
Denis, Maurice, 123
Denver Art Museum, 77, 167n39
Derain, André, 97, 127
des Cars, Laurence, 267
The Descent from the Cross (Rubens), 44, **45**
Desert X AlUla (2024), 275, **275**
Dessins et croquis de Manet provenant de son atelier (1893), 115
de Stäel, Nicholas, 158
de Strooper, Liesbeth, 99
Detroit Institute of Arts, 92n36
de Vlaminck, Maurice, 97, 127
Dia Art Foundation (New York), 182, 267
Diaconus, Paulus, 16
Diamonstein, Barbaralee, 189, 191
Diana and Her Companions (Vermeer), 46
Diaz, Al, 265
Díaz, Porfirio, 147
DiCaprio, Leonardo, 69
Diebenkorn, Richard, 196
Diego y yo (Kahlo), 270
digital art, 258, 261
digital transformations, 254–60
Dinner at Gertrude Stein's: The French Collection Part II, #10 (Ringgold), 206
The Dinner Party (Chicago), 206
Dior, 255
diplomacy, cultural, 276
Les Distractions de Dagobert (Carrington), **269**, 270
Documenta exhibition (1982), 265
Dodson, Howard, 170
Doig, Peter, 278
Dominguín, Luis Miguel, **223**
Donatello, 19–20, 22
Dorsey, Thomas A., 174
Dossin, Catherine, 194
Dostoyevsky, Fyodor, 253
Double Merge (Gilliam), 182, **182**
Double Negative (Heizer), 197
Double White Map (Johns), 203
Doucet, Jacques, 125, 127
Douglas, Aaron, 173, **173**
Dove, Arthur, 145
Downtown Gallery (New York), 145, 174
Drape (Gilliam), 181–82
Drawing Center (New York), 176, 267
Drexler, Rosalyn, 206
Dreyfus, Alfred, 120
drip paintings, 149, 153, 154, 158, 187
Driskell, David C., 169, 170, 254
Drouin, René, 192
Druick, Douglas, 121
Du Bois, W. E. B., 170, 171
Dubuffet, Jean, 158
Duchamp, Marcel, 152, 154, 196
Dufy, Raoul, 97, 120, 133
Dumas, Ann, 117
Duncanson, Robert S., 144
Duomo, 22
Duo Yun Xuan Auctions Co. Ltd., 236–37
Durand-Ruel, Flavie, 106, 113, 117, 118, 121, 133, 138
Durand-Ruel, Paul, 9, 95, **103**, 103–9, 118, 121, 133, 138, 144, 276–78
Durand-Ruel, Paul-Louis, 106
Durand-Ruel & Sons, 108
Dürer, Albrecht, 27
Dutch art, 39, 49–50, 77
Dutch art market, 37
Dutch East India Company, 38
Dutch Golden Age, 36–51, 85–86, 276
Dutch Republic, 37–39, 50, 53
Dutilleul, Roger, 127
Duveen Brothers, 72
Duveen, Henry, 72
Duveen, Joseph, 70, 72–73, **73**, 74
Dwan Gallery, Los Angeles, 180, 196
Dwan Gallery, New York, 196–97, **197**
Dwan Light Sanctuary, 197
Dwan, Virginia, 196–97, **197**, 198
Dwek, Claudia, 229–30
Dykstra, Natalie, 76

E

Eakin, Hugh, 137
Eakins, Thomas, 143
Early Baroque period, 12–33
Earth art, 196
Earthworks (Dwan Gallery, 1968), 196–97
Eastern Roman Empire, 14
East-West/West-East (Serra), 273–74
eco-certifications, 272
École de Paris (School of Paris), 129–30
economic growth, 70–71
Edict of Milan, 14, 15

Edict of Nantes, *57*
educators, 170–74, 176
Egan, Charles, 143, 155, 158, 189
Charles Egan Gallery (New York), 155, 186
Egyptian art, 173
eighteenth century, 86–90
Eighty Years' War, 38
Eleanor of Naples, 25
Elisabeth of Valois, 81
Elvis series (Warhol), 201
Embiricos, George, 274
Emin, Tracey, 213
Endeavor, 278
England, 17, 50
Envelope (Château de Versailles), 59
Environmental art, 196
environmental concerns, 272
Epitaph to Something's Gotta Give (Boty), 206
Erased de Kooning Drawing (Rauschenberg), 186
Ernst, Jimmy, **160**
Ernst, Max, 148, 150, **151**, 152, 154, 269, 270–71
Escobar, Marisol, 191, 205
Esquire, 191
Essenhigh, Inka, 271
Este, Ercole I d', 25
Este, Isabella d', 13–14, 25–26
Estes, 13, 21
Ethiopia Awakening (Fuller), 172
Euclid, 28
Evans, George, **181**
Everydays: The First 5000 Days (Beeple), 257, **257**
exhibitions. *See also specific exhibitions by name, artist, venue*
  blockbuster, 220–33
  institutional, 266–67
  solo, 281n24
Experimental Workshop (New York), 148
Exposition Picasso (Galeries Georges Petit, 1932), **132**, 133, 137
Exposition rétrospective d'oeuvres de Cézanne (Salon d'Automne, 1907), 117
Exposition Universelle, 96, 104
The Eye Is the First Circle (Krasner), 164

F

Family of Saltimbanques (Picasso), 129, **129**
Fantastic Art, Dada, Surrealism (MoMA, 1936–37), 135, 148, 270
Fantastic Women: Surreal Worlds from Meret Oppenheim to Louise Bourgeois (2020), 281n24
Farber, David, 187
Faustina, 26
fauves (wild beasts), 97, 123
Feast of the Rosary (Dürer), 27
Federal Art Project (FAP), 145–47, 173
Feigenbaum, Gail, 70, 73
female patronage, 13, 25–26, 82
Femme au chapeau (Woman with a Hat) (Matisse), 123
Fenway Court (Boston), 75
Ferragosto (Twombly), 188
Ferus Gallery (Los Angeles), 180, 190, 196, 199–201
Ficino, Marsilio, 22
Field, Hamilton Easter, 135
Le Figaro, 98
Figure in Movement (Bacon), 262
Fillette à la corbeille fleurie (Young Girl with a Basket of Flowers) (Picasso), 124
Fini, Leonor, 270
Finlay, Victoria, 19
Fiorio, Maria Teresa, 67
First Group Showing (Works in Black & White) (Spiral, 1965), 175
Fischer, John, 156
Fischer, Konrad, 198
Fitzgerald, F. Scott, 126
FitzGerald, Michael, 122, 124, 129, 136, 137
Flag (Johns), **186**, 187
Flag on Orange Field (Johns), 187
Flags series (Johns), 187, 189, 190, 193
Flavin, Dan, 191
Flechtheim, Alfred, 128
Florence, Italy, 20–24, 29
Floyd, George, 263
Fondation Cartier (Paris), **217**, 218
Fondation Giacometti, 240
Fondation Louis Vuitton (Paris), 134, 167n39, 266
Fontana, Lavinia, **82**, 82–83, 92n36
Fontana, Lucio, 227–28, 230, 231
Force, Christel H., 113, 114
For the Love of God (Hirst), 214–15, **215**
Fortune magazine, 174
Foster and Partners, 276
Fouquet, Nicolas, 60
Four Friends (Toor), 255
Four Seasons (Bonnard), 134
Four Seasons restaurant (New York), 156
Fourth Annual Exhibition of Painting and Sculpture (Stable Gallery, 1955), 187
Fra Angelico, 75
Fragonard, Jean-Honoré, 74
Fraissex du Bost, Antoinette, 192
France, 50, 52–61, 90, 165, 275
Franchetti, Tatiana, 188
Francis (Pope), 267
Francis I, 32, 58
Francis, Sam, 165
Franco, Francisco, 224
Frankenthaler, Helen, 147, 158, 161–63, **163**, 164, 167n39
free markets, first, 36–51
Freeze (Port of London Authority, 1988), 213–14
Frelinghuysen, Alice Cooney, 78
French Academy (Académie Française), 56
French Barbizon school, 74
French & Company, 163
French East India Company, 54
French garden, **58**, 59
French Revolution, 57, 58, 86, 89
Frescobaldi, Marchesi, 84
frescoes, 15, 20, 23, 24, 28–30, 156
Frick Coke Company, 73–74
Frick Collection (New York), 70, 74–75
Frick, Henry Clay, 71, 73–75, 79
Friedan, Betty, 204
Frost at Louveciennes (Sisley), 134
Fuller, Meta Vaux Warrick, 172

G

Gabriel, Mary, 146, 159, 162–63
Gaea (Krasner), **162**

Gagosian, 188, **215**, 215–16, 237–38, 255, 264, 278
Gagosian, Beverly Hills, 218
Gagosian, Larry, 192, 221, 265–66, 277
Gagosian, London, **215**, 225
Gagosian, New York
  Ewa Juszkiewicz: In vain her feet in sparkling laces glow (2020–21), **271**
  Isabel and Other Intimate Strangers: Portraits by Alberto Giacometti and Francis Bacon (2008), 225
  Lucio Fontana: Ambienti spaziali (2012), 230
  Picasso & the Camera (2014–15), 225
  Picasso and Françoise Gilot: Paris–Vallauris, 1943–1953 (2012), 225
  Picasso and Marie-Thérèse: L'amour fou (2011), 225
  Picasso: Mosqueteros (2009), 221–24, **225**, 225–27, 231
  Piero Manzoni: A Retrospective (2009), 221, 227–28, 230–32, **231**, **232**
Gainsborough, Thomas, 79
Galenson, David W., 103
Galerie Bernheim-Jeune, 109
Galerie Berthe Weill (Paris), 120, 122
Galerie Daniel Templon (Paris), 266
Galerie de l'Effort Moderne (Paris), 131
Galerie des peintres flamands, hollandais et allemands (Le Brun), 46
Galerie Huit (Paris), 165
Galerie Rive Droite (Paris), 193
Galeries Georges Petit (Paris), **132**, 133, 137
Galileo Galilei, 22
Gallerani, Cecilia, 26
Galleria Apollinaire (Milan), 228
Galleria Continua (Beijing), 237
Gallerie degli Uffizi (Florence), 92n47
galleries, 185, 237–38, 253, 254, 273, 276–79. *See also specific galleries by name*
  American, 144
  Castelli-Sonnabend model, 197–98, 277
  commercial, 179–81, 198, 220–33, 268
  mega-galleries, 277
  in New York, 202
gallerists, 143
Gallery 32 (Los Angeles), 181, **181**
Gallery Climate Coalition (GCC), 272, **272**
Gamin (Savage), **172**
Gandini, Manuela, 193
Garçon au gilet rouge (Boy in a Red Waistcoat) (Cézanne), 116, **116**, 137
Gardner, Isabella Stewart, **75**, 75–77
Gardner, John Lowell "Jack," Jr., 76
Isabella Stewart Gardner Museum (Boston), 70, 77
Garnier, Charles, 102
Garnier Frères, **102**
The Gates of Paradise (Ghiberti), 21
Gauguin, Paul, 113–14, 117, 121, 123, 133, 274
gay artists, 262
Gego (Gertrud Goldschmidt), 267
Gehry, Frank, 276
Geldzahler, Henry, 198, 200
Gemäldegalerie (Berlin), 67
gender disparities, 268
Generation Z (Gen Z), 236, 247–48, 261–62
genius (concept), 28–29
genre painting, 37, 47–48
Gentileschi, Artemisia, 81, 83–85, **84**, 92n36, 92n49, 268
Gentileschi, Orazio, 81, 83–85
The Geographer (Vermeer), **47**
George III, 65, 195
Germany, 116, 126, 128, 137, 165, 243, 267
Gerritse, Bregje, 118
Gerson, Noel B., 45
Gertrude Stein and Pablo Picasso: The Invention of Language (Musée du Luxembourg, 2023–24), 126
J. Paul Getty Museum (Los Angeles), 67, 77
Geuna, Elena, 229
Gherardini, Lisa, 31
Ghiberti, Lorenzo, 21, 28
Ghirlandaio, Domenico, 23
Ghotmeh, Lina, 275
Giacchetti, Gian Ambrogio, 54
Giacometti, Alberto, 217, 225, 240, 241
GI Bill (Servicemen's Readjustment Act of 1944), 165
Gilbert, 195
Gilded Age, 70–71, 73–75
Gilliam, Sam, 181–82, **182**
Gilot, Françoise, 223, 225
Giocondo, Francesco del, 31
Giotto, 9, 19–20, **20**, 68
Girl before a Mirror (Picasso), 136
Girl with a Pearl Earring (Vermeer), 47
Girl with Pink Rose (Strider), 206
Giuliani, Rudolph, 214
Glaber, Rodulfus, 17
Glackens, William James, 137, 138
Glaswall, Mrs. H. W., 190
Gleyre, Charles, 97
global art fairs, 254
global art market, 252–81
Gluckman, Richard, 225–26
Gobelins family, 54
Gobelins manufactories (Manufactures Royales des Meubles de la Couronne, Royal Manufactories of Furniture of the Crown), 54–56
gold, 13, 19, 27
Golden Lions, 185
Golden, Thelma, 267
Goldman Sachs, 279
Gold Marilyn Monroe (Warhol), 201
Goldschmidt auction (Sotheby's, 1958), 116
Goldschmidt Collection, 116
Goldschmidt, Gertrud. *See* Gego
Goldschmidt, Jakob, 116
Gomès, Henriette, **223**
Góngora y Argote, Luis de, 223
Gonzaga, Elisabetta, 26
Gonzaga, Federico II, 29
Gonzaga, Francesco, 25
Gonzagas, 13, 21
Gonzaga, Vincenzo, 33, 44
Goode Bryant, Linda, 169, 179, 180, **180**
Gopnik, Blake, 201
Gorky, Arshile, 145, 147, 159
Gothic architecture, 17–18
Gothic style, 22
Gottlieb, Adolph, 160, **160**, 202
Goya, Francisco de, 77–79, 221
Goyen, Jan van, 48
Gozzoli, Benozzo, 19, 24, **24**
Grafton Galleries (London), 109
Graham-Dixon, Andrew, 32–33
Grande Halle de la Villette (Paris), 244
grande manière (grand manner), 56
Grand Palais, Paris, 92n35, 222, 244
Grand Prize for Painting (Venice Biennale), 185, 195

Grand Tour, 49–50
Great Criticism series (Wang), 244
Great Depression, 143, 146–47, 172, 173, 202
Great Migration, 173–74
El Greco, 78, 137, 221
Greenberg, Clement, 143, 149, 151–54, **157**, 157–59, 163
Green Target (Johns), 189
Gregory the Great, 15
Gris, Juan, 127
The Gross Clinic (Eakins), 143
Guanajuato, Mexico (Motley), 174
Guangda Art Museum (Hangzhou), 241
Gu Dexin, 244
Guernica (Picasso), 136, 137, 149
Guggenheim Abu Dhabi, 276
Guggenheim, Benjamin, 150
Peggy Guggenheim Collection (Venice), 150
Guggenheim Jeune gallery (London), 150, 151
Solomon R. Guggenheim Museum and Foundation, 221, 231, 267
Guggenheim Museum Bilbao, 188
Guggenheim, Peggy, 143, 150, **150**, 151, 151–53, **153**, 154, 155, 194, 270, 277
Guilbaut, Serge, 161
Guild of Saint Luke, 46, 48, 85
guilds, 27
Guillaume, Paul, 129–31, 138
The Guitar Player (Vermeer), 46
Guston, Philip, 196, 202
Gutenberg, Johannes, 22
Gweong-Gweong (Yue), 245, **245**

H

Haak, Bob, 39, 40, 43, 46, 49, 50
The Hague, Holland, 50
Haight, Charles Coolidge, 78
Halpert, Edith, 145, 174
Halsey, Lauren, 266
Hals, Frans, 39, 48, 85
Hamilton, Richard, 187
Hammons, David, 169, 176–77, **177**, 180
Hampton Institute, 176
Hands Up (Boafo), 255, **256**
Jack Hanley Gallery, 258
Hansberry, Lorraine, 174
Hao, Zheng, 241
The Happy Couple (Leyster), 85
Hardouin-Mansart, Jules, 59
Harlem Artists Guild, 170, 171
Harlem Community Art Center, 170, 172, 174
Harlem on My Mind: Cultural Capital of Black America, 1900–1968 (Metropolitan Museum of Art, 1969), 178, **178**, 179
Harlem Renaissance, 144, 169–70, 173, 183n12, 264–65
Harmon Foundation, 170
Harmon, William E., 170
The Harp (Lift Every Voice and Sing) (Savage), 171
Harper's, 173
Harper's Magazine, 156
Hartigan, Grace, 147, 161
Hastings, Thomas, 74
Haus der Kunst (Munich), 246
Hauser, Arnold, 10, 16, 23, 28, 47, 49, 53, 56
Hauser & Wirth, 237–38, 264, 278
Haussmann, Georges-Eugène Baron, 102
Havemeyer, Henry Osborne "Harry," 77
Havemeyer, Louisine, 77–78
Havemeyers, 70
Haxall, Daniel, 279
Hayes, Jeffreen, 171
Haystacks (Meules) (Monet), 104, 105
Hébuterne, Jeanne, 110
Hegra (Mada'in Saleh), 275
Heizer, Michael, 197
Held, Al, 165
Heller, Ben, 190
Helter Skelter I (Bradford), 264
Hemingway, Ernest, 126
Henrietta Maria of France, 65
Henry IV, 45
Heracllitus, 28
Hermitage Museum (St. Petersburg), 79, 123, 134
Herning Kunstmuseum (Denmark), 230–31
Herzog & de Meuron, 241
Hesse, Eva, 192
Hessel, Katy, 78
Hewitt, Catherine, 88, 90
Higgie, Jennifer, 85, 109
Hille, Hermann, 137
Hines, Earl, 174
Hirshhorn Museum and Sculpture Garden (Washington, DC), 182
Hirst, Damien, 211–18, 253, 261, 273, 274
- *Beautiful Inside My Head Forever* auction (Sotheby's, 2008), 211–12, **212**, **213**, 217, 218
- *Cherry Blossoms* (Fondation Cartier, 2021–22), **217**, 218
- *The Complete Spot Paintings, 1986–2011* (Gagosian, 2012), **215**, 215–16
- *The Currency*, 216–17
- *Freeze* (Port of London Authority, 1988), 213–14
- *For the Love of God*, 214–15, **215**
- *The Miraculous Journey*, 274
- Newport Street Gallery (London), 216
- *Pharmacy* auction (Sotheby's, 2004), 214
- *The Physical Impossibility of Death in the Mind of Someone Living*, 214
- Spot Challenge, **215**
- Spot paintings, **215**, 215–17
- *Treasures from the Wreck of the Unbelievable* (Venice, 2017), 216, **216**, 218
- *Veil Paintings*, 218

historical paintings, 89
History of Alexander (Gobelins), 55
History of the King (Gobelins), 55
history painting, 49
Hockney, David, 262
Hofmann, Hans, 147
Hofstede de Groot, Cornelis, 85
Holland, 49–50
Hollar, Wenceslaus, 63, **64**, 65
Hollingsworth, Mary, 13, 19–20, 22, 23, 31
Holofernes (Sirani), 83
Holy Roman Empire, 16, 17
Homem, Antonio, 195
Homestead massacre, 74
Hommage à Pablo Picasso (Paris, 1966), 222
Homme à la pipe (Picasso), 227
Hong Kong, 235, 237, 238, 249
Hong Kong Palace Museum, 241

Hook, Philip, 49, 95, 108
Hopper, Edward, 147
Hoptman, Laura, 267
The Horse Fair (Bonheur), 88, **88**
Hoschedé, Alice, 105
Hôtel Drouot (Paris), 108, 121, 128
Houses of Parliament (Monet), 104
Howard, Olivia, 262
HOW Art Museum, 241
How Will I Know (Whitney, 2020–21), 255
Huang Rui, 250n11
Huang Yong Ping, 244
Hudson River School, 143
Hulst, Titia, 37, 39, 48, 145
Hultén, Pontus, 193
Hunter, Sam, 155
Huntingtons, 70
Hunt, Richard, 181

I

Ibrahim, Mariane, 255
Icons of Modern Art (Fondation Louis Vuitton, 2016–17 and 2021–22), 134
Akira Ikeda Gallery (Tokyo), 266
Ileana Sonnabend (Kender and Shunk), **194**
imperialism, 56
Imperial Palace (Beijing), 239
Impressionism, 56, 77, 94–111, 165, 276–78
Impression, soleil levant (Impression, Sunrise) (Monet), 99, **99**, 103
Works in Oil and Pastel by the Impressionists of Paris (1886), 108
Incense Road Museum (Saudi Arabia), 275
Indian Art of the United States (MoMA, 1941), 148–49
inequality, 70–71
Inferno (Dante), 191
Infinity Mirror Room–Phalli's Field (Kusama), **204**
Infinity Mirror Room series (Kusama), 205
Ingres, Jean-Auguste-Dominique, 132, 145
Innocent VIII, 29
The Inspiration of Saint Matthew (Caravaggio), 33
Instagram, 53, 247, 254–55, 257
Institute of Contemporary Art (Philadelphia), 202
Instragrammable art, 255, 257
Interchange (de Kooning), 164
interior scenes, 37, 47–49
International Association of Art Critics, 226
International Exhibition of Modern Art (69th Regiment Armory, 1913), 119, 135, 145
International Exhibition of the New Realists (Janis Gallery, 1962), 202
international fairs, 238
International Klein Blue (IKB), 228
International Program (MoMA), 159
Internet access, 248
In This Case (Basquiat), 265
Irascibles, 160, **160**
Isaacson, Walter, 31
Isabel and Other Intimate Strangers: Portraits by Alberto Giacometti and Francis Bacon (Gagosian, 2008), 225
Isabella Steward Gardner (Sargent), **75**
Italian miracle *(miracolo italiano)*, 228
Italy, 17, 137, 228
Grand Tour of, 49–50
Renaissance, 13, 22, 48

J

Martha Jackson Gallery (New York), 163
Jackson, Suzanne, 181, **181**
Jacques Seligmann & Co., 125
Jagger, Bianca, 212
James II, 65
Sidney Janis Gallery, 158, 202
Janis, Sidney, 143, 158, 159, 202
Japan, 243
Japanese prints, 101–3
Jasper Johns and Kurt Schwitters (Ferus Gallery, 1960), 190
Jatta, Barbara, 267
Jeu de Palme (Paris), 47
Jewish Museum (New York), 163, 189–91
Jiang Qing, 236
Jimson Weed/White Flower No. 1 (O'Keeffe), 270
JNBY, 241
Johns, Jasper, 185, 186–87, 189–90, 193, 199, 261, 277
Double White Map, 203
Flag, **186**, 187
Flag on Orange Field, 187
Flags series, 187, 189, 190, 193
Green Target, 189
Jasper Johns and Kurt Schwitters (1960), 190
Numbers series, 189
Sixteen Americans (MoMA, 1959–60), 190
Small False Start, 261
Targets series, 187, 189
Target with Four Faces, 189
Two Flags, 190
White Flag, 187
White Numbers, 189
Johnson, James Weldon, 183n7
Johnson, Philip, 155–57, 198, 201
John VIII Palaeologus, 24
John XII, 17
Jones, Kellie, 179–81
Jopling, Jay, 214, 218
Joseph and Potiphar's Wife (Rossi), 80
Joseph II, 24
Joyeux Noël (Egan Gallery, 1954), 186
Jozefacka, Anna, 135
Judd, Donald, 188, 191, 207n7
Judgment of Paris (Raphael), 98
Judith (Sirani), 83
Julien, Isaac, 278
Julien Levy Gallery, 148
Julius II, 25, 28–31, 53
Just Above Midtown (JAM), 169, 172, 179, 180, **180**
Just What Is It That Makes Today's Homes So Different, So Appealing? (Hamilton), 187
Juszkiewicz, Ewa, 271, **271**

K

Kahlo, Frida, 270
Kahnweiler, Daniel-Henry, 113, 122, 124, 127–28, 131–33, 135, 140n29
Kakar, Arun, 268
Kameyama, Shigeki, 167n46

Kandinsky, Wassily, 151, 189
Kann, Rodolphe, 72
Kantor, Paul, 196
Karp, Ivan, 185, 191, 198, 199, **199**, 201–2
Kars, Georges, **120**
Kauffman, Angelica, 81, 89, 92n36
Kawamura Memorial DIC Museum of Art (Sakura, Japan), 156
KAWS, 241
Kazakina, Katya, 255–56
Keller, Georges, 116
Kelly, Ellsworth, 165, 191
Kelly, Simon, 105
Kempers, Bram, 19, 29
Kemp, Martin, 67
Kender, János, **194**, 195
key opinion leaders (KOLs), 248
Kienholz, Edward, 196
Kiesler, Frederick John, 152
King, Martin Luther, Jr., 175
Kleeblatt, Norman, 157
Klein, Hélène, 125
Klein, Yves, 176–77, 196, 227, 228, 231
Klimt, Gustav, 69
Kline, Franz, 147, 158, 159, 196, 203
Klingemann, Mario, 259–60
Kloveniersdoelen, 41
Klumpke, Anna, 88
M. Knoedler & Co., 78
Knoedlers, 70
Alfred A. Knopf, 233n1
Knuijt, Maria Simonsdr. de, 46
KOLs (key opinion leaders), 248
Koolhaas, Rem, 274
Koons, Jeff, 195, 261
Korean War, 186
Kramář, Vincenc, 127
Krasner, Lee, 146, 147, 152, 153, 159, 160, **162**, 162–64, 167n39
Krauss, Rosalind, 271
Kress Collection, 73
Kress, Samuel H., 70, 79
Kunstmuseum Basel (Switzerland), 182
Kuntz, Warren E., 66
Kurokawa, Kisho, 119
Kusama, Yayoi, **204**, 205, 231

L

Labille-Guiard, Adélaïde, 86
Lady Day II (Gilliam), 182
Lady with an Ermine (Leonardo), 26
Lady Writing a Letter with Her Maid (Vermeer), 46
Lagraulas, Jean Bilhères de, 29
Land art, 196, 197
Landau, Felix, 196
landscape, 37, 40–41, 143, 144
Language III (Dwan Gallery, 1969), **197**
Lanskoy, André, 158
lapis lazuli, 9, 19
Larionov, Mikhail, 134
Last Judgment (Giotto), 20, **20**
Lastman, Pieter, 41
The Last Supper (Nelli), **80**, 81
Latin manuscripts, 16
"laughing man" self-portraits (Yue), 245
Lau, Joseph, 247
Lawrence, Jacob, 171, 173–74, 181, 264–65
Lawson-Tancred, Jo, 260
lazulite, 19
Le Brun, Charles, 55–56, 59, 60, 95
Le Brun, Jean-Baptiste-Pierre, 46, 89
Leduc, Marie, 243–44
Leo Castelli (Warhol), **192**
Lee, Simon, 238
Lefèvre, André, 127
Léger, Fernand, 127, 133, 158, 189
Lehman Brothers, 212, 226
Lehmann Maupin, 238
Leiden, Holland, 41, 50
Le Nôtre, André, 59, 60
Leo III, 16
Leonardo da Vinci, 25, 32, 63, 265
  Benois Madonna, 64, 71
  Lady with an Ermine, 26
  Mona Lisa, 31, 79
  Painter at the Court of Milan (National Gallery, 2011), 67
  Salvator Mundi, 63, **64**, 64–69, **66**
  The Virgin of the Rocks, 31, 67
Leo X, 24, 25, 37
Lepic, Ludovic Napoléon, 101
Leroy, Louis, 99
Lesser, Casey, 268
Le Vau, Louis, 56, 59, 60
Level, André, 113, 124, 127, 128–29
Julien Levy Gallery (New York), 270, 271
Levy, Julien, 148
Lewis, Ben, 63, 64, 67
Lewis, Edmonia, 144
Lewis, Norman, 147, **148**, 161, 171, 172, 175, 264–65
Leyster, Judith, 39, 85
The Liberation of Aunt Jemima (Saar), 178
Liberty Porcelain (Toor), 255
Lichtenstein, Roy, 185, 187, 191, 193, 199, 205
Life magazine, 159, 160, **163**, 164, 191, 194
Lift Every Voice and Sing (The Harp) (Savage), 171
Li Lin, 241
Li Ma, 236
Lippard, Lucy, 187
Li Shuang, 250n11
Little Galleries of the Photo-Secession, 144
Liu Yiqian, 240, 247
The Lives of the Most Excellent Painters, Sculptors, and Architects (Vasari), 28–29
Livingston, Jane, 271
Loan Exhibition of Masterpieces by Old and Modern Painters (M. Knoedler & Co., 1915), 78
Locke, Alain, 170
Locomotion (Clark), **165**
La logica del vegetale–Metamorfosi (Vegetal Logic–Metamorphosis) (Penone), **275**
Lombards, 14, 16
Longhi, Roberto, 92n49
Long Museum (Shanghai), 240
Long Museum Chongqing, 240
Long Museum Pudong, 240
Long Museum West Bund, 240
Lope de Vega, 223
Lorenzo the Magnificent, 23
Los Angeles, 1972: A Panorama of Black Artists (LACMA, 1972), 179

Los Angeles County Museum of Art (LACMA), 173, 179
Betye Saar: Call and Response (2019–20), 183n11
Los Angeles, 1972: A Panorama of Black Artists (1972), 179
Los Angeles to New York: Dwan Gallery, 1959–1971 (2017), 197
Sculpture of Black Africa: The Paul Tishman Collection (1968), 179
Two Centuries of Black American Art (1976–77), 170
Women Artists: 1550–1950 (1976), 78
Los Angeles Modern Auctions, 206
Los Angeles Museum of History, Science, and Art, 173, 196
Los Angeles Negro Art Association, 173
Los Angeles Public Library, 172, 173
Los Angeles to New York: Dwan Gallery, 1959–1971 (2017), 197
Louisiana Museum of Modern Art (Humlebaek, Denmark), 193
Louis IX, 18
Louis XII, 25, 31, 65
Louis XIII, 56, 58
Louis XIV, 33, 53, 56–57, 59, 60, 95
Louis XIV (Rigaud), 56–57, **57**
Louis XIV visite la Manufacture des Gobelins, 15 octobre 1667 (Saint-André), **55**
Louvre, 56
Louvre Abu Dhabi, 69, 276, **276**
Loving, Alvin, 181
Low Countries, 38
Lozano, Lee, 205
Lucas, Martine, 87
Lucas, Sarah, 213
Lucretia (Gentileschi), 81
Ludwig, Irene, 193
Ludwig Museum (Cologne), 193
Ludwig, Peter, 193
Luijten, Hans, 117, 118
Luther, Martin, 37
Luxembourg, 38
luxury goods market, 247

M

M50 Art District (Shanghai), 241
Maar, Dora, 271, 281n24
Machine Hallucinations (Anadol), 258–59
Macy's, 270
Made in Heaven (Koons), 195
Ma Desheng, 242–43, 247, 248, 250n11
Madonna and Child (Madonna of Bruges) (Michelangelo), 29–30
Maës, Antoine, 55
Maestri di Pietra e Legname (Masters of Stone and Wood) guild, 27
Magi Chapel frescoes, 24, **24**
Magiciens de la terre (Magicians of the Earth) (Centre Pompidou, 1989), 243–45, **244**
A Maid Asleep (Vermeer), 72
Maingon, Claire, 97
Les Maîtres de la peinture contemporaine (Masters of Contemporary Painting) (Zervos), 133
Malanga, Gerard, 200
Malatesta, Sigismondo Pandolfo, 24
Malaysia, 243
Malevich, Kazimir, 134
Le Mal oublié (Tanning), 271
Malvasia, Carlo Cesare, 83
Mañach, Pedro "Pere," 120, 122
Manchester Art Gallery, UK, 281n24
Manet, Édouard, 76, 77, 96–97, 101, 103, 104, 107–9, 221
A Bar at the Folies-Bergère, 108
Le Déjeuner sur l'herbe, 98, **98**, 109
Dessins et croquis de Manet provenant de son atelier (1893), 115
Goldschmidt auction (Sotheby's, 1958), 116
Olympia, 100, **100**, 109
Portrait of Victorine Meurent, 109
Manifesto of Realism, 96
Mansel, Philip, 57, 59
Mantegna, Andrea, 25, 26
manufactories, royal, 54–55
Manufactures Royales des Meubles de la Couronne (Royal Manufactories of Furniture of the Crown) (Gobelins), 54–56
manuscripts, 16
Manzoni, Piero, 221, 227–28, **228**, 228–30, **230**, 230–32, **231–32**
Mao (Warhol), 247
Mao Zedong, 236
Marani, Pietro, 67
Marie Antoinette, 87–89
Marilyn series (Warhol), 201
Marin, John, 145, 154
Marisol (Marisol Escobar), 205
Marlborough Galleries, 157
Marquesa de Pontejos (Goya), 79
Marquet, Albert, 97
Marquis, Alice Goldfarb, 135
Marron, Donald, 198
Marshall, Kerry James, 176, 264, **264**
Marshall Plan, 161
Martel, Charles, 17
Marter, Joan, 161, 164
Martin, Agnes, 161, 191
Martin, Jean-Hubert, 244
Martin Luther (Workshop of Lucas Cranach the Elder), **38**
Martin, Trayvon, 263
Martin V, 31
The Martyrdom of Saint Matthew (Caravaggio), 32
The Massacre of the Innocents (Rubens), 81
Mastry (MCA Chicago, 2016), 264
Mathaf, the Arab Museum of Modern Art (Qatar), 274
Pierre Matisse Gallery (New York), 148, 271
Matisse, Henri, 78, 97, 122–24, 126, 131, 135, 137, 145, 165
Blue Nude: Memory of Biskra, 123
Le Bonheur de vivre (The Joy of Life), 123, 138
The Dance, 134, 138, **138**
Femme au chapeau (Woman with a Hat), 123
Matisse et Picasso (1918), 130–31
The Music, 134
Seated Riffian (Le Rifain assis), **138**
Matisse, Pierre, 148
Matta, Roberto, 148
Matthews, Miriam, 172, 173
Mayer, Marc, 265
Mayer, Salvator, 120
Mazarin, Cardinal, 55, 57, 60
Mazzarino, Giulio, 55

Mazzoli, Emilio, 265
McAndrew, Clare, 254
McKinsey & Company, 262
Medici, Cosimo de', 19, 21–24
Medici, Cosimo III de', 50
Medici, Giovanni di Bicci de', 21
Medici, Giuliano, 23, 24
Medici, Lorenzo the Magnificent, 23–24
Medici, Maria de', 45
Medicis, 13, 18, 21–24, 84, 156, 273
mega-galleries, 277
Megliorini, Ferdinando, 54
Megliorini, Orazio, 54
Mehretu, Julie, 264, 279
Meis, Morgan, 187
Mellon, Andrew, 70–72, 79, 116
Mellon Collection, 73
Mellon, Paul, 79
memento mori, 43, 215
Memories of Passersby I (Klingemann), 260
Méneux, Catherine, 99
Las Meninas (Velázquez), 222
Merda d'artista (Artist's Shit) (Manzoni), 229, **232**
Merisi, Michelangelo. *See* Caravaggio
Metamorphoses (Ovid), 76–77
Metapurse, 257
Metropolitan Museum of Art (New York), 72, 74, 77–79, 125, 135, 144, 145, 179, 264, 267
  American Painting Today, 1950, 160
  Cecily Brown: Death and the Maid (2023), 266
  Harlem on My Mind: Cultural Capital of Black America, 1900–1968 (1969), 178, **178**, 179
  The Harlem Renaissance and Transatlantic Modernism (2024), 183n12
Meules (Haystacks) (Monet), 104, 105
Meurent, Victorine, 98, 100, 109, **110**
Mexican Muralism, 143, 147–48
Mexican pottery, 135
Mexico, 243
Micas, Nathalie, 88
Michelangelo, 24, 28, 29, 42, 44, 53, 78, 81, 156
  David, 24, 29
  The Deluge, 30
  Madonna and Child (Madonna of Bruges), 29–30
  Pietà, 29
  Sistine Chapel frescoes, 29–31, **30**
  Venus and Cupid, 26
Michelle LaVaughn Robinson Obama (Sherald), 263, **263**
Middle Ages, 12–35
The Migration Series (Lawrence), 173–74
The Milkmaid (Vermeer), 47
The Mill (Rembrandt), 71
millennials, 236, 247–48, 257, 261–62
Miller, Dorothy C., 143, 159
Miller, Lee, 271
Milwaukee Art Center, 188
Minimal art, 188
Minimalism, 165, 191, 196, 222, 261
miracolo italiano (Italian miracle), 228
The Miraculous Journey (Hirst), 274
Mirvish, David, 198
Mitchell, Joan, 147, 158, 162–65, 167n39, 196
Mitterrand, François, 242
M+ Museum (Hong Kong), 241
Mnuchin Gallery, 177
models, 109–10
Moderna Museet (Stockholm), 193
modern art market, 112–41
modernism, 113–14
Modesti, Adelina, 83, 92n47
Modestini, Dianne, 66, 67
Modigliani, Amedeo, 69, 110, 120, 129, 131, 137, 138, 240, 247
Mohammed bin Salman, 69, 274–75
Mona Lisa (Leonardo), 31, 79
Mona Lisa (Warhol), 79
Monconys, Balthasar de, 46
Mondrian, Piet, 189
Monet, Claude, 97, 99, **99**, 101, 103–5, **105**, 108, 133, 241
monopsony, 52–61
Montecassino Abbey, 15
Montefeltros, 13, 21
Monte, Francesco Mario del, 43
Monumenta commissions (Grand Palais, 2016), 244
Morandi, Giorgio, 241
Morgan, Jessica, 267
Morgan, J. P., 71, 74
Morgan Library & Museum (New York), 70
Morisot, Berthe, 77, 101, 109
Morozov, Ivan Abramovich, 113, 127, 133, 134, 134
Morozov, Mikhail, 113, 127, 133, **134**
Morris, Robert, 192
Moscheroni, Alessandro, 30
Moscheroni, Giovanni, 30
Moscow City Gallery (Moscow), 133
Moser, Mary, 89
Mosqueteros (Musketeers) (Picasso), 221–24
Motherwell, Robert, 151, **160**, 202
Motley, Archibald John, Jr., 174, **174**
Moulin de la Galette, 109
Mountains and Sea (Frankenthaler), 164
Mousquetaire à la pipe (Picasso), 227, **227**
Muhammad Dervish Khan, 81, 89
Mural (Mehretu), 279
Mural (Pollock), **153**
Murphy, Rysia, 278
Murrell, Denise, 183n12
Musée d'Art Moderne de la Ville de Paris, 281n24
Musée de l'Orangerie (Paris), 105, 131
Musée de Montmartre (Paris), 281n24
Musée d'Orsay (Paris), 88, 98, 100, 107
Musée du Louvre (Paris), 26, 31, 33, 45, 56, 64, 69, 104, 125, 150, 222, 267
  Louvre Abu Dhabi, 69, 276, **276**
  Salon Carré, 96
Musée du Luxembourg (Paris), 86–87, 106, 108, 126
Museo di Palazzo Grimani (Venice), 167n39
Museo Nacional Centro de Arte Reina Sofía (Madrid), 136
Museo Nacional del Prado (Madrid), 85, 92n36
Museum of Art, Carnegie Institute (Pittsburgh), 78
Museum of Contemporary Art Chicago (MCA Chicago), 264
Museum of Contemporary Art, Los Angeles (MOCA), 193, 264
Museum of Fine Arts, Boston, 67, 109
Museum of Fine Arts, Houston, 163, 182
Museum of Islamic Art (Qatar), 274
Museum of Modern Art (MoMA), 119, 125, 135–36, 143, 145, 149, 152, 153, 155, 157–60, 164, 174, 176, 180, 186, 189, 191, 201, 267

Betye Saar: The Legends of "Black Girl's Window" (2019–20), 183n11
Cubism and Abstract Art (1936), 135
Fantastic Art, Dada, Surrealism (1936–37), 135, 148, 270
Ileana Sonnabend: Ambassador for the New (2013), 194
Indian Art of the United States (1941), 148–49
International Program, 159
Lee Krasner: A Retrospective (1983), 163
Meret Oppenheim: My Exhibition (2022–23), 281n24
The New American Painting (1958–59), 159, 194
Picasso: Forty Years of His Art (1939–40), 136–37
Refik Anadol: Unsupervised (2022–23), 258–59
Sixteen Americans (1959–60), 190, 191
museums, 202. *See also specific museums by name*
blockbuster exhibitions, 137, 220–33
in China, 238–41
curators, 278
directors, 267
exhibitions in commercial galleries, 220–33
The Music (Matisse), 134
My Bed (Emin), 213

N

Nabataeans, 275
Nadar, 99
Nafea faa ipoipo? (When Will You Marry?) (Gauguin), 274
Tibor de Nagy gallery (New York), 163
Naifeh, Steven, 148, 152
Naissance de Vénus (Birth of Venus) (Cabanel), 100, **100**
Nanas series (Saint Phalle), 205
Nantong Museum (China), 238–39
Napoleon I, 96
Napoleon III, 96, 100, 102
The Nation, 153, 158, 160
National Art Museum of China (Beijing), 242, 243, **243**
National Association for the Advancement of Colored People (NAACP), 170, 173
National Gallery (London), 31, 67, 84, 92n36, 241
National Gallery of Art (Washington, DC), 47, 70, 73, 77, 79, 129, 156, 197, 243
National Gallery of Victoria Triennial, 260
National Geographic, 191
National Portrait Gallery (Washington, DC), 263
National Urban League, 173
Native American art, 143, 147, 148–49, 266–67
Native Americans, 71, 144
natura morta, 43
Nauman, Bruce, 192
Nazi Germany, 116, 126, 128, 165, 267
Nelli, Plautilla, 80, **80**, 81
Nelson-Atkins Museum of Art, Kansas City, 77
Nelson, Jonathan K., 27
Nengudi, Senga, 169, 180
Neo-Dada, 185
Netherlands, 38–40, 47
Nevelson, Louise, 161
The New American Painting (MoMA, 1958–59), 159, 194
New Art Dealers Alliance, 277–78
New Deal, 146, 173
New Gallery (New York), 164
Newhouse, S. I., 261, 262
Newman, Barnett, 147, 154, 158, **160**, 187, 203
New Museum (New York), 206, 267
The New Negro, 170
Newport Street Gallery (London), 216
New World Development Company, 239
New York City, New York, 108, 161, 202–3, 222, 277
Abstract Expressionism, 142–67
Harlem Renaissance, 169–70, 173, 183n12
SoHo neighborhood, 192
New Yorker, 152, 191, 240
New York Herald Tribune, 160
New-York Historical Society, 144
New York Public Library, 74, 171, 173
New York School, 147, 158–60
New York State Pavilion (World's Fair, 1964–65), 201
New York Times, 69, 155, 160, 226, 231
New York World's Fair, 171
NFTs (non-fungible tokens), 216–17, 257, 258, 261, 272
Nicholas II, 71
Nicolaes Ruts (Rembrandt), 41, 74
"Night Art Museum" initiative (HOW Art Museum), 241
Night Journeys (Krasner), 163
The Night Watch (Rembrandt), 41
Nine Discourses on Commodus (Twombly), 188
nineteenth century, 86–90
Ninth Street Show (1951), 162–64, 186, 189
No. 14, 1960 (Rothko), **154**
noblesse de robe (nobility of the robe), 60
noblewomen, 80–81
Nochlin, Linda, 78, 82–83, 204
non-fungible tokens (NFTs), 216–17, 257, 258, 261, 272
Norberg-Schulz, Christian, 15
North, Michael, 39, 49
Nosei, Annina, 265
Annina Nosei Gallery (New York), 265
Nouveau Réalisme, 193
nouveaux riche, 71
Nouvel, Jean, 274, 276
Nu couché (Reclining Nude) (Modigliani), 240
Nude, Green Leaves and Bust (Picasso), 217
Number 1, 1949 (Pollock), 155
Number 1, 1950 (Lavender Mist) (Pollock), **149**
Number 1A, 1948 (Pollock), 155
Number 17, 1951 (Pollock), 164
Numbers series (Johns), 189
nuns, 80–81
Nuova pittura cinese (New Chinese Painting) (1993), 246
Nymphéas en fleur (Water Lilies in Bloom) (Monet), 104, **105**

O

Obama, Barack, 263
Obama, Michelle, 263, **263**
Odoacer, 14
O'Hara, Frank, 186
O'Keeffe, Georgia, 145, 147, 268, 270
Oldenburg, Claes, 187, 205

old masters, 70, 78–81, 268
Olivier, Fernande, 110
Olympia (Manet), 100, **100**, 109
Olympic Sculpture Park (Seattle), 249
One Hundred Layers of Ink series (Yang), **244**
online sales, 254
Oppenheim, Meret, 281n24
Opportunity, 173
Orange, Red, Yellow (Rothko), 164
Oriental America (Brockman Gallery, 1969), 181
Orozco, José Clemente, 147, 148
Orsini, Clarice, 23
Osservatore Romano, 196
Otis Art Institute, 176
Otto I, 16, 17
Ottoman Empire, 39
Otto of Saxony, 16
Ovid, 76–77
Oxford University, 18

P

Pace, 238
Pacific Railroad, 71
The Painter's Studio (Courbet), 96
Painting (de Kooning), 158
Pakistani artists, 255
Palace Museum (Beijing), 236, 239
Palais de l'Industrie (Paris), 97
Palais des Papes (Avignon), 224, **224**, 226
Palais de Versailles, 56, 58–60
Palatine Chapel, 16
Palazzo Barbaro (Venice), 75
Palazzo Grassi (Venice), 216, **216**
Palazzo Venier dei Leoni (Venice), 150, **150**
Pand market, 49
Panorama gallery (Amsterdam), 118
Panza di Biumo, Giuseppe, 193
Papal States, 13
Paris Agreement, 272
Paris Commune, 96
Paris, France, 29, 95, 113, 276, 277
  American artists in, 165, 171
  Gertrude Stein's apartment, 123, **123**, 124, 126
  redesign, 102, **102**
Parish, Alex, 63, 67
Paris Salon (1801), 90
Paris University, 18
Parks, Gordon, 163
Parsons, Betty, 143, 154, 194, 277
Betty Parsons Gallery (New York), 154–55, 163, 186
Parsons School of Design (New York), 186
Parthenon, 53
Partisan Review, 158
Pasadena Museum of Art, 190
Le Passage (Sage), 271
Passaggio a Oriente (Passage to the Orient) (1993), 246
Pasternak, Anne, 267
Pastoral Concert (Titian), 98
The Pastry Chef (Le Pâtissier) (Soutine), 131, 137
Past Times (Marshall), 264, **264**
Patinir, Joachim, 40
Le Pâtissier (The Pastry Chef) (Soutine), 131, 137
patronage
  Church, 14–15
  female, 13–14, 25–26, 82
  private, 18–22, 31, 60
  in Qatar, Saudi Arabia, and Abu Dhabi, 273–76, 279
  Renaissance, 13, 18, 19–20, 273, 276
  royal, 16
  state, 60
Patry, Sylvie, 108
Patton, Sharon F., 175, 181
Pavillon du Réalisme (Pavilion of Realism), 95, 96
Pazzi conspiracy, 23
Peace of Münster, 38
"La Peau de l'Ours" (the Skin of the Bear) auction (1914), 113, 128–29
Peeters, Clara, 44, 85
Peggy Guggenheim Collection (Venice), 150
Pei, I. M., 79, 274
Peintres Femmes, 1780–1830: Naissance d'un combat (Women Painters, 1780–1830: The Birth of a Battle) (Musée du Luxembourg, 2021), 86–87
Pennsylvania Academy of the Fine Arts (Philadelphia), 166n1
Penny, Nicholas, 67
Penone, Giuseppe, **275**
People's Republic of China (PRC). *See* China
Péret, Benjamin, 269
Perls, Frank, 196
Perrotin, 238
Perugino, Pietro, 25
Peters, Mrs. Donald, 190
Petit Palais, Paris, 222
Petukhov, Alexey, 133
Phantasy II (Lewis), **148**
Pharmacy (Sotheby's, 2004), 214
Phidias, 53
Philadelphia Museum of Art, 119, 196, 261
Philip, Duke of Anjou, 56
Philip II (Philip Augustus), 38, 56
Philip II of Spain, 77, 81
Philip, Lord Wharton (Van Dyck), 79
Philip V of Spain, 83
Phillips auction house, 205, 235, 237, 256, 273
Phillips Collection (Washington, DC), 174
Phillips, Lisa, 267
Phillips London, 255, 264
Phillips New York, 177, 256, 264
photography, 271
The Physical Impossibility of Death in the Mind of Someone Living (Hirst), 214
Picabia, Francis, 130
Picasso, Claude, 223
Picasso, Pablo, 69, 78, 110, 117, **121**, 121–22, 127, 137, 145, 185, 189, 212, **223**, 242
  Acrobat and Young Harlequin, 137
  The Acrobat's Family with a Monkey, 123
  Armory Show (New York, 1913), 135
  The Ascetic, 137
  Blue Period, 120, 122, 123
  Claude and Paloma, 247
  Composition: The Pheasants, **138**
  dealers, 113
  Les Demoiselles d'Avignon, 124–25, **125**, 127, 133, 136, 137
  Exposition Picasso (Galeries Georges Petit, 1932), **132**, 133, 137
  Family of Saltimbanques, 129, **129**
  Fillette à la corbeille fleurie (Young Girl with a Basket of Flowers), 124
  Forty Years of His Art (MoMA, 1939–40), 136–37

Gertrude Stein and Pablo Picasso: The Invention of Language (Musée du Luxembourg, 2023–24), 126
Girl before a Mirror, 136
Guernica, 136, 137, 149
Hommage à Pablo Picasso (Paris, 1966), 222
Homme à la pipe, 227
The Last Years, 1963–1973 (Guggenheim, 1984), 221
market for, 226–27
Matisse et Picasso (1918), 130–31
The Mediterranean Years (1945–1962) (Gagosian, 2010), 225
Mosqueteros (Gagosian, 2009), 221–24, **225**, 225–27, 231
Mosqueteros (Musketeers), 221–22
Mousquetaire à la pipe, 227
Nude, Green Leaves and Bust, 217
Peintures et dessins: 1969–1970 (Palais des Papes, 1970), 224, 226
Picasso and Françoise Gilot: Paris–Vallauris, 1943–1953 (Gagosian, 2012), 225
Picasso and Marie-Thérèse: L'amour fou (Gagosian, 2011), 225
Picasso & the Camera (Gagosian, 2014–15), 225
Portrait de l'Homme à l'epée et à la fleur, **222**
Portrait of Gertrude Stein, 125, **126**
promotion of, 113, 122–24, 131–37
Rose Period, 129
Three Women, 123, 133
20 Years in the Evolution of Picasso, 1903–1923 (Jacques Seligmann & Co., 1937), 125
Two Women Seated at a Bar, 123
Vollard Suite, 122
Young Acrobat on a Ball, 123
Young Woman Holding a Cigarette, 138
Picasso, Paloma, 223
Piero della Francesca, 75
Pietà (Michelangelo), 29
Pilat, Agnieszka, 260
pilgrimage routes, 18
Pinacoteca Agnelli (Turin), 205
Pinault, François, 216
Pincus-Witten, Robert, 188
Pindell, Howardena, 169, 180
Pinkertons, 74
Pino, Paolo, 82
Pissarro, Camille, 96–97, 101, 103, 104, 108
Pittura/Panorama: Paintings of Helen Frankenthaler, 1952–1992 (Museo di Palazzo Grimani, 2019), 167n39
Plato, 22, 28
Pliny the Elder, 80
"Poesie" (Titian), 76–77
Pointillism, 218
Poiret, Paul, 127
The Polish Rider (Rembrandt), 74
Political Pop, 244–45
Pollock, Jackson, 105, 146–49, 151, 152, **153**, 154, 155, 158–59, **160**, 163, 187, 189
Autumn Rhythm (Number 30), 159
Mural, **153**
Number 1, 1949, 155
Number 1, 1950 (Lavender Mist), **149**
Number 1A, 1948, 155
Number 17, 1951, 164
The She Wolf, 153
Shimmering Substance, 153
Stenographic Figure, 152
Young Painters in U.S. and France (1950), 158
Pompeii, Italy, 156
Pop art, 165, 185, 187, 188, 191, 193, 194, 202–6, 222, 261, 278
Political Pop, 244–45
The World Goes Pop (Tate Modern, 2015–16), 204
Pope, John Russell, 74–75, 79
Poplars (Monet), 104
porcelain, 72, 76
Port of London Authority, 213–14
Portrait de l'Homme à l'epée et à la fleur (Picasso), **222**
Portrait of a Cardinal (El Greco), 78
Portrait of a Man with Arms Akimbo (Rembrandt), 81
Portrait of Ambroise Vollard (Cézanne), **115**
Portrait of an Artist (Pool with Two Figures) (Hockney), 262
Portrait of a Young Artist (Rembrandt), 74
Portrait of Bianca degli Utili Maselli and Her Children (Fontana), **82**
Portrait of Dr. Gachet (Van Gogh), 107
Portrait of Gertrude Stein (Picasso), 125, **126**
Portrait of Mme. Berthe Weill, Art Dealer (Kars), **120**
Portrait of Victorine Meurent (Manet), 109
portraiture, 37, 39–40
The Postman (Van Gogh), 138
Pousette-Dart, Richard, **160**
Poznanskaya, Anna, 133
Prakash, Lakshmi, 262
Prak, Maarten, 48
Predis, Ambrogio de, 31
Predis, Evangelista de, 31
Prestage, 65
prices, 72, 129
for abstract paintings, 154, 155, 161, 164, 194
for African American artworks, 174, 177, 178, 182
for American art, 159, 203
auction records, 53, 63, 68, 69, 71, 81, 91n10, 104, 107, 116, 167n46, 174, 182, 205–6, 217, 229, 232, 245, 255, 261, 262, 264, 265–66, 270–71
fixed scale, 121, 127
for Impressionist paintings, 108
for old masters paintings, 46, 49–50, 81, 85
for Pop art, 188, 194, 201
Prince of Wales, 90
Prince, Richard, 261
private academies, 90
private patronage, 18–22, 31, 60
Prix de Rome, 56
Procession of the Magi (Gozzoli), 24, **24**
The Procuress (Vermeer), 46
professional artists, women, 80–83
professionalization of women artists, 86–90
The Progress of Love (Fragonard), 74
Prometheus (Orozco), 148
propaganda, 31, 53
Proposte monocrome, epoca blu (Monochrome Proposition, Blue Epoch) (Galleria Apollinaire, 1957), 228
Proust, Marcel, 47
Pruitt, Rob, 231
public auctions, 254
public collections, 267
public commissions, 171

Public Works of Art Project, 173
Punta della Dogana (Venice), 216, **216**
Pushkin State Museum of Fine Arts (Moscow), 134
Putzel, Howard, 152, 154

Q

Qatar, 67, 273–74, 279
Qatar Museums Authority, 274
Qatar National Library, 274
Qatar National Museum, 274
Quarles, Christina, 271
Queen's House (Greenwich), 85
Quek Jie Ann, 247–48
quilts, 205–6
Quinn, John, 135
Quinn, Marc, 213
Quistelli, Lucrezia, 80, 82

R

Rabinow, Rebecca, 123
Raboteurs de parquet (The Floor Scrapers) (Caillebotte), 106, **106**
racism, 70–71
Raimondi, Marcantonio, 98
Rainbow Mojo (Saar), 178
The Raising of the Cross (also called Elevation of the Cross) (Rubens), 44
Random House, 233n1
The Rape of Europa (Titian), 76–77
Raphael, 29–31, 42, 44, 53, 75, 241
  Alba Madonna, 79
  Judgment of Paris, 98
  The School of Athens, 28, **28**
Rauschenberg, Robert, 185–86, 189–90, 195–96, 231
  Bed, **190**, 191
  Black Paintings, 186
  Combines, 190–91, 193, 203
  Erased de Kooning Drawing, 186
  Red Paintings, 186
  Robert Rauschenberg exhibition, Venice Biennale, 1964 June 21 (Kender and Shunk), 195
  ROCI (Rauschenberg Overseas Culture Interchange), 243
  Short Circuit, 187
  Sixteen Americans (1959–60), 191
  Thaw, 203
  White Paintings, 186
Rawsthorne, Isabel, 225
Raysse, Martial, 196
The Reader (Amos), **175**
realism, 143
  Cynical Realism, 244–45
  Manifesto of Realism, 96
  Nouveau Réalisme, 193
  Pavillon du Réalisme (Pavilion of Realism), 95, 96
  Regional Realism, 146–47
  Socialist Realism, 242
Rech, Almine, 237–38
Red Gate Gallery (Beijing), 237
Redmond, Roland L., 160
Redon, Odilon, 123
Red Paintings (Rauschenberg), 186
Red Vineyard at Arles, Montmajour (Van Gogh), 118
refusés ("refused" artists), 96–97
Regional Realism, 146–47
Reinhardt, Ad, **160**
rejected commissions, 32–33
relics, 18
Rembrandt van Rijn, 39–42, 49, 50, 71, 76, 78, 221, 223, 241
  The Anatomy Lesson of Dr. Nicolaes Tulp, 41–42, **42**
  Aristotle with a Bust of Homer, 72
  The Mill, 71
  Nicolaes Ruts, 74
  The Polish Rider, 74
  Portrait of a Man with Arms Akimbo, 81
  Portrait of a Young Artist, 74
  Self-Portrait, 74
Remembering (Ai), 246
Renaissance, 22, 48, 53, 269
  artist's status in, 26–29
  Carolingian, 16
  patronage in, 13, 18, 19–20, 21–26, 273–74, 276
René, Denise, 194
Renoir, Pierre-Auguste, 97, 101, 103, 104, 106, 108, 123, 137
  Bal du moulin de la Galette (Dance at the Moulin de la Galette), 107, **107**
  Goldschmidt auction (Sotheby's, 1958), 116
Renovatio Carolingia (Carolingian renovation), 16
Renzo Piano Building Workshop, 241
Restany, Pierre, 193
Rewald, John, 107
Reynolds, Joshua, 79, 89
Rice, Dan, 156
Richardson, John, 122, 125, 127, 128, 131, 222, **223**, 224–26, 233n1
Richelieu, Cardinal, 56
Richter, Gerhard, 261
Rietveld, Gerrit, 119
Rigaud, Hyacinthe, 56–57, **57**
Rijksmuseum, 46, 47
Ringgold, Faith, 175, 205–6
Ritual (Lewis), 265
Rivera, Diego, 147, 270
robber barons, 71
Robbins, Anne, 101
Robson, A. Deirdre, 145, 161, 202
Roché, Henri-Pierre, 125
ROCI (Rauschenberg Overseas Culture Interchange), 243
Rockefeller, Abby Aldrich, 135, 155
Rockefeller, David, 123
Rockefeller, John D., 71
Rockefeller, Peggy, 123
Rockefellers, 70
Rococo style, 60
Rodchenko, Alexander, 134
Rodin, Auguste, 145
Roe, Sue, 96, 101
Rokeby Venus (Velázquez), 100
Roldán, Luisa Ignacia (La Roldana), 83
The Roll Call (Thompson), 90
Roman basilicas, 15, 28, 29, 31, 37
Roman Catholic Church, 14–15, 37, 39, 196, 276
  Benozzo Gozzoli's Magi Chapel frescoes, 24, **24**
  Giotto's Scrovegni Chapel frescoes, 9, 19–20, **20**
  Sistine Chapel, 23, 28, 29–31, **30**
Roman Empire, 13, 14
Romanesque architecture, 17

Rome, Italy, 25, 29, 31
Rooftop Party with Ghosts 1 (Toor), 255
Roosevelt, Franklin D., 79, 146
Roosevelt, Theodore, 145
Roque, Jacqueline, 222, **223**
The Rose (Twombly), 188
Rosenberg, Alexandre, 131
Rosenberg, Harold, 143, 152, **157**, 157–58
Rosenberg, Léonce, 131
Rosenberg, Paul, 113, 131–34, 137, 277
Rosenblum, Robert, 190
Rosenquist, James, 187, 191
Rosenthal, Norman, 214
Rosenwald Fellowship, 171
Rosenwald, Lessing J., 79
Rosler, Martha, 206
Ross, Charles, 197
Rossi, Properzia de', 80
Rothko Chapel, Houston, **156**, 157
Rothko, Mark, 105, 145, 147, 151, 153, 154, 156–58, **160**, 202
  No. 14, 1960, **154**
  Orange, Red, Yellow, 164
  Young Painters in U.S. and France (1950), 158
Rotterdam, Holland, 50
Rouault, Georges, 120
Rouen Cathedral (Monet), 104
Rousseau, Henri, 133
Rovere, Giuliano della, 31
Royal Academy of Architecture (Académie Royale d'Architecture), 56
Royal Academy of Arts (London), 89–90, 92n36, 214
Royal Academy of Dance (Académie Royale de Danse), 56
Royal Academy of Painting and Sculpture (Academie Royale de Peinture et de Sculpture), 55–56
Royal Collection, 65
Royal Commission for AlUla, 275
Royal Fireworks (Frankenthaler), 164
royal manufactories, 54–55
Royal Manufactories of Furniture of the Crown (Manufactures Royales des Meubles de la Couronne) (Gobelins), 54–56
royal patronage, 16
Roy, Pierre, 130
Rubens, Peter Paul, 33, 42, 44–45, 221
  The Descent from the Cross, 44, **45**
  The Massacre of the Innocents, 81
Rubens, Philip, 44
Rubin, William, 198
Ruisdael, Jacob van, 41
Ruiz-Picasso, Bernard, 225, 226
Rupf, Hermann, 127
Russia, 133, 134, 137
Russian Revolution, 134
Ruysch, Rachel, 44, 85–86, **86**
Rybolovlev, Dmitry, 67–69

S

Saadiyat Island, Abu Dhabi, 276, 281n31
Saar, Betye, 169, 177–78, 183n11
Saatchi, Charles, 214
Saatchi Collection (London), 214
Saenredam, Pieter Jansz, 48
Sage, Kay, 269, 271
Sagot, Clovis, 123
Saint-André, Simon Renard de, **55**
Saint-Denis, France, 17
Sainte-Chapelle (Paris), 18
Saint John (Donatello), 19–20
Saint Mark's Basilica (Venice), 18
Saint Matthew and the Angel (Caravaggio), 32–33
Saint Peter's Basilica (Rome), 18, 28, 29, 31, 37
Saint Phalle, Niki de, 196, 205
Saito, Ryoei, 107
Salai, 65
sales value, 161
Salmon, André, 124–25
Salon d'Antin, 124–25
Salon d'Automne (Autumn Salon), 97, 117, 121, 122–23, 128
Salon de Paris, 96
Salon des Indépendants (Salon of the Independents), 97, 118, 127
Salon des Refusés (Salon of the Refused), 56, 95, 96–97, 101, 144
Salon of Contemporary Negro Art (New York), 172
Saltzman, Cynthia, 71, 76
Salvator Mundi (Hollar), 63, **64**, 65
Salvator Mundi (Leonardo), 63, **64**, 64–66, **66**, 67–69
SAMO©, 265
San Francisco Museum of Modern Art, 167n39, 186
Sangallo, Giuliano da, 23
San Paolo fuori le mura (Saint Paul Outside the Walls), 15
Santa Caterina di Cafaggio (Florence), 81
Santa Maria della Carità, Padua, 18–20, **20**
Santa Maria della Scala (Rome), 33
Santa Maria Maggiore, 15
Santa Pudenziana, 15
Santa Sabina, 15
Santiago de Compostela (Spain), 18
Saraceni, Carlo, 33
Sargent, John Singer, **75**, 75–76, 144
Sarmant, Thierry, 54
Saudi Arabia, 69, 273, 274–75
Saudi Arabia Museum of Contemporary Art (SAMoCA), 275
Saudi Vision 2030, 274–75
Savage, Augusta, 170, **171**, 171–72, **172**, 173, 174
Savage Studio of Arts and Crafts, 170, 171–72
Savonarola, Girolamo, 23–24
Savonnerie, 54
Saxons, 14
Scaccia, Beatrice, 271
Schama, Simon, 188
Schapira, Ileana, 192, 194–95
Schirn Kunsthalle Frankfurt, 281n24
Schneider, Tim, 218
Schomburg Center for Research in Black Culture, 171
The School of Athens (Raphael), 28, **28**
School of Paris, 196
Schuffenecker, Émile, 117
Schwitters, Kurt, 190
Schwob, Lucy. *See* Cahun, Claude
Scott, William Edouard, 174
Scrovegni Chapel (Santa Maria della Carità, Padua), 9, 19–20, **20**

Scrovegni, Enrico, 20
Scrovegni, Reginaldo, 20
Scull auction (Sotheby Parke Bernet, 1973), 203
Scull, Ethel, 198, 203
Scull, Robert, 190, 198, 203
sculptors, 27, 83
sculpture, 15, 17, 83, 130, 205
Sculpture of Black Africa: The Paul Tishman Collection (LACMA, 1968), 179
Scultura viventi (Living Sculptures) (Manzoni), 229, **230**
Scuola dei Tedeschi (School of the Germans), 27
Seagram Building, 156
Sears, Willard T., 75
Seated Riffian (Le Rifain assis) (Matisse), **138**
Seattle Art Museum (SAM), 249
Seattle Asian Art Museum, 249
secondary markets, 211, 217–18, 253, 256, 258, 260 273
Secrest, Meryle, 72
Sedley, Catharine, 65
Seedbed (Acconci), 195
Self (Quinn), 213
Self-Portrait (Meurent), 109, **110**
Self-Portrait (Rembrandt), 74
Self-Portrait as the Allegory of Painting (La Pittura) (Gentileschi), **84**
Self-Portrait at the Easel (Anguissola), 82
Self Portrait in a Straw Hat (Vigée Le Brun), **87**
Seligmanns, 70
Selldorf, Annabelle, 226, 230
Selldorf Architects, 75
Sensation (Royal Academy of Arts, 1997), 214
Serra, Richard, 192, 273–74
Servicemen's Readjustment Act of 1944 (GI Bill), 165
Seurat, Georges, 113
Sforza, Galeazzo Maria, 24
Sforza, Ludovico ("il Moro"), 25
Sforzas, 13, 21
Shadows (Warhol), 240
Shakespeare, William, 223
Shanghai Biennale, 246
Shanghai Cultural Relics Management Commission, 237
Shanghai Metro, 241
Shanghai Museum, 236
Shaw, Anny, 278
Shchukin, Sergei, 113, 123, 124, 127, 133–34, **134**
Sheffield, Charles Herbert, 65
Sheffield, John, 65
Sherald, Amy, 263, **263**, 264
Sherman, Cindy, 261
The She Wolf (Pollock), 153
Shimmering Substance (Pollock), 153
Short Circuit (Rauschenberg), 187
Shunk, Harry, **194**, 195
Sidney Janis Gallery, 158
Sidra Medicine (Qatar), 274
Signac, Paul, 113
Silk road, 19
Silver Car Crash (Double Disaster) (Warhol), 261
Simmons, Laurie, 259
Simon, Robert, 63, 66, 67
Sinclair, Anne, 132
Siqueiros, David Alfaro, 147, 148
Sirani, Elisabetta, 83
Sisley, Alfred, 97, 101, 103, 104, 108, 134
Sisters in Pink (Taku), 256
Sistine Chapel, 23, 28, 29–31, **30**
Sixteen Americans (MoMA, 1959–60), 190, 191
Sixtus IV, 29, 30
Skin of the Bear ("La Peau de l'Ours") auction (1914), 113, 128–29
Sluijter, Eric Jan, 49
Small False Start (Johns), 261
Small, Zachary, 257
Smee, Sebastian, 124
Smith, David, 189
Smith, Gregory White, 148, 152
Smith, Jaune Quick-to-See, 266–67
Smith, Roberta, 221, 226
Smithson, Robert, 197
soak-stain technique, 164
Socialist Realism, 242
social media, 248, 255
social status, 72
Societe Anonyme des Artistes Peintres, Sculpteurs, Graveurs, etc. (Anonymous Society of Painters, Sculptors, Engravers, etc.), 99–103
Société des Artistes Français (Society of French Artists), 109
Société le Droit des Femmes (Society for the Rights of Women), 90
Société Nationale des Beaux-Arts (National Society of Fine Arts), 110
Socle du monde (Base of the World) (Manzoni), 231
soft sculptures, 205
Solanas, Valerie, 200
Solomon, Alan, 191, 198
Solomon, Deborah, 148
Ileana Sonnabend Gallery (Paris), 193–98, 201
Sonnabend, Ileana, 185, 189, 192–95, 197–99, 277
  Castelli-Sonnabend model, 197–98, 277
  Ileana Sonnabend (Kender and Shunk), **194**
  Ileana Sonnabend: Ambassador for the New (MoMA, 2013), 194
Sonnabend, Michael, 190, 193, 195
Sotheby Parke Bernet, 203
Sotheby's, 67, 69, 235, 237, 248, 273
Sotheby's London, 81, 217, 232, 271
  20th Century Italian Art auction (1997), 229–30
  Damien Hirst: Beautiful Inside My Head Forever auction (Sotheby's, 2008), 211–12, **212**, **213**, 217, 218
  Goldschmidt auction (1958), 116
  Pharmacy auction (2004), 214
Sotheby's New York, 81, 104, 107, 164, 174, 178, 188, 205–6, 212, 227, 229, 255, 261, 262, 264, 265, 270
Soulages, Pierre, 158
Soutine, Chaïm, 129, 137, 138
Spain, 38, 136, 137
Spanish painting, 77
Spaulding, John, 135
Spawforth, Tony, 59–60
Sperone, Gian Enzo, 198
Spiral collective (New York), 175
Spiral Jetty (Smithson), 197
Spot Challenge (Hirst), **215**, 216
Spot paintings (Hirst), **215**, 215–16
Springford, Vivian, 161
"Spring Salons for Young Artists" (Art of This Century, 1943), 152

Stable Gallery (New York), 163, 164, 187, 188, 201, 202
stained-glass windows, 15
Staller, Ilona (La Cicciolina), 195
Stamos, Theodoros, **160**
Stanze (Vatican), 28, 31
Star Axis (Ross), 197
The Starry Night (Van Gogh), 114
the Stars (Xing Xing), 242, **243**
state patronage, 60
State Tretyakov Gallery (Moscow), 133
Statuary in Wood by African Savages: The Root of Modern Art (291, 1914), 130, **130**
St. Charles Gallery (New Orleans), 63, 66
Stedelijk Museum (Amsterdam), 119, 193
Steichen, Edward, **130**
Steinberg, Leo, 190
Stein, Gertrude, 113, 122–26, 133, 138
  apartment, 123, **123**, 124, 126
  Gertrude Stein and Pablo Picasso: The Invention of Language (Musée du Luxembourg, 2023–24), 126
  Portrait of Gertrude Stein (Picasso), 125, **126**
Stein, Leo, 113, 122–24, 133, 138
Stella, Frank, 191, 193, 231
Stenographic Figure (Pollock), 152
Sterne, Hedda, 160, **160**
Stevens, Alfred, 107
Stevens, Mark, 155
Stiattesi, Pierantonio, 84
Stieglitz, Alfred, 130, 135, 144–45
Still, Clyfford, 146, 151, 153, 154, 158, **160**
still life, 37, 43–44
Still Life with a Skull and a Writing Quill (Claesz), **43**
Still Life with Flowers in a Vase on a Ledge with a Dragonfly, Caterpillar, and Butterfly (Ruysch), **86**
stockpiling, 117
stonemason (comacine) masters, 26–27
Stone, Richard, 213–14
Stourton, James, 116
Strider, Marjorie, 206, **206**
Strike (Pinacoteca Agnelli, 2023), 205
Strinati, Claudio, 48
St. Thomas, 101
Studio Museum (Harlem), 179, 182, 267
Study for Portrait of Lucian Freud (Bacon), 262
Suger, Abbot, 17
Sullivan, Mary Quinn, 135
Sundaresan, Vignesh, 257
Sun King. *See* Louis XIV
Surrealism, 143, 148, 152, 165, 192, 222, 268–71
  L'Amour fou: Photography and Surrealism (Corcoran, 1985), 271
  Angels of Anarchy: Women Artists and Surrealism (Manchester Art Gallery, 2009–10), 281n24
  Fantastic Art, Dada, Surrealism (MoMA, 1936–37), 135, 148, 270
  Fantastic Women: Surreal Worlds from Meret Oppenheim to Louise Bourgeois (2020), 281n24
  Surréalisme au féminin? (Musée de Montmartre, 2023), 281n24
Susanna and the Elders (Gentileschi), 85
Swan, Annalyn, 155
Swann Galleries, 263
Sweeney, James Johnson, 153, 154, 159
Swynnerton, Annie, 89
Symphony in White, No. 1: The White Girl (Whistler), 144
Syson, Luke, 67
Szeemann, Harald, 246
Sze, Sarah, 267

T

Taku, Emmanuel, 256
A Tale of Two Women Painters: Sofonisba Anguissola and Lavinia Fontana exhibition (Prado, 2016), 92n36
Taliban, 19
Tang dynasty art, 137
Tanguy, Père, 115, 117, 152
Tanguy, Yves, 151, 269, 271
Tanner, Henry Ossawa, 144
Tanning, Dorothea, 150, 269, 270–71, 281n24
tapestries, 54, 55, 72, 76, 205–6
Targets series (Johns), 187, 189
Target with Four Faces (Johns), 189
La Tartaruga (Rome), 188
Tas, Sara, 118
Tasseau, Vérane, 128
Tassi, Agostino, 83–84
Tate Modern (London), 156, 204, 267, 281n24
Taylor, Francis Henry, 160
Teicher, Max, 278
Tek, Budi, 240
Temkin, Ann, 194
TFP Farrells and Arup, 241
Thannhauser, Heinrich, 117, 128
Thaw (Rauschenberg), 203
Theodosius I, 18
The Pastry Chef (Le Pâtissier) (Soutine), 137
This Is Tomorrow (Whitechapel Gallery, 1956), 187
Thompson, Don, 72, 109, 278
Thompson, Elizabeth (Lady Butler), 90
Thompson, Jennifer A., 106
Thoré-Bürger, Étienne-Joseph-Théophile, 46
Three Women (Picasso), 123, 133
Tibet, 243
Tiffany, Louis Comfort, 78
Timelapse (Guggenheim Museum, 2023), 267
Times Square Show (1980), 265
Tinari, Philip, 242
Tinterow, Gary, 77, 122
Tintoretto, 44
Tippoo Sahib, 89
Titanic, 150
Titian, 25, 29, 42, 44, 75, 76–77, 98, 100, 241
tokenization, 258
Toklas, Alice B., 126
Tomkins, Calvin, 185, 186, 189, 191, 193, 198, 202–3
Tomlin, Bradley Walker, **160**
Tool Paintings series (Lozano), 205
Toor, Salman, 255
Toulouse-Lautrec, Henri de, 109, 122, 123, 145
Tour of Holland, 49–50
Toward Mont Sainte-Victoire (Cézanne), 138
Toyen, l'écart absolu (Musée d'Art Moderne de la Ville de Paris, 2022), 281n24
Treadway Toomey Auctions, 174
Tremaine, Emily and Burton, 198
Los Tres Grandes (the Three Greats), 147–48
Tretyakov, Pavel and Sergei, 133
Treves, Letizia, 85, 92n36
Triptych II (Beach Girl) (Strider), **206**

Trubetskoy Palace (Moscow), 133–34
Tucker, Marcia, 164
tulip mania, 39
Twain, Mark, 70
Twitter (now X), 247
Two Centuries of Black American Art (LACMA, 1976–77), 170
Two Flags (Johns), 190
Twombly, Cy, 188, 203, 207n7, 265
Two Women Seated at a Bar (Picasso), 123
Tyrannosaurus rex, 91n10

U

UBS, 254, 258, 262, 278–79
UCCA Clay, 240, **240**
UCCA Dune, 240
UCCA Edge, 240
UCCA Group, 240
Uhde, Wilhelm, 127
Uhovski, Valentine, **215**
Ullens Center for Contemporary Art (UCCA), 240, **240**
Ullens, Guy, 240
Ullens, Myriam, 240
ultra-contemporary artists, 268
ultramarine blue, 13, 19, 27
Uncertain Future (Jack Hanley Gallery, 2022), 258
UNESCO World Heritage Sites, 275
Union Pacific Railroad, 71
United Arab Emirates (UAE)
  Abu Dhabi, 275–76
  Saadiyat Island, 276, 281n31
United States, 90, 134–37, 143–45, 275
  economic growth, 187
  Federal Art Project (FAP), 145–47, 173
  GI Bill (Servicemen's Readjustment Act of 1944), 165
  Gilded Age, 70–71
  Great Depression, 146–47
  museums, 238
  Pop art, 187
  unemployment, 146, 166n4
  Works Progress Administration (WPA), 146, 170–74
United Talent Agency (UTA), 278
United World College–USA, 197
universities, 18
University of Texas at Austin, 78
Unsupervised (Anadol), 258–59
Untiled (Twombly), 188
Untitled (New York City) (Twombly), 188
Untitled, 1956 (Parks), 163
Untitled, 1959–60 (Bontecou), 205
Untitled, 1976 (Calder), 79
Untitled, 1982 (Basquiat), 53, 265, **266**
Untitled, 2000 (Hammons), 177, **177**
urbanization, 70–71
USSR, 243

V

Vacation (New York), 277
Vail, Lawrence, 150
Valadon, Suzanne, 109–10
validation, 278
valuation, 13, 27, 49, 260. *See also* prices
Van Berckhout, Pieter Teding, 46
Vandals, 14
Vanderbilt, Alva, 71
Vanderbilt, Cornelius, 71
van der Doort, Abraham, 65
van der Rohe, Ludwig Mies, 156
van de Velde, Willem the Elder, 48
van Dongen, Kees, 97
van Dyck, Anthony, 45, 79
van Eyck, Jan, 79
van Gogh-Bonger, Johanna, 117, 118–19, **119**
Van Gogh Foundation, 119
Van Gogh Museum (Amsterdam), 118, 119
van Gogh, Theo, 118–19
van Gogh, Vincent, 114, 117–19, 121, 133, 135, 241
  Goldschmidt auction (Sotheby's, 1958), 116
  Portrait of Dr. Gachet, 107
  The Postman, 138
  Red Vineyard at Arles, Montmajour, 118
  The Starry Night, **114**
  Vase with Fifteen Sunflowers, 69
van Goyen, Jan, 41
van Hoogstraten, Samuel, 41
Vanity Fair, 173
van Mieris, Frans, 48
van Ruijven, Pieter Claesz., 46
van Uylenburgh, Gerrit, 46
van Uylenburgh, Hendrick, 41, 42, 46, 49
van Veen, Otto, 44
Varo, Remedios, 269–70
Vasari, Giorgio, 28–31, 80–82
Vase with Fifteen Sunflowers (Van Gogh), 69
Vatican Museums, 28, 267
Vauxcelles, Louis, 127
Vaux-le-Vicomte, 60
Velázquez, Diego, 100, 221, 222, **222**
Venezuela, 243
Venice Biennale, 155, 159, 163, 182, 193, 243, 246, 264, 266
  Aperto (Open) section, 246
  French Pavilion, 196
  Grand Prize for Painting, 185, 195–96
  Nuova pittura cinese (New Chinese Painting) (1993), 246
  Passaggio a Oriente (Passage to the Orient) (1993), 246
  Robert Rauschenberg exhibition, Venice Biennale, 1964 June 21 (Kender and Shunk), 195
Venice, Republic of, 13
Venus and Cupid (Michelangelo), 26
Venus of Urbino (Titian), 100
Verhaecht, Tobias, 44
Vermeer, Johannes, 39, 46–47, 49, 72, 76
Vernon Branch Library, 173
Veronese, 44
Versailles, 56, **58**, 58–60
Vervoordt, Axel, 237–38
Victoria, 89
Victoria and Albert Museum (London), 26
Vida Americana: Mexican Muralists Remake American Art, 1925–1945 (Whitney, 2020–21), 147–48
Vietnam War, 187, 206
View of Delft (Vermeer), 46, 47
View of Toledo (El Greco), 78
Vigée Le Brun, Élisabeth Louise, 81, 86, 87, **87**, 88, 89
Les Vingt (Les XX), 118

The Virgin of the Rocks (Leonardo), 31, 67
Visigoths, 14
Viviano, Catherine, 271
Vlieger, Simon de, 48
Vogel, Carol, 211, 212
Vollard, Ambroise, 113–24, 131, 133, 138, 277
Vollard Suite (Picasso), 122
Voltaire, 60

W

Wadsworth Atheneum Museum of Art (Hartford), 92n36, 144
Walker, Margaret, 174
Walkers With the Dawn and Morning (Mehretu), 264
Walking Man I (Giacometti), 217
Wallace, Brian, 237
Wang Guangyi, 244
Wang Jianlin, 247
Wang Keping, 250n11
Wang Wei, 240
Ward, Eleanor, 187
Warhol, Andy, 78, 79, 185, 187, 191, **199**, 199–202, 205, 266, 277
  Campbell's Soup Cans, 199–201, **201**
  Death and Disaster series, 201
  Death in America (Sonnabend Gallery, 1964), 193
  Elvis series, 201
  Factory, 200, **200**, 202
  Gold Marilyn Monroe, 201
  Leo Castelli, **192**
  Mao, 247
  Marilyn series, 201
  Mona Lisa, 79
  Shadows, 240
  Silver Car Crash (Double Disaster), 261
  White Disaster (White Car Crash 19 Times), 261
Washington Square Gallery (New York), 128, 135
Water Lilies (Monet), 104, 105
WeChat, 248
Weill, Berthe, 120, **120**, 122
Wellesley College, 135
Werner, Michael, 278
Wesselmann, Tom, 187
West Bund Art & Design, 238
Westermann, Mariët, 267
Western Roman Empire, 14–15
Western Schism, 31
Weyant, Anna, 271
Whistler, James McNeill, 75–76, 144
Whitaker, Amy, 257, 258
Whitechapel Gallery (London), 163, 187, 190
White, Charles, 174, 176, **176**
White Cube gallery, China, 238
White Cube gallery, London, 214, 215
White Disaster (White Car Crash 19 Times) (Warhol), 261
White Flag (Johns), 187
Whitehall, London, 45
White House Artificial Intelligence Council, 259
White Numbers (Johns), 189
White Paintings (Rauschenberg), 186
Whitney Museum of American Art (New York), 164, 179, 188, 261, 266–67
  Annual Exhibition: Contemporary Painting (1959–60), 190
  Biennial (1983), 265
  Contemporary Black Artists in America (1971), 179
  How Will I Know (2020–21), 255
  Vida Americana: Mexican Muralists Remake American Art, 1925–1945 (2020–21), 147–48
Wickham, Annette, 89
Widener, Joseph E., 79
Widener, Peter Arrell Brown, 71
Wildenstein, Georges, 113, 131–34
Wildensteins, 70
Wiley, Kehinde, 255, 263
Williams, William T., 181
William the Conqueror, 17
Winkelmann, Mike. *See* Beeple
Winter Landscape with Ice Skaters (Avercamp), **40**
Woman as Landscape (de Kooning), 164
Woman I (de Kooning), **155**
women art dealers, 194–95
women artists, 44, 83–90, 261, 266–71
  31 Women (Art of This Century, 1943), 154, 270
  Abstract Expressionists, 143, 161–64
  Angels of Anarchy: Women Artists and Surrealism (Manchester Art Gallery, 2009–10), 281n24
  Dutch Golden Age painters, 85–86
  Fantastic Women: Surreal Worlds from Meret Oppenheim to Louise Bourgeois (2020), 281n24
  group shows, 281n24
  By Her Hand: Artemisia Gentileschi and Women Artists in Italy, 1500–1800 (Detroit Institute of Arts, 2021–22), 92n36
  Impressionists, 77, 101
  institutional exhibitions, 266–67
  models turned artists, 109–10
  Native American, 266–67
  noblewomen, 80–83
  nuns, 80–83
  old masters, 78–81, 268
  Peintres Femmes, 1780–1830: Naissance d'un combat (Women Painters, 1780–1830: The Birth of a Battle) (Musée du Luxembourg, 2021), 86–87
  photographers, 271
  Pop era, 204–6
  professionals, 80–83
  sculptors, 83
  solo exhibitions, 281n24
  Surréalisme au féminin? (Musée de Montmartre, 2023), 281n24
  Surrealists, 268–71
  ultra-contemporary, 268
  Women Artists: 1550–1950 (LACMA, 1976), 78
  Women of Abstract Expressionism (Denver Art Museum, 2016), 167n39
women collectors, 75–78
Women of Algiers (Delacroix), 222
women patrons, 13–14, 25–26, 82
women's suffrage, 78, 90
Wong, Tanley, **215**
Woodard, Beulah, 173
Wood, Grant, **146**, 147
Woodruff, Hale, 175
Wool, Christopher, 261
Workshop of Lucas Cranach the Elder, **38**
workshops, 45, 81
Works in Oil and Pastel by the Impressionists of Paris (1886), 108
Works Progress Administration (WPA), 146, 170–74
The World Goes Pop (Tate Modern, 2015–16), 204

World Health Organization (WHO), 280n1
World Inequality Database, 71
World's Fair (1964–65), 201
World War I, 128, 130, 131, 135
World War II, 145, 149, 192, 228
Wright, Richard, 174
Wu Hung, 246
Wu Jian, 241
Wu, Kejia, 235–37

X

Xing Xing (the Stars), 242, **243**
Les XX (Les Vingt), 118

Y

Yang Jiechang, 244, **244**
Yau, John, 162
YMCA, 170
Young Acrobat on a Ball (Picasso), 123
Young British Artists (YBAs), 212–14
young collectors, 235–36, 247
Young Painters in U.S. and France (1950), 158
Young Woman Holding a Cigarette (Picasso), 138
YouTube, 211
Yue Minjun, 245, **245**
Yun Cheagab, 241
Yusaku Maezawa, 53
Yuz Foundation, 240–41
Yuz Museum (Shanghai), 240

Z

Zayas, Marius de, 130
Zayed National Museum (Abu Dhabi), 276
Zeckhauser, Richard J., 27
Zeller, Robert, 270
Zervos, Christian, 133
Zhang Jian, 238
Zhang Xiaogang, 244–45, **245**
Zimmerman, George, 263
zips, 187
Zöllner, Franck, 67
Zoo Bandit Killed (Drexler), 206
Zucchi, Antonio, 89
Zucker, Jill, 262
Zwirner, David, 237–38, 264, 278

PHOTOGRAPHY

p. 20: © Gabrielle Croppi/Scala, Florence, Italy; p. 24: Photo Scala, Florence, Italy, courtesy Ministry of Cultural Heritage and Activities and Tourism, Italy; pp. 28, 30: © Governorate of the Vatican City State–Directorate of the Vatican Museums; p. 33: © classicpaintings/Alamy Photo Stock; pp. 38, 43, 88: Metropolitan Museum of Art, New York; p. 40: Rijksmuseum/Oursana, 2021/Wikimedia Commons; p. 42: Mauritshuis, The Hague, Netherlands; p. 45: Odecalchi, 2024/Wikimedia Commons; p. 47: Städel Museum, Frankfurt, Germany; pp. 55, 121: © Heritage-Images/TopFoto/IPA; p. 57: FDRMRZUSA, 2021/Wikimedia Commons; p. 58: © MBessaha/Shutterstock; pp. 64 (left), 105: © Christie's Images/Scala, Florence, Italy; p. 64 (right): © Trustees of the British Museum c/o Scala, Florence, Italy; p. 66: Josh Nefsky, courtesy Dianne Modestini, © 2011 Salvator Mundi LLC; p. 68: incamerastock/Alamy; p. 73: Everett Collection; p. 75: © Isabella Stewart Gardner Museum/Bridgeman Images; p. 80: 2026 © Photo Scala, Florence, Italy; p. 82: Lavinia Fontana, *Portrait of Bianca degli Utili Maselli and Her Children*, c. 1604–05, oil on canvas, 39 × 53 ¼ inches (99.1 × 135.3 cm), Fine Arts Museums of San Francisco, Museum purchase, Margaret and Will Hearst, Lisa and Douglas Goldman Fund, John A. and Cynthia Fry Gunn, Dagmar Dolby, and The Roscoe and Margaret Oakes Endowment Income Fund in celebration of the Legion of Honor centennial. Photo: Randy Dodson, courtesy Fine Arts Museums of San Francisco; p. 84: Royal Collection Trust/© His Majesty King Charles III, 2026/Bridgeman Images; pp. 86, 266, 269: Courtesy Sotheby's; p. 87: © Bridgeman Images; pp. 98, 107: © RMN-Grand Palais/Mathieu Rabeau/Dist. Photo Scala, Florence, Italy; p. 99: Paris 16, 2013/Wikimedia Commons; pp. 100, 106: © RMN-Grand Palais/Hervé Lewandowski/Dist. Photo Scala, Florence, Italy; p. 102: Library of Congress, Geography and Map Division; p. 103: Photo Archives Durand-Ruel © Durand-Ruel & Cie; p. 110: © Museum of Fine Arts, Boston. All rights reserved/Scala, Florence, Italy; pp. 114, 125, 136, 148, 155, 162, 186, 190, 201: © Museum of Modern Art, New York/Scala, Florence, Italy; p. 115: CC0 courtesy Paris Musées/Petit Palais, Musée des Beaux-Arts de la Ville de Paris; pp. 116, 129: Courtesy National Gallery of Art, Washington, DC; p. 119: © World History Archive/Alamy; p. 120: © Maxime Champion Delorme and Collin du Bocage; p. 123: © Granger/Shutterstock; pp. 126, 149, 222 (left): © akg-images/Mondadori Portfolio; p. 130: Ross Archive of African Images, Yale University Art Gallery, New Haven, Connecticut; p. 132: © G-P.F. Dauberville & Archives Bernheim-Jeune; p. 134 (left): Siren-Com, 2024/Wikimedia Commons; p. 134 (right): © TopFoto/IPA; p. 138: © 2026 The Barnes Foundation; p. 146: © Art Institute of Chicago/Art Resource, New York/Scala, Florence, Italy; p. 150: Everett/Shutterstock; p. 151: © Album/Fine Art Images/Mondadori Portfolio; p. 153: George Karger, courtesy Solomon R. Guggenheim Foundation Archives, New York; p. 154: San Francisco Museum of Modern Art/Bridgeman Images/Helen Crocker Russell Fund purchase; p. 156: Smiley N. Pool/Houston Chronicle via Getty Images; p. 157 (left): Denver Post via Getty Images; p. 157 (right): © Jeff Lowenthal. All rights reserved 2026/Bridgeman Images; p. 160:

© Nina Leen/The LIFE Picture Collection/Shutterstock; p. 163: Courtesy and copyright the Gordon Parks Foundation; p. 165: Thomas Barratt; p. 171: National Archives, photo H-HNE-20-87/Wikimedia Commons; p. 172: Cleveland Museum of Art; p. 173: © Photo Scala/SPL History; p. 174: © Chicago History Museum/ Bridgeman Images; p. 175: Emma Amos, *The Reader*, 1967, oil on canvas in artist's frame, 41 ⅛ × 61 ⅛ inches (104.5 × 155.3 cm), Crystal Bridges Museum of American Art, Bentonville, Arkansas, 2019.23. Photo: Edward C. Robison III; p. 176: Collection of the Hampton University Museum, Hampton, Virginia; p. 177: © Phillips Auctioneers LLC; p. 178: Jack Manning/The New York Times/Redux; p. 180: © Dawoud Bey, courtesy the artist and Sean Kelly, New York/Los Angeles; p. 181: Gregory Wiley Edwards, courtesy the artist and Ortuzar, New York; p. 182: Courtesy David Kordansky Gallery; p. 192: Christie's Images, London/Scala, Florence, Italy; p. 194: Shunk-Kender © J. Paul Getty Trust, Ileana Sonnabend portrait, unidentified location, c. 1960s, Getty Research Institute, Los Angeles (2014.R.20). Gift of the Roy Lichtenstein Foundation in Memory of Harry Shunk and János Kender; p. 195: Shunk-Kender © J. Paul Getty Trust, Robert Rauschenberg exhibition, Venice Biennale, June 21, 1964, Getty Research Institute, Los Angeles (2014.R.20) Gift of the Roy Lichtenstein Foundation in Memory of Harry Shunk and János Kender; p. 197: Dwan Gallery records, 1959–c. 1982. Archives of American Art, Smithsonian Institution; p. 199: Sam Falk/The New York Times/Redux; p. 200: © Fred W. McDarrah/MUUS Collection via Getty Images; p. 206: Private collection, US, courtesy Galerie Gmurzynska; p. 212: Daniel Berehulak/Getty Images; p. 213: Courtesy Sotheby's/Multiplesinc; p. 214: © Nils Jorgensen/Shutterstock; p. 215 (top): Courtesy Arte Svelata; pp. 215 (bottom left), 225, 232: Gagosian archives; p. 215 (bottom right): Tanley Wong; pp. 216–17: Prudence Cuming Associates Ltd; p. 222 (right): Museo Nacional del Prado, Madrid © Photo MNP/Scala, Florence, Italy; p. 223: © André Gomes/ © RMN-Grand Palais/Art Resource, New York; p. 224: David Douglas Duncan Papers and Photography Collection, © Harry Ransom Center, University of Texas at Austin; p. 227: Courtesy MutualArt; p. 228: Frank Philippi, Piero Manzoni, Milan, 1959, Collection Fotomuseum Antwerpen, Belgium, P/2012/97/1 © 2026 Artists Rights Society (ARS), New York/SABAM, Brussels; p. 230: © Fondazione Piero Manzoni, Milan; pp. 231, 271: Robert McKeever; p. 240: Zhu Di, Agent Pay; p. 243: Courtesy Li Xiaobin; p. 244: Fei Dawei Archive, courtesy Fei Dawei and Asia Art Archive; p. 245 (top): Courtesy Christie's Hong Kong; p. 245 (bottom): Courtesy Pace Gallery; p. 246: Courtesy Ai Weiwei Studio; p. 256: © 2021 Christie's Images Limited; p. 259: Robert Gerhardt, © Museum of Modern Art/Licensed by Scala/Art Resource, New York; p. 263: Amy Sherald, *Michelle LaVaughn Robinson Obama*, 2018, oil on linen, 72 ⅛ × 60 ⅛ inches (183.2 × 152.7 cm), National Portrait Gallery, Smithsonian Institution. The National Portrait Gallery is grateful to the generous donors who made these commissions possible and proudly recognizes them at npg.si.edu/obamaportraitstour; p. 267: David Heald © Solomon R. Guggenheim Foundation, New York; p. 272: Courtesy Gallery Climate Coalition, https://galleryclimatecoalition.org; p. 275: © Lance Gerber, courtesy Desert X; p. 276: © Hufton+Crow; p. 277: © 2026 Sam de Groot (graphic design), courtesy Carlos/Ishikawa, London.

ARTWORKS

pp. 121, 123, 125–26, 129, 132, 136, 222 (left), 223–25, 227: © 2026 Estate of Pablo Picasso/Artists Rights Society (ARS), New York; p. 130: © 2026 Estate of Edward Steichen/Artists Rights Society (ARS), New York; p. 138: (top to bottom): © 2026 Succession H. Matisse/Artists Rights Society (ARS), New York, © 2026 Estate of Pablo Picasso/Artists Rights Society (ARS), New York; p. 148: © Estate of Norman Lewis, courtesy Michael Rosenfeld Gallery LLC, New York; pp. 149, 153, 162: © 2026 Pollock-Krasner Foundation/ Artists Rights Society (ARS), New York; p. 151: © 2026 Artists Rights Society (ARS), New York/ ADAGP, Paris; pp. 154, 156: © 1998 Kate Rothko Prizel & Christopher Rothko/Artists Rights Society (ARS), New York; p. 155: © 2026 Willem de Kooning Foundation/Artists Rights Society (ARS), New York; p. 163: © 2026 Helen Frankenthaler Foundation, Inc./ Artists Rights Society (ARS), New York; p. 165: © The Estate of Ed Clark. Courtesy the Estate and Hauser & Wirth; p. 172: © Augusta Savage; p. 173: © 2026 Heirs of Aaron Douglas/Artists Rights Society (ARS), New York; p. 174: © Estate of Archibald John Motley Jr. All rights reserved 2026/ Bridgeman Images; p. 175: © 2026 Emma Amos/ Artists Rights Society (ARS), New York; p. 176: © Charles White Archives; p. 177: © 2026 David Hammons/Artists Rights Society (ARS), New York; p. 182: © 2026 Estate of Sam Gilliam/Artists Rights Society (ARS), New York; p. 186: © 2026 Jasper Johns/ Artists Rights Society (ARS), New York; pp. 190, 195: © 2026 Robert Rauschenberg Foundation/Artists Rights Society (ARS), New York; pp. 192, 201: © Andy Warhol Foundation for the Visual Arts, Inc./ Licensed by Artists Rights Society (ARS), New York; p. 197: (left to right): Arakawa, *Untitled No. 2*, 1968, Art Institute of Chicago. Gift of Virginia Dwan, 1988; Arakawa, *Marriage Announcement to Annina Nosei (Untitled - Letter to John Weber)*, 1966; Arakawa, *Statement*, 1968. All works by Arakawa © 2026 Reversible Destiny Foundation, Reproduced with permission of the Reversible Destiny Foundation, © Robert Bruce Newman, © Estate of Walter De Maria, © Charles Frazier, © 2026 Luis Camnitzer/ Artists Rights Society (ARS), New York; p. 204: © Yayoi Kusama; p. 206: © Estate of Marjorie Strider/ courtesy Galerie Gmurzynska; pp. 212–17: © Damien Hirst and Science Ltd. All rights reserved/DACS, London/Artists Rights Society (ARS), New York 2026; pp. 228, 230–32: © 2026 Artists Rights Society (ARS), New York/SIAE, Rome; p. 243: Qu Lei Lei; p. 244: © Yang Jiechang; p. 245 (top): © Zhang Xiaogang, courtesy Pace Gallery; p. 245 (bottom): © Yue Minjun, courtesy Pace Gallery; p. 246: © Ai Weiwei; p. 256: © 2026 Amoako Boafo/Licensed by Artists Rights Society (ARS), New York p. 257: Beeple Studios; p. 259: © Refik Anadol Studio; p. 264: © Kerry James Marshall, courtesy the artist and David Zwirner, London; p. 266: © Estate of Jean-Michel Basquiat. Licensed by Artestar, New York; p. 267: © Sarah Sze; p. 269: 2026 Estate of Leonora Carrington/Artists Rights Society (ARS), New York; p. 271: © Ewa Juszkiewicz; p. 275: © Giuseppe Penone.

Trading Beauty: Art Market Histories
from the Altar to the Gallery
Valentina Castellani

Gagosian
980 Madison Avenue
New York, NY 10075
+1 212 744 2313
gagosian.com

All original quotations not in English have been translated by the present author unless otherwise noted.

Editor: Priya Bhatnagar
Print production manager: Shiori Kawasaki
Editorial coordinator: Helen Redmond
Chief creative officer: Alison McDonald

With thanks to Andisheh Avini, Anna Collins, Owen Conway, Maren Frey, Brett Garde, Paris Gilstrap, Lauren Gioia, Ella Huzenis, Ines Kang, Lauren Mahony, Sophie McLellan, Diana Poussin, Alexandra Samaras, Gianna Ting, Rita Yirui Wang, Kira Webb, and Michael Wilson

Copy editor: Richard Slovak
Indexer: Pilar Wyman

Design concept: Sofia Salvatori
Layouts and typesetting: Philipp Hubert, New York
Color separations and printing: Longo, Bolzano, Italy

An Italian edition of this book is published by Allemandi Editore.

Cover: Maurizio Cattelan, *Envy*, 2025
Photo: Laura Veschi

Distributed by Rizzoli International Publications
49 West 27th Street, 4th Floor
New York, NY 10001
rizzoliusa.com

ISBN: 978-1-968417-02-4
Library of Congress Control Number: 2025950645